QATAR

DAVID B. ROBERTS

Qatar

*Securing the Global Ambitions
of a City-State*

HURST & COMPANY, LONDON

First published in the United Kingdom in 2017 by
C. Hurst & Co. (Publishers) Ltd.,
41 Great Russell Street, London, WC1B 3PL
© David B. Roberts, 2017
All rights reserved.
Printed in India

Distributed in the United States, Canada and Latin America by
Oxford University Press, 198 Madison Avenue, New York, NY 10016,
United States of America.

A Cataloguing-in-Publication data record for this book
is available from the British Library.

9781849043250 *hardback*

This book is printed using paper from registered sustainable
and managed sources.

www.hurstpublishers.com

CONTENTS

ACKNOWLEDGEMENTS

Only after completing a PhD and having undergone the tortuous process of converting the thesis into a book can you appreciate the quantity of thanks that needs to be distributed to compensate, in however insignificant a fashion, all the people who have helped, facilitated, informed, clarified, supported, and taught the author along the way.

Firstly, I must thank the University of Durham and the Centre for the Advanced Study of the Arab World (CASAW) for granting me four years of PhD funding. Sincere thanks to my supervisor Dr Christopher Davidson for the years of invaluable advice, suggestions, and guidance. My thanks too to Professor Anoush Ehteshami and Dr Elisabeth Kendall for acquiescing to my sojourn to Qatar University half-way through the PhD. Thanks also to Dr Afshin Shahi, Professor Emma Murphy, Dr Lorraine Holmes, and Dr Lucy Abbott for their help and advice over the years at Durham.

At Edinburgh University, many thanks to Dr Jonathan Featherstone, a fantastic Arabic teacher, and in Cairo to Ben Taylor, Ed Kehoe, Majid Robinson, and Rachel Thomas for their help in wrestling with the Hans Wehr Arabic-English dictionary.

Thanks also to Qatar University and their Arabic for Non-Native Speakers course for the tuition and for allowing me to spend such an invaluable period of time in Qatar. Eternal thanks to Charlie Gandelman and Jared Koch for making the dorms in Doha liveable. Dr Steven Wright at Qatar University deserves particular mention. Without him I would have missed this opportunity, while his support and advice during my years in Qatar have been invaluable.

For my initial return to Qatar, I must thank Dr Jonathan Eyal and Professor Michael Clarke at the Royal United Services Institute (RUSI). My time with RUSI in Qatar was crucial in cementing my understanding of the country and

ACKNOWLEDGEMENTS

offered me the chance to observe and understand far more about Qatar than I would have been able to by myself.

In this incarnation with RUSI, and subsequently with King's College London in Qatar, a great many people deserve sincere thanks. They include Dr Abdullah Baabood, Alex Munton, Dr Andreas Krieg, Professor Gerd Nonneman, Hussein Abdullah, Justin Alexander, Dr Khalid Al-Mezaini, Dr Mari Luomi, Dr Mark Farha, Mark Thomas, Professor Mehran Kamrava, Michael Stephens, Robert Baxter, and Dr Tim Bird. As for my Qatari and diplomatic friends, I shall not do you the disservice of including your names here, but you know who you are: *shukran jazeelan*.

As for the production of the book itself, I must thank the editors at Hurst for their patience and the various peer reviewers for their detailed, useful comments.

Lastly, I must thank Stefi Roberson for following us around the world so assiduously, my mother for doing so much to set things up for me so well back in Middlesbrough, and also Josh Roberts, Don Bathie, and John Constable.

This book is dedicated to my long suffering wife Elizabeth, for her perennial support and brutal editing. Thanks for putting up with years of rambling about Qatar and the peripatetic lifestyle, and apologies for deciding to study Qatar rather than Hawaii.

London, December 2015

ABBREVIATIONS AND ACRONYMS

ADIA	Abu Dhabi Investment Authority
APOC	Anglo-Persian Oil Company
Aramco	Arabian America Oil Company (Now Saudi Aramco)
Centcom	United States Central Command
CMC	Central Municipal Council
CFI	Canal France International
CIE	Companion (of the Order of) the Indian Empire
DFI	Doha Film Institute
FCO	Foreign and Commonwealth Office (UK)
FDI	Foreign Direct Investment
GECF	Gas Exporting Countries Forum
GCC	Gulf Co-operation Council
IOC	International Oil Company
IS	Islamic State
IPC	Iraq Petroleum Company
IRA	Irish Republican Army
KIA	Kuwait Investment Authority
KSA	Kingdom of Saudi Arabia
LNG	Liquefied Natural Gas
MCM	Million Cubic Metres
MENA	Middle East and North Africa
MIA	Museum of Islamic Art (Doha)
MICE	Meetings, Incentives, Conferences, and Exhibitions (sector)
MOF	Ministry of Finance
NAM	Non-Aligned Movement
NGL	Natural Gas Liquefaction

ABBREVIATIONS AND ACRONYMS

OECD	Organisation for Economic Co-operation and Development
OIC	Organisation of Islamic Countries
OPEC	Organisation of Petroleum Exporting Countries
QF	Qatar Foundation
QFC	Qatar Financial Centre
QGPC	Qatar General Petroleum Company
QIA	Qatar Investment Authority
QMA	Qatar Museums Authority
QMDI	Qatar MICE Development Institute
QNCC	Qatar National Conference Centre
QSI	Qatar Sports Investment
QSTP	Qatar Science and Technology Park
RAF	Royal Air Force (UK)
SNC	Syrian National Council
SOCAL	Californian Standard Oil Company
SWF	Sovereign Wealth Fund
TNC	Transitional National Council (Syria)
UAE	United Arab Emirates
UAR	United Arab Republic (1958–1961)
UNESCO	United Nations Educational, Scientific and Cultural Organisation
UOG	UAE Offsets Group

NOTE ON NAMES AND TRANSLITERATION

Technically speaking, one could refer to Qatar's ruler as 'His Highness the Emir, Sheikh Tamim bin Hamad bin Khalifah Al Thani.' This type of naming convention denotes that Tamim's father is called Hamad and his grandfather Khalifah. This convention serves two broad purposes. Firstly, it can—as in this case—directly link a person to a prestigious lineage. Secondly, it is a useful way of discerning specifically who a person is, given for example that 'Hamad Al Thani' could be any one of dozens of people in any given Qatari context.

Yet this book does not wish to mirror the impenetrable name-suffused prose of much of the press in the Gulf. Indeed, such a system can become cumbersome. Rather, on first mention of a protagonist in each chapter, s/he is referred to by his/her full name with one middle name (for example, Hamad bin Khalifah Al Thani). Subsequently in the same chapter, s/he is referred to simply as, for example, Hamad bin Khalifah. Occasionally, if s/he is referred to multiple times in the same paragraph, or it is otherwise clear who is being referred to, 'Hamad' alone has been used. Similarly, Saudi Arabia, for example, is referred to as the Kingdom of Saudi Arabia, Saudi Arabia, or even 'Riyadh' as the prose dictates.

LIST OF FIGURES

INTRODUCTION

When writing about Qatar, it has become customary for global media to note that the country resembles a mitten or a thumb, and that it is about the size of Yorkshire or Connecticut.[1] That the state follows the strict Wahhabi creed of Islam is also noted as a key point, and one juxtaposed against Doha's newly sprouted buildings (an 'artificial forest' in the words of one BBC News article), shimmering or glittering in the sunshine.[2] Al Jazeera, the embattled Doha-based regional news network, also merits a mention, as does Qatar's controversial success in the race to host the 2022 FIFA World Cup. Finally, Qatar's prominent role in the Arab spring uprisings that began in late 2010 spawned hundreds of articles. These were often positive at the start of the uprisings. However, they quickly turned increasingly negative as Syria and Libya descended into civil war and Qatar stood accused of meddling and supporting extremist Islamic groups.[3]

Throughout this rollercoaster of public opinion, journalists and editors unerringly resorted to the near permanent clichés of Qatari coverage, describing it as a state with a maverick foreign policy and 'punching above its weight.'[4] Always more entertaining with its titles, *The Economist* preferred to describe Qatar as a 'bouncy bantam,' a 'pygmy with the punch of a giant,' engaging in 'flying carpet diplomacy,' and haughtily as 'too rich for its own good.'[5] Clichéd analysis aside, however, there have been some superb articles over the years: Worth's 2008 *New York Times* article remains relevant, while Eakin's 2011 *New York Review of Books* article is still arguably the best summary of Qatar's 'strange power.'[6] But too often articles note facts alone and, faced with what appears to be a confusing and contradictory array of issues, coherent and persuasive analysis remains scarce.

While there is some merit to noting Qatar's size (if not its shape), the country's location is arguably of greater importance. The state is defined by its

72km land border with Saudi Arabia and 270km sea border with Iran; the latter runs through the world's largest gas field, which the two countries share. In terms of land mass, Qatar is approximately 187 times smaller than Saudi Arabia and 144 times smaller than Iran. In terms of population, Qataris are outnumbered approximately 1:68 by Saudis and 1:272 by Iranians.[7]

In terms of military strength, Qatar on its own is exponentially outnumbered. Even ignoring the fact that Qataris are a minority within their own armed forces (accounting for around 20 to 30 per cent), and ignoring Iran's paramilitary units and Basiji forces[8] and Saudi Arabia's paramilitary forces and internal security forces, 'Qatar' is outnumbered approximately 1:18 by Saudi Arabia and 1:46 by Iran.[9]

The same yawning discrepancies in the basic building blocks of power (or at least power as it is traditionally conceived) have been present for centuries. From the late eighteenth century, when Qatar's modern history can be said to have begun, the typical policy of the principal sheikh on the Qatari Peninsula was to seek security either with a local tribal alliance or under the aegis of an external guarantor. Leaders in Qatar needed to concentrate their limited resources on shoring up alliances and adjusting them where possible to secure protection with greater autonomy. Until the 1960s, this left few resources over with which to engage in a wider foreign policy, or anything but the most meagre domestic development. Indeed, Qatar developed a reputation for being 'known for being unknown' and 'the most boring place in the Gulf.'

These adages, which spread throughout the Gulf over the decades, summed up Qatar, a country that seldom entered international consciousness before the 1990s. The state's role in the Ottoman Empire's denouement was negligible, it played no meaningful role in World War One, World War Two or the Cold War, and it did not play an active part in Arab affairs, aside from sporadic donations of foreign aid when oil revenues allowed. Yet against this quietist historical background and as the 1980s wore on, Qatar began to eschew this modus operandi and embarked on a new, provocative course of action in both foreign and domestic politics. In short, the state has changed more in the past 30 years than in the previous 300.

Domestically, following a bloodless coup in 1995, censorship laws were relaxed, municipal elections were called, women were enfranchised, and a new emphasis on education was prioritised. Doha-based regional television news network Al Jazeera was established in 1996. Meanwhile, a change in external relations began in 1988 with the establishment of diplomatic relations with China and the Soviet Union, unusually without waiting for Saudi Arabia to take the lead. Relations were subsequently cultivated with Iran and Israel, a deeply anti-establishment policy for a previously stalwart Gulf Co-operation Council (GCC) state such as Qatar, while a broad set of agreements, including one allowing US forces to be based in Qatar, was reached in 1992. Concurrently, Qatar expanded its aid and political support to groups such as Hamas, the main Palestinian Islamist movement, and Shia movement Hezbollah in Lebanon. In the 2000s, the state extended its influence by mediating not only in the Gulf (Yemen) and the Levant (Lebanon), but also in the Horn of Africa (Eritrea), West Africa (Mauritania), East Africa (Sudan), and North Africa (Libya).

Diverse international relations formed a part of efforts to boost Qatar's visibility across the region. The state also focused on increasing its soft power by promoting Al Jazeera and hosting world-class sporting and cultural events, as well as some of the largest conferences in the world: these included the 'Doha Round' of World Trade Talks in 2001 and the eighteenth Conference of the Parties (COP 18) climate change conference in November 2012.

Until the Arab spring uprisings, Qatar tended to avoid establishing one-sided, divisive relationships, preferring instead to use its reputation as a relatively unbiased and 'inoffensive' state to great effect. However, with its heavy diplomatic, material, and military support for rebel forces in Libya for example, the state jettisoned its previously (mostly) neutral status. Support for Qatar's ploys against then Libyan ruler Muammar Al Gaddafi and Syrian President Bashar Al Assad was initially widespread, but consistent financial and political support for many of the emerging Muslim Brotherhood governments and parties around the region became deeply divisive. Unsurprisingly, given the post-revolutionary tumult, many of the new Muslim Brotherhood-dominated governments soon struggled, and opposition movements emerged, particularly in Egypt. By so visibly supporting these Muslim Brotherhood actors, Qatar was tarred by association, and even the once region-leading Al Jazeera saw its ratings plunge, largely because of its association with the Qatari state and the assumed Muslim Brotherhood-supporting line that it was widely believed to be toeing.

The genesis of and rationale behind the transformation of Qatar's domestic and international policies, which culminated in its provocative actions during the Arab spring, resists immediate explanation. More specifically, it is not immediately clear how these policies were designed to secure the Qatari state, given that they occasionally appeared to actively undermine Qatar's interests and even security. For example, Qatar's long-running policy of supporting

Islamists backfired when GCC allies Saudi Arabia, the United Arab Emirates (UAE), and Bahrain withdrew their ambassadors from the state in March 2014 in an unprecedented sign of irritation over Qatar's policies.

The first step towards understanding Qatar's so-called 'maverick' policies both before and during the Arab spring is to delineate exactly what they were. When juxtaposed against the state's historical practices, eight policies that are either new in character or type are evident: close relations with the US; gas policies; international mediation and negotiation; 'taboo' international relations; international investments; Al Jazeera; soft power policies; and Qatar's Arab spring policies. All of these stemmed from the rise to power of a new generation of leaders in the late 1980s, and will be the initial focus of attention. Bringing the book up to date, a detailed examination will be undertaken of Qatar under the youthful Emir Tamim bin Hamad Al Thani that considers how his emerging rule is shifting existing policy patterns to secure the state. The conclusion examines the primary motivating factors underpinning Qatar's extraordinary rise to prominence, and how these policies coalesce to form a plan to underwrite the security and prosperity of the Qatari state. A clear three-way interaction between the domestic, regional, and international levels becomes apparent.

Domestically, policies emerge from a surprisingly unconstrained Qatari elite that derives little direction from anything that could be described as public sentiment. Although Qatar seeks regional and international powers to guarantee its security, these guarantor states very rarely actively direct or shift Qatar's policies. Qatar may be a small state and a weak one by many metrics, but its policies have often been fiercely independent, belying traditional 'realist' assumptions as to the de facto impotence of small states.

Nevertheless, Qatar's region has been decidedly conflict-prone in recent decades and has proved to be a recurring source of concern for the state's leaders. As a result, securing the state from regional threats is a thread that runs throughout most, if not all, of Qatar's foreign policies.

Foreign and security policies emerging from the domestic arena, often in large part in reaction to regional stimuli, are then crucially both enabled and constrained by factors at the international level. As a small state, particularly in the 1990s and 2000s, Qatar had to wait for international politics to present opportunities for it to act because it was not sufficiently strong to force through its policies. For example, the state's controversial diplomatic relations with Israel rested largely on the whims of international (and regional) politics. Wider détente with Israel in the early 1990s created an opening that Qatar exploited to pursue increasingly close relations with the Jewish state. The state weathered difficulties and pressures to abandon these ties as the 1990s progressed, but was eventually forced to curtail its relations by a wider change in the international landscape—Israel's Operation Cast Lead in 2008–2009.[10] This pattern repeats itself: Qatar takes advantage of openings in international relations, but subsequently finds that it is not sufficiently resilient to resist international pressures.

The book concludes with an appreciation of the emerging trends that have become evident under Emir Tamim bin Hamad. Fundamentally, both the emir's approach and those of his father, Sheikh Hamad bin Khalifah Al Thani, are analysed in terms of their efficacy in securing the state. The book overall provides an anatomy of the rise of Qatar on the world stage.

A framework for analysis

To crisply and clearly analyse the vast changes in Qatar's politics, a structured approach devised by Professor Gerd Nonneman will be used. This conceptual framework for analysing the foreign policies of Middle Eastern states assesses how the policies are conditioned by the domestic, regional, and international environments. Underpinned by a rigorous theoretical pedigree and one not beholden to any one perspective, Nonneman's framework offers a systematic way of analysing policies that is sufficiently flexible to be used in this analysis, in which not all the policies in question are traditional 'foreign' policies (though an international dimension is almost always present). Adept use of this framework highlights the importance of the interplay between policy thrusts at the domestic level from the Qatari elite. These often stem from regional concerns, but are fundamentally facilitated or stifled by contextual factors in the international realm.

Early in the development of his framework for analysing foreign policy in Middle Eastern states, Nonneman notes the following sine qua non of international relations:

> The central pursuit of most MENA [Middle East and North Africa] regimes remains that of domestic survival—and the search for legitimacy, acquiescence, and control to assure this, in turn supported by a search for resources to deploy in this domestic quest.[11]

In pursuit of this central and abiding goal, foreign policy is but one of many tools in the armoury of states seeking to secure their survival. Contributing to foreign policy formulation at the domestic level, Nonneman notes that there are several direct and indirect factors to consider, including the nature of the state, the state's capabilities, the intra-state decision-making system(s), and decision-makers' perception of their role.

Each of these points is applicable to the Qatari context, though there needs to be a subtle change of emphasis. Although Nonneman's typology is an aggregate typology for Middle Eastern and North African countries, Qatar is far from an average MENA state. The state's population is the smallest in the region, while it also has the world's largest royal family per capita and, according to the International Monetary Fund (IMF), the world's highest gross domestic product (GDP) per capita.[12]

As such, the role of the ruling Al Thani family needs to be emphasised. For most of Qatar's leaders until Khalifah bin Hamad Al Thani (r. 1972–1995), the wider Al Thani family was often a hindrance, exerting huge pressure on the leader for favourable policies, larger stipends, or otherwise a greater share of the state's wealth by virtue of the fact that they were royal family members.[13] As outlined in greater detail below, Khalifah struggled but nevertheless successfully began the process of diversifying his support base from the royal family alone to the wider Qatari public, releasing him from their pressure to a degree.[14] His son, Hamad bin Khalifah Al Thani (r. 1995–2013), continued this trend in the late 1980s, when he actively sought to further diversify his sources of legitimacy.[15]

For modern leaders such as Hamad bin Khalifah and his son Tamim (r. 2013–) therefore, while it would be naive to discount the importance and influence of different groups within the ruling family,[16] such groups nevertheless represent a far less vocal and influential bloc than one might expect. Instead, in a state with only approximately 270,000 citizens, a conservative ethos, and a tribal ethic, modern leaders are strongly positioned and enjoy relative freedom of action. While it should not be over-emphasised, the Qatari elite is unusually unencumbered relative to other MENA states and can imprint its personality on wider state policies, as has clearly been the case in the 1990s, 2000s, and 2010s.

Leaders and other domestic actors are products of their environment, and whether the state is fundamentally secure or not is a concern that will affect policy formulation. The issue of 'basic security' takes many forms, ranging from the physical security of borders, towns, or the Al Thani family's place in society, to questions of economic resilience and development. Qatar's history shows that different leaders draw different conclusions when faced with broadly the same set of circumstances. For example, Khalifah bin Hamad sought security in a fundamentally different way to his son Hamad. In essence, the former sought to secure Qatar hiding under the auspices of Saudi Arabia, while the latter sought security through a wide array of extra-regional entanglements.[17] Drawing on limited in-depth interviews and an examination of available data facilitates a rounded discussion, below, of the impact of generational differences and close familial ties on the two leaders' different policy outlooks.

Nonneman's framework cautions that the state's capabilities at the behest of the leadership (for example, fiscal, technological, demographic capabilities) must be factored in to understand decision-making. Indeed, this aspect is important in grasping the change in Qatari policies. As the state's gamble on liquefied natural gas (LNG) began to pay off, particularly after the millennium, the opportunity cost for engaging in a 'luxury' foreign policy (for example, mediation or giving extensive foreign aid) reduced.

Questions as to the 'nature of the state' also require analysis of more esoteric notions, such as the level of consolidation of national identity and the legitimacy of the ruling elite. Ruling elites can bolster their legitimacy and help consolidate national identity by overtly seeking to take charge and defend an issue of national sensitivity. This can be effected through foreign policy, as occurred in Morocco with the irredentist cause of the reintegration of the 'Spanish Sahara' (the Western Sahara issue today), a deeply resonant concern for Moroccans. As Willis and Messari note, 'by adroitly placing himself symbolically and politically at the head of the Saharan campaign, Hassan II [Morocco's then ruler] saw both his legitimacy and that of the Monarchy as an institution rise substantially.'[18] Following this logic, particular foreign policies will be highlighted in terms of their domestic effects, specifically as they affect emerging identity issues.

In terms of the regional level, Nonneman notes that this refers not only to an actor's immediate regional environment, but also to trans-geographical phenomena that are particularly significant in a Middle Eastern context.[19] As for the former, the Gulf region, as well as the wider Middle East, has vacillated for decades amid the ebb and flow of various currents of thought: decolonisation, pan-Arabism, and Islamism have waxed and waned, and while each country has been affected by these (and other) waves in different ways, none have been immune. In particular, a small country such as Qatar for most of its history has had to heed the flow and act accordingly. These factors represent constraints on but also provide opportunities for Qatar's elite, and are particularly salient in understanding Qatar's 'Islamist-supporting' policies during the Arab spring.

Aside from pan-regional movements, Qatar has been acutely aware of its neighbours, who have been both a source of threats and have also presented opportunities to counter threats in equal measure. Time and again, the issue of differentiation for Qatar comes to the fore. The state finds itself nearby city states such as Abu Dhabi, Dubai, and Manama that are similar to it in a variety of ways, and the commensurate desire to differentiate Qatar is noted through key policies.

The international level in Nonneman's analysis is understood in broadly two ways. It refers straightforwardly to countries beyond Qatar's regional area and it can be more abstractly be seen as the vast flow of policies, alliances, opportunities, and threats to which the state is subject. Traditional small state theory would suggest that smaller states are incapable of resisting the dominant flow at any given moment, and that they tend to be compelled to follow a regional consensus because of their size.[20] However, scholars have questioned this type of assumption, at times explicitly in relation to Qatar.[21] Indeed, a direct relationship can be seen between the changing international context and some of Qatar's most important foreign policy actions. Pan-global events and phenomena such as the end of the Cold War, the ramifications of the September 2001 attacks on the US, or the globalisation-inspired communications revolution gave Qatar, it is argued, crucial ideas and also a certain room to manoeuvre that provided a lynchpin facilitating and otherwise underpinning many of its new policies.

Key terms

State branding

The concept of state branding arises time and again in this analysis. Indeed, various organs of the Qatari state and many of the policies examined can be viewed as aimed at forging a brand for Qatar. As such, it is important that this concept is clearly understood.

Branding as a concept for products and services, from Coca Cola to FedEx shipping, has a long history, but the concept has only been explicitly transferred to the state level relatively recently. Academic study of state branding[22] and associated concepts of country equity[23] and public diplomacy has increased significantly since the millennium. Indeed, *The New York Times* in 2005 listed nation-branding as among 'the year's most notable ideas.'[24] Van Ham, one of the pioneers of this field of research, describes it as follows: 'A brand is best described as a customer's idea about a product; the 'brand state' comprises the outside world's ideas about a particular country.'[25]

Although academic study of place-branding may be relatively new, it is not a new topic. Indeed, Olins, in a 2002 article for the *Journal of Brand*

Management argues that France, for example, had undergone numerous 'rebranding exercises', from Louis XIV via Bonaparte's empire to the Fifth Republic today.

> The Tricolour replaced the Fleur de Lys, the Marseillaise became the new anthem, the traditional weights and measures were replaced by the metric system, a new calendar was introduced, God was replaced by the Supreme Being, and the whole lot was exported through military triumphs all over Europe. In other words the entire French package was changed.[26]

Olins concludes that 'you may not like the term, you may prefer to talk about a new or reinvented nation or state, but if revolutionary France was not a new brand I do not know what is.'[27]

It is important to find ways to differentiate oneself from the homogenised crowd, particularly in the context of the Gulf, which contains numerous small states or city-states, all of which are remarkably similar in terms of language, history, culture, geography, economics, politics, and society. Adopting 'strategic marketing and management tools (to undertake) conscious branding' is one key way in which this can be done.[28] Aside from a banal desire to 'be different,' put simply, every dollar of foreign direct investment (FDI) and every engineer that goes to Abu Dhabi is one dollar and one engineer that does not go to Doha, and one of the goals of branding can be to affect exactly this kind of balance.

Van Ham also notes that a country's 'culture, political ideals, and policies' are a key part of brand-creation.[29] Aside from these intangible attributes, in assessing the more practical aspects that form a state's brand it is useful to examine the attributes that businesses find attractive when looking to relocate their premises. Indeed, Gulf states are competing, often directly with each other, to attract multinational businesses. Examining what businesses look for in a host country is therefore a sensible approach to take when deconstructing the attributes of a state's brand.

Kotler and Gertner undertook just such a study and noted that, on a general level:

> A country's image results from its geography, history, proclamations, art and music, famous citizens and other features...Most country images are in fact stereotypes, extreme simplifications of the reality that are not necessarily accurate.[30]

More specifically, however, they note that for companies looking for a new location, the following set of criteria is important:

- Local labour market
- Access to customer and supplier markets
- Availability of development site facilities and infrastructure

- Transportation
- Education and training opportunities
- Quality of life
- Business climate
- Access to research and development (R&D) facilities
- Capital availability
- Taxes and regulation (clarity)[31]

It is possible to discern that a number of policies Qatar has pursued in its modern era can be seen as directly targeting these attributes. This suggests, implicitly at least, that one of the key motivations behind the state's 'unusual' set of policies from the early 1990s onwards was to create and develop a brand for the country to increase its attractiveness to international commerce.

While endowing one's state with a distinct brand to obtain advantage has always been important, it arguably became even more important as the twentieth century progressed. Despite numerous positive impacts, the internationalisation of commerce has also resulted in, as Olins puts it, 'a very harsh and turbulent commercial environment [in which] the nation that makes itself the most attractive wins the prizes—others suffer.'[32]

Qatar's status as a young state can be both advantageous and disadvantageous. It had to start with little or no brand identity, and then engage in a commensurate struggle, firstly to define its space and then propagate its brand in a world of more established competitors. Equally, it did not have a negative brand perception to counter and had a blank state to start with.[33] Indeed, Tarek Atrissi, the designer tasked with developing a new 'corporate' identity for Qatar, noted that the state 'did not have an existing national identity... [something that] made [my job] easier.'[34] This lack of a noticeable 'brand perception' was also useful in facilitating Qatar's mediatory activities as a state without historical baggage to complicate relations.

Lastly, it must be noted that, as with Olins' example of France, a significant audience for the rebranding exercise is in fact internal. Here, there is an interesting confluence of the 'foreign policy' aspects of the study and the other parts of the puzzle with both an external and internal dimension.

Soft power

Inextricably linked to state branding is the concept of 'soft power.' First espoused by Joseph Nye in the early 1990s (though its antecedents go back centuries),[35] the notion was used to explain that the US's power rested not only on its superior 'hard power' facilities (primarily its military), but also soft power, namely its ability to persuade states to follow the US's path rather than threatening or coercing them to do so. Nye identified three fonts of soft power stemming from culture, political values, and foreign policies.[36] Under this rubric, he identified US educational institutions teaching numerous foreign leaders and future businesspeople, as well as US culture (via Hollywood) familiarising people with American traits, as two key fonts of US soft power.[37]

In the Qatari context, many of the emergent policies can be seen as boosting Qatar's soft power. Indeed, two of Qatar's flagship undertakings were the establishment of Al Jazeera and the promotion of education through the establishment of US educational institutions in Doha, both of which mirror the US's twin traditional sources of soft power: education and media projection. Moreover, sporting ventures are a central means for Qatar not only to publicise itself, but also to 'reiterate its adhesion to the universal values of democracy, solidarity, and human rights,' as one scholar put it regarding Qatar's hosting of the 2006 Asian Games. This directly echoes Nye's discussion on the promotion of values and political culture as sources of soft power.[38]

For Qatar to pursue a soft power approach is an obvious if not a necessary policy. There are fewer than 300,000 native Qataris, to pick just one limiting factor, while Qatar will always struggle to project hard power. However, the state can invest in activities and policies that boost another aspect of power. This is the context of Al Jazeera, for example—a savvy, asymmetric use of financial power to augment Qatar's soft power.

Not only has soft power become a fixture on the international politics lexicon in recent decades, despite difficulties in defining this nebulous issue, but the concept of Qatar building its soft power capacities has become something of a trope in public writings on the state. Indeed, a wide variety of articles and analysis pieces in recent years have focused specifically on Qatar's various fonts of soft power.[39]

Book plan

Chapter 1 surveys Qatar's modern historical experience to highlight four recurring themes: the (slow) evolution of the Qatari state; balance in international relations with the changing of alliances; Saudi Arabia's regional dominion; and the notion of Qatar as the *Kaaba Al Madiyoom* (literally, 'Kaaba of the dispossessed', figuratively a 'Mecca for exiles'). Highlighting factors of continuity from the eighteenth century to the present demonstrates a consistency of strategic approach amid tactical policy changes.

This chapter draws on hitherto unused sources (freedom of information requests from the British Foreign and Commonwealth Office), alongside a range of interviews in Qatar. Overall, the book offers the most detailed account to date of the intricate relationship between Qatar and Saudi Arabia in the 1960s and of the transition to Hamad bin Khalifah in the late 1980s. This is a singular blind-spot in Qatar's modern history, which often results in authors suggesting that changes only began to happen in 1995, whereas in fact they had begun at least seven years' earlier.

Chapters 2 through 8 delineate key policy themes that have been evident since the late 1980s and which are the foundation of the modern Qatari state, namely close relations with the US, gas policies, international mediation, 'taboo' international relations, international investments, Al Jazeera, and soft power policies. While many of these policies have historical echoes—Qatar had limited gas policies in the 1950s, and sporadically sought to burnish its soft power credentials in the 1960s and 1970s—the scale of the modern policy is either of a different magnitude, or the policy itself is new to Qatar.

These chapters adopt the same systematic approach. Initially, each policy theme is fleshed out in detail. In an integrated and synthesised fashion, each is then analysed in turn using the Nonneman tripartite framework as the guiding principles. As noted above, the tripartite framework is specifically designed to provide an analytical framework for examining policies in the Middle East context. In turn, therefore, Qatari domestic, regional, and international concerns are considered in the formation and execution of each policy. Only in Chapter 6, which focuses on international investments, is the structure altered, because the necessary regional considerations are too similar to the international considerations to warrant separating them. Chapter 7, which examines Al Jazeera, focuses on the network from 1996 to 2011 alone because the Arab spring proved a watershed moment in its existence. Al Jazeera's seesawing history from the start of the Arab spring is dealt with in Chapter 9.

Indeed, Chapter 9 focuses on Qatar's policies during the Arab spring, and begins with an account of the state's role in the uprisings. Rather than offering a simple narrative account of what the state did, it examines how Qatar exerted its influence, and there is a focus on how Qatar used its media assets ('the revolution will be televised'), its financial assets ('chequebook diplomacy'), and its personal and institutional links ('personal relationships and Islamist connections'). Subsequently, the chapter examines the complex reasons why Qatar acted as it did during the Arab spring, informed by Nonneman's tripartite taxonomy.

Chapter 10 assesses the reign of Qatar's current emir, Tamim bin Hamad. Still in the early stages of his rule, there is as yet no sufficient body of evidence to specifically determine his proclivities and policies. Initially, Tamim's rule was swiftly diverted by his GCC allies when he was forced to address a diplomatic and regional crisis precipitated by the withdrawal of the Saudi, UAE, and Bahraini ambassadors from Doha. However, by examining this incident and noting in detail the domestic-oriented nature of his concerns in his first 24 months in office, a picture of the rudiments of a 'Tamimi' approach emerges.

The book concludes by examining the continuity and change in threats that the state faces and how Qatar's elites have reacted to these pressures. In particular, consideration is given to examining how the same (often regional) motivating factors led different elites to derive vastly different conclusions. The idiosyncratic quirks of the Hamad bin Khalifah-led elite, alongside the vastly new international arena that the end of the Cold War heralded, are highlighted as important determinants of Qatari policy. Lastly, considered conclusions are drawn as to the success, both to date and in future, of Qatar's attempt to secure its global ambitions under Tamim.

1

QATAR IN HISTORICAL CONTEXT

Several books on Qatar and its modern politics have been written in recent years,[1] and there is consequently no need to plot the state's history merely for form's sake. Instead, the approach taken in this chapter provides not a historical narrative, but rather a chapter of analysis dived into several themes: the state's slow evolution; the perennial importance of balance and changing alliances; the looming role of Saudi Arabia; and Qatar as a Mecca for regional exiles.

This approach has several advantages. Context is necessary in understanding Qatar's modern politics, and subsequent chapters of the book focus in great detail on discrete policy areas. This initial section provides readers with a holistic picture of the state's emergence to contextualise these policies in a manner that avoids a simplistic narrative approach.

This opening chapter allows recurring themes in Qatar's politics to be emphasised by showing the change and continuity in a historical context. Only juxtaposed against an appreciation of Qatar's slow historical growth and quiescent policies can its radical, taboo-breaking modern politics truly be grasped. Nevertheless, as the subsequent analysis highlights, while modern policies may by highly unusual by historical standards, the core motivations underpinning their employment often have historical resonance. Similarly, it is only with this historical perspective emphasising the near perennial importance of seeking a balance among allies, that Qatar's Arab spring policies—by which the state sought to support certain sides as never before—can really be seen in relief as a deeply ahistorical Qatari policy.

It is also important to plot the slow evolution of the state itself. This is because the state's capabilities (or lack thereof) are often of vital importance in directly shaping policy. As such, the laboured, incomplete, and slow establishment and maturation of the Qatari state needs to be highlighted in some detail.

It is certainly worth highlighting the dominating influence that Saudi Arabia (and its forbearer states) has had on Qatar's evolution. Actors from modern-day Saudi Arabia have provided both challenges and answers to Qatar's security. In particular, relations between Saudi Arabia and Qatar were one of the most important factors galvanising Qatar's young leadership in the 1980s to instigate a series of transformational, paradigm-shifting policies.

Another consistent policy thread has been evident from Qatar's formative years through to the present day, namely Qatar as the '*Kaaba Al Madiyoom*', a phrase that translates as 'Kaaba of the dispossessed.' It was used by Qatar's most revered historical leader, Jassim bin Mohammed Al Thani (r. 1878–1913), to describe how Qatar repeatedly played host to an array of regional banished leaders, fleeing criminals, exiled religious figures, and other waifs and strays. Just as the Kaaba, the central focus of the Great Mosque in Mecca, is a lure to Muslims around the world, so, in its own way, was Qatar a draw to those in need of respite. In turn, these regional exiles that Qatar took in over the years became important—if not pivotal—conduits through which the state supported a range of groups around the region. This was particularly evident during the Arab spring, where exiled religious leaders and Al Jazeera contacts became, in essence, the de facto Qatari foreign ministry.

Lastly, this chapter allows for an opportunity to fill in the gaps in existing scholarship on specific areas of Qatar's history. Interviews in Doha and newly disclosed primary documents from the British Foreign and Commonwealth Office (FCO) are used to provide the greatest detail yet on two important but under-researched periods in Qatar's history. Saudi-Qatari relations in the period before Khalifah bin Hamad Al Thani took power (before 1972) are poorly understood, given Saudi Arabia's importance to Qatar in the 1970s and 1980s as a state providing de facto protection. Equally, the transition to Hamad bin Khalifah Al Thani in the late 1980s is an important era about which only the broader brush strokes of the historical narrative are known. The FCO records allow more details about this era to be fleshed out to plot the shift of power from Khalifah bin Hamad to his son and allies as the 1980s progressed.

The (slow) evolution of the Qatari state

There are few specific records of activity on the Qatari Peninsula before the mid-eighteenth century, leading one Arab historian to conclude that 'its inhabitants led a peaceful life and confronted no major events thought worthy of historical recording.'[2] It was not until the arrival of the Ottomans in Qatar in 1871 that evidence of the establishment of formal bureaucratic systems emerged.[3]

The Ottomans anointed Jassim bin Mohammed Al Thani, the man today revered as Qatar's founding father, *Kaymakam* or governor of the state. As well as being tied into the regional administrative and bureaucratic centre in Hufuf, in modern-day Saudi Arabia, the first professional bureaucracy was started in Qatar. New posts were created and staffed by Ottomans, including a treasurer, an accounts officer, a deputy *kaymakam*, regional administrators for Udeid and Zubarah, a harbour master, an Arabic-speaking secretary, a claims tribunal, and a correspondent clerk conversant in Arabic and Turkish.[4] Records of these activities were kept, while the administration of Qatar's outlying villages and towns was formalised and written down.[5] This not only institutionalised the role of Doha as the capital but, in conjunction with the use of Ottoman flags to denote the furthest reaches of Qatari territory, contributed to the formalisation of Qatar as a separate entity.

Through a combination of public and private funding, the Ottomans encouraged the founding of rudimentary schools and mosques throughout Hasa (the east and south-east region of modern-day Saudi Arabia that formerly included Qatar).[6] With the defeat of the Ottomans by Jassim's native forces at the battle of Wajbah in 1893, Ottoman suzerainty of Qatar was de facto ended. The British took over the Ottoman role in both a de jure and de facto sense on 3 November 1916, though even here the underdeveloped nature of the state was clear. Qatar did not sign up to several of the articles of the protectorate treaty (VII, VIII & IX), including one requiring the ruler to protect British citizens in his charge, such was the lack of confidence in Qatari authority to be able to fulfil such demands.[7]

The extent of this underdevelopment once again became clear when Qatar's oil industry proved so difficult to get off the ground.[8] All of the necessary equipment (weighing 100,000 tonnes), skilled manpower, and most of the surrounding infrastructure including basic roads had to be imported and constructed before exports could begin.[9] Such was the lack of alternative industry or employment that 'almost everyone who had any significant income at all in the later 1940s drew it from the oil company; for five days of the week the entire life of Doha seemed to drain away to Dukhan, the oil-company town on the other side of the peninsula.'[10]

From a low point of an estimated 10,000 people living on the peninsula in the 1930s, the oil industry resuscitated Qatar.[11] As oil income increased as the 1950s and 1960s progressed, the resulting wealth was distributed, cementing the traditional economic bargain between the ruler and his subjects. However, Al Thani leaders had to carefully balance maintaining a pliant public through building and improving the state's infrastructure, creating jobs, and distributing benefits, with maintaining support within the wider ruling family. Indeed, the demands of the wider family became increasingly rapacious as oil revenues increased. Ministries were hived off and handed to sections of the family, payments were made, and land was distributed firstly to royals and then to all Qataris.[12]

Unsurprisingly for such a young, developing state, international affairs remained initially concerned with the immediate region, though foreign visits increased from the mid-1950s onwards. For example, Colonel Anwar Sadat of Egypt visited Doha twice in 1955, as did King Saud of Saudi Arabia.[13] As Qatar opened up, it became increasingly affected by international movements. 1956 saw a rash of pro-Egyptian demonstrations during which protesters, angry at the UK's intervention against Egypt in Suez, threw stones at the British Political Residency. There was also a 'partial strike in sympathy with the Algerians, the sabotage of oil installations...and a general increase in the strength of Egyptian propaganda and of its local agents.'[14] In April 1963, meanwhile, the union proposed by Egypt, Syria, and Iraq prompted popular demonstrations and a strike. Two of the strike leaders were Nasser bin Abdullah Al Misnad and Hamad bin Abdullah Al Attiyah. The latter, a diehard 'radical and Nasserite' in the 1960s,[15] was imprisoned (having been arrested by chief of police Mohammed bin Abdullah Al Attiyah, his full brother) over his role in the 1963 demonstrations and died in prison in 1965.[16] Nasser Al Misnad, in common with many of the protest organisers, was briefly imprisoned (for around a year at the same time as Hamad bin Abdullah Al Attiyah) and then exiled. Within a few weeks, with vague promises of reforms and the leaders arrested, the strike fizzled out.[17]

In contrast to the rapacious policies of Ahmed bin Ali Al Thani (r. 1960–1972), Khalifah bin Hamad Al Thani (r. 1972–1995) from early on appeared to understand the longer-term importance of placating ordinary Qataris. During labour unrest in the 1950s, he nominally acted as their champion. He also put himself forward as a pan-Arabist while remaining privately cordial with the British.

On independence day in September 1971, Ahmed bin Ali did not even return to Qatar to sign the documentation or celebrate independence, preferring instead to remain in Geneva. The exorbitantly expensive lifestyle and impunity with which he and his son Abdul-Aziz bin Ahmed Al Thani conducted themselves contributed to Khalifah bin Hamad being immediately recognised as emir when he took over on 22 February 1972, when Ahmed bin Ali was on one of his many foreign excursions.[18] Saudi Arabia also quickly recognised Khalifah bin Hamad's ascension, most likely according to the terms of an agreement he fostered in Riyadh in 1965 (as discussed in greater detail below). Following a modicum of caution from the British, Khalifah bin Hamad was accepted as the legitimate ruler, if for no other reason than the British had long since tired of dealing with Ahmed (a 'singularly useless individual' according to one British official).[19]

Khalifah bin Hamad swiftly proved himself quite a different leader to his predecessors. Internally, he became the first modern Qatari leader to stand up to the Al Thani family and their ever increasing demands. With a history of supporting 'popular' movements and policies, he quickly bolstered his reputation as a leader for all Qataris and not just the wider Al Thani family. He cut royal family benefits; transferred his stipend of the budget (25 per cent) to the state's coffers; increased social aid by 30 per cent, old age pensions by 25 per cent, and armed forces and civil servant pensions by 20 per cent; cancelled outstanding housing payments and built 2,500 free housing units within a year; implemented an amended provisional constitution; established an advisory council; further sought to secure state jobs for Qataris; and continued to 'pour large amounts of money' into all social services.[20]

In addition to these direct distributive policies and attempts to include Qataris in the emerging bureaucracies, Khalifah bin Hamad also sought to engender a civic myth. This proved difficult. Not only was there significant competition for 'belonging' (such as pan-national, familial and tribal identities, as well as the notion of belonging to one Islamic *umma*)[21] but there was also a limited amount of 'civic resources' on which to draw: Qatar had experienced neither a glorious battle for independence nor any other overly auspicious historical moments. As a result, Khalifah bin Hamad sought to 'find' Qatar's history. In 1975, a museum was established, furnished with artefacts from newly undertaken archaeological digs, and from 1972 onwards the Information Ministry controlled and added to Qatar's historical narrative.

Externally, Khalifah bin Hamad indicated an appreciation of the importance of the wider world. He placed an advertisement in *The Times* of London in May

1972 titled 'The Era of Reform'[22] and significantly expanded Qatar's diplomatic network. Diplomatic relations were established, the first ambassadors hosted, and delegations (often presidential or prime ministerial) were received from Belgium, Brazil, Burundi, the Comoros Islands, Congo, Egypt, Finland, Gabon, Indonesia, Mali, Malta, Morocco, Palestine, North Korea, Senegal, Switzerland, Syria, Trinidad and Tobago, and Uganda in 1974, 1975, and 1976 alone.[23] Qatar also donated millions of dollars to a variety of causes, ranging from UNESCO to struggling countries to the Arab Peace Force in Lebanon.[24]

These international relations, civic myth-building ventures, and the vast increase in the state's bureaucracy were funded by rising oil prices. In 1971, oil revenue was $300 million. In 1973, it doubled to $600 million, before rising to $2 billion the next year with almost flat production.[25] However, by the early to mid 1980s, oil prices had fallen and budget deficits were run, charges for healthcare, water and electricity were introduced, and 3,000 government employees were laid off.[26]

It was around this time that Khalifah bin Hamad's son and crown prince Hamad bin Khalifah Al Thani began to exert influence, having being appointed heir-apparent and minister of defence on 31 May 1977. As early as 1986, the British ambassador to Qatar noted Hamad bin Khalifah's increasing assertiveness:

> A further decline in Sheikh Khalifah's drive and decisiveness in 1987 seems almost inevitable. The days when he was the sole arbiter...are apparently over. Sheikh Hamad, the Crown Prince, takes more and more decisions without first obtaining the approval of his father. He will gain increasing prominence here.[27]

The British ambassador's annual review for 1987 refers to Hamad bin Khalifah continuing to 'consolidate his authority, especially over the North Field project and military procurement, through his small network of relatively competent and honest young Qatari executives who face a difficult task in clearing up the inefficient administration.'[28] The next year's report notes that this delegation of authority to Hamad had reached 'an apparently irretrievable extent ... speculation is now even heard about Sheikh Khalifah's own position.'[29]

Aside from prosaic changes, such as the change from the Islamic lunar calendar to the Gregorian tax year calendar, deeper change benefitting Hamad bin Khalifah was crystallised in 1989 in a cabinet reshuffle.[30] Growing difficulties between Hamad bin Khalifah and his father's brother, the then interior minister Khalid bin Hamad Al Thani, prompted the first wholesale ministerial reshuffle since 1972. Seven ministers were relieved of their positions and eleven newcomers appointed.[31]

The creation of 'Supreme Councils' became a feature of the state under Hamad bin Khalifah. These in essence were new versions of existing ministries, but ones controlled by dynamic Qataris loyal to Hamad. The supreme councils—of planning, health, and education—were another means by which Hamad bin Khalifah could consolidate his power and bypass existing sclerotic ministries to implement changes he wanted to push through.

However, domestic economic expansion had to be based on secure foundations. Relations between the US and Qatar became increasingly strong after operations Desert Shield and Storm, which were put in place to to protect Saudi Arabia and liberate Kuwait after Saddam Hussein's 1990 invasion. Aside from deteriorating regional relations (most notably with Saudi Arabia, outlined in detail below) forcing the resort to an external guarantor of security, it is difficult to emphasise enough the importance of the invasion of Kuwait as a driver of Qatar's subsequent actions. Indeed, the British ambassador in Doha at the time of the invasion remarked that both Emir Khalifah and Crown Prince Hamad had commented specifically on the issue: 'The Amir [sic] and the Crown Prince have made much of the way in which the invasion of Kuwait has changed permanently Qatar's political alignments.'[32] The analogy with Kuwait—a small, intrinsically defenceless, hydrocarbon-rich country surrounded by larger states with whom it had sporadically antagonistic relationships—was plainly not lost on the Qatari elite.

Another cabinet reshuffle in 1992 saw the dismissal of 'those Ministers who had long ceased attending their offices' and, as with the 1989 reshuffle, breathed new life into the Qatari government and allowed Hamad to install key allies.[33] Abdullah bin Hamad Al Attiyah, a close friend of Hamad bin Khalifah and a son of the aforementioned 1960s protest leader, played a key part in Qatar's growth, efficiently overseeing the evolution of the state's liquid natural gas (LNG) industry.

In an apparent attempt to reassert his authority, Khalifah bin Hamad sought to lead an official state visit to Egypt and to Tunisia and then on to Geneva in summer 1995. Through an intermediary, Hamad bin Khalifah informed his father the Emir that he could only do so with the authority and guidance of his government. And that if he chose to ignore the request, there would be changes afoot. Scoffing at the highly plausible notion of his son replacing him (and forgetting how he himself had come to power), he chose to continue with his plans and flew on. On landing, he was informed that his son had overthrown him and had recalled the plane to Qatar. Attempts to corral regional support against Hamad bin Khalifah were initially greeted with sympathy and support, but were ultimately ineffective.[34]

In common with his father before him, Hamad bin Khalifah (r. 1995–2013) sought to placate Qatar's citizens on becoming emir, and consciously began to remake ruling politics with a more progressive slant. He decoupled the position of prime minister from that of the emir, and separated the state and ruling family's finances (no doubt a pointed move, considering that his father retained an estimated $3 billion-$12 billion of Qatar's finances in his personal accounts in Europe).[35] The Doha Stock Market was established in June 1995 and opened in May 1997 on the IMF's advice, the 'liberalising' tenor of which chimed with the thrust of Qatar's policies.[36] Moreover, new legislation facilitating foreign investment was introduced and state assets were privatised, starting with the Qatar Electricity and Water Company taking control of power generation and desalination plants in February 1998.[37]

No minister for information was appointed in the 1996 cabinet reshuffle, and the ministry responsible for censorship was officially disbanded in March 1998. Al Jazeera began broadcasting in 1996 in a further sign of a new era of openness. It is difficult to over-emphasise the ground-breaking role that Al Jazeera played. Never before in the Middle East had such a relatively independent indigenous news source been allowed to operate.

In November 1995 it was announced that the Central Municipal Council (CMC), which until then had been directly appointed, would become an elected body. More surprisingly, the Emir Hamad bin Khalifah announced on 29 November 1997 that women could vote and stand for CMC office, a first in the Gulf.[38] Following a few false starts, 280 candidates—including eight women—in 1999 registered for the twenty-nine seats, while an estimated 87 per cent of registered Qataris participated in the polls. However, no women were elected to office.[39] Lambert notes that the election spurred 'a country-wide phenomenon of government officials replacing appointed bodies with elected ones,' including direct elections to the Chamber of Commerce.[40]

These progressive policies were mirrored on the international stage. While Qatar had made sporadic attempts to mediate with Iraq and Kuwait, in Palestine, and with US-led sanctions against Iraq between 1993 and 1999, it was not until after the turn of the millennium that it systematically engaged in public mediation across the MENA region.[41]

Qatar in 2006 donated $50m to the newly elected Hamas-led government in Palestine, adding to its longer-term support for the Palestinian Islamist movement.[42] Hamas leader Khaled Meshaal has lived periodically in Doha and has direct access to Qatar's leadership. Later in 2006, Qatar sought to use this relationship to broker a Palestinian unity government, though this attempt was ultimately unsuccessful.[43] Similarly, the state sought to use its relations with Israel to mediate with Hamas, but this also failed.[44] In late 2012, Hamad became the first international leader to visit Gaza since Hamas's 2007 takeover, a startling move even in the context of Qatar's energetic and surprising foreign policy.

Aside from widespread changes in traditional Qatari foreign policies, the new elite also undertook a raft of new approaches in a range of spheres, including commerce and energy, and in terms of what could be described as 'softer' policies. The decision to focus on Qatar's gas reserves took over a decade to come to fruition, but eventually paid dividends. Qatar became the world's biggest LNG exporter in 2006 and remains by some distance the world's largest LNG supplier, though Australia appears set to assume this mantle from around 2018.[45] LNG-derived revenue was one of the central factors allowing Qatar to undertake the diverse and expensive range of new policies that this book examines.

After almost a decade of LNG revenues, Qatar in 2005 established its Sovereign Wealth Fund (SWF), the Qatar Investment Authority (QIA). The fund quickly became one of the most recognisable SWFs in the world, and in the late 2000s and 2010s became famous for frequently taking large stakes in blue-chip companies such as Volkswagen and Porsche, Harrods, and Shell. The QIA is but one of the mechanisms that can be understood as adding to and propagating a brand to boost Qatar's soft power. Such power rests on the power of attraction, according to soft power's modern intellectual father, Joseph Nye.[46]

Viewed in this light, various other Qatari policies can be seen as key fonts of the state's soft power. Facilitated by LNG revenues, Qatar's relentless push to host a range of world-level sporting events (for example, football (soccer), athletics, golf and tennis) is a primary method of boosting the state's attraction across the world. At the very least, under the rubric of 'no publicity is bad publicity,' the events have certainly put Qatar on the proverbial map.[47] Similarly, Qatar's pursuit of international acclaim in the world of culture with the purchase of art and the hosting of film premieres, film festivals, and world-class museums is aimed at publicising the state in a positive manner.

Of more recognisable relevance to building a brand is Qatar's pursuit of the international business market. As well as the QIA being a leader of the brand, billions of dollars have been invested in efforts to boost Qatar's development of Doha as a centre for the Meetings, Incentives, Conferences, and Exhibitions (MICE) industry. In addition to tourist infrastructure such as top-class hotels and recreation areas, Qatar has also built two world-class conference centres, and a world-spanning and award-winning airline, Qatar Airways. During Hamad bin Jassim Al Thani's tenure at the foreign ministry in particular, there was a sense of an almost bottomless budget to host the largest and most prestigious conferences. Qatar has hosted some of the largest conferences in the world, including the eponymous 2001 'Doha Round' World Trade Organisation talks and the 2012 COP 18 conference.

Aside from being the location of Qatar's large conference centre, Education City is populated by several US and British university campuses. These universities, which are based in Doha, are—alongside New York University in Abu Dhabi—indisputably the best universities in the Middle East, and form part of the plan to encourage and facilitate the transition to a knowledge-based economy in Qatar. Other parts of the Qatar Foundation (QF), the overarching body behind Education City, include Qatar Science and Technology Park (QSTP), a centre for innovation, research and design designed to provide an outlet for Education City students and burnish Doha's image as a hub of innovation and opportunities for businesses.

While the energy, sporting, education, cultural, and MICE policies evolved over time, Qatar's foreign policy stance changed swiftly during the Arab spring. Whereas the state previously had a reputation for being something of an inoffensive, neutral state—which proved useful in mediation efforts—it quickly became partisan in the Arab spring, clearly and proudly supporting one side over the other. This support was most clearly initially evident in the Libyan uprising, when Qatar supported anti-Gaddafi forces in a variety of ways.[48]

Elsewhere in the aftermath of the Arab spring-inspired regime changes, Qatar sought to expand its support by whatever means possible. Particularly in Tunisia and Egypt, this took the form of channelling cash and material support via established contacts, typically Islamists associated with the Muslim Brotherhood. However, as the promise of the Arab spring began to wane, so too did Qatar's reputation. The state's strong relations with the Muslim Brotherhood-led government of Mohammed Morsi in Egypt were replaced by deeply antagonistic relations with the government of new president Abdel Fatah El Sisi after he took power. In Syria, meanwhile, Qatar—in common with all international actors—was powerless to prevent the civil conflict from intensifying, but attracted particular attention for its support for a range of Islamist groups in the country. Not only was Qatar viewed as making the situation worse by arming untrustworthy groups, but it also gained a reputation as a state that tolerated the financing of bona fide terrorist groups such as Jabhat Al Nusra. This narrative was particularly effectively championed by the media in late 2013 and 2014, and broadly coincided with the February 2014 withdrawal of three GCC ambassadors (from Saudi Arabia, the UAE and Bahrain) from Doha.

This was the international situation that confronted Emir Tamim bin Hamad Al Thani soon after he took over from his father in June 2013. As one might expect, his overarching focus was initially on domestic matters, mirroring the immediate priorities of his father and grandfather as their power increased. Externally, whether through luck or good judgement, his administration dealt professionally with the regional isolation enforced by Saudi Arabia, Bahrain and the UAE. Moreover, as the Saudi Arabia and UAE-led war in Yemen intensified as 2015 progressed, Qatar sent a small contingent of its troops to Yemen as well as supporting the mission with its air force assets.

Overall, Tamim bin Hamad's focus has remained primarily internal. His speeches on assuming power and opening parliament in 2013, 2014, and 2015 are all odes to thriftiness; exhorting Qataris to work hard for their state. In 2015 he went as far as to charge that Qatar's generous welfare state had created a "dependency on the state to provide for everything," something that would change as the overall fiscal picture became more difficult.[49] Rhetorically at least, Tamim bin Hamad is, therefore, as revolutionary as his father, but in a different context.

Balance and the changing of alliances

A recurring theme in Qatar's modern political history has been that of its leadership perennially seeking some form of balance in its regional and international relationships, consistently and quickly switching alliances when necessary. This was evident from the very beginning of Qatar's modern history in the late eighteenth century. At that time, there was competition to control the young but growing and increasingly rich town of Zubarah (a small town on Qatar's west coast) and the more established island of Bahrain. After evicting Persian-allied forces from Bahrain in the 1790s, Utub tribes—a group that had recently arrived from Kuwait and came to challenge in the Zubarah-Bahrain region—were attacked by Persian forces between 1777 and 1801. In 1799, the Sultan of Muscat also attacked Bahrain, forcing the Utub to seek protection from their former adversaries, the Persians.[50] However, this tactic failed. Muscat took Bahrain in 1800 and the Utub escaped to Zubarah, where they sought assistance from another power with whom they had also recently been fighting, the Wahhabis, to regain control of Bahrain. Pleased to be offered the opportunity to extend their influence, Wahhabi forces joined the Utub to retake Bahrain. The Al Khalifah—the leading family in the Utub tribal group—was reinstalled in Manama under a Wahhabi 'tribal commonwealth' in 1802.[51]

However, the Al Khalifah were far from diligent Wahhabi subjects and sought ways to extract themselves from the relationship, including (unsuccessfully) seeking British assistance in 1805.[52] With some of the Al Khalifah leadership having been summoned to the Wahhabi capital Diriyah to be punished for their recalcitrance, other Utub went to Muscat for help. Always eager to attack Wahhabis, Muscat took advantage of Egyptian advances down the Wahhabi western flank and destroyed Zubarah and took Bahrain in 1811, expelling the Wahhabis.[53] With the Al Khalifah restored once again to the throne under Muscat's aegis and the withdrawal of troops back to Oman, the ruling Utub enjoyed reasonable independence, despite nominal overlordship by both the Wahhabis and Muscat.

As weaker actors in a region of larger, predatory powers, the Al Khalifah and the wider Utub tribe were forced to be dextrous in their foreign dealings. Although the Al Thani were yet to emerge as leaders in Qatar, this is the milieu in which they were brought up, socialised, and educated, and in which they lived. One of the few notes in Arabic or English on Muhammad Al Thani, one of the first mentioned Al Thani sheikhs, notes that he 'was aware of the balance of power in the eastern part of the Arabian peninsula,' according to a Qatari scholar.[54] This kind of alliance-swapping was not unique to Qatar, but is a central feature of the politics on the peninsula. What is relatively unique to Qatar is the combination of the number of actors seeking influence on the peninsula, and the initial lack of any already established hegemonic presence.

The courting of Ottoman and later British forces is a logical evolution stemming from the basic necessities of the region. On 13 September 1868, Sir Lewis Pelly, the British Political Resident, formally signed a treaty with Muhammad bin Thani as the leader of 'all residing in the province of Qatar' but still under Al Khalifah rule.[55] A complex series of tribute payments was then arranged, indicating the multi-layered nature of the protection system.[56] At this time, therefore, Al Thani leaders juggled the Ottomans, the Al Khalifah in Bahrain, and the British to their best advantage.

After signing the Trucial Agreements in 1916, Qatar's dependence on the UK increased, and the emirate sought to carefully extract as many concessions as possible. When the UK asked for the Royal Air Force (RAF) to open an emergency landing-strip in Qatar, Abdullah bin Jassim Al Thani (r. 1913–1949) demanded meaningful protection assurances in return, having previously been deceived by the British.[57] A deal was eventually struck, and Qatar remained under the broad aegis of the British until independence in 1971.

Still seeking balance and aware of the basic disparities in size, relations with Saudi Arabia were continually assured and improved (as discussed in more detail below). Overall, Qatar rested under Saudi Arabia's aegis from 1971 until the late 1980s. Indeed, the lack of evidence of Qatar's elite in some way seeking to diversify this dependence is unusual and ahistorical. Under the influence of a new generation of leaders from the late 1980s onwards, Qatar would return to its historical policy of cultivating wider relationships.

Qatar reinvigorated its support for the Non-Aligned Movement (NAM) in the late 1980s, and Hamad bin Khalifah attended the NAM summit in Belgrade in 1988. Equally, towards the end of the decade, Qatar began to actively and quickly deepen ties with states such as Iran, China, and the Soviet Union. Interestingly, this occurred just as Qatar's relations with the US were deteriorating after the state had been 'caught' acquiring Stinger missiles on the black market. The British ambassador to Qatar at the time described these kinds of relations 'as a signal of its [Qatar's] wish not to appear beholden to the West or subservient to Saudi leadership, [so] Qatar established diplomatic relations with a curious range of countries of no relevance to its needs.'[58] The subsequent British ambassador was of the same opinion, noting that while the Soviet and Chinese Ambassadors were 'charming,' they made no impact.[59] Moreover, the tenor of the British ambassadorial reports noted the increasing power of Crown Prince Hamad bin Khalifah, with Ambassador Nixon noting that he detected 'the Crown Prince's hand behind surprising shifts in Qatar's relationship with the superpowers.'[60]

Two factors immediately flow from this statement, which fits closely with the thrust of emerging Qatari domestic political realities and long-term foreign policies. Firstly, at this stage Qatar was not a particularly valuable US ally. If, therefore, the elite felt that even a modest association or imbalance whereby Qatar was overtly associated with the US should be corrected, this had potentially huge implications for the state in the 1990s. For when Qatar became one of the central locations for US forces and there were real, evident, and widely known commonalities of interest and relationships between Doha and Washington, if one uses the same logic (namely that Qatar must diversify its interests to avoid being too overtly viewed as being in one camp), this offers a powerful explanatory factor for Qatar's foreign policy explosion as the 1990s progressed.

Secondly, the ambassador's contention that it was Hamad bin Khalifah who was in charge of establishing relations with China and the Soviet Union, is persuasive. Khalifah bin Hamad's disposition became ever more cautious as the 1980s progressed to the point of a deep inertia, a problem Hamad was to counter with various ministerial changes. Moreover, Khalifah bin Hamad's own foreign policy motivation was, as identified by a former British ambassador, to follow the GCC lead, and he would have been highly unlikely to have abandoned this stance for no apparent reason. In 1990, Qatar was similarly outspoken when it became the first GCC country to condemn Iraq's invasion of Kuwait.[61] While this may seem a sensible reaction for Qatar, perhaps seeing worrying analogies in the invasion, it is nevertheless another indicator of a sea-change in its foreign policy. Far from its traditional 'wait and see' approach, Qatar was becoming far more forthright in its own opinions.

The close US-Qatar relationship that exists today stems from basic ties being reset by the exigencies of operations Desert Shield and Desert Storm. In June 1992, Qatar and the US concluded an agreement 'that provided for US access to Qatari bases, pre-positioning of United States materiel, and combined military exercises.'[62] In addition to seeking US security agreements, Qatar sought to vastly increase its wider international relations, a plan motivated by acrimonious relations with Saudi Arabia and Qatar's obvious increasing dependence on US protection. In particular, beginning in the early 1990s, Qatar developed new alliances that were starkly at odds with its previously predictable politics. Aside from newly invigorated and deepened relations with the US, contact was augmented with Iran and Israel. Trade deals, bilateral visits, military co-operation agreements, and discussions over importing water from Iran characterised the relationship with Tehran, while a thawing of frozen relations, discussions on LNG sales and opening trade offices, signing aviation pacts, and elite visits were discussed with Israel.[63] However, neither relationship progressed as far as initially envisaged. No water supply or LNG deals were reached, and such plans were eventually dropped. Relations subsequently ebbed and flowed, though all sides benefited from maintaining the public facade of a strong, working relationship.

Saudi Arabia's regional dominion

A quick glance at a map of the Gulf highlights the vast discrepancy in size between Saudi Arabia and the other Gulf states, as well as the kingdom's dominant position. As the region's history demonstrates, this dynamic is of central relevance to understanding the evolution of Qatari politics. At the outset of Qatar's modern history, with the migration of Utub tribes south to the Qatari peninsula from Kuwait, almost immediately there were marauding raids from forces based in modern-day Saudi Arabia to cope with. The Qatari Peninsula, with its small, sporadic coastal towns with no overarching ruler, at the time was left to 'total subjugation...by the Su'udi [sic] state.'[64] As noted above, this Wahhabi authority over Zubarah and Bahrain persisted for some decades, but was challenged by, for example, its subjects (the Al Khalifah) refusing to send a tribute in 1808.[65] The following year, the Wahhabis reasserted their control by appointing Abdullah bin Ufaysan as quasi-governor of Bahrain and Qatar and reinforcing him with troops, while the Al Khalifah rulers were summoned to the Wahhabi capital for punishment.[66] However, this iteration of the Al Saud-Wahhabi pact failed, and was not re-established until 1902, when the Wahhabis consolidated their state for the third and final time.

Faced once again with a power emerging with overwhelming force from the central Arabian Peninsula, Qatar's then leader, Jassim bin Mohamed Al Thani (r. 1878–1913), had to ally with the emerging Saudi Wahhabi forces in lieu of any other options. Jassim went as far as to welcome this new power, embracing the Wahabbis' stricter religious stance 'by conviction' and sending them tribute (though he had little choice in this).[67]

Subsequently, Ibn Saud (the founder of modern Saudi Arabia, Abdul-Aziz ibn Saud), acted as if the Qatari Peninsula was a natural part of his territory. In 1905, while visiting Qatar on a tour to 'explore the country belonging to my [sic] father and grandfather,' he effected a resolution of a dispute between Jassim and tribes residing in Qatar (the Al Murrah, the Bani Hajir, and the Ajman).[68] As Goldberg notes, in doing so he clearly assumed 'the role of a sovereign...[treating] them as his subjects.'[69] Fully believing the adage that the towns on the coast belonged to Qatar and that the desert belonged to him (Ibn Saud), the British, though nominally in charge of Qatar's external affairs, were unable to intercede.[70] They did not want a confrontation that they were not prepared for and feared that Ibn Saud could 'eat up Qatar in a week.'

Saudi dominance was facilitated by the fact that there were no set borders, as pro-Bahrain historian Jawad Al Arayed demonstrates.[71] Al Arayed notes that, up until 1934, the Qatari leader assumed that existing treaties with the British only covered control of the coastal areas of Qatar, clearly insinuating that the leader had little (if any) control of the interior, a reasonable conclusion supporting Ibn Saud's desert-town adage.[72] Nor should it be forgotten that, despite British agreements, Abdullah bin Jassim (r. 1913–1949) still paid a tribute of some 100,000 riyals (approximately $30,000) a year to Ibn Saud to stay his hand.[73] Moreover, the Qatari Peninsula was encroached on 'at least once' by Aramco geologists under Saudi guard looking for oil.[74]

No oil was found in Qatar's hinterland, which was both explicitly and implicitly claimed by Ibn Saud. While oil was discovered on Qatar's western coast at Dukhan, an area theoretically under Qatari control, so incomplete was the Qatari state that Saudi tribes extracted taxes from residents of Qatar Petroleum Company's camp at Dukhan, as well as Murrah tribespeople near Zubarah, as late as 1949.[75]

Saudi Arabia's de facto suzerain role continued in parallel with the UK's de jure role throughout the 1950s and 1960s. As one commentator noted, 'though no desire to get rid of the British protective agreements could be discerned, the Resident noted that Qatar's foreign policies often closely reflected the reaction in Saudi Arabia.'[76]

In 1965, Khalifah bin Hamad Al Thani, the then crown prince but who also had a vast portfolio, went to Riyadh with Hassan Kamal for talks over Qatar's border.[77] The agreement reached with Saudi minister of petroleum affairs Ahmed Zaki Yamani rode roughshod over existing understandings of the border. It gave Saudi Arabia previously unclaimed land, breaking the land link between Qatar and the Trucial States (later the UAE), by giving Saudi Arabia access to the Gulf south of the Qatar Peninsula. London firmly believed that this land belonged to Shakhbut bin Sultan Al Nahyan (r. 1928–1966), the ruler of Abu Dhabi, who was also under British protection at the time.[78] Although Khalifah gave up vestigial Qatari claims to Khor Al Udeid, the land at the centre of a long-running dispute, the agreement gave Qatar a generous swathe of land nearby, even if it lost its contiguous link to the Trucial States. The US consul-general in Dhahran noted that the new agreement effectively gave Qatar seventy-five square miles of land 'previously...regarded as falling within the Aramco [Saudi oil] concession.'[79]

Off-the-record interviews in Doha with protagonists aware of these negotiations suggest that more was at stake here than simply land. Khalifah bin Hamad, while crown prince, still understandably feared being usurped (for what would have been the third time) in respect of being appointed emir. According to one source, part of the 1965 agreement included understandings by Saudi Arabia to support Khalifah's ascension to the Qatari throne and his continued rule in return for a certain Qatari deference to the kingdom.[80] In essence, Khalifah was seeking personal assurances from the Saudi elite in respect of his own position and for Qatar more generally. The historical record of Khalifah's tenure demonstrates that he acted on this kind of understanding. Indeed, he followed Saudi Arabia on practically all significant international issues.[81] As well as following the kingdom's lead in various 'regional and global issues', Metz notes that Qatar was the only other country to observe the full forty days of mourning after the death of Saudi Arabia's King Faisal in 1975 and King Khalid in 1982.[82] As the Saudi-US relationship deepened with increasing training and supplying of weapons, an in-depth special report in *The Times* of London described Qatar as being 'glad to accept the Saudi military umbrella, facilitated by the United States, particularly in the summer of 1984.'[83] A bilateral defence agreement was also signed in 1982 and Riyadh often acted as an interlocutor for Qatar in regional disputes. Indeed, the 1986 dispute over the Fasht Al Dibal reef, claimed by Qatar and Bahrain, was innovatively settled by Saudi Arabia by dredging the entire reef.[84]

The relationship was not characterised by a significant degree of reciprocity. A 1974 border agreement between Abu Dhabi and Saudi Arabia, which was made public in 1995, ate into Qatari territory near Khor Al Udeid to the tune of 15 littoral miles,[85] highlighting Riyadh's disregard for Qatari autonomy and bolstering the notion of Qatar operating as 'but an adjunct to Saudi Arabia.'[86] J B Kelly even noted in 1976 that Qatar was isolated and that Saudi Arabia was in a position to, 'should the political occasion arise—outright absorb the sheikhdom within [its] domain.'[87] This did not need to be explained to Khalifah. Former British ambassador to Qatar Colin Brant (1978–1981) summarised a conversation with Khalifah in which he noted that 'Qatar being a small country, he [Khalifah] has to discern the path that the other Gulf countries are treading, and follow it after them.'[88]

The 'tanker war' of the late 1980s (when Saudi Arabia and other Gulf states were forced to seek US help to reflag their oil tankers to avoid attacks by Iran) provided the first inkling that Saudi Arabia was not necessarily so powerful. Such concerns were brutally confirmed by Iraq's invasion of Kuwait in 1990 and Saudi Arabia's decision to ask the Western coalition to launch Operation Desert Shield to protect the kingdom. If Saudi Arabia could not protect itself, no Qatari leader could reasonably expect the state to be protected should the need arise. A change in Qatar's foreign policy orientation was in the offing. In a region experiencing regular, serious military conflicts, finding a suitable leviathan to protect Qatar was essential.

US-Qatar relations, which were reset by operations Desert Shield and Storm, were crucial for a number of reasons, not least the swiftly deteriorating relationship between Qatar and Saudi Arabia. Aside from mounting rhetorical differences and Saudi Arabia's blocking of (previously agreed) Qatari intra-Gulf gas pipelines, Saudi troops or tribes loyal to Saudi Arabia on 30 September 1992 attacked a border post at Al Khaffus in Qatari territory, killing a Qatari soldier and an Egyptian soldier serving in the Qatari army, and capturing a third.[89] A Saudi tribal sheikh was also killed, according to some reports. Qatar immediately and publically cancelled its 1965 border agreement with Saudi Arabia and withdrew 200 Qatari soldiers from the GCC Peninsula Shield force.[90] Egyptian mediation calmed the situation, but only temporarily. In 1993 and 1994, more deadly border clashes took place, while Qatar boycotted the GCC annual summit in 1994 and refused to sign a mutual security pact.[91] Okruhlik and Conge note that these Saudi-Qatari tensions:

> ...were less about the land itself and more symptoms of the multi-layered tension between the two countries. It gave Qatar a pretext for expressing its bitterness over the Saudi Arabian hegemony within the GCC and Saudi Arabia a chance to express its displeasure over Qatar's independent manoeuvres.[92]

After being usurped by his son in 1995, there were at least two attempted coups to restore Khalifah bin Hamad in 1995 and 1996, and Saudi Arabia is suspected of involvement in at least one, if not both of them. In the first attempt, in late 1995, it is rumoured (somewhat implausibly) that the Syrian government sought to use Lebanese Druze based in Saudi Arabia to topple the new emir.[93] A more sizable attempted coup allegedly took place the following year, when an estimated 2,000 mercenaries led by a former French special forces commander in Khalifah's personal guard were accused of being supported and supplied by Saudi Arabia and other local powers. On 20 February 1996, more than 100 people, including army officers and police, were arrested in Doha, the Emiri guard was mobilised, and the farcically organised coup was put down.[94]

Relations between two countries remained bitter for decades. Al Jazeera's relentless sniping at Saudi Arabia was one of the factors that led the kingdom to remove its ambassador, Hamad Al Tuwaimi, from Doha in September 2002.[95] Al Tuwaimi returned in 2008 during a period of détente, and bilateral relations subsequently improved, particularly as Al Jazeera toned down its coverage of Saudi Arabia.[96] Nevertheless, the see-sawing continued. As the Arab spring soured in 2013 and 2014, relations deteriorated once again. This time, in conjunction with the UAE and Bahrain, Saudi Arabia recalled its ambassador from Doha in March 2014, only for diplomatic relations to be restored the following November.

'Kaaba Al Madiyoom'

Whether looking at Qatar's earliest or most modern relations, a curious thread links them together, namely that the Qatari Peninsula has always been a location for regional exiles who have occasionally had a significant impact on Qatar's policies. This notion, expressed in a poem by Qatar's modern founder Jassim bin Mohammed Al Thani, refers to the proto-state as a *Kaaba Al Madiyoom*, a 'Kaaba of the dispossessed', a place to which exiles gravitate.

A key reason why the Wahhabis wanted to control the Qatari Peninsula in the late-eighteenth century was that it was a haven for those escaping their clutches.[97] Throughout the nineteenth century, a lack of central control meant that the peninsula maintained a semi-lawless feel, with absconding exiles and pirates heading to Qatar as a place of 'respite.' Disaffected sheikhs from Abu Dhabi,[98] deposed Abu Dhabi leader Muhammad bin Shakhbut,[99] notorious outlaw Jassim bin Jabr Raqraqi, numerous pirates,[100] and countless manoeuvring sheikhs from Bahrain[101] all sought protection or at least boarding at towns in Qatar.[102] This reputation eventually led to the British bombardment of Al Bida (the early 'Qatari' capital) in 1841 as punishment for hosting piratical elements.[103] There was no meaningful overarching authority in Qatar at the time. Not only could the British not find such an authority with whom to discuss the situation, but—had there been one—would likely have used its control to avoid incurring the wrath of the powerful British. Similarly, the apparent abrogation of practical responsibility by Bahraini leaders suggests that they too had little control over Qatar.

The first time British records mention a member of the Al Thani is on 27 March 1841, when Muhammad bin Thani was asked not to host absconding or criminal elements in the town of Fuwairit.[104] While stemming fundamentally from an inability to prevent such elements from coming to Qatar, Jassim bin Mohammed in his poetry turned this notion of Qatar as a haven for exiles, pirates, and undesirables of all types into a virtue.

This trait is not confined to the nineteenth century. Two men wanted for questioning on terrorism charges following an explosion at a Shell petrol station in Matrah (Oman) in March 1961, as well as the sinking of the British ship *Dara*, absconded to Qatar. Moreover, an active policy of giving jobs to exiles from Egypt, Syria, and Iraq in the 1950s and 1960s in particular is clearly evident.[105] These exiles, driven out of countries such as Egypt because of their Muslim Brotherhood sympathies, were welcomed by all Gulf states (not only Qatar) and used their often higher levels of education to establish and staff key ministries, particularly the proto-education ministry in Qatar.

Individuals such as Abdul Badi Saqr, Yusuf Al Qaradawi, Abdel Moaz Al Sattar, and Kemal Naji were particularly important in the education sector.

Qatar's need for educated bureaucrats saw the recruitment of other groups of people too. For example, a number of individuals who would in time come to occupy senior positions in the Palestinian liberation movement—Mahmoud Abbas, Rafiq Shaker Al Natshah, Kamal Adwan, and Mohammed Yusuf Al Najjar—were all based in Qatar for a time.[106] Nor has the importing of talent ceased. Hamas leader Khaled Meshaal has lived sporadically in Qatar since 1999, as have the controversial Indian artist M F Husain and former Iraqi foreign minister Naji Sabri Al Hadithi. Former Chechen leader Zalimkhan Yandarbiyev also lived in Doha from 1999 until his assassination by the Russians in 2004. Other 'guests' have included Omar bin Laden, a son of former al-Qaida figurehead Osama bin Laden; much of former Iraqi president Saddam Hussein's family; controversial Islamic preachers such as Canadian national Bilal Philips and US national Wagdy Ghoneim; deposed Mauritanian president Maaouya Ould Sid Ahmed Taya and his family; Abbasi Madani, the former leader of the Islamic Salvation Front in Algeria; prominent Libyan cleric Ali Al Sallabi; and former Arab-Israeli member of the Knesset (Israeli parliament) and avowed pan-Arabist Azmi Bishara.[107] Nor is this trope forgotten with Qatar's newest leader: Tamim bin Hamad, on assuming power, specifically referred to maintaining Qatar as the *Kaaba Al Madiyoom* in his speech.[108]

2

CLOSE RELATIONS WITH THE US

Securing close relations with as militarily potent a state as the US is an obvious ploy for a small state such as Qatar in a volatile region. However, this should not conceal how much this relationship, which emerged in the early 1990s, broke with the previous status quo. Indeed, facts on the ground have a power of their own. Today, the US has maintained a significant military presence in the Gulf for nearly a quarter of a century, while the size and importance of bases used by the US military in Qatar, Bahrain, Kuwait, the UAE, Oman, and previously in Saudi Arabia, are well-known and can give a misleading impression as to the longevity of the US presence.

On 21 April 1980, the US signed an agreement to use Omani military facilities, driven in part by the need for a regional base from which to launch its ultimately unsuccessful attempt to rescue hostages from the US embassy in Tehran.[1] Subsequent renewals of the agreement expanded the remit, though the facility remained a small, underdeveloped, and a mostly insignificant outlier base. Even taking into account the defence relationship between the US and Saudi Arabia in the 1960s and 1970s, which encompassed the provision of hundreds of trainers and billions of dollars of equipment sales, the depth and presence of the US footprint in the Gulf following operations Desert Shield and Storm in no way compared with the pre-1990 era. Indeed, the relationship between the US and most of the states in the Gulf was characterised by either hostility or apathy, with US support for Israel a particular bone of contention. This changed towards the end of the 1980s as the tanker war continued to take its toll, and US help was increasingly sought. Contingent on further US support, the rulers of Qatar, Bahrain, Kuwait, and Saudi Arabia in 1987 considered upgrading their co-operation with the US to, in the words of Western military officials, a 'long-term presence' in the region.[2] According to *The New York Times*, Qatar had officially agreed to store US equipment by 1987.[3]

Nevertheless, US support for Israel remained contentious, and relations with Qatar were almost broken off in the late 1980s as a result of a dispute over the state's acquisition of Stinger missiles and missile launchers. In June 1988, an individual at the US embassy in Bahrain watching coverage of Qatari National Day celebrations noted several Stinger anti-aircraft missiles on parade, and it subsequently transpired that Qatar had bought thirteen such missiles on the black market.[4] The US, concerned at this illegal activity and proliferation, put pressure on Qatar to return the weapons to the US and pass on details of their origins.[5] Several protests by US ambassador Joseph Ghougassian and a visit by then Assistant Secretary of State for Near Eastern and South Asian Affairs Richard Murphy failed to resolve the dispute. The fact that Washington did not provide Qatar with economic or military aid meant that the US had no leverage.

That Crown Prince Hamad bin Khalifah Al Thani, the then minister of defence, refused to hand over the weapons was unsurprising. Although the Qatari elite would have resented the US's demands, they were also irritated at Washington's willingness to sell seventy such missiles and fourteen missile launchers to Bahrain in December 1987 while at the same time selling none to Qatar.[6] One suggestion, among others, has been that the US refused to sell the equipment to Qatar because the state's armed forces were 'unable to deploy and use the sophisticated weapon system correctly and that the Qataris would be unable to provide adequate security for the Stingers.'[7] Qatar's justification for procuring the missiles was that it needed them because of the threat from Iran, the same argument Bahrain had used. However, this cut little ice with Washington, with one theory suggesting that Qatar had bought the weapons from Iran in the first place.[8]

Interestingly, and indicative of the unusual, proactive types of foreign policy that would come to characterise Hamad bin Khalifah's reign, there was a flurry of activity between Qatar and communist bloc states as relations with the US came under strain. On 9 July 1989, Qatar established diplomatic relations with China without waiting for Saudi Arabia to take the lead, an unusual step, and at the end of the month withdrew from talks with the US over the Stinger missile dispute.[9] A few days later, on 1 August, diplomatic relations were established with the Soviet Union and Minister for Foreign Affairs Ahmed bin Said Al Thani visited Moscow the following month.[10] Qatari officials also made known that they were considering buying Chinese Silkworm missiles and even offered the Soviet Union 'the same shore facilities enjoyed by the US Navy in Bahrain.'[11] Meanwhile, Qatar upgraded the office of the Palestinian Liberation Organisation (PLO) in Doha to an embassy on 7 January 1989, while relations with Yugoslavia were established on 24 August 1989 and with Cuba in December 1989.[12] Crown Prince Hamad described the moves as merely an effort by Qatar 'to balance relations and world powers.'[13]

The eventual restoration of bilateral ties with the US was not prompted by these provocative initiatives towards states broadly hostile to US policies in an area of explicit US national interest. Rather, the 2 August 1990 invasion of Kuwait, as with so much else in the Gulf, changed the character of the bilateral relationship entirely. Within a few weeks of the invasion, Qatar's leaders had approved the deployment of 'friendly' forces in the state.[14] A squadron of US F-16C fighter jets and almost 1,000 personnel from the 401st Tactical Fighter Wing were deployed to Qatar, alongside 26 CF-18 fighter bombers from the Canadian Air Force, though their presence—as with the wider US presence today—remained conspicuous by its absence from any apparent day-to-day presence in Qatar.[15] France also sent eight Mirage F1s to Qatar as part of the force build-up.[16]

Qatar became an increasingly important US ally as the prominence of the Gulf grew. The growing US presence in Doha and the security co-operation that accompanied it were *a sine qua non* facilitating its diverse and controversial policies that were to come.

The emergence of close US-Qatar relations in the early 1990s denoted a significant change from their previous hostile relations from the late 1980s. Not since the British left in 1971 had Qatar cultivated a relationship that included the active military presence of a capable, foreign power on its soil.[17] There is no evidence to suggest that the US provided Qatar with a catch-all security 'guarantee.' However, the build-up of relations and the US's increasing investment in Qatar in terms of military-to-military co-operation and basing (see below) provided at the very least a certain deterrent capacity. Compared with whatever tacit security-related understandings with Saudi Arabia existed in the 1970s and 1980s, Qatar from the early 1990s onwards was hosting ever more troops and important bases for the world's leading military power. More to the point, the US had just unequivocally demonstrated its willingness to use military force in defence of a fellow small Gulf state (Kuwait). It would have been surprising had Qatar's leadership not found comfort and security in deepening relations with the US.

Qatar signed a defence co-operation agreement with the US on 23 June 1992. The agreement provided the framework for 'access to Qatari bases, pre-positioning of United States materiel, and combined military exercises.'[18] Doha International Air Base (or Camp 'Snoopy', as it came to be known because people were forever peering into the base, given its proximity to downtown Doha) was based at Doha International Airport between 1991 and 1993, and again between 1996 and 2003. Qatar built the Al Udeid air base at a cost of around $1 billion when the state did not even have a meaningful air force. The base was clearly constructed (it was completed in 1996, though it would later be expanded and updated) to encourage Washington to seek ever deeper co-operation. However, the facility formally remains a Qatari air force base.

This gambit laid the foundations for a close bilateral relationship. 'Within hours' of Hamad bin Khalifah taking power in 1995, the US implicitly recognised his rule, giving the new regime 'almost immediate international legitimacy.'[19] Furthermore, following the arrests of 100 people believed to have been conspiring to reinstall Khalifah bin Hamad in early 1996, the US and France participated with Qatari forces in two joint military exercises brought forward in the wake of the arrests.[20] The joint Qatari-French exercise, which involved two warships, took place on 2 March 1996, while the US-Qatar exercise, dubbed 'Eastern Maverick 96', took place two weeks later, involving three US warships and 300 US marines storming ashore.[21] In July 1996, a sixty-day exercise took place involving more than 1,000 US airmen, US fast-jets, and refuelling aircraft.[22] In December 1996, Qatari armed forces and the US Navy participated in exercise 'Eastern Maverick 97'.[23] The number of exercises and the willingness to bring them forward following a foiled coup attempt underlined both the concern and the eagerness of the US (and France) to shore up Hamad bin Khalifah's rule. Interestingly, Qatar preferred to take part in these exercises and withdrew from planned joint Gulf Cooperation Council (GCC) manoeuvres the same year, the first time in the regional body's history that joint military exercises has been conducted without one member state.[24]

Al Udeid air base expanded significantly over the years, particularly after US access to the base was formalised in 2000.[25] Initially, with only one runway (though one that also happened to be one of the longest in the Middle East, at 15,000 feet), Qatar in the late 2000s agreed to pay for a second runway, as well as a $400 million 'state-of-the-art regional air operation centre', taking additional Qatari spending on bases for US use to at least $700 million.[26] Initially, Al Udeid was designed as a back-up to the main Combat Air Operations Centre (CAOC) for the US military, based at Prince Sultan Air Base in Saudi Arabia, for use in the event that the Saudi authorities restricted what could be directed from the base.[27] Somewhat inevitably, the CAOC in April 2003 was permanently moved to Al Udeid, and the base became the logistical heart of US military operations in Iraq and Afghanistan. Indeed, it was regarded as 'the principal power projection node in US plans to defend the Gulf', and 10–15 per cent of its staff were relocated from Florida to Qatar.[28]

Opened near Al Udeid in August 2000, Camp As Sayliyah is the US's largest prepositioning hub outside continental America, with sufficient storage for a heavy armoured brigade, a divisional base, and more than 10,000 soldiers.[29] As Sayliyah housed the forward headquarters of US Central Command (CENTCOM) from 2003 before it transitioned to Al Udeid in 2009.[30] These two facilities are critical to US interests in the wider Middle East. Were MacDill Air Force Base in Florida, where CENTCOM's headquarters are based, to be struck by a natural disaster, the body's temporary headquarters would move to Qatar rather than another base in the US.[31] Other US bases in Qatar include 'Falcon 78', an ammunition storage depot, while Qatar in 2012 became a host alongside Israel and Turkey of the most sophisticated US X-band radar system.[32]

Qatar does not charge the US for use of these bases and has historically paid one of the highest proportions of US costs. According to the US Department of Defense's 'Allied Contributions to the Common Defense' reports, Qatar both directly and indirectly paid 43 per cent of the US's costs of stationing its troops in Qatar in 1999, and 61.2 per cent in 2004.[33]

Securing the revolution

Qatar has never been able to guarantee its own security by itself. As outlined in the previous chapter, the state's early history is one of rotating alliances and agreements under which the sheikh in Qatar sought to guarantee his position, his descendants' rights to power, and some notion of territorial security with as little external interference as possible. One effect of this pattern of seeking external protection was that, with the exception of skirmishes with local tribes reasserting their dominion over a reluctant village, a notable military victory at Wajbah, and sporadic skirmishes with local forces, a Qatari military force was rarely called on to defend the homeland. There were no regular, professional, trained military forces in Qatar from the beginning of the modern Qatari state in the late eighteenth century through to the turn of the twentieth century. The police and armed forces came into being under British tutelage in the late 1940s and early 1950s, but at no time in the twentieth century was a Qatari meaningfully charged with protecting his country.

Rather, while the British were dominant in the Gulf, claims and counterclaims were made to the British resident, who wielded significant power and would demand and receive reparations or unseat a tribal leader as he saw fit. After the British left in 1971, although there may have been some vestigial hope that they could return in an emergency (as they had when Kuwait was threatened immediately after independence in 1961), Qatar removed the key source of potential concern by seeking close relations with Saudi Arabia, even if it did so at the expense of some autonomy.

Central to this decision was the personal proclivity of the emir. Khalifah bin Hamad Al Thani was content to remain under the aegis of Saudi Arabia. Without the capabilities to defend Qatar because of the state's small population, larger neighbours, and a lack of ethos of a professional military, Khalifah opted to reach an arrangement with Saudi Arabia.[34]

However, his son, crown prince and eventual usurper Hamad bin Khalifah repeatedly demonstrated that he both could not and would not remain under Saudi Arabia's aegis. His conception of his role as an emerging leader could not be squared with reliance on the kingdom. No compelling evidence has emerged that adequately explains the fundamental reason for his anti-Saudi Arabia proclivity. Whether this intrinsic desire reflected a man from a younger generation unwilling to have both his country and his rule tethered, a different appreciation of Qatar's security situation because of his military background, or increasing tensions with Saudi Arabia in the early 1990s, the result was the same for Hamad. Unlike his father, who had a track record of seeking accommodation with Saudi Arabia, and with no solution to Qatar's existential security concerns to be found in the domestic realm, Hamad resolved to assuage Qatar's security concerns by looking outwards.

As a military man who had studied at Sandhurst, the British military academy—or even just a leader with a reasonable grasp of his strategic environment—there was an obvious importance in forging as close a relationship as possible with a state as potent as the US before embarking on his most iconoclastic policies from the 1990s onwards. Indeed, after overthrowing his father in 1995, there was at least one attempted counter-coup by Saudi Arabia. Hamad bin Khalifah knew very well that Saudi Arabia would seek to restore the status quo, and cultivating US relations was one way of underpinning his rule.

Equally, opting for a greater alliance with the US over one with Saudi Arabia reflected Qatar's overarching orientation under Hamad bin Khalifah. Under his auspices, the old, traditional Gulf-modelled education system was abandoned in favour of the RAND Corporation-led, US-inspired educational system. In higher education, Hamad and his most prominent wife, Moza bint Nasser Al Misnad, who headed the Qatar Foundation, did not look to a leading Saudi Arabian university or even an Arab one, but rather to the likes of Virginia Commonwealth, Texas A&M, and Georgetown University.

This chapter has deliberately sought to emphasise that the security agreement with the US stemmed almost exclusively from Hamad bin Khalifah and his close allies. While the early 1990s saw limited pro-democracy demonstrations in Qatar, overall there is little evidence to suggest that following a US model, whether in terms of security provision or education, stemmed from any widespread, grassroots-inspired movement. Nor was there any meaningful, established mechanism through which to channel public sentiment into policy circles. Foreign policy decisions, particularly those regarding security and defence, were and have continued to be almost exclusively the prerogative of Qatar's most senior elites. It is consequently no coincidence that improving relations with the US mirrored Hamad bin Khalifah's wider preferences. Geography aside, Qatar under Hamad reflected American values and ideas more than Saudi ones.

With neighbours like these...

Khalifah bin Hamad took power within six months of independence in 1971, having already established an understanding with Saudi Arabia regarding Qatar's security.[35] Evidently he was not perturbed by both his and Qatar's relative lack of autonomy in following Saudi Arabia's line. His stewardship was energetic at the beginning, when he sought to alter the ruling bargain to relieve the stifling pressure of his extended family. There were also flurries of embassy openings and aid-giving, though nothing that could be described as systematic. Despite hints of 'Nasserist-style' popularity in his past, he was a typical Gulf ruler, solid, slow to change, patriarchal, and conservative.

The same could not be said of his son, Hamad bin Khalifah. Although he too inherited a basic need to seek security for Qatar externally, it became increasingly obvious that he would not toe the Saudi line. However, before the split with Saudi Arabia became evident, the 1990–1991 Gulf War was to have a deep effect on Qatar.

When Iraq invaded Kuwait on 2 August 1990 and took over the small Gulf state within forty-eight hours, Qatar—in common with the rest of the region—looked on in astonishment. For the state, the parallels were both obvious and also deeply concerning. Qatar too was a small, energy-rich country with a small native population. It was also flanked on two sides by much larger neighbours with a history of belligerence and against whom it could not hope to offer any resistance.

Qatar's relationship with Iran has historically not been overly antagonistic, with the exception of proxy skirmishes centuries ago and sporadic threats from Tehran. However, in common with all the Gulf states, Qatar harboured concerns over Iran, particularly after the country's 1979 revolution. This was, after all, a fervently anti-monarchical, anti-Sunni, revolutionary Shia regime that stood accused of exporting terrorism and unrest to the Gulf in the 1980s. Iran's military capabilities were also manifest.

Worse still, Qatar shared the world's largest gas field with Iran. By developing its side of the largely sea-based gas field, Qatar opened another vector of concern in that it could be accused (as Kuwait had been) of extracting more than its fair share. Indeed, Qatar's hugely expensive investment in the field would fundamentally change the dynamic of bilateral relations, with Iran being contiguously joined to the source of Qatar's future wealth. In such a precarious position, Qatar made what many may see as an understandable decision to seek support in the form of a closer relationship with the US. Only with this type of capable military force on the Qatari Peninsula could Doha acquire some peace of mind in respect of its relationship with Iran.

Aside from a hiatus of a few decades, Qatar's historical relations with Saudi Arabia were far from harmonious, given marauding Wahhabi raids in the eighteenth, nineteenth, and twentieth centuries. Although concerns over Qatar's security in respect of Iran and Saudi Arabia would have to be termed low-probability, high-impact events, the likelihood of Iraq invading Kuwait would have been characterised in exactly the same manner. Moreover, given the slow deterioration in relations with Saudi Arabia in the early 1990s and increased tensions around the border at Al Udeid (the town rather than the base) that culminated in border skirmishes in 1992 and 1993, the prospect of a larger conflagration between Saudi Arabia and Qatar was becoming more likely. Hamad bin Khalifah noted this himself in an interview with Lebanese newspaper *As Safir* in 2009, in which he described Qatar as 'not ready to face the burdens' of confronting Saudi Arabia in the early 1990s.[36]

Even if Qatar was content to remain under Saudi Arabia's aegis, between the tanker war and its humiliating request for foreign troops for operations Desert Shield and Desert Storm, Saudi Arabia could evidently not protect itself sufficiently. Furthermore, in terms of subsequent developments in the US-Qatar relationship, as well as Qatar being open to hosting increasingly important US bases, the US had no option but to leave Saudi Arabia in 2003. The presence of US troops in the kingdom was placing the bilateral relationship between Washington and Riyadh under increasing strain. This was another example of the regional situation facilitating a key aspect of Qatari foreign policy.

Any notion that an often-mooted pan-GCC military force might offer Qatar any measure of security has long been, in reality, as unrealistic as any putative Saudi security guarantees. In reality, the GCC force has perennially suffered from some combination of a lack of interoperability, poor training, and issues of control at elite levels. Lastly, any notion that Qatar could use its oil and future gas wealth to buy support through foreign aid was routed with the invasion of Kuwait. Exactly these kinds of understandings had underpinned Kuwaiti foreign policy for decades, but they did not save it from a devastating invasion. In particular the Palestinians, in the form of PLO leader Yasser Arafat, despite being significant recipients of Kuwaiti largesse, had turned their backs on Kuwait and supported Iraq's invasion. This was a bitter blow for Kuwait and instructive for any other state that had faith in such reciprocity. The experience seemed to underline that the only secure means of guaranteeing security was with that most basic but effective of deterrents— military might.

The opportunity the Carter Doctrine needed

In the 1970s, US President Richard Nixon employed a 'twin-pillar' policy towards the Gulf, namely delegating the region's security to regional 'policemen' Iran and Saudi Arabia. This allowed Washington to support these client states, and by extension regional security, while at the same time remaining aloof. This approach was successful until Iran's 1979 Islamic revolution effectively emasculated the policy.

The US subsequently required a new strategy for the region's security. Not only did it need to replace its now defunct policy, but, with its 1979 invasion of Afghanistan, the Soviet Union had also come within a few hundred miles of the Gulf. In the feverish atmosphere of the Cold War, this development agitated Washington,[37] while the region itself was becoming ever more important to the world economy and oil supply. From 1985 onwards, following a period in which the risk had been shared more equally, the world once more became significantly more dependent on Gulf oil.[38]

US President Jimmy Carter in 1980 inaugurated his eponymous doctrine, which declared that the US would defend what it viewed as its national interests in the Gulf with force. This laid the ground for the US to acquire an increasing foothold in the region as the 1980s progressed. While at least $3.2 billion of military services had been sold to Saudi Arabia in the 1970s, the Iraq-Iran war from 1980 onwards augmented Saudi fears, allowing the US to increase its support. Eventually, Washington sold a (theoretical) Gulf-wide air defence system worth $50 billion that included the stationing of five AWACS planes in Saudi Arabia, allowing for $14 billion of bases to be established and augmented throughout the country. Overall, around 10,000 US civilian and several hundred military advisers were present in Saudi Arabia by the end of the decade.[39] As US Defence Secretary Caspar Weinberger's classified 1984–1988 'Defence Guidance Report' noted, this formed part of a concerted plan to facilitate the introduction of US forces to the region if needed to defend Saudi Arabia and maintain regional stability.[40]

These arrangements were secret and there was little official commentary regarding the development of US-Gulf relations until the latter part of the decade. Although hard to imagine today following more than two decades of cheek-by-jowl relations between the US and Gulf states, few Gulf states in the 1980s were disposed to co-operate with Washington.[41] Some considered Kuwait an overt ally of the Soviet Union and even a 'conduit' for Moscow to showcase the benefits of communist friendship.[42] However, the invasion of Afghanistan, a Muslim country, cooled Kuwait's relations with the Soviet Union, and it moved to a position of superpower non-alignment. Qatar was not disposed to either superpower and became positively anti-US following the Stinger missile dispute in the late 1980s.

It took Kuwait's threat to seek Soviet assistance to reflag its oil tankers during the tanker war, as well as the realisation that Washington could provide protection much more effectively, before the US finally engaged significantly with the Gulf. The US had been building up its forces in the Indian Ocean, based in Diego Garcia, and sent around fifty ships to the Gulf to reflag tankers, project its power, and make a statement of intent.[43]

Iraq's invasion of Kuwait finally provided the US with the opportunity it needed. Up to this point, Saudi Arabia in particular had wanted to conceal its increasingly close relations with Washington, and would only countenance an overt relationship if it encountered an unprecedented challenge. Iraq's invasion of Kuwait provided just such a challenge. Qatar at this stage was a passive actor, and it took the US's slowly increasing focus on the Gulf, incrementally closer relations, and the Kuwait invasion-induced paradigm shift in the region's international relations for the US to become a palatable actor with whom to engage and for Qatar's leadership to feel it needed to call on US assistance. The invasion of Kuwait asked new existential questions of Qatar, while simultaneously providing the answer.

3

GAS POLICIES

Decades before the discovery in 1971 of a huge gas field shared with Iran, Qatar had formulated plans to use associated gas (gas found with oil) for domestic power generation. However, these plans foundered, while early plans to liquefy gas and ship it to Japan—which had been mooted as early as 1960—took decades to come to fruition.[1] In the 1960s and early 1970s, gas was typically seen as an annoyance to be flared off, or burned away.[2] Nevertheless, such sentiments were to evolve. By 1974, only 66 per cent of gas was flared and by 1979 just 5 per cent.[3] This shift primarily reflected the completion of the first natural gas liquids plant (NGL 1) in 1975, four years after work began. The plant broke associated gas down into useful products such as propane, butane, and gasoline, some of which was then exported.[4]

However, the plant was beset by problems and in 1976 suffered a huge leak of 14,000 barrels of propane that was not properly repaired. On 3 April 1977, the plant exploded as 236,000 barrels of propane leaked, engulfing storage for 125,000 barrels of butane. The ensuing fire burned for eight days, killing six people, and at the time was the most expensive accident in the history of the gas industry worldwide, costing insurers $68 million (approximately $568 million as a total economic cost in 2014 dollars).[5]

Although NGL 2 was completed in 1979, the earlier explosion had cast a pall over the gas industry in Qatar. Even though Shell in 1971 discovered an enormous gas field shared between Qatar and Iran that would come to be known as the North Field for Qatar and South Pars for Iran, gas was so unattractive that the overriding emotion on discovering the field was one of disappointment that it was not an oilfield.[6] The NGL 1 accident further prompted the Qatari elite to consider cutting back rather than diversifying into gas, slowing any meaningful plans to develop the field.[7] Although in the 1970s and 1980s Qatar's oil was expected to run out by the end of the millennium, this was not a sufficiently pressing concern to reduce the fixation on oil to the detriment of gas.[8] The oil price spike of the 1970s further insulated the oil industry and undercut the argument for diversification. Annually, Qatar made $2 billion in 1975 from oil alone, rising to more than $5 billion by 1980.[9] Neither could Japanese interest in investing in Qatar's gas industry in the 1970s snap Qatar's elite out of an anti-gas mind-set.[10] These factors, along with concerns over continuing global gas demand, led Doha-based diplomats to suggest that the North Field would be left 'until the late 1980s.'[11] And so it proved.

As the 1980s progressed, oil prices fell and Qatar endured a relatively difficult financial period, sustaining successive budget deficits for the first time and financing debt through external borrowing.[12] The state did not even announce a budget for 1986–1987 as the deficit grew.[13] Lethargy, inaction, and institutional difficulties surrounding decision-making characterised Qatari action in a difficult regional climate. However, a three-part plan to develop the North Field eventually emerged in the 1980s.

Phase one was concerned with exploiting the field for domestic use. It was launched in 1987 following several delays stemming from poor work quality and a hostile regional environment. On the twentieth anniversary of Qatar's independence and the field's discovery, production on the North Field began in 1991.[14]

Phase two focused on the creation of a regional pipeline-based gas grid, which was scheduled to come on-line by 1996. This plan was cheaper than engaging in the liquefied natural gas (LNG) industry and was the preferred choice at the time.[15] Not only would it boost Qatar's importance were it to become a significant regional gas supplier, but the cost, at around $2 billion, was more manageable than a global LNG hub and spoke system. Discussions between GCC oil ministers took place in 1988. At the annual GCC summit the following year, the idea of piping North Field gas to Saudi Arabia, the UAE, Kuwait, and Bahrain was approved, while at the 1990 summit the 'GCC Nations agreed to nearly all the essentials for the regional pipeline, except the price.'[16] However, this concept soon foundered as regional competition, rivalries, and war came to the fore. Grand plans for pipelines to Israel, India, and Pakistan persisted for several years before they were also abandoned.[17]

The third phase of the plan focused on LNG. However, progress was slow following discussions in 1982 between Qatar and Shell, British Petroleum (BP), and Total (then CFP), which were offered 7.5 per cent equity stakes in a joint venture to exploit the North Field for LNG. Following Shell's withdrawal in 1984, a joint-venture agreement to export LNG to Japan was signed, providing BP and Total with a 7.5 per cent stake each in the Qatargas LNG plant.[18] Nevertheless, Qatar's demands slowed the negotiations and made it almost uneconomical ('marginal', as one oil company executive put it),[19] while the escalating conflict between Iran and Iraq and the attendant tanker war disincentivised the external parties.[20]

Nevertheless, amid growing LNG competition stemming from South Korea and Taiwan entering the LNG market (on the demand side) in 1986 and 1990 respectively, there was pressure on Japan to secure long-term contracts. Japan's *sogo shosha*—general trading companies such as Mitsubishi and Marubeni—which had been operating in Qatar for decades, acted as 'the glue' between the Japanese state, Japanese regional gas companies, and Qatar during

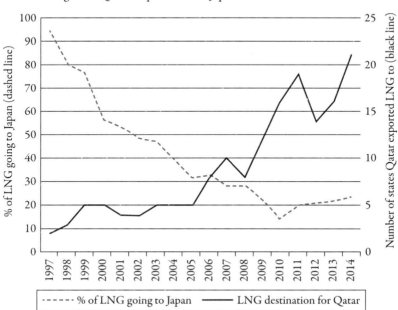

Figure 1: Qatar's dependence on Japan and LNG destinations

Source: Natural Gas Information 2000–2014.[21]

negotiations in the late 1980s and 1990s.[22] Overall, Japan played a significant role in the development of Qatar's LNG industry.

> In addition to Japanese end customers, Japanese *Sogo Shosha* brokering the deals, Japanese firms involved in the construction of the apparatus, the Japanese Government oversaw key financing. The Government-led Export-Import Bank of Japan (J-EXIM) provided the majority of the $3bn for the first LNG 'train' in Qatar along with other Japanese banks.[23]

The Japanese persevered despite the Iran-Iraq War, the tanker war, the invasion of Kuwait, the flight of skilled personnel from the Gulf, repeated infrastructure problems in Qatar, and BP withdrawing in 1992 and being replaced by Mobil. Finally, in January 1997, Japan received its first LNG from Qatar.

As highlighted in Figure 1, in the first year of LNG exports, more than 95 per cent of Qatari LNG went to Japan, though the percentage of LNG exports to Japan fell as Spain and Korea (particularly from 2000 onwards) imported more LNG and Qatar diversified its export markets.

Korea and Japan proved the mainstay for Qatari LNG exports until 2004, when India started to import significant quantities of LNG. In the late 2000s, the UK also began to import sizeable amounts of LNG from Qatar, and was the leading buyer of Qatari LNG in 2010 and 2011. With new LNG trains coming online in 2006 and 2009, Qatar significantly diversified its suppliers to include Brazil, Chile, Kuwait, Luxembourg, and Mexico.

When Qatar entered the LNG market in 1997, the state exported 4 per cent of the world's LNG that year while Indonesia was by far the world's largest LNG supplier, and Algeria and Malaysia were also significant suppliers.

Subsequently, Qatar became a mature, then a powerful and then a dominant supplier, with an ever-growing share of the global LNG market. With its fourteenth train coming online in January 2011, its market share leapt to 31 per cent, accounting for almost 90 per cent of the increase in the LNG trade in 2011.[24] By 2013, Qatar was by far the largest LNG producer in the world, a position it is expected to retain until the late 2010s.

The abandoned phase-two plan to establish a network of regional pipes was revived in the late 1990s. Saudi objections blocked any northward pipes to Bahrain and Kuwait, but the kingdom's objections to a pipe going to the UAE and then on to Oman were tenuous and ultimately ignored. A subsection of the Emirati Ministry of Defence—the UAE Offsets Group (UOG)—and the Qatari Dolphin Group were created in 1999 to oversee and administer the new project piping Qatari gas to the UAE and on to Oman.[25] The desire on the Emirati side was multi-faceted. Politically, the move would increase regional integration between Qatar, the UAE, and Oman, while economically it made some sense, given foreseeable energy shortages in the UAE. The project called for a 370km pipe to be laid from Qatar's processing facilities at Ras Laffan on the east coast to Abu Dhabi, and the construction of new facilities at a cost of $3.5 billion.[26]

As Dargin notes, January 2004 was 'a truly historic moment in that it was the first ever cross-border gas transmission in the history of the GCC.'[27] The Dolphin project subsequently came up to speed, supplying 2 billion cubic feet per day (bcf/d) of natural gas to the UAE, approximately 30 per cent of the federation's daily demand as of 2012.[28] Although the UAE has sought to maximise the pipe's capacity, which can supply up to 3.5 bcf/d to meet surging domestic demand, negotiations have proved difficult. Emir Hamad bin Khalifah had to intervene to force Qatar Petroleum (QP) to lower its price. Considering that Qatar can sell the gas for a higher price via LNG, persuading the Qatari elite to once again accept a loss to supply the UAE will be hard.

A new elite with new vision and capabilities

Despite these difficulties, there was a certain inevitability about Qatar's move into the LNG market. As noted above, this has been an espoused goal of the state since the 1960s. However, there is significant difference between remarking on a goal and mortgaging the country to engage in a risky paradigm-shifting venture.

Khalifah bin Hamad appeared unwilling to take gas seriously. His focus was dominated by oil and, as Abdullah bin Hamad Al Attiyah noted, the discovery of the largest gas field in the world mostly within Qatari territory was greeted in some quarters with disappointment. Indeed, the timidity of the old regime in pursuing such a policy is summed up by Dargin, who discretely describes Khalifah bin Hamad as 'far less aggressive in promoting the country's resource development.'[29]

LNG began to be taken seriously and progress was made in the mid to late 1980s as the new elite led by Hamad bin Khalifah rose to power. The international flavour of LNG policy, making Qatar crucial to leading countries around the globe, was exactly the type of policy that could be expected from the new elite, with its drive to internationalise the state.

Although Khalifah bin Hamad and his elite would have eventually sought to develop Qatar's LNG capacity, nothing about their priorities, working practices, or outlook suggests that they would have pursued this opportunity with anything like the speed and success of their successors. Part of this assertion reflects an issue of vision as much as a question of personnel. In terms of the former, the old elite's actions were characterised by caution and a resolutely intra-regional mind-set. The decision to mortgage Qatar's future income, which was taken in the early 1990s when the new elite was running the country in all but name, is the type of risky decision that came to characterise their tenure and bears little resemblance to old policies. Equally, aside from a spate of embassy openings and rounds of distributing foreign aid when economic circumstances allowed, the old elite seldom sought prolonged and involved interaction with states outside the Gulf. Deeply and inextricably intertwining Qatar's economy with that of Japan, Spain, Korea, and subsequently the UK, is a feature associated with the new rather than the old elite.

In respect of personnel, Khalifah bin Hamad for much of his tenure was the personification of a hands-on ruler, and in the 1970s and early 1980s insisted on signing all cheques of $50,000 and over.[30] Such a lack of delegation of responsibility has a deleterious effect on efficiency and severely impinged on long, complex negotiations. Indeed, it is no wonder that Hashimoto et al conclude that this kind of 'lack of institutionalized decision-making in Qatar likely stalled progress in negotiating the complexities of LNG development.'[31] They proceed to quote a Shell executive who worked in Qatar at the time as noting that the situation was also vastly complicated, and made worse by the presence of 'advisers' who 'were not unnaturally intent on protecting their positions and so raised question after question to justify their presence.'[32]

Although Qatar remained plagued by the overbearingly top-down nature of politics, a younger, more energetic elite intent on pursuing LNG as a crucial part of their plan to bolster Qatar's independence naturally placed more emphasis on LNG. Moreover, in the person of Abdullah bin Hamad Al Attiyah, the new elite installed a trusted executive who doggedly, effectively, and professionally focused on Qatar's gas industry.

Both the old and the new elite felt pressure to use the gas industry to diversify Qatar's oil income to maintain the ruling bargain and the generous Qatari welfare state. The key difference was that the new elite was more dynamic in pursuing such a goal, as opposed to suffering from the lethargic reluctance to change that often characterises ageing Arab governments. As many changes as the new elite brought to Qatar, they did not seek to alter the basic ruling bargain. This understanding demands that the citizens do not agitate for a political say in how the country is run, and in return receive cradle-to-grave welfare support from the government while paying no taxes. This system can only function with a successful rentier economy, which typically requires significant oil or gas revenues for the state to distribute. Bolstering this bargain by offering the public more and better services for free is an obvious goal of government in Qatar, and one that getting the LNG industry up and running meets.

Moreover, although this bargain was strong in Qatar in the 1990s, it suffered in the 1980s when the constriction in global oil prices and production meant that services and jobs had to be cut and charges introduced. It was clear that the source of the state's income needed to diversify to maintain the rentier bargain, without even considering the added dimension of the new elite's vast array of plans. New LNG policies were the key to unlocking Hamad bin Khalifah vision for Qatar.

Escaping Saudi Arabia's "gravitational pull"

Once more, Saudi Arabia was of key importance in influencing the decision-making hierarchy in Qatar and informing major policy changes. Following the 1988 and 1989 GCC summits that initially welcomed Qatar's regional gas initiatives, Saudi Arabia's elite changed its position over the subsequent few years, for a variety of reasons.

Firstly, as Figure 2 shows, Saudi Arabia's own gas reserves increased substantially towards the end of the 1980s. From 4.19 trillion cubic metres (tcm) in 1987, by 1989 the kingdom's reserves had increased by more than 1 million cubic metres, or around 30 per cent, to 5.2 tcm, as indicated by the circle on the graph below. With the potential for more to come, this reminded Saudi policy-makers that the kingdom itself might want to become a gas exporter in future, and that allowing Qatar to expand into this area could restrict such opportunities. Indeed, Saudi Arabia in the early 1980s implemented a 'Master Gas' system in an attempt to collect more associated gas from oil production, underlining an increasing awareness of gas as a potential energy alternative.[33]

Secondly, Saudi Arabia was unhappy to see the younger elite increasingly take the lead in Qatar and engage in policies such as seeking to build relations with Iran. Similarly, without waiting for Saudi Arabia to take the lead, Qatar established diplomatic relations with the Soviet Union and China in 1988, and burnished its NAM credentials throughout the late 1980s, indicating increased distancing from Saudi leadership.[34] The Saudi elite viewed stymying these new gas initiatives as a means of 'putting Qatar in its place.'

Thirdly, these emerging bilateral issues were consolidated by border skirmishes in 1992, 1993, and again in 1994 that resulted in deaths on both sides.

Figure 2: Saudi Arabia's proved gas reserves, 1980–1998

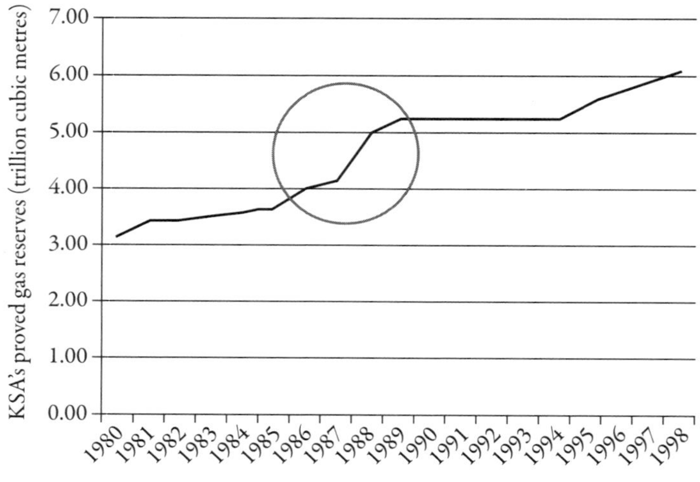

Source: BP Statistical Review of World Energy 2010.[35]

Moreover, Qatar's 1995 coup severely damaged relations with a conservative Saudi state that was unwilling to countenance a son usurping his father, and at least one Saudi-supported counter-coup ended bilateral relations in all but name. Even without this dislocation in the bilateral relationship, the new Qatari elite had shown that it was unwilling to remain dependent on Saudi Arabia. It knew that Riyadh would never have sanctioned its policy orientation—progressive and international—and understood that Qatar was not benefitting from tacit protective agreements in place.

LNG policies were crucial in facilitating the state's escape from Saudi Arabia's 'gravitational pull', as Dargin puts it, in two ways.[36] Firstly, they allowed Qatar financially to engage in a range of policies through which it sought to expand beyond its previously Saudi-dominated external relations to the wider international community. Pursuing these policies helped Qatar become a meaningful international actor rather than merely a small-scale regional player. Secondly, they deliberately intertwined Qatar with a number of key international countries in an inextricable and crucial energy-economic nexus. Qatar was diversifying its international alliances and no longer needed to toe Saudi Arabia's line.

Surging demand in Oman and particularly the UAE was a catalyst in reanimating the phase-two intra-regional pipeline project.[37] Curiously for energy exporting states—and particularly so for the UAE given its prodigious oil and gas supplies—both countries have experienced domestic energy shortages in recent decades.[38] This partly stems from the evident preference to sell energy abroad for a higher price given the high opportunity cost of producing it under cost (i.e. subsidised) for the local market. Importing gas from Qatar was one way to square this circle to prevent Oman and the UAE suffering from, at one stage, 'substantial gas shortages.'[39] As Dargin notes, this potentially places Qatar in a strong position, theoretically increasing Qatar's influence in the region.[40]

Moreover, this position as an important gas supplier could come in useful. Relations between the UAE and Qatar deteriorated severely in 2014 and the UAE led the isolation of Qatar within the GCC. Though this situation was resolved with the return of the UAE, Saudi, and Bahraini Ambassadors in November the same year, the fact that Qatar is an important supplier of fuel to the UAE gives Qatar's elite some leverage if relations seriously deteriorate again.

An international perspective

Expected growth in Asian economies facilitated Qatar's decision to invest heavily—in the form of debt—in the LNG industry. Between 1975 and 1996, LNG demand from the Asia-Pacific region was strong, at around 3.31bcm per year. This was a significant amount, given that it was greater than the capacity of the average LNG train at the time (i.e. new demand required the creation of the equivalent of one new train per year).[41] Between 1980 and 1992, the gross national product of 11 key Asian countries (Japan, Korea, Taiwan, China, Hong Kong, Singapore, Indonesia, Malaysia, Thailand, Philippines, and India) grew by an average of just under 5 per cent per year, with many countries outstripping this rate.[42] Such growth rates have a commensurate effect on energy demand, which also experienced healthy growth.[43] This level of economic growth would necessarily have to be fuelled by growth in energy imports, and the Asia-Pacific region is relatively 'poor in resources, particularly oil and gas.'[44] Oil from the Middle East would form a part of the answer, but LNG would come to play an increasingly prominent role too. LNG was viewed as a relatively clean fuel as far back as 1974, and the premium placed on avoiding dirtier fuels subsequently only increased.[45] In the mid-1980s, some observers even expected gas to become the world's leading fuel, such were its intrinsic advantages.[46]

In the mid-1990s, only Japan, South Korea, and Taiwan in Asia were importing LNG. Estimates from the Institute of Energy Economics in Japan suggested that LNG demand from these countries would double by 2010, but were in fact significantly wide of the mark. Demand from these three countries alone increased by 480 per cent, from 65 to 314 billion cubic metres (bcm) of LNG imports, between 1992 and 2010.[47]

However, this was just the beginning. By 2010, China and India had become significant customers, importing 17 per cent of Qatari LNG.[48] Although judging in hindsight should be done with a degree of caution, sufficient evidence suggested that LNG demand would be significant should Qatar develop such a capacity.

Much Western literature focusing on the meaning of the end of the Cold War unsurprisingly discusses the watershed event as a victory for capitalism. This means different things to different people, but there is often a sense that the fall of the Berlin Wall either precipitated or was the harbinger of an era of increased globalisation. In such an age, some observers believed that the autonomy of the state was under threat, while others hyperbolically touted 'the end of geography.'[49] Increased economic trade in this brave new world would 'create positive economic interdependencies that contribute to global stability, prosperity, and security.'[50] Or, as Bergsten, writing in *Foreign Affairs*, put it, 'the international position of individual countries will derive increasingly from their economic prowess rather than their military capability.'[51]

With hindsight, one can see hubris and excitement colouring the thoughts of policy practitioners. For example, the imminent stagnation of Japan as a

Figure 3: Actual vs estimated LNG imports from Japan, Korea and Taiwan

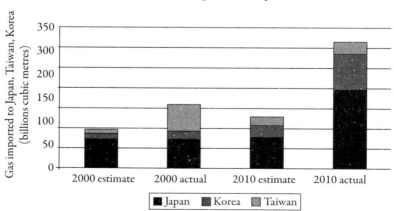

Source: IEA Natural Gas Information, Koyama[52]

state that had been assumed would take over from the US as the world's largest economy made a mockery of analysis predicated on Japan, along with the US and Europe, forming part of a new tri-polar world. Nevertheless, the international environment had changed significantly. The constrictions that the Cold War fostered, such as the zero-sum nature of international relationships and an unusually acute preoccupation with security, were either gone or no longer as acute.

Such changes created space for countries such as Qatar. In the most basic terms, Qatar could not have exported LNG to Italy, Korea, and the US, as it did in 1999, without pinning its colours to the non-Soviet mast. Long negotiations with Israel or Qatar's (albeit limited) attempts to build a pipeline to transport gas through Pakistan to India further suggest that Qatar sought to use gas as a tool to overcome tensions and, at the very least, prompt discussions and interaction. Qatar's budding international relations and consolidation of its LNG trade put the state in a position of importance it would otherwise not have had.

Such ties could possibly prove useful in matters of hard security too. The more Qatar taps its shared field with Iran and the more revenue it derives from it, the more it becomes vulnerable to Iran. Incidents in the mid-2000s displayed a willingness by Iran to attack and steal equipment from unmanned rigs, doubtless confirming long-held Qatari fears.[53] Although the range of basing agreements and security-related co-operation initiatives between Qatar and the US provide some deterrence for the state, possessing a web of influential international actors increasingly dependent on Qatar for gas has its own benefits too.

Firstly, by building capacity to become a key supplier of gas to countries across the world, Qatar plays an important role in some of the world's leading states. In 2013, the state provided Argentina with 14% of its LNG, Belgium 40%, Brazil 4%, Canada 83%, Chile 5%, China 38%, France 19%, India 85%, Japan 18%, South Korea 33%, Kuwait 86%, Mexico 23%, Spain 23%, Taiwan 50%, Thailand 74%, the UAE 84%, the UK 93%, and the US 8%.[54]

Even though Qatar occasionally only accounts for a small proportion of a state's LNG imports and LNG is, of course, not the only energy source for a country, the state is evidently crucial to several countries. Most notably, taking into account the role of LNG in each state and Qatar's contribution to it, the emirate is acutely important to states such as Belgium, China, France, India, Japan, South Korea, Spain, Taiwan, and the UK. These are financially, militarily, diplomatically, and politically powerful states that depend heavily on

Qatar's continuing prosperity and security. In 2013–2014, Qatar's importers also included four permanent members of the UN Security Council and three non-permanent members (Argentina, Korea, and Chile). This encapsulates Qatar's foreign policy thrust to enhance its security by enmeshing the state in the energy nexus of many of the world's most influential countries.

Secondly, Japan has historically enjoyed positive relations with Iran. Were relations between Qatar and Iran to escalate to the point at which LNG production and shipping were threatened, Japan would be forced to use its relations with Iran to seek some form of a workable accommodation to avoid quickly running short of gas. The same applies to all Qatar's LNG customers. In the case of the UK, Qatar has made security of supply a concern of the first order: if the UK wants its gas and there is Iranian aggression, the UK needs to 'keep the lights on' and join with the international community to find a solution. This type of corollary remains of key importance to Qatar in becoming such a prolific energy exporter.

4

INTERNATIONAL MEDIATION
AND NEGOTIATION

Qatar's mediation activities under emirs Hamad bin Khalifah Al Thani and Tamim bin Hamad Al Thani have been qualitatively and quantitatively different from the policies of their predecessors. Historically, there have been examples of individuals in exile coming to the Qatari Peninsula, and occasionally some form of informal 'mediation' ensuing between disgruntled parties. Similarly, there have been isolated examples of, for example, Ahmed bin Ali Al Thani (r. 1960–1972) hosting more formal negotiations with disputants from the UAE or, more interestingly, playing a small role in the culmination of Algerian independence from France in March 1962.[1] In this instance, during final negotiations with France for independence in 1962, Ahmed bin Ali provided the Algerian delegation with the use of his palace in Vienna, funds to cover expenses, and secure telephone lines, the very definition of providing good offices.[2] However, prior to Hamad bin Khalifah's initiatives, there is no evidence of any systematic attempt to make Qatar a state known for its mediation, and certainly not in the wider Middle East. In short, mediation is clearly a policy of the new era.

Before discussing Qatari mediation further, it is important to grasp what mediation actually is. After a suitable definition has been arrived at, three of the most influential instances of Qatari mediation will be discussed. Conclusions as to why Qatar involved itself in these issues will then be fleshed out to better explain why the state has developed a role for itself as a mediator, and how this helps secure its global ambitions.

As with any such all-encompassing term, mediation can be defined widely, for example, 'by the sought outcome (settlement, end to hostilities...); against other forms of dispute settling (arbitration, litigation...) or according to sought attributes of a mediator such as neutrality or impartiality.'[3] Following an earlier study of Qatari mediation, a broader definition will be used that encompasses the state's diverse activities. Mediation will be understood as 'a form of conflict management in which a third party assists two or more contending parties to find a solution without resorting to force.'[4]

The question then arises as to how the mediator mediates, as there is a continuum of involvement ranging from facilitation[5] through formulation to manipulation.[6] Typically, facilitation is more passive, with the mediator relaying messages and arranging meetings, as opposed to manipulation, where progress is theoretically maintained through 'the "introduction of an element of power" and the mediator is overall far more active, dynamic and "forceful" in the process.'[7] In between these two poles, the mediator is involved in suggesting ways to proceed, reframing questions and offering proposals, but not in coercing or cajoling the disputants.

Qatar's forays into mediation in the Arab world, the Horn of Africa, and North Africa run the gamut of these definitions. In May 2008, the political situation in Lebanon was deteriorating rapidly following 18 months of parliamentary gridlock and mass demonstrations in which around ten people were killed,[8] while escalating clashes between Shia movement Hezbollah and the Lebanese government clearly highlighted the Shia movement's strength. It was at this point that Qatar stepped in and flew politicians from all sides to Doha for five days of intense negotiations. This is classic example of manipulation in the mediation process. Qatar certainly facilitated the negotiations, providing a relatively neutral setting for the parties to come together, while its leadership provided suggestions and ideas. However, reports from the negotiations indicated that Hamad bin Khalifah and his foreign minister, Hamad bin Jassim Al Thani, were practically locked away in the Sheraton Hotel, cajoling, pressuring, and discussing options and ways forward.[9] Qatar in this instance has been credited with bringing Lebanon 'back from the brink' by stabilising Lebanese politics temporarily at least.[10]

Qatar took a more reserved position in Sudan. From 2008 until interim agreements in 2010 and subsequent iterations of discussions, Qatar was a primary facilitator of negotiations between warring parties in the conflict in the western Darfur region. The state provided years of good offices to all sides to come to Qatar to negotiate an agreement. Indeed, 'Darfur Protocol' signs festooned several of downtown Doha's five-star hotels for a number of years. Initially, Minister of State for Foreign Affairs Ahmed bin Abdullah Al Mahmood knew 'nothing whatsoever' about the conflict, but he soon became a key figure in the process.[11] However, compared with Lebanon—the Qatari leadership had grown up learning about Levantine politics and the actors were already known to them—the Darfur negotiations were more aloof, and Qatar significantly leveraged the expertise of foreign experts to assist the talks.[12] In short, Qatar's role in the Darfur negotiations involved less manipulation, aside from last-minute negotiations when agreements were due to be signed.

More recently under Hamad bin Khalifah and particularly Tamim bin Hamad, Qatar has repeatedly acted as a negotiator to secure the release of hostages being held by a variety of extremist groups around the Middle East. Most widely known from a Western perspective is Qatar's role in the release in August 2014 of US journalist Peter Theo Curtis in Syria and in the release of the last US serviceman being held by the Taliban in Afghanistan, Bowe Bergdahl, who returned home in June 2014.[13] In Syria in 2013 and 2014, meanwhile, Qatar helped secure the release of 48 Iranians being held by Syrian rebels,[14] 45 Fijian peacekeepers,[15] 13 Greek Orthodox nuns,[16] and 30 Turkish diplomats and security officials,[17] while in Yemen it negotiated the release of a Swiss woman captured by tribes in the west of the country in early 2013.[18] In Eritrea, Qatar presided over successful negotiations to secure the release of a Djiboutian soldier from the government in September 2014,[19] while in June 2015 it negotiated the release of four Tajik border guards whom the Taliban had captured.[20]

As will be argued below, these hostage negotiations can be viewed either as discrete incidents or as part of a much wider mediation strategy. Both suggestions accord with the reasons that the literature on mediation offers as to why states engage in mediation.

> The motives for initiating individual mediation may include (a) a genuine desire to change the course of a long-standing or escalating conflict and promote peace, (b) a desire to gain access to major political leaders and open channels of communication, (c) a desire to spread one's ideas and enhance personal standing and professional status.

> Where mediators represent an official government...motives...may include: (a) a clear mandate to intervene in disputes [i.e. state is constitutionally mandated to do so], (b) a desire to do something about a conflict whose continuance may adversely affect their own political interests, (c) being approached directly by one or both parties... (d) the wish to preserve intact a structure of which they are a part...

(e) viewing mediation as a way of extending and enhancing their own influence and gaining some value from the conflict.[21]

In the case of Qatar, where politics is so elite-dominated and where a group of no more than three of four people formulate and put new policies into action, one must consider 'personal' motivations alongside 'state' motivations. As will be discussed, many of these other motivations apply to the Qatari example, but the importance of 'enhancing their own influence', a typical motivating factor according to the literature, is a recurring theme.

A very 'Hamadian' policy

Reasons stemming from the domestic level as to why Qatar engaged and continues to engage in mediation initiatives naturally focus on the leadership's influence. This is to be expected given the dominance of Qatar's modern elites, how few other domestic influences can be seen as having an impact on foreign policy, and how much mediation is a strategy of choice as opposed to necessity. Indeed, it is hard to avoid the reflection in Qatar's forays into mediation of the overarching tone of Qatar under Hamad bin Khalifah. Mediation is an archetypal Hamadian policy.

Before Khalifah bin Hamad came to power, Qatar was little more than a quickly growing village with an Al Thani leader at the helm who appeared to spend as much time abroad as in Doha. Ironically, the only time that Qatar engaged in any form of extra-regional mediation was when Ahmed bin Ali's penchant for living in Europe presented an opportunity (on his very doorstep) to offer good offices in support of Algerian independence negotiations in 1962.

More generally, before Hamad bin Khalifah began to exert influence in Doha, there were few examples of Qatari leaders overly engaging in extraneous foreign affairs such as mediation. Indeed, for a state grasping with the need to build rudimentary ministries and systems, as Qatar was for much of the twentieth century, there was seldom spare capacity and little elite desire to involve Qatar in any type of international mediation, aside from spurts of embassy openings or international aid-giving when budgets allowed. It would also be fair to note the more conservative disposition of Hamad bin Khalifah's predecessors, which militated against 'risky' international manoeuvres. In short, it is unsurprising that Qatari leaders did not engage in any significant wider mediatory forays, and in keeping with their character and ruling temperament.

Like his father before him, on taking over in 1995, Hamad bin Khalifah built on existing attempts to popularise himself and his rule. He continued to use rentier policies distributing wealth for support, but also took steps to disperse power, enfranchise women, modernise the education system and the constitution, and significantly open up domestic debate by removing overt censorship. These policies pointed to the direction in which he was seeking to take the state, namely on a clearly more 'liberal' tack. In this context, fostering a reputation for Qatar as a state seeking to bring peace through mediation has progressive echoes of Hamad's domestic direction of travel.

Moreover, particularly in the pre-Arab spring era, Qatar expanded its relations with regional states as an inoffensive, 'neutral' actor. This established Qatar's reputation as a state that was willing to bear the financial and reputational cost of facilitating peace internationally, highlighting a sense of burgeoning international statesmanship that Hamad bin Khalifah's long-serving and dynamic foreign minister, Hamad bin Jassim Al Thani, personified. And, particularly with Qatar's modus operandi so often involving cheque-book diplomacy, it was little surprise that the state cultivated close relations with several governments and individuals keen to build ties with a munificent small state.

Hamad bin Khalifah sought to indelibly inscribe these progressive notions in respect of foreign policy into Qatar's constitution. Article seven of the constitution that was drawn up under his aegis and approved by a plebiscite in 2003 notes that:

> The foreign policy of the State is based on the principle of strengthening international peace and security by means of encouraging peaceful resolution of international disputes; and shall support the right of peoples to self-determination; and shall not interfere in the domestic affairs of states; and shall co-operate with peace-loving nations.[22]

Just as policies notionally aimed at a domestic audience can have an impact abroad, so too can foreign policies be designed to resonate at the domestic level; as former US House of Representatives speaker Thomas O'Neill noted, 'all politics is local.' From Qatar's support for the Palestinian cause through the Palestinian Islamist movement Hamas, to wide-ranging mediation initiatives, the state was undertaking policies that frequently played well at home.[23]

Although the frequency and depth of Qatar's mediation was new, there was a distinct echo in such policies of Qatar's historical role as a *Kaaba Al Madiyoom*. Both infer a certain unusual openness to discussions with all sides in a conflict. However, striking echoes aside, there is no proof that Hamad bin Khalifah actively sought to build on this historical trait by expanding from hosting exiles—a 'light' version of offering good offices—to fully-fledged facilitation, formulation, and manipulation. Tamim bin Hamad's explicit referral on taking power to maintaining Qatar's role as the *Kaaba Al Madiyoom* suggests a desire to actively build on a historic Qatari trait,[24] and neither leader would be the first to hark back to a trait in a country's past to forge some link of historical continuity to the present. However, the leap from correlation to causation cannot be made in this instance. Nevertheless, Qatar's penchant for hosting exiles proved useful, both in its mediation efforts and in its Arab spring policies.

Issues of finance at the domestic level are also important. A prosaic but crucial point is that Qatar began to accrue more money than it could spend, particularly in the late 2000s. With such a situation comes not only a search for ways to spend the excess funds, but also a lower threshold for deciding whether to engage in a particular activity or not. In this context, mediation became a 'luxury' item that Qatar could easily afford without any serious opportunity cost considerations.

Linked to this, Gulbrandsen seeks to link Qatari business interests and Qatari mediation efforts.[25] He rightly notes that, in Lebanon in 2007, when the country's political crisis was at its height, Qatar was the fourth-largest investor in the country.[26] He also notes that Qataris are known to have personal property and business interests in Lebanon, while the country's proximity to Syria, where Qatar also had significant investments, further intimates that 'business diplomacy,' driven by a desire to secure Qatar's investments, may have been a motivating factor. This argument is all the more plausible when considering that the Qatari elite's small size means that such an elite can direct state policy to significantly reflect its own personal motivations should it choose to do so.

While Qatari elite investment in Lebanon and Syria is likely to have been a factor in the decision to mediate, splitting the vexatious issues of correlation and causality in this case is—once again—difficult. Money was certainly not the only factor. If Qatar mediated or otherwise intervened everywhere either it or its elite had investments, its foreign policy would be even more active than it already is. Gulbrandsen provides more sporadically compelling statistics in respect of the depth of Qatari investment in Yemen and Sudan, but the question of causality remains problematic.[27]

Finally, the ever-present but nevertheless ephemeral issue of reciprocity also needs to be examined. There is frequently a sense in Qatari foreign policy that the state is building relations with a view to stockpiling credit to be cashed in at some stage. Take the example of Sudan, juxtaposed against Qatar, which is one of the most food insecure nations on earth that imports at least 90 per cent of its food from abroad, while Sudan was once known as the 'bread basket of Africa.'[28] Or consider the potential utility of having solid relations with the Sudanese government in September 2014 when Qatar faced regional pressure needed to deport or repatriate Muslim Brotherhood leaders, some of whom are believed to have gone to Sudan.[29] The mediation process cost Qatar up to $2 billion, but the state nevertheless showed deep commitment despite numerous setbacks. Even when Sudanese President Omar Al Bashir was being attacked in the Western press and indicted as a war criminal, Qatar stuck by his side.[30] There is therefore a sense that Qatar in this instance and others like it engaged for wider reasons that hint towards issues of reciprocity but which are nevertheless hard to pin down.[31]

Expanding a regional presence

Kuwait in the 1970s pioneered the role of a small Gulf state seeking to engage in a range of international relations, using its financial largesse to bolster causes deemed worthy to engender a positive, non-aligned reputation.[32] Indeed, Kuwait's oil money has long been used for foreign and even defence policy, to the extent where 'virtually every time a danger presented itself, Kuwait responded with foreign aid.'[33]

While Kuwait was actively using its financial largesse in the Middle East to support friendly causes, Qatar was decades behind in terms of development. From the eighteenth century onwards, Kuwait—the 'Marseilles of the Gulf' as Goldberg memorably describes it[34]—was more established and advanced, while Qatar was still a collection of small, mostly poor villages. There was consequently little opportunity for Qatar to emulate such a foreign policy until later in the twentieth century. As oil began to flow more vigorously in the 1970s and oil prices rose steeply in line with the regional crises noted in Chapter 1, Khalifah bin Hamad engaged in sporadic attempts to burnish Qatar's international image, notably by following the Kuwaiti example and offering international aid. However, there was no paradigm shift in Qatar's foreign policies, more a peripatetic desire to dabble internationally when the international climate was favourable and funds were available.

Yet it was this quietist regional history that helped Qatar when it sought to become a mediator. By virtue of being such a restrained international actor, Qatar could credibly claim that it hardly had any 'axe to grind' on the international scene. Unlike Saudi Arabia, which by virtue of its size and geopolitical self-image had long had defined policies, allies, and enemies around the region, Qatar presented a relatively blank slate.

Saudi Arabia was one of many would-be mediators that failed in Lebanon in 2008. A key reason for its failure is that its history in the region meant that it could not possibly be viewed as impartial. In particular, Hezbollah, one of the protagonists in the negotiations, would not accept a meaningful mediatory role for Saudi Arabia. By contrast, Qatar had no history of animosity towards the Shia movement and had been seeking to diversify its international contacts and open lines of discussion and support with all parties. Qatar was therefore in the almost unique position of being able to call Tel Aviv and Tehran in the morning and the hills of southern Lebanon and the Washington Beltway in the afternoon.[35] Its ability to be an interlocutor in negotiations that required the acquiescence and support of diverse actors such as Israel, Iran, and the US provided it with a comparative advantage that it used to good effect. In this sense, Qatar sought to fill a gap in regional politics.

It is also possible to view Qatar's forays into regional mediation as a means of calming regional tensions, particularly in respect of Iran.[36] Arab-Persian animosity stems from perennial questions of identity, culture, and religion. The modern twist, stemming from Iran's 1979 revolution, heightened concerns and highlighted the differences between conservative Sunni monarchies and proselytising republican Shia revolutionaries.

The Gulf states' reaction to Iran and its international politics has varied. Saudi Arabia typically leads a staunch block that seeks to contain Iran wherever possible, and accommodation and negotiation, while occasionally undertaken, is the exception rather than the rule. Abu Dhabi has increasingly followed Saudi Arabia's path, while Kuwait occasionally falls into place (though the state's effervescent and independent-minded parliament provided its foreign policies with ever more balance as the 2000s progressed). Bahrain also follows Riyadh's path and has done so with additional enthusiasm since Arab spring protests erupted in the kingdom's capital in February 2011. By contrast, Oman and Qatar have largely eschewed the Saudi line for decades, and both believe that it is in their best interests to attempt to deal with Iran constructively. Although this is not to say that bilateral relations with Iran are necessarily warm, Oman and Qatar have normally reached a different conclusion to the 'Iranian equation' to that reached by Saudi Arabia. Several instances of Qatari mediation may be viewed in this context, namely one in which Qatar has sought innovative and non-confrontational ways to address Iran's growing influence.

Although Qatar has a positive relationship with Hezbollah that has allegedly extended to supporting the movement financially and certainly politically, this does not mean that it wants to see an Iranian proxy take untrammelled power in Lebanon.[37] Hezbollah is clearly a power to be reckoned with in the country, and Qatar's relationship with it stems not from ideological conviction but rather a sober reflection on the realities of power in the Levant. Simply ignoring such realities would be of little benefit to Qatar, just as such an approach has done Saudi Arabia little good.

Aware of the realities of power in Lebanon, as demonstrated by Hezbollah in the run-up to Qatar's mediation in 2008, Qatar sought to salvage the situation by enshrining de facto Hezbollah power in a more de jure fashion. Qatar, it can be argued, undertook a damage-limitation exercise aimed at preventing Hezbollah from fomenting further civil strife and gaining a position from which the Iran-backed group could push for further gains in the face of a weak and divided Lebanese state and army.

In the case of Qatar's negotiations in Yemen, which began in the late 2000s, the Iran link is more tenuous. The Houthis, the group that launched several uprisings since 2004 and seized control of the Yemeni capital Sanaa in late 2014, are Zaidi Muslims, a sect widely (though not universally) viewed as closer to Shia than Sunni Islam. Despite their differences, Iran is often simplistically portrayed as a natural, religiously-aligned supporter of the Houthi cause. Such an assumption has been fed by documented visits by Houthi leaders to Iran, as well as sporadic reports of weapons shipments and other forms of support.[38] In this context, it could be suggested that Qatar's desire to seek some form of equitable solution in Yemen formed part of a wider desire to shore up the troubled country to prevent the unchecked growth of Iranian influence in a failing state. Qatar's joining in with the UAE and Saudi-led war against the Houthis in Yemen in 2015 does not stem from any visibly voluntary change in Qatar's preferred modus operandi. Instead, it must be seen in the context of the 2014 pressure heaped on Qatar by Saudi Arabia and the UAE to reform its foreign policies, conform to the GCC line, and join their campaign against regional threats. In light of such pressures, and given that Emirati, Saudi, Bahraini, and Qatari soldiers are on the ground and suffering casualties in Yemen, it is inconceivable that Doha could maintain extensive links to the Houthis while they were at war with their GCC allies and, of course, Qatar too.

Finally, in terms of the wider Sudanese Horn region, Iran has historically supplied weapons to Sudan, and has explicitly sought to augment bilateral relations since the mid-2000s in particular.[39] The Iranian dimension in Sudan came to light following strikes on weapon-smuggling convoys bound for the

Gaza Strip and on a munitions factory in the Sudanese capital Khartoum.[40] Meanwhile, although reports of Iran developing a military base in Eritrea appear groundless, Eritrea has certainly significantly increased its profile vis-à-vis Iran through a raft of agreements.[41] More generally, Iran has been active in pushing senior diplomatic visits to Africa, at least partly to seek support in the face of a hostile international community.[42] It remains to be seen how much more pliant regional politics will become for Iran in light of the 2015 nuclear agreement. But Iran's charm offensive worked to some degree, with Iran receiving notable diplomatic support in respect of its nuclear programme before the P5 + 1 deal. Iran has also been accused of supplying weapons throughout the region, often with the aim of bolstering anti-Israel groups.[43]

Just as in the case of Qatar's mediation in Yemen, there is logic behind the notion that Qatar may be attempting to assert itself in the Sudanese Horn region. Involving itself in the machinations of the Darfur conflict, with all the personal contacts that such a course of action will necessarily generate, is potentially a sensible approach to develop relations and knowledge in what may be a region of strategic interest. Similarly, by investing in Sudan in the form of mediation (in terms of time, money, and effort), Qatar is shoring up its relations across the country, which may prove useful as a foil against Iranian encroachment. This means at the very least that Qatar is not the only Gulf state investing in the area, in some small way diluting Iran's opportunities to dominate.

Unencumbered and important

The Cold War prevailed for most of Khalifah bin Hamad's reign (1972–1995). Its dynamics set the overarching tone of international relations, imposing a set of constraints on the international system that were both implicitly and explicitly acted on. The place of states, their role in the system, the limits to their actions, and the expectations on them were set. With the end of the Cold War came a transformation of these fundamental issues. Stern and Druckman briefly summarise some of the effects of this paradigm shift.

> The end of an era of bipolarity, a new wave of democratization, increasing globalization of information and economic power, more frequent efforts at international co-ordination of security policy, a rash of sometimes-violent expressions of claims to rights based on cultural identity, and a redefinition of sovereignty that imposes on states new responsibilities to their citizens and the world community.[44]

Simultaneously, in the colourful words of former Central Intelligence Agency (CIA) director James Woolsey, the end of the Cold War meant that conflicts that had been pent up were released, and the dragon of the Soviet Union had been slain only to be replaced by a 'jungle of snakes.'[45] This change in the international system and in the type and number of conflicts 'opened the door for small state facilitation in conflict resolution.'[46]

An approach positing that the Cold War international system was not broadly conducive to small state mediation tallies with a grasp of the region's basic history. Under the duress of Cold War bipolarity, in which assisting or even maintaining positive relations with a particular state was potentially sufficient to pin one's colours to the wall, with all the ramifications of being readily identified with one particular camp, it is understandable that a small, relatively defenceless state such as Qatar would not pursue such a course of action. Yet with more conflicts finally escaping their Cold War-based repression, something of a 'target-rich' environment emerged for actors seeking to engage in mediation. Empirically, Yilmaz notes that, from 1948 to 1978, thirteen peacekeeping forces were established, though the number did not increase between 1978 and 1988. However, twenty new missions were created between May 1988 and October 1993. By December 2008, notes Yilmaz, a total of sixty-three had been created.[47] Such statistics highlight the explosion of smaller conflicts that the end of the Cold War era heralded, as well as the ability of and the necessity for the international community to react and do something about them.

Following the end of the Cold War, the next paradigm-altering event for the Middle East was the September 2001 attacks on the US. After 9/11, the US viewed the Arab world from a basic, Manichean perspective; as US president George W Bush put it, 'you're either with us or against us.'[48] Qatar was one of the states that was seen—though not without a couple of crises—as an Arab state 'on America's side.' Support in the War on Terror, not least through increased basing agreements, meant that Qatar had more latitude to act than other states as the decade progressed. Certainly, angry statements occasionally emanated from the US, including an admonishment by former presidential candidate Senator John Kerry that 'Qatar cannot continue to be an American ally on Monday that sends money to Hamas on Tuesday.'[49] Yet the US in time came to realise that Qatar, though not perfect, was nevertheless a useful ally. Qatar fostered a niche role for itself as an interlocutor between the US and some of the more problematic Arab regimes and Muslim groups with whom it regularly engaged, often in the pursuit of mediatory activities.

The case of the opening of the Afghan Taliban office in Qatar, which was initially mooted in late 2011, provides an interesting example of Qatar seeking to position itself as a key interlocutor.[50] In light of the drawdown of US and international coalition troops in Afghanistan, and given the difficulties of finding suitable representatives from the Taliban with whom to negotiate, an opening appeared for an intermediary to bring the two sides together. Qatar, with Germany's assistance, put forward the proposal, which was eventually accepted. Despite several apparent 'cancellations' of the office, it was de facto working in Qatar from late 2012 and formally opened in mid 2013, only to close within a week of opening.[51] Despite the office's closure, Qatar in June 2014 was still able to play a critical role in a prisoner exchange with the Taliban for the last captured US serviceman in Afghanistan, Bowe Bergdahl.

Qatar exists to fulfil such a niche role. Exiting Afghanistan was of critical importance to the US, which had expended much 'blood and treasure' in the conflict and did not want to see its efforts come to nothing. As unpalatable as some may find them, negotiations at the very least form an important part of attempts to ensure a more stable Afghanistan. By facilitating a potentially key avenue for talks on such a critically important topic, Qatar was reminding the US, as well as the wider international community, of the almost uniquely important role that it can play.

The repatriation of a captured US serviceman as a result of Qatari efforts provided empirical proof of the small state's usefulness in maintaining these relations. A similar logic can be seen with other hostage-rescue actions by Qatar. For example, securing the release of US journalist Peter Theo Curtis from extremists in Syria was an action that few states could have undertaken, once again reinforcing the importance of Qatar and its web of connections.

5

TABOO INTERNATIONAL RELATIONS

ISRAEL, IRAN

Relations between the Gulf states and Iran were poor during the 1980s. Aside from the Iran-Iraq war fostering a sectarian dynamic in the region, attacks spilled over to focus on the region's shipping in the form of the 1984–88 tanker war. However, Qatar escaped relatively unscathed, and only on three occasions were its ships targeted by Iran (twice) and once by Iraq (presumably by mistake). Other Gulf states were not as lucky: Saudi Arabian and Kuwaiti ships were targeted at least eleven times each.[1]

Nevertheless, Qatar repaired its relations with Iran more quickly than any other Gulf state, with the possible exception of Oman, and took the lead in regional actions, in contrast to its hitherto more conservative approach. Initially, the rapprochement was signalled by a raft of high-level visits. Iranian foreign minister Ali Akbar Velayati visited Qatar on 1 June 1987 and on 12 April 1988, while deputy Iranian foreign minister Ali Mohammed Besharati visited Doha on 9 November 1988 as a part of a wider schedule of visits to the Gulf.[2] Going beyond Doha merely being a stop-off on a regional visit, specific bilateral matters were soon discussed. Iranian oil minister Gholam Reza Aghazadeh came to Doha on 9 January 1990 to discuss jointly developing the two countries' shared gas field, and a joint plan worth $3 billion was drafted in November the same year.[3] As a sign of improving relations after a break of more than a decade, Qatar and Bahrain on 1 January 1991 restored a freighter and passenger shipping link to the south-western Iranian port of Bushehr.[4]

After ratifying a range of agreements, Hamad bin Khalifah Al Thani in November 1991 led a sizable delegation to Iran for a four-day visit, and welcomed the resumption of diplomatic relations between Iran and Saudi Arabia, stating that Iran must 'have a say in any security architecture devised for the region in the post-crisis era.'[5] Other initiatives launched during this period included discussions over the construction of a $1.5bn, 770km pipe to transport fresh water from the lake behind the Shahid Abbaspour Dam on the River Karun, Iran's largest river, to Qatar.[6] Defence co-operation was also discussed in December 1991, when Iranian defence minister Akbar Torkan visited Doha.[7] There were subsequent visits in May 1992 by Iranian vice-president Hassan Habibi, 'regarded by the Iranians as a 'watershed' event in the relations of the two countries', and by Qatar's interior minister to Iran the same month.[8] Qatar's then-new foreign minister and Hamad bin Khalifah's closest political ally, Hamad bin Jassim Al Thani, also spent two weeks in Iran in 1993.[9]

As unusual as these positive relations were, they did not occur in a vacuum. The death of Iran's supreme leader and the figurehead of the country's 1979 revolution Ayatollah Khomeini in 1989 and the rise of his successor, Ayatollah Khamenei, and President Akbar Hashemi Rafsanjani, were turning 'the doctrines and the practices of Iranian foreign policy on their heads.'[10] Qatar sought to take advantage of this changing situation at a time when the two countries needed to delineate and develop their giant shared gas field.

Following a border skirmish between Qatar and Saudi Arabia in 1992, a report by *Misr Al Fatah* claimed that Qatar in retaliation had signed a $13 billion agreement with Iran to construct 'ports, jetties, and roads in Qatar', even noting that 'the Qatari leadership requested Iranian protection against Saudi threats.'[11] Similarly, following an alleged coup attempt in Qatar in 1995, reports emerged suggesting that Iran had pledged to send 30,000 troops to defend Emir Hamad bin Khalifah.[12] In reality, these reports (particularly the latter) were exaggerations if not outright speculation. However, they nevertheless highlighted not only the feverish climate of the time, but also the potential as seen by some for Qatar's relationship with Iran. Indeed, Hamad bin Khalifah himself hinted that he believed a rapprochement with Iran could help bring the US to the negotiating table, the implicit threat being that if the US would not discuss bolstering Qatar's security then maybe Iran could.[13]

Continuing Qatari attempts to bolster relations with Iran included using the state's diplomatic role on the UN Security Council in 2006 to vote against Resolution 1696, which censured Iran and called on the Islamic Republic to cease nuclear enrichment. The resolution passed easily, but Qatar nevertheless sent a strong message of support to Iran. The following year, Qatar abstained on Resolution 1757, which sought a tribunal to investigate the assassination of former Lebanese prime minister Rafic Hariri, a move that also played well in Tehran (and with the Syrian government, Iran's key ally).

In 2007, Qatar invited Iranian president Mahmoud Ahmadinejad to attend the GCC's annual summit, the first time an Iranian leader had been invited and much to the chagrin of other GCC attendees. 2008 saw Qatar's intervention in Lebanon, as discussed in the previous chapter; some observers interpreted this as Qatar aiding Lebanese Shia movement Hezbollah, while unverified but nevertheless plausible reports suggested that Qatar was sending up to $100m per year to Hezbollah.[14] 2009 saw numerous bilateral visits, including one to Iran by Hamad bin Khalifah and the chief of staff of the Qatari armed forces. That visit culminated in agreements on joint border and related security arrangements, while an unspecified military co-operation agreement was signed the following year.[15]

The frequency of such actions often went far beyond mere posturing and can be interpreted as Qatar seeking some kind of balance with the US, as Hamad bin Khalifah explicitly noted in 1990.[16] In particular, the flurry of activity in the late 2000s mirrored the depths of the regionally unpopular US-led intervention in Iraq from 2003, which was being run and supplied from the US base in Qatar. The mid and late 2000s were also a time of tense Qatari-US relations, when visa and customs issues at Al Udeid began to significantly affect bilateral relations as well as the US's ability to operate from the base.[17] As a wider part of Qatar's perennial desire to balance relations, keeping a channel open to Tehran neatly balanced the state's role in the military operations in Iraq, and at the very least highlighted that Qatar was not a slavish supporter and facilitator of the US.

There are also various incidental examples of Qatar pursuing a balance that, when taken together, reinforce this overarching pattern. For example, when former US Secretary of State Hillary Clinton in 2010 delivered a strong and at times anti-Iran speech at the Doha Forum, one of Qatar's large internationally-orientated conferences, Qatar allowed several Iranian warships to dock in Doha at the same time, as Press TV—a television network affiliated with the state-owned Islamic Republic of Iran Broadcasting—proudly reported.[18] Similarly, Qatar refused a request by US president George W Bush's administration to close Iranian banks in Doha. While not allowing any new ones to open, the Qatari government announced that it would allow 'in classic Qatari fashion' the existing Iranian bank in Qatar to open another branch on the same day US Treasury Secretary Henry Paulson visited the state in mid-2008.[19] Former US Ambassador Joseph LeBaron noted that this behaviour 'does not satisfy either the US or Iran, but it exemplifies how the Al Thani leadership tries to maintain balance between competing interests.'[20] However, as much as such examples hint at cooperation between Qatar and Iran, questions persist as to how meaningful the relationship is and whether it is in fact more of a public relations exercise. As Hamad bin Jassim noted about his Iranian counterparts, 'they lie to us, and we lie to them.'[21]

At the same time as Qatar was developing its relations with Iran in the late 1980s and early 1990s, it was also bolstering ties with Israel. Stemming from the November 1991 Madrid peace conference, Qatar signalled that it was willing to end its boycott of the Jewish state. Slowly thereafter, the state increased its levels of recognition of Israel until it became 'the first GCC state to offer de facto recognition of Israel by launching trade relations.'[22] The 1993 Oslo Accords between Israel and the Palestinians further facilitated relations, and several visits ensued. This culminated in Hamad bin Khalifah attending the 'Oslo 2' signing ceremony, Qatar's minister of information attending the funeral of assassinated Israeli prime minister Yitzhak Rabin in 1995, and Rabin's successor, Shimon Peres, visiting Qatar in April 1996. Peres's visit laid the ground-work for the official opening of an Israeli trade office in Doha on 24 May 1996, less than a kilometre from the Emiri Diwan (royal court).[23]

While the trade office focused primarily on telecommunications and aviation, Israel also sent a large trade delegation to the Milipol military and police trade fair in November 1996.[24] Although relations were inevitably somewhat strained and unusual (even if US retailer 'Toys 'R Us' sold F-16 toy airplanes with Israeli markings in Doha), both sides were optimistic and set about slowly building ties.[25] The most important commercial deal focused on LNG, with US energy company Enron acting as the key interlocutor between the two states. Discussions began in 1993 and eventually failed in 1998, but they nevertheless highlighted a willingness on Qatar's part, at one stage at least, to integrate itself into Israel's economy.

The trade office in Doha struggled in the face of Arab criticism. Qatar managed to resist Arab pressure to close it until November 2000, when it was scheduled to host the Organisation of Islamic Countries (OIC) summit, after which it was to assume the presidency of the body. Violence in the Palestinian Territories, exacerbated by Israeli Prime Minister Ariel Sharon's provocative visit to the Al Aqsa mosque on Jerusalem's Temple Mount worsened relations, and Saudi Arabia and Iran threatened to boycott the event unless the Israeli office was closed. Qatar announced the office's closure on 9 November 2000.[26] However, according to leaked US diplomatic cables, it 'never effectively closed. In fact, Israeli personnel remained in Qatar, maintaining a low profile until normal operations of the office resumed.'[27]

Without an official announcement, the office 'reopened' and was led by Israeli ambassador Roi Rosenblit from 2006 to 2009. The period saw sporadic elite interaction, such as Israeli foreign minister Tzipi Livni speaking at the Doha Forum on Democracy, Development and Free Trade on 14 April 2008.[28] However, in reaction to Israel's December 2008 Operation Cast Lead in the Gaza Strip, Qatar officially closed the office and broke off diplomatic relations. Subsequent overtures by Qatar to reopen the office in 2010 and 2011 were rejected by Israel and stymied by Egypt.[29] Finally, leaks from the Israeli Foreign Ministry in 2011 indicated a firming of Israel's stance against Qatar and the complete closure of the office facility.[30]

Such relations with Israel and Iran would simply have been impossible had Qatar continued to operate under Saudi Arabia's auspices. Yet there was also a deepening of relations with other regional actors that, while not as unique, still contrasts with Qatar's more traditional, conservative diplomatic history. Notably, the state in 1995 announced its intention to open an office in Gaza, mirroring its increasing interest in the wider MENA region, to act as a centre from which to monitor the increasing amount of money it was spending there.[31] Meanwhile, building on Qatar's long-term relationship with Hamas Secretary-General Khaled Meshaal, Hamad bin Khalifah in 2012 became the first leader to visit Hamas-controlled Gaza since the Islamist movement won Palestinian parliamentary elections in 2006 and took over the strip the next year. Again, to facilitate the dispersal of Qatari aid, Hamad announced the (re)opening of an office in Gaza.

Aside from Hamas and long-term contacts with the Palestinian Authority, Qatar has an ambiguous relationship with Hezbollah, the specifics of which are hard to discern. The state has supported and protected the group diplomatically and politically, while there have also been suggestions that it has supported it financially too.[32] Such a supportive relationship with a Shia group such as Hezbollah is unusual in Qatar's history, and is another feature of Qatar's policies under the new elite, which maintains that it needs to speak to all sides and deal with the realities of whomever holds power.

A young, new perspective

With so much power vested at the pinnacle of the Qatari state among just a handful of individuals, personality preferences inevitably shape policy. However, it is hard to accurately weigh the influence of this intangible variable. In Qatar, there is no culture of leaders publicly explaining policy decision-making in any depth or with candour, and no local media scrupulously investigating and interrogating policy trends. There are also no official governmental white papers and a crucial lack of insightful, useful, in-depth interviews with protagonists. Faced with such limiting factors, analysis must instead rest on a triangulation of available evidence, combining an assessment of leaders' backgrounds and preferences with state policy, drawing judicious conclusions along the way.

In understanding the genesis of these policies, it is sensible to start with the milieu in which they were formed. Firstly, as he rose to power, there were a surprising lack of impediments to Hamad bin Khalifah's freedom of action. There was no discernible media pressure and no domestic legislative checks and balances. Furthermore, the native population was small and imbued with the strict Wahhabi doctrine, which contributed to fostering a broadly conservative approach in a society where basic pressure to conform to the leader's approach already existed. Although there would doubtless have been discussion of Qatar's evolving policies towards Israel and Iran, this remained confined to the private sphere. Even when a small democratically-inspired protest movement erupted in the 1990s, this was short-lived and did not come close to taking root. Moreover, as Hamad bin Khalifah's policies became ever more taboo-breaking, he still faced remarkably little discernible push-back from domestic society. Although later in his reign Hamad bin Khalifah had to contend with dissent over his education policies, practically no opposition or protest was ever mustered in respect of foreign policy. As in French politics to this day, Qatar's foreign relations remain predominantly *la domaine réservé*.

But these facilitating factors are only part of the answer, and there still needs to be an account of fundamentally why Hamad bin Khalifah would be minded to pursue such unusual policies as seeking ahistorically positive relations with Iran and Israel. Many of the key motivating factors stem from the regional level (discussed below), but it is also important to look at Hamad himself and his coterie of allies. When a leader is as profoundly influential as he was in Qatar, some focus must fall on the individual.

Initially, it is noticeable just how unusual this emerging Qatari elite was in terms of the age of its members. When it became increasingly obvious that

Hamad bin Khalifah was effectively running Qatar, or at least its dominant personality, in the late 1980s, he was in his late thirties. When he took formal power in 1995, he was forty-three, a generation younger than most of his fellow Gulf rulers. His peers were seventy-two in Saudi Arabia, seventy-six in the UAE, sixty-nine in Kuwait, sixty-two in Bahrain, and fifty-four in Oman.[33] Meanwhile, Hamad bin Jassim, arguably his closest political ally, was in his late twenties as relations were developing with Iran, thirty-two when he became foreign minister, and thirty-five at the time of the 1995 coup. Moza bint Nasser, Hamad bin Khalifah's second wife, who was to play an instrumental role in influencing his policies, is the same age as Hamad bin Jassim. The extent to which 'age' was a determining factor in policy-making is hard to elucidate but, without the dogma imbued in Gulf leaders by decades of staid, conservative intra-regional politics, it is not necessarily surprising that a fresh elite would take such a fresh approach.

Regional 'omnibalancing'

Saudi Arabia's central importance in determining or at least serving to shape Qatar's foreign policy was evident in Qatar's diversification of its relations with Israel and Iran. As the state's relations with Saudi Arabia soured in the early 1990s, the US broadly took up the mantle of offering some level of implicit protection or at least deterrence. However, Qatar still faced more subtle challenges. Having rested under the aegis of Saudi Arabia for so long, and with the two countries' histories being so intertwined and Qatar having undertaken such little autonomous activity over the years, there was an abiding need for the Qatari elite to differentiate itself. Seeking improved relations with Iran and Israel was a pronounced way of doing this.

Nothing about traditional Saudi Arabian values and policies chimes with Hamad bin Khalifah's world-view or proclivities, and he appears to have had no time for the rigidity that characterises the core of the Saudi state. Nor did he believe that women should play an anonymous, subservient role. Had he followed the Saudi line, he would never have entrusted control of the multi-billion-dollar-backed engine of social and educational change in Qatar, the Qatar Foundation, to his wife. Nor would he have enfranchised women to vote, having announced in 1997 that he 'saw nothing wrong with it,'[34] nor would he have sat beside his wife in an interview with US television network CBS's '60 Minutes' in 2003, leaving Qataris in 'complete shock—and not because of the emir's ruminations on the freedom and democracy...rather

[Qataris] were focused on the woman sitting beside him. It was the first time that the vast majority of them had seen any of their first ladies.'[35] Such progressive policies are hard to imagine in a Saudi Arabian context. Similarly, Hamad bin Khalifah's policies indicated a pluralist world-view that prized debate and discussion among all actors, friend or foe, also something not typically found in the Saudi context.

Were Hamad bin Khalifah to have consciously drawn up a range of policies that would cause the most friction with Saudi Arabia, the list would have been likely to have included offering women a prominent place in public discourse, opening up the political arena with elections, improving relations with Iran, and establishing and improving relations with Israel.[36] Qatar, which for so long had been seen as little more than an appendage of Saudi Arabia, was resolute in its desire to separate itself from any association with the kingdom and engage in policies that were essentially the exact opposite of Saudi Arabia's. Such policies made crystal clear the emerging gulf between Qatar and Saudi Arabia, to reinforce the separation that Hamad sought.

Aside from this focus on Saudi Arabia, other dynamics in the Gulf were changing. A decade after the Iranian revolution, in the aftermath of the Iran-Iraq War, and with the death of Ayatollah Khomeini in 1989, an opportunity for change came. Following Khomeini's death and the exhaustion of the war, the Islamic republic 'downplayed its desire to spread its ideological message across the Gulf by propaganda and subversion.'[37] The early years of Rafsanjani's presidency, starting in 1989, represented a period of rapprochement with Arab states and even Saudi Arabia.[38] With an Iranian leadership open to improving relations and with the cover of the GCC's lessening anti-Iran tone, Qatar took advantage of this to normalise relations with Iran.

Yet with or without a brief window of improved relations, the development of the North Field mandated that relations with Iran would have to change. If Qatar was to develop and extract gas from the joint field, relations would have to be amicable if the state and those investing in the field were to have confidence that Iran would not interfere. It is under this rubric that a (Qatari) call for the UN secretary-general to intervene and calm relations between Iran and Iraq in 1985 can best be understood.[39] Furthermore, as Qatar mortgaged itself to pay for the necessary investment in the field, the state became increasingly reliant on future revenues from the field by shipping gas through the Strait of Hormuz, and its vulnerability to Iran consequently increased.

Qatar has occasionally used commercial diplomacy to improve relations with Tehran. Importing water represented one attempt to tie the Islamic republic into commercial ventures to edge towards normalising the bilateral relationship. However this, in addition to a mooted plan to jointly invest $3 billion in the shared gas field in 1990, which came to nothing, and another similar venture in the late 2000s, which was similarly unsuccessful, were the extent of such overtures.[40] Political and diplomatic realities appear to be one thing, important commercial dealings another. Understandings to establish some form of gas troika with Iran and Russia were initially welcomed by the other two states, but Qatar has proved sanguine in reality.[41] Although Qatar hosts the secretariat of the Gas Exporting Countries Forum (GECF), a group established in 2001 with the theoretical goal of becoming 'the OPEC' of the gas world, this has yet to emerge as a significant body. Volatile relations with Russia and fluctuating relations with Iran have been important contributors to the body's relative ineffectiveness.

Just as the brief regional rapprochement with Iran helped Qatar, so too the 1991 Madrid Peace talks, the 1993 Oslo Accords, and the Israel-Jordan peace treaty signed in 1994 heralded a period of active negotiation between Arabs and Israelis that provided cover for Qatar to improve relations with Israel. Although this did not prevent Qatar's GCC allies from lambasting the state for engaging with the Jewish state, particularly as Arab-Israeli relations soured, it offered initial rhetorical cover and an opportunity to engage.

The best lens through which to understand these policy gambits is one of balance, or what the academic literature refers to as 'hedging.'[42] Qatar shored up relations with Iran as its relationship with Saudi Arabia flagged. Similarly, as the state's relationship with the US became ever deeper and more security and defence-orientated as the military base was established, expanded, and populated during the 1990s, balancing this West-leaning relationship with continued Iranian support had a logic to it. However, not to go too far, striving to establish relations with Israel shows how Qatar sought to balance its relationship with Iran, while relations with groups such as Hamas and Hezbollah can be seen as balancing Israel. Another way to view this curious circle of regional balancing is by viewing Qatar as a state intent on using its international relations to cast itself in as favourable a light as possible, striving to support all regional actors to remove itself, theoretically at least, from the region's conflicts.

New policies for a new era

The invasion and subsequent liberation of Kuwait and the end of the Cold War came at a seminal moment for Qatar's emerging elite. As previously noted, the elite had been accruing and consolidating power since the mid 1980s with policy initiatives, cabinet reshuffles, and the creation of new, influential supreme councils. Halfway through this consolidation of power, between 1989 and 1991, the dominant structural system in the world changed more than at any time since the end of World War Two.[43] US President George H Bush summed up the aspirations of the resultant 'new world order' in his post-Gulf War speech to the US Congress.

> And now, we can see a new world coming into view. A world in which there is the very real prospect of a new world order. In the words of Winston Churchill, a 'world order' in which 'the principles of justice and fair play...protect the weak against the strong.' A world where the United Nations, freed from cold war stalemate, is poised to fulfil the historic vision of its founders. A world in which freedom and respect for human rights find a home among all nations.[44]

The sense of optimism that greeted the fall of the Iron Curtain should not be forgotten. The tone of the new age, of collective action, of upholding international law and norms as exemplified by the defence of Kuwait was, at the start of the decade at least, deeply positive.[45] The cleavages and fears of the Cold War had vanished, and while they would be replaced by new concerns (the 'jungle of snakes'), they would not, it was believed, be as existentially pressing. The embodiment of the change that the end of the Cold War heralded can be found in Francis Fukuyama's contention that history itself was at an end.[46]

While Bush's speech outlined an optimistic agenda for a new era, the promise of the 'New World Order' soon lost its lustre. Nye notes that when 'reality intruded [and] grand schemes turned into a liability', the White House soon decided to turn down 'the rhetorical volume.'[47] Similarly, in an essay rejecting the assumed importance of the end of the Cold War for the Middle East, Karsh notes that it was not long before 'euphoric predictions of a "New World Order" and the "End of History"....[were]...buried in the alleys of Sarajevo and the killing fields of Rwanda and Chechnya.'[48] Similarly, as Karsh cautions, it is important to refrain from blithely assuming that the end of the Cold War in the Middle East had the same dramatic impact as it did on the West and the Soviet bloc.

Exactly what impression this lofty rhetoric had on Qatar's young elite is difficult to say. What is clear, however, is that this kind of rhetoric—an appeal to and a pursuit of higher ideals—characterised the state's approach across the policy spectrum under Hamad bin Khalifah. From domestic concerns with grand social and educational goals as embodied in the Qatar Foundation, to

Qatar's diversification of international relations to previously forbidden states such as Iran and Israel, such policies encapsulated the ethos of the new, post-Cold War age. Whether the elite believed in this change or not, the West had 'won' and it would have made sense to mirror the US's rhetoric to show the world's sole remaining superpower that Qatar sought to follow this vision.

Aside from rhetoric, the end of the Cold War would necessarily herald changes in the basic structural framework of the international system.[49] Replacing the bipolar system that had so dominated politics, security, and economics, other systems that had been previously subsumed would emerge. In 1993, Cerny posited that the end of the Cold War would reinvigorate alternative dynamics and systems (regionalism, statism and multilateralism).[50] Whatever the new system would be termed, it would inevitably be characterised by a greater diffusion and decentralisation of power.[51] In this new world, there would be greater opportunities for small states to act assertively to expand their influence.

Although the structural dynamics of the Cold War and the post-Cold War system may not have been discussed in such technical ways in Hamad Bin Khalifah's diwan or majlis, to a practitioner, the differences were obvious. Leaving aside the lofty aspiration inherent in the new era, a leader was freer to make his own decisions without the Cold War zero-sum constraints of having to seek to balance US, Soviet, and non-aligned blocks. Certainly difficulties were still present and balance still had to be maintained with other actors. However, not having the concern of alienating one of the two superpowers in the febrile Cold War atmosphere was liberating.

Amid these strategic changes in the nature of international politics, tactical factors were also important. With the perennial need to seek guarantees against deteriorating relations with Saudi Arabia, Qatar sought to open a dialogue with the US. However, although the paradigm was shifting with operations Desert Shield and Desert Storm, and even though the US wanted an opportunity to engage with the Gulf states, this took some time to come to fruition. From Qatar's perspective, this meant that initial overtures for some closer security-aligned engagement with the world's lone superpower were, according to Hamad bin Khalifah, rebuffed.[52] Needing to secure such US relations, Hamad noted that relations were boosted with Iran and Iraq to provoke the US into coming to the negotiating table. Eventually, the US became more amenable when Qatar made overtures to Israel.

This explanation makes sense. For the US, it could extract a concession to boost regional support for Israel, its strongest ally in the Middle East, while such a gamble was not difficult for Qatar to undertake if it was confident of the US's desire for basing options in the Gulf. Nevertheless, given the state's subsequent augmenting of relations with Iran, the initial overtures cannot solely have been to force the US's hand. The perseverance that the elite showed in maintaining such a relationship indicates that this policy chimed with its own proclivities, rather than being merely the result of tactical pressure alone.

6

INTERNATIONAL INVESTMENTS

As Qatar's diplomatic relations expanded after Hamad bin Khalifah Al Thani came to power, the state's gas ventures also came online and the state accrued more money than it could spend. Qatar consequently became an increasingly active financial actor internationally. Unlike Kuwait, which established the fund that would become its Sovereign Wealth Fund (SWF) in 1953, Qatar's SWF—the Qatar Investment Authority (QIA)—was not founded until 2005. Investment had previously been undertaken on a smaller scale by a team working under the auspices of the Ministry of Finance, and leaked US government cables note that the ministry continued to run the QIA until late 2007.[1]

The QIA was initially run by former Prime Minister and Foreign Minister Hamad bin Jassim Al Thani until 2013, when he retired from all public roles in Qatar and the new leadership took over. Emir Tamim bin Hamad Al Thani became chairman and promoted former chief executive Ahmed Al Sayed to chief executive officer. Another shake-up was announced in December 2014, when Abdullah bin Mohammed bin Saud Al Thani replaced Al Sayed and Tamim bin Hamad stepped down from the board of directors.[2]

Although the QIA is the dominant Qatar-based financial investor, there are several smaller funds and other actors to note, if only not to confuse which institution has acquired what. As crown prince, Tamim bin Hamad established the Qatar Sports Investment (QSI) fund. Active across sports industries, this was the entity that acquired French football club Paris Saint-Germain in 2011, rather than the QIA as is often reported.[3] The Qatar Foundation (QF), the charitable entity founded and run by the emir's mother, Moza bint Nasser Al

Misnad, has its own SWF. Founded in 1995, the QF's stated aim is to foster a knowledge-based economy in Qatar and its fund, which was augmented with a new, separate legal framework in 2010, is designed to underpin this central task. The QF holds the government's stake in the Vodafone telecoms operation in Qatar, while a 5 per cent stake in India's largest mobile phone operator Bharti Airtel, worth $1.26 billion, is its other most notable investment.[4] Qatar Petroleum International (QPI) is another large, Qatar-based state institutional investor. Founded in 2006, its explicit goal is to invest in both upstream and downstream energy ventures to expand Qatar Petroleum's (QP) footprint across the world.[5] The Qatar Armed Forces also runs its own fund. While most of its investment takes place within the state, it has emerged as a purchaser of high-profile hotels in Europe in recent years.[6]

With no direct state involvement, a variety of large family-run funds invest across sectors, typically focusing on banking, sport, and luxury goods. Qatari individuals have also made significant purchases in their own right. For example, Abdullah bin Nasser Al Thani bought Spanish football club Malaga in 2010. This adds to a sometimes confusing picture of financial actors, both in Qatar and around the region. For example, the *Financial Times* in September 2014 referred to a Middle East SWF acquiring expensive apartments in London.[7] However, as Victoria Barbary, the former director of the Institutional Investor's Sovereign Wealth Centre tweeted, 'Sovereign wealth funds don't buy apartments. Read: "Middle Eastern Royal."'[8]

A basic difficulty when analysing 'Qatar' as an actor investing internationally is the pervasively opaque nature of such investments.[9] If information is released as to which entity did the acquiring, much comprehensive information related to price, rationale, or such matters is seldom provided. Even basic details such as the date that the QIA was founded are widely misreported in academic papers, highlighting the difficulties that experts face in getting to grips with the fund.[10]

Inevitably, in terms of size and an apparent preference for publicity, the QIA garners the most attention among Qatari investment institutions. The authority is divided into different entities that control different areas. Qatari Diar is a real-estate development company, Qatar Holding focuses on strategic private and public equity or direct investments, and Hassad Foods focuses on agribusiness investments. The QIA's stated goal is to develop investments to secure Qatar's long-term financial future through economic diversification.

The QIA has focused on acquiring (often large) stakes in some of the world's most prominent companies. These include Agricultural Bank of China, Barclays

Bank, Cegelec, Credit Suisse, Harrods, Heathrow Airport Holdings, Hochtief, Iberdrola, Lagardère Group, London Stock Exchange, Miramax Films, Porsche and Volkswagen, Sainsbury's, Santander Brazil, Shell, Siemens, Tiffany, Uber, Vinci and Xstrata, as well as various high-end property deals with a particular focus on London, Paris, and increasingly Washington DC.

The QIA under Tamim bin Hamad has been somewhat calmer and less active, and has undergone a slight change of focus. This is unsurprising, given that any state in the world, let alone one as small as Qatar, would miss as forceful and effective a seasoned diplomat, politician, and investor as Hamad bin Jassim.[11]

In addition to 'headline' changes, there was also a rash of hiring across the QIA, most notably in key positions such as head of strategy (Steffen Frank, formerly head of strategy at Deutsche Bank), head of Asia real estate (Jason Chew, previously managing director for Greater China at Pramerica Real Estate Investors), and head of mergers and acquisitions (Michael Cho, previously head of Asia mergers and acquisitions for Merrill Lynch in Hong Kong).[12] The Asia-focused experience of several of the newcomers reflected a perception within Qatar's elite that the QIA was too exposed to Europe and needed to readjust. This change of emphasis was confirmed by a review by new chief executive Abdullah bin Mohammed in 2015.[13] Although there was no radical switch and the QIA continued to invest in Europe, this refocusing had an effect. This included the launch of a $10 billion fund, in conjunction with CITIC Group Corp, to focus on Asia, with another $15–$20 billion expected to be invested in Asia, according to former CEO Ahmed Al Sayed.[14] Meanwhile, Qatar in April 2015 won the race to host the Middle East and North Africa's first Renminbi Clearance Centre, joining world financial centres such as Hong Kong, Singapore, Frankfurt, and London.[15] This came after the Qatar Central Bank signed a RMB 35bn ($5.6bn) swap agreement in November 2014.[16] These agreements mean that claims from around the Middle East in Chinese renminbi can now be settled in Qatar, bolstering the state as a key financial centre.

Particularly under Hamad bin Jassim's tenure, the QIA arguably enjoyed unusual prominence compared to its size. Estimates vary and accurate conclusions are difficult to reach because of the secrecy of most SWFs, but the QIA is clearly by no means the largest SWF in the world. Studies and reports vary significantly as to the extent of assets under QIA control, with estimates ranging from $125bn to around $300bn.[17] Either way, this is smaller than the Norway Government Pension Fund, the Abu Dhabi Investment Authority, the China Investment Corporation, or the Kuwait Investment Authority. Nevertheless, the QIA retains a surprising prominence in the international press relative to these other older and larger SWFs.

This is not happenstance, but rather a part of an orchestrated plan to gain prominence, particularly under the stewardship of Hamad bin Jassim, who established the QIA's reputation as 'the worlds most aggressive deal hunter.'[18] The QIA achieved this in part by having unusually close relations with the financial media, as well as focusing on taking often large stakes in high-profile companies.[19]

Simple, domestic diversification

Amid the 'razzmatazz' and controversy of some Qatari investments, the basic guiding principle underlying them must not be forgotten: the QIA is there to make money for the state. Diversification of income sources is a sensible approach to safeguarding the existing socio-economic bargain, which calls for the state pay for a vast array of expensive cradle-to-grave entitlements for its citizens.[20] When the 2008 global economic crisis threatened to seriously undercut continued domestic economic expansion and impinge on opportunities for Qataris, the QIA invested in Qatar's economy, more directly playing an internal role. In the same way that the QIA acts as an endowment for future generations, the same logic underpins the QF fund, albeit that its goals are to a greater extent confined to supporting the organisation itself. The QPI follows a similar logic, diversifying Qatar's hydrocarbons concerns for the overarching, longer-term benefit of the state.

Compared with most SWFs, which tend to seek smaller stakes in a wider range of companies or which engage in obtuse financial deals to make money, many QIA investments are relatively easy to understand. While behind the scenes there is complex debt-restructuring, the QIA on the surface has a reputation for being a 'champion of a much more active role...making fewer, large and visible investments in both equities and, even more, in iconic real-estate deals.'[21] Not only this, but many of the companies in question deal in tangible goods and services that Qataris can easily recognise, such as luxury hotels in Europe, German car manufacturers, Tiffany, and Harrods. Or, if they are not tangible goods, the investment is often in household names (such as Heathrow Airport's holdings, Shell and Siemens). As with all SWFs, the QIA is spending the country's money, the inheritance for future generations of Qataris. Although overall purely financial motives are doubtless the key determinant in the choices of investment, such a strategy means that Qataris at the very least know the outlines of how their money is being spent. Even though Qataris are far from a vociferous, influential constituency, particularly in respect of matters concerning their state's foreign relations (or investments), this allows the elite to demonstrate how they are spending the peoples' money, given the lack of transparency at the QIA.[22]

It is impossible to understand the QIA's early years and why it chose to invest as it did without appreciating the importance of Hamad bin Jassim. 'HBJ', as he is colloquially known in Doha, has been a life-long confidant and ally of Hamad bin Khalifah. He was the beneficiary of Hamad bin Khalifah's first cabinet reshuffle in 1989, when he was given the prominent position of minister of municipalities. He had previous experience of this role, having acted as the director of the office of the previous two ministers of municipalities, Mohammed bin Jaber Al Thani (1972–1983) and Khaled bin Abdullah Al Attiyah (1983–1989). This ministerial role is important in the Gulf states; in the oil era, land was one of the key ways in which wealth was transferred from the state to the individual. Given that all Qataris are entitled to a free plot of land on which to build a house (backed by subsidised loans from the government), this land can technically be in downtown Doha or in the depths of Qatar's inhospitable hinterland. The minister of municipalities consequently has huge potential influence, and the role is bestowed on trusted allies. Hamad bin Jassim's pedigree and role from an early age was that of a trusted individual who acted as an important interlocutor and mediator, cajoling support for Hamad bin Khalifah during the 1980s and thereafter, even when he moved to the foreign ministry in 1992.[23] By 1993, the British ambassador to Qatar viewed Hamad bin Jassim as 'the third most powerful man in the state', and by the time of the 1995 coup he was widely seen as the 'most important' ally of Hamad bin Khalifah, delivering the support of key Al Thanis.[24]

Hamad bin Jassim's prominence and power only subsequently increased, and he developed and consolidated a reputation as Qatar's leading businessman.[25] He was the natural choice to lead the state's nascent SWF in 2005. The point to note here is that he did not only lead the SWF as a titular head, but rather as the emir's central confidant and ally. Hamad bin Jassim's secure, imperiously influential personality dominated the QIA entirely.[26]

Although a shrewd businessman, Hamad bin Jassim is not a banker or an accountant trained in abstract financial machinations; rather, he bought what he instinctively understood and took advantage of opportunities presented to him as he travelled the world as Qatar's foreign minister. One deputy ambassador in Doha recalls that, on arriving in his country's capital on an official visit, Hamad bin Jassim was presented with around ten large (multi-billion dollar) investment opportunities in his country, one of which the QIA subsequently acquired.

Linked to this is the context of the QIA within Qatar, which only increased the importance of Hamad bin Jassim's role. In common with all organisations in Qatar, the QIA lacks skilled Qatari functionaries in senior positions because there are simply not enough qualified Qataris. Foreigners fill the breech, but the situation as a whole contributes to creating a top-heavy working environment. In turn, this means that there is an overriding sense of investors such as the QIA seeking the 'lowest hanging fruit' and being directly led by its leadership. While this is changing, the QIA historically tended to opt for more obvious, more high-profile investments in lieu of a fully-staffed and trained team of investment bankers. As so often, what Qatar does, which investment it goes for, or which side it supports is perhaps to a surprising degree conditioned or at least shaped by the state's bureaucratic structures and limitations.

Establishing and burnishing an international reputation

In their typology of SWFs, Dixon and Monk develop and refine existing categories, leading them to introduce concepts such as the rentier SWF, the moral SWF, and the postcolonial SWF.[27] As a classical rentier state, QIA naturally fits into the category of rentier SWF, saving money to prolong the expensive social bargain. However, it equally fits into other categories. In particular, the QIA resembles the authors' description of a postcolonial SWF. The authors note that:

> In a global system of 195 countries, postcolonial states, particularly small ones, can be easily overshadowed and homogenized within their broader cohort. As a result, postcolonial states may seek to separate themselves and gain wider reception from more powerful cohorts of states...the SWF can provide a state with increased capacity to a) engage with more powerful states through investment in the markets of the latter, and b) engage with institutions such as multinational firms or other non-governmental organizations that may possess significant if not implicit power in the global economy and thus the political sphere. The postcolonialist SWF is a means of increasing a state's capacity to engage, thus partially improving the country's perceived sovereignty deficit.[28]

Alongside the simple goal of seeking to secure financial returns, other motivating factors, as Dixon and Monk suggest, are readily identifiable. That Qatar owns 20 per cent of the London Stock Exchange and 20 per cent of Heathrow

Airport's holding company, not to mention an estimated £20 billion of other investments in London, means that the state has bought more than just stocks and shares.[29] Rather, Qatar has tied itself into two of the UK's most critical hubs—its stock exchange and key airport—and will have a say in decisions surrounding them for as long as it holds the equity. Qatar's importance and visibility is therefore increased and entrenched across segments of the British economy, while its moves to take these positions in the first place highlight both statesmanship and business know-how.[30] With more than £20 billion invested in a country's capital, the QIA's leadership can doubtless arrange a meeting with any investor, company, or politician in the city, and with such access and such investment comes influence. Former British prime minister Tony Blair has acted on behalf of the QIA on several occasions, notably in relation to the huge merger deal between mining companies Xstrata and Glencore in 2012.[31]

Although the extent to which Qatar can affect British policies or secure votes in international organisations is debatable, the UK and France, two of the countries in which Qatar has invested the greatest amounts, were the two countries that initially supported Qatari calls to arm the Syrian opposition.[32] Other calculations are obviously present and common interests exist, but the lure of Qatari investment in straightened economic times cannot be ignored.[33] Similarly, Qatar's deep importance to the UK in respect of investment and gas sales is one of the reasons why the UK rethought its security commitments and foreign policy towards the Gulf states in 2013 and 2014.[34] These ideas found their final form in the UK's December 2014 announcement of its 'return to east of Suez' with the establishment of a permanent naval base in Bahrain. This was a clear indication of the UK shifting its foreign policy to find favour with Gulf elites.[35]

Outside governmental relations, the QIA is a crucial tool in building a financial and business-related reputation for the state. Indeed, there is a sense that Qatar's elite longs to be known to as a 'kingmaker of corporate Britain', as a British broadsheet referred to it in 2012.[36] Even accounting for a certain hyperbole, such sentiments signal that Qatar is a central financial power in one of the world's most important financial centres, and this is where Qatar wants to be. Building and buying the tallest buildings in London—the Shard and Canary Wharf—speaks to this desire to position Qatar both physically and metaphorically in London. Given the historic UK-Qatar connection, the Anglophile nature of Qatar's leadership, the global economic downturn, and Qatar's huge financial reserves, there cannot be an influential trader or banker in London who is unfamiliar with Qatar or the QIA.

However, it is not only the UK that has such a close relationship with Qatar. There is a Francophile streak in the Qatari elite too, stemming from decades of close business contacts, military sales, and the Qatari penchant for acquiring property in France under beneficial tax regimes.[37] Qatar's investments in France have mounted steadily, if not quite matching the scale and depth of investments in the UK.[38] Prime property on the Champs Élysées in Paris, a string of luxury hotels, and important French conglomerates have also been acquired, along with the aforementioned Paris Saint-Germain football club. As ever, these acquisitions are expected to be financially sound and profitable, while they also cement ties with an important state with a seat on the UN Security Council, as well as an important military presence in the Gulf.

The question of Qatari political influence in France is equally interesting. In particular, there are concerns that Qatar used its relationship with key members of the French elite to boost its prospects of winning the right to host the FIFA World Cup in 2022.[39] It has been reported that former French president Nicolas Sarkozy in November 2010 hosted a lunch for then Crown Prince Tamim Bin Hamad, Sebastian Barzan, the head of the fund controlling Paris Saint-Germain (Colony Capital), and Michel Platini, the president of football's European governing body UEFA. There, it has been alleged, a multi-layered deal was arranged that led to Tamim bin Hamad's QSI acquiring Paris Saint-Germain, as well as significant Qatari investment in French football (via television rights), while Platini switched his support to Qatar's bid to host the 2022 World Cup.[40] Sepp Blatter, the embattled former President of FIFA, football's world governing body, has also spoken about this Platini–Sarkozy–Tamim deal.[41] That Platini's son also works for QSI as a lawyer is another curious coincidence.[42]

UEFA has rejected and denied such accusations. However, this type of tangential and esoteric quid pro quo is characteristic of Qatar's relations, namely establishing and bolstering bilateral ties so that it can extract support on important matters as and when it needs it.

Qatar was the leading buyer of European property in 2011 and 2012, driven primarily by purchases in London and Paris.[43] However, its investment is far from confined to the UK and France. Even before its more extensive focus on Asia following the 2013 leadership transition, the QIA took large stakes in companies in China, as well as acquiring a licence to invest up to $5 billion in Yuan-listed Chinese companies.[44] Elsewhere, the QIA established a $5 billion fund to invest in Greece in the middle of the 2008 financial crisis, and sought up to $10 billion of investment in Malaysia and up to $1 billion in Vietnam.[45]

Such large investments will give Qatar significant influence in these smaller countries. While the state may make a profit, such investments will also bolster relations to prepare for the day when Qatar can call in its quid pro quo.

Finally, a European diplomat based in Qatar noted the profound effect that a significant QIA purchase had in his home country. He described his phone as subsequently 'ringing off the hook,' with business delegations curious to know about this country called Qatar.[46] This deal and others that soon followed were directly responsible for numerous trade delegations coming to Qatar to seek business opportunities. Numerous goals of Qatar's policy are visible in this example, including Qatar boosting its visibility, encouraging further investment and opportunities for Qatari investment, and making Qatar a recognised and more important state to a key European country.

7

AL JAZEERA

1996–2011

This chapter examines the inception and development of news network Al Jazeera until the beginning of the Arab spring uprisings. Given the organisation's prominence during the uprisings from 2011 onwards, its role as a 'tool' of Qatari policy during this era will be discussed in Chapter 9, which deals specifically with these tumultuous events.

The concept of a new Qatar-based television channel dates back at least to August 1994 and was first envisioned by then crown prince Hamad bin Khalifah Al Thani.[1] Following discussion and debate as to the format and the overarching holding company (namely whether to use Qatar's existing television network or create a new entity entirely), Al Jazeera Arabic aired its first programme on 1 November 1996, and 'the very nature of Arab journalism began to change.'[2] Although not an overnight success, Al Jazeera within two years had made inroads into traditional news media coverage, and was noted as 'the most influential Arab TV channel.'[3] When the network's cameras were the only ones broadcasting from Baghdad as Operation Desert Fox struck the Iraqi capital in December 1998, Al Jazeera came to the fore.[4] Subsequently, it became a fixture of the Middle East's cultural landscape and prompted a paradigm shift in Arab media.

Al Jazeera was truly revolutionary. Never before had there been an Arab television news network as outspoken, outlandish, watched, or influential. Media outlets had previously tended to be distrusted and dismissed as little more than uncritical government propaganda outlets, and while the BBC, Voice of America, and France's Radio Monte Carlo broadcast popular radio broadcasts in Arabic, these were nevertheless foreign in origin.[5] Al Jazeera was the first network to successfully tap the latent Arab desire for locally-based television news with a semblance of impartiality, while the fact that its coverage was so salacious merely added to its appeal.

Al Jazeera courted controversy (and viewers) by showing video messages from Al Qaida figurehead Osama bin Laden (just as US network CNN did), though it did not show beheadings as is sometimes claimed.[6] It also interviewed Israeli spokespeople for the first time on an Arab channel, a popular but controversial move.[7] Al Jazeera's reputation garnered countless exclusives across the world, including the destruction of the giant Buddhas in Bamiyan (Afghanistan) in March 2001, while the Al Jazeera brand has been noted as one of the most recognised in the world.[8] The network has also caused practically every Arab state to complain to Qatar's emir at some stage, while the Algerian government in January 1999 went a step further by shutting down power to the capital Algiers and other major cities to prevent an Al Jazeera interview with a dissident diplomat and exiled journalist from being broadcast.[9]

Much of Al Jazeera's success was based on two fortuitous instances of happenstance. Firstly, a Saudi consortium and the BBC on 24 March 1994 signed a ten-year agreement to establish BBC Arabic,[10] though the arrangement predictably soon foundered. An interview with a prominent Saudi cleric suffered a mysterious power failure in January 1996, while a BBC Panorama documentary aired months later that was critical of Saudi Arabia proved the final straw.[11] BBC Arabic was replaced by the Disney channel, and a whole newsroom—presenters, producers, researchers, and technicians—found itself looking for work. Al Jazeera, which at the time was still largely on the planning table in Doha, gladly took advantage of this serendipity and hired 120 trained BBC journalists.[12]

Even after Al Jazeera was up and running, however, its audience was small. It was limited by the capacity that the Arab Satellite Corporation's satellite could offer, a limited 'Ku-Band' transponder, and coveted a strong but and unavailable 'C-band' transponder that would augment the number of viewers who were able to receive the Al Jazeera signal.[13] Happily for Al Jazeera, Canal France International, while meant to be showing a children's educational show one afternoon in July 1997, instead broadcast half an hour of *Club Privé au Portugal*, a hard-core pornographic film, to up to thirty-three million Arabs.[14] CFI consequently lost its C-band transponder and Al Jazeera took up the contract, increased its airtime to seventeen hours per day, and never looked back.

After moving to round-the-clock coverage in 1999, the Al Jazeera brand expanded to encompass almost 20 separate channels, including Al Jazeera Sports (a brand that later became beIN SPORTS) from November 2003; Al Jazeera Mubasher (live), a C-Span-like channel, in April 2005; Al Jazeera Children's Channel in September 2005; Al Jazeera English in November 2006; Al Jazeera Documentary Channel in 2007; Al Jazeera Misr Mubasher, a twenty-four-hour channel dedicated solely to Egyptian coverage that was launched in 2011 but shut down by the Egyptian military in 2013; Al Jazeera Balkans in 2011; Al Jazeera America in 2013 (but which closed in 2016); and Al Jazeera Turk in 2014.

Despite belonging to the same overarching brand and reporting ultimately to the same controlling editors, flagship channels Al Jazeera Arabic and Al Jazeera English are poles apart. From the beginning, the English channel was a slick production similar in appearance to US and UK-based rivals, with staff being hired from the major Western television organisations, including household names such as David Frost. Pursuing viewers in the same market as the BBC and CNN, its tone and style were similar, even if its focus was more of a 'global south orientation.'[15] Compared with Al Jazeera English's more reserved character, Al Jazeera Arabic's coverage could be described as sensationalist and provocative, a true adherent to the media cliché of 'if it bleeds, it leads.'[16] When Arab states complain to Qatar's emir about Al Jazeera, they are almost always referring to Al Jazeera Arabic.[17]

In terms of reach and influence, Al Jazeera English pales compared with Al Jazeera Arabic. This is often forgotten or ignored from a Western-based perspective, and many may watch the Al Jazeera English broadcasts and fail to see what all the fuss is about. A brief focus on some of the lead shows in Arabic, by contrast, in particular *Al Itijah Al Muakis* ('The Opposite Direction') and the (now cancelled) platform for Sheikh Yusuf Al Qaradawi, *Al Shariaa wa Al Hayaa* ('Sharia [Islamic religious law] and Life') shows a different side to Al Jazeera. The former is a fast-paced debating show that often pits representatives from opposite ends of the spectrum against each other. Bahry describes 'The Opposite Direction' as 'undoubtedly the most popular and most controversial political talk show in the history of Arab television.'[18] While the format itself was not new, it was the novelty of seeing some of the guests on the show that was the change. Erik Nisbet, a US-based academic who has focused on anti-Americanism in Arab media, writes that Al Jazeera 'took press freedom to the extreme,' noting that some of its guests could be the equivalent of a major US network inviting members of the Ku Klux Clan on to a prime-time discussion show.[19] Though shrill and not a perfect analogy, there is some truth to such a comparison.

Al Qaradawi's show is an updated version of a programme he broadcast on Qatari domestic television in the 1970s. The original show—*Hadi Al Islam* ('Guidance in Islam')—marked the beginning of his television career and made him a household name in Qatar. Generally apolitical in tone, Qaradawi used his pedigree as one of the most gifted theologians to come out of Al Azhar University in Cairo to discuss the Quran and its implications for modern life. This was the exact premise of *Al Shariaa wa Al Hayaa*. As the audience for Qaradawi's Al Jazeera show grew, his reputation as a theologian increased significantly and he became arguably the most noted and famous preacher in the Middle East. At its peak, his show garnered an estimated audience of sixty million.[20]

Vanguard of the Qatari revolution

Any examination of the milieu in which Al Jazeera was created must take account not only of the core motivations of the elite, but also the other factors that allowed and facilitated its creation. These represent different sides to the same coin. Taken together, they allow for a richer, more rounded explanation of Al Jazeera's creation.

Firstly, as is so often the case with these more iconoclastic policies, the pliant domestic arena in which the policies were created and implemented needs to be noted. In the late 1980s and 1990s, it is difficult to point to any significant domestic force that needed to be reckoned with. Small pro-democracy protests in 1991 were ignored, and while there were doubtless difficulties between the new, emerging generation and the old generation they were replacing, these seldom came out into the open.

Although the ease with which the new elite established its policies in the 1990s should not be exaggerated, the fact remains that it made wholesale changes to Qatar's domestic and international orientation with almost no demonstrable public complaint. Al Jazeera is but one outcome of this relatively pliant atmosphere, in which the emir's whims could be enacted with relative ease. An important corollary to this is the inorganic nature of Al Jazeera's birth, which in no way reflected wider Qatari society. Aside from the aforementioned brief pro-democracy protests in the early 1990s, there is scant evidence for any yearning for liberalisation in Doha. Al Jazeera's attitude towards including Israelis in the conversation, fostering debate on political topics, and discussing women's rights and controversial religious issues was at odds with Qatar's intrinsic conservatism. As so often, the Al Jazeera project was almost entirely elite-driven.

Secondly, although financial returns had yet to be realised in the mid 1990s, Qatar's leadership was increasingly confident that its liquefied natural gas (LNG) gamble was paying off. The initial grant of money for Al Jazeera was an estimated $137 million, while the network's annual running costs were estimated at between $25 and $100 million. The launch of Al Jazeera English, meanwhile, called for investment of up to $1 billion.[21] With Qatar's $500 million acquisition of Al Gore's Current TV in January 2013 and the subsequent expansion of Al Jazeera America, the cost of the overall Al Jazeera venture leapt once again. The various other Al Jazeera spin-offs, such as the children's channel, the documentary channel and most notably the hugely expensive failure that proved to be Al Jazeera America—added to the loss-making enterprises. Al Jazeera has also struggled to offset its costs with advertising. Historically, given its poor bilateral relations with Qatar, Saudi Arabia put unbearable pressure on companies advertising on Al Jazeera to pull out, driving up costs for the network.[22] Similarly, a negative view of Al Jazeera particularly from right-wing elements, meant that initially advertisers were concerned about associating their brand with the new American enterprise.[23] Later on, even when the brand proved itself not to be toxic, the fact that its viewing figures were so low also put off advertisers.[24] In short, the opportunities for subsidising Al Jazeera America's expensive running costs were relatively limited.[25]

That Qatar can afford luxuries such as a television network stems from the state's hydrocarbon resources, a basic but crucial enabler. However, it is also important to distinguish between Al Jazeera and its subsequent spin-offs, because they originated in different fiscal environments. The original Al Jazeera show in Arabic was aired in an era in which Qatar was still in hock to international banks and energy companies. Although oil reserves meant that the state was comfortably well-off, the wealth associated with Qatar today was not present at the time. In short, the decision to branch out in the 2000s was taken in a much more pliant, comfortable fiscal environment in which more money was available for 'whim-like' policies. Indeed, the state had more money that it could spend, as reflected by the creation of its sovereign wealth fund in 2005. By contrast, Qatar in 1996 was experiencing more straightened times. In such circumstances, initiating a venture that would cost half a billion dollars by the turn of the millennium looks less like a whim and more like a firm policy-orientated choice.

One of the central tenets of the new Qatari policies in the 1990s was a desire to be both seen and heard. Al Jazeera is the apogee of this thrust, aimed at shattering the old cliché of Qatar being 'known for being unknown.' The network gave Qatar a uniquely powerful comparative advantage over all other Arab states, and allowed news 'live from Doha' to be disseminated across the region.

Al Jazeera's creation was also a savvy asymmetric move. Although Qatar lacks a large population, a significant land-mass, a potent military, or a diaspora to exert influence, it has money. While having money confers a certain amount of power, the creation of Al Jazeera and the network's remarkable popularity in the early 2000s meant that Qatar became pre-eminent in the region in a particular role, the first time that it had led the region in any sphere.

Born in 1952, then emir Hamad bin Khalifah had grown up in a world of revolutionary Nasserist rhetoric. State borders were seemingly weakened by pan-national radio broadcasts by pan-national movements, such as *Sawt Al Arab*, an important medium of information propagation in its era.[26] While important to refrain from after-the-fact rationalisations, there is a striking resemblance between one of Hamad bin Khalifah's early ideas—Al Jazeera—and *Sawt Al Arab*. Both were revolutionary uses of available technology in the Middle East, while both were also uniquely powerful and viewed as the key medium of imbibing information by huge numbers of Arabs around the region.[27] The fact that Hamad grew up in an internationalised climate punctuated by pan-regional phenomena cannot be ignored as an instigating factor in the development of ideas (such as promoting Al Jazeera and pursuing new, in-depth international relations) that were subsequently reflected in his policies.[28]

Defence and offense

Qatar's international dynamic in the 1950s, 1960s, 1970s, and 1980s exuded a logic of deliberately eschewing international attention. However, this strategy was deeply challenged in the early 1990s, particularly by the invasion of Kuwait. For a small, mostly defenceless state, realising that invasion is possible, that it has actually happened just a few hundred kilometres to the north, and that the devastation wrought is as profound as may have been feared, must have been a most sobering experience. Drawing the conclusion that anonymity—Qatar's previous default mode—was potentially a deeply detrimental quality would be entirely logical. A corollary to this conclusion would be a need to find ways to augment the state's visibility. In the event of a 'Kuwait-style' catastrophe, the Qatari leader would not want to be appealing to Western leaders for help while international commentary wakes up to discover that there is a state in the world beginning with the letter 'Q.' Several of the new elite's strategies were aimed at reversing Qatar's previous anonymity, with Al Jazeera a central plank in their desire to actively publicise the country.

These concerns were far from necessarily academic. In the mid 1990s relations between Saudi Arabia and Qatar deteriorated from rhetorical sparring into border skirmishes and alleged Saudi support for counter-coups in Qatar. The Qatari administration had legitimate grounds to believe that a Kuwait-style invasion scenario was not likely but also not impossible, or at least no less likely than Iraq invading Kuwait had appeared in 1989. That the US by the mid 1990s had signed up to some level of security-focused training and basing agreements with Qatar was reassuring. However, at no stage were there any explicit defensive agreements. Also, there must have been lingering fears that Saudi Arabia could do to Qatar's emir what he himself had done to his father, namely effect a swift political 'decapitation' and present an immediate fait accompli.

Against such an antagonistic regional backdrop and reflecting a strong desire to persist with its iconoclastic policies, creating an international media platform makes sense for Qatar. If the state needed to broadcast escalating concerns, call for help, or create a certain international noise to avoid any swift, silent takeovers, Al Jazeera plays a certain defensive or even deterrent role.

It can also be argued that Al Jazeera has an offensive aim too. The Qatari elite knew perfectly well what would happen if it gave a BBC-trained crew carte blanche in respect of editorial control: naturally, the seasoned reporters would pursue the most salacious topics in the region. Without any explicit boundaries, the sacred cows that had up until then been unassailable suddenly became fair game. Burgeoning audience figures showed that Al Jazeera's desire to poke, prod, and report on elite politics across the Gulf and the wider Middle East region was wildly popular.

In this context, Al Jazeera can be seen as one of Qatar's most significant means of antagonising Saudi Arabia. While the state had no diplomatic, economic, or military weight with which to bully as large a state as the kingdom, it could—through Al Jazeera—embarrass Saudi Arabia with coverage of disputes within its royal family and by speaking to Saudi dissidents. Whether instigated purposefully by the elite or a natural but expected corollary of unleashing Al Jazeera, this was certain to cause friction between Saudi Arabia and Qatar. Aside from any personal animus or desire to strike back at Saudi

Arabia, it was a prime way of reminding the Riyadh elite that Qatar was an independent state and that it would no longer do as it was told.

Al Jazeera can also be seen as influencing the region's wider politics. Giving Al Qaradawi, the leading cleric associated with the Muslim Brotherhood Islamist movement, access to Al Jazeera, and by extension tens of millions of viewers, was a political decision. As much as this burnishes Al Qaradawi's reputation, so too it cements Qatar's status as a key location in some of the region's key conversations. Indeed, members of Qatar's elite do not support Al Qaradawi because they are secretly Muslim Brotherhood members themselves, but rather because of realpolitik. Understanding the central role that religion plays in the region, Qatar pragmatically facilitated a quasi-spokesman one of the most popular, best organised, and relatively moderate political parties in the Middle East, as well as its role as an interlocutor.

A new channel for a new era

'News framing' is a standard technique in fields associated with media analysis and social psychology that seeks to categorise eras in news coverage. An infamously difficult topic to specifically define, a 'news frame' refers to the whole normative structure at a given time that provides the backdrop, assumed values, and typical narratives that coalesce into any given 'frame.' As Norris notes, 'frames represent stereotypes.'[29] In terms of the Cold War frame, she identifies the key characteristics:

> The Cold War frame highlighted certain events as international problems, identified sources, offered normative judgements, and recommended particular policy solutions. Specifically, the Cold War frame depicted international events in terms of rivalry between two major superpowers and ranged other countries into 'friends' and 'enemies' of these superpowers. Warfare in Vietnam...or Afghanistan could be interpreted as internal power struggles provoked by religious, ethnic, or regional civil wars...Alternatively, these conflicts could be seen in terms of international rivalry for global ascendency...interests were defined in large part by virtue of opposition to Soviet allies. This led to a policy framework in which American involvement in the Middle East, Latin America, or Southeast Asia was justified by a policy of containment.[30]

Eras change and with them news frames. Norris highlights that the end of the Cold War provided a clearly identifiable change in backdrop, assumed values (for example, of the 'enemy'), and typical narratives, which changed significantly as the US news frame entered the post-Cold War world.[31] In the context of the Middle East, there is no similarly detailed qualitative and quantitative study as Norris's. However, the media revolution(s) that occurred in the Arab world in the 1990s manifestly stemmed from the emancipation of the post-Cold War era.[32]

Specifically in relation to Al Jazeera, in addition to the other instances of happenstance already mentioned (Qatar having the funds and also a leadership interested in establishing such a television network), the network needed the end of the Cold War era to be established. It would have been too difficult to attempt to tread a neutral line amid Cold War rivalries, which would have resulted in either an emasculated network or one that angered one of the superpowers, not an appealing prospect for an intrinsically defenceless state that sought to pursue some notion of non-alignment. These profound changes in the international system allowed Qatar to position itself such that it was fundamentally able to host an entity like Al Jazeera.

More generally, it was the international lacuna in the Middle East media landscape that allowed Qatar to steal a march on the competition and be the first to establish a professional and popular media organisation. The power of the media had only recently been demonstrated to great effect in the Middle East during Operation Desert Storm. Although the definition is contested, the eponymous 'CNN effect' entered the lexicon as a phrase to describe the vastly increased range, popularity and in some cases impact of media in the post-Cold War world.[33] Definitions aside, a doctorate in media studies was not required to see the revolution in television coverage unfolding with CNN's coverage of Operation Desert Storm.

However, no such media organisation was indigenous to the Middle East, and Qatar moved to fill the gap by establishing Al Jazeera. As a result, the state benefitted from 'first mover' status. As well as controlling what was the Middle East's most powerful media outlet for several years, until competition inevitably reduced Al Jazeera's market share, founding the network mirrored the ethos of the age. What better way to evidence Qatar's desire to reorient itself along broadly progressive lines than by founding and supporting an iconoclastic, revolutionary, popular television news network.

8

SOFT POWER POLICIES

MICE, SPORT, CULTURE, AND EDUCATION

This chapter examines a range of 'soft power' policies used by Qatar, including in the meetings, incentives, conference, and exhibitions (MICE) sector; the sports industry; cultural promotion; and domestic education. Although each has a discrete genesis and goal, a central thread ties them together, and a compelling case can be made for these policy areas being designed to contribute quite specifically to promoting a Qatari form of soft power in the guise of a coherent brand. While there have certainly been instances of, for example, Qatar seeking to promote indigenous culture in the 1970s by encouraging archaeological projects to dig up and then display the state's history, the emphasis on such issues as the 1990s and 2000s progressed was demonstrably of a different magnitude.

The MICE industry is widely regarded as a lucrative sub-sector of tourism, with MICE visitors seen as unusually high spenders at the 'blue-chip' end of the industry.[1] Amid a wider trend to shift marketing focuses 'away from simply increasing the numbers of tourists to enhancing "the quality" associated with tourism growth,'[2] the MICE sector is 'one of the fastest growing segments of world tourism.'[3]

Asia and Australasia have emerged as hives of MICE activity, while cities such as Singapore, Bangkok, Hong Kong, and Sydney have increased their capacity to attract more MICE industry events, to accrue knock-on economic and other benefits.[4] More recently, Dubai has entered the crowded market along with Doha, with Doha currently coming of age in terms of its MICE industry potential. Plans many years in the making are coming to fruition, providing Qatar with world-leading MICE infrastructure. The state's $2 billion Qatar National Convention Centre (QNCC), which opened in December 2011, embodies Qatar's push to augment its MICE credentials under the banner of the Qatar Foundation (QF), while its award-winning airline Qatar Airways is used to spread Qatar's brand and fly tourists and businesspeople to Doha.

Although the marketing hype predictably describes the QNCC as having been 'built to be one of the most sophisticated convention and exhibition centres in the world', there is some justification to this hyperbole. No expense has been spared on the cavernous centre, from its ostentatious 'Sidra tree' external design, to its curved escalators (which serve no real purpose beyond allowing the QF to state that they are the first in the Middle East), to the multi-million dollar 30 x 33ft Louise Bourgeois spider sculpture, to the centre's 'first in the Middle East' LEED gold environmental rating.[5] AEG Ogden, the QNCC's management company, insists that it exceeded its first-year targets within seven months, boasting an estimated economic impact of almost $32 million, generated from 128,000 visitors attending 128 events in the first seven months of operation.[6] At the end of 2012, Qatar hosted the UN Framework Convention on Climate Change conference (COP 18), one of the largest conferences in the world, showcasing the state's ability to host world-level events.

Qatar's desire to attract important conferences is not new. In 2001, the state hosted the Doha World Trade Organisation (WTO) round of negotiations, and 'the Doha round' entered the vernacular of international finance. The state also inaugurated a 'permanent committee for organising conferences' in 2004 under the auspices of the Ministry of Foreign Affairs. The committee oversees up to fifteen significant conferences per year, including Qatar's regular 'Inter-faith Dialogue,' the 'US-Islamic World Forum,' and the 'Doha Forum.' The US-Islamic World Forum and the Doha Forum entered their 12th and 15th iterations respectively in 2015.

The elite-led push to make Qatar a centre for discussion and dialogue knows few bounds. Tens of conferences are arranged each month by some ministry, supreme council, or organisation. As well as the aforementioned regular forums, which attract Qatari and senior international ministers, other conferences include the Pipeline Integrity Management Forum, the Underground Infrastructure and Deep Foundations Conference, and key mini-conferences or 'contact groups' focused on Libya and Syria. Qatar also hosts (and pays for) conferences for institutions of which it is neither a member nor a candidate for membership. These include the Extractive Industries Transparency Initiative, whose 2009 conference was supported by the Ministry of Foreign Affairs.[7] Aside from the QNCC, the Qatar Tourism Authority opened its own 'world class' conference centre in autumn 2015. The fact that almost 10 per cent of Qataris could be seated in these two convention centres highlights how Qatar's ambitions are firmly set on international markets.

Underpinning these projects to attract MICE industries is a reputed $17 billion investment in the state's tourism infrastructure for the construction of meeting facilities, resorts, and hotels.[8] Equally, between Stenden University and the QF-sponsored MICE Development Institute (QMDI), Qatar is building infrastructure capacity in hospitality management and associated areas to train people to facilitate its push to become a world-class MICE destination.

Another mechanism for boosting Qatar's popularity and spreading its message has been the hosting of sporting events. For such a small state that, compared with its regional peers, has been so underdeveloped for much of its history, Qatar has a curiously strong reputation for hosting such events. According to one academic, until the 1960s the state was the only regional state to have a stadium with a grass pitch, which hosted iconic events, such as one of Muhammad Ali's open-air boxing fights in 1971 and a football match between Brazilian football legend Pele's Santos FC and Qatar's oldest club, Al Ahli, in 1973.[9] Qatar also hosted the fourth Gulf Cup, a regional football tournament, in 1976. Meanwhile, under the direction of then Crown Prince Hamad bin Khalifah Al Thani, in 1980 the state became a member of the International Olympic Committee.[10]

Qatar hosted the Asian Cup (football) tournament in 1988 and the FIFA Under-20 football World Cup in 1995, and has hosted an annual Association of Tennis Professionals (ATP) event since 1993, the same year *The New York Times* reported on Qatar making a move to be a 'sports capital.'[11] However, the volume of sporting tournaments based in the state increased significantly after the millennium. The 2000s saw Qatar host regional (Asian) handball, basketball, sailing, indoor athletics, and fencing championships, as well as world table tennis and weightlifting tournaments. The state also hosts top-class annual tennis, golf, motor-racing, equestrian, and athletics events.

In 2006, Qatar hosted the Asian Games, the largest sporting event to be held in the country to date, and in 2011 hosted the Asian Football Cup, another large and prestigious sporting event. However, winning the right to host the 2022 FIFA World Cup, the second largest sporting event on earth, represents the pinnacle of Qatar's sport hosting ambitions. Despite the negative publicity Qatar has experienced following its successful bid, this has not reduced its desire to host such global events. Witness Qatar's successful bid to host the World Athletics Championship in 2019, which it was awarded in November 2014.

A key aspect of Qatar's plan to make itself a world centre for sport is investment in sporting infrastructure, and Doha boasts one of the world's best sporting hubs in the form of its Aspire Zone. A complex including a sports-injury hospital and one of the world's largest indoor sporting arenas fit for multiple sports, Aspire acts as an international academy for athletes at both youth and professional levels.[12] This investment has extended to not only paying large sums to persuade older football stars to play in Qatar's domestic league (among them former Barcelona players Pep Guardiola and Ronald De Boer, Argentina's Gabriel Batistuta and Brazilian player Nene), but also paying athletes to change nationality to represent Qatar in tournaments and attracting top-class football teams to Aspire for mid-season breaks.

In terms of wider cultural sponsorship, the Qatari government has undertaken a variety of initiatives that, when taken together, constitute a cohesive policy for garnering a reputation for Qatar as a cultural hub. Overtly promoting Qatar as a cultural hot-spot is a direct, planned elite-led project comprising different strands. The New York-based Tribeca film festival first came to Qatar in 2009, and held an annual event in Doha until 2012 under the auspices of the Doha Film Institute.[13] Against the backdrop of emerging film industries and competing festivals in Dubai and Abu Dhabi, the festival attracted Hollywood stars, film premieres, and international media coverage.[14] One reason for partnering with such a well-known festival was to catalyse the start of a Qatari 'film industry,'[15] and there has been significant progress towards this goal; the 2012 Tribeca festival in Qatar screened a total of 19 films made in the state.[16] However, subsequent funding crises and the Tribeca's withdrawal from the partnership has resulted in festivals being cancelled and an exodus of staff.[17]

Despite Qatar's relative youth as a country, the state has quickly developed a world-wide reputation in the art world. The Museum of Islamic Art on Doha's corniche contains an impressive array of artefacts from all walks of Islamic heritage. I M Pei was coaxed out of semi-retirement to design the museum and provided with carte blanche, while luminaries including Damien Hirst, Jeff Koons, Robert De Niro and Ronnie Wood attended the glitzy opening in 2008.[18]

Saud bin Mohammed Al Thani was one of the world's most prolific art-buyers in the 1980s and 1990s, and his collection forms the basis of Qatar's credentials as an art hub.[19] Today, the personification of Qatar's push into the art world is Sheikha Al Mayassa bint Hamad Al Thani, a daughter of Hamad bin Khalifah Al Thani and Moza bint Nasser Al Misnad, and the sister of Emir Tamim bin Hamad Al Thani. She too has become one of the largest art-buyers in the world with a taste for Mark Rothko, Francis Bacon, Andy Warhol, and Paul Cezanne, for whose 'The Card Players'—a painting depicting gambling and drinking—she paid the highest price ever for a work of art sold at auction, approximately $250–$300 million, more than double the then auction record for an art sale.[20] In total, Sheikha Al Mayassa is believed to have amassed a $1 billion collection, to add to existing works in Qatar bought by Saud bin Mohammed for more than $1.5 billion in the 1990s and 2000s.[21] Unsurprisingly, at the height of the spending spree in the late 2000s and early 2010s, Qatar was the leading buyer in the global art market.[22] Sotheby's opened its first Middle East office in the state in 2008, and Doha is now, along with London, New York, and Tokyo, a stopping-off point for exhibitions on major Sotheby's art sales tours.[23]

As well as being the third place after Los Angeles and Versailles to host a significant Takashi Murakami exhibition (for which the Museum Authority built an exhibition hall on Murukami's orders), Qatar has the influence to obtain objects from museums that even the US's established institutions cannot procure, as with the 'Gifts of the Sultan' exhibition.[24] The Qatar Museums Authority (QMA) also seeks to lavishly sponsor key retrospectives in some of the world's most established museums, as it did for the Damien Hirst retrospective at London's Tate Modern in 2012.[25] Overall, Qatar has more than a passing desire to establish a reputation in the art world. Rather, the funds spent and infrastructure created to sustain Qatar's cultural industries are clear evidence of a consistent, elite-led policy to put the state at the forefront of this industry.

The same sense of a well-funded and evident policy is found in Qatar's education sector. Since Hamad bin Khalifah came to power in 1995, the education system has changed beyond recognition. Spearheading this educational revolution has been his most prominent wife, Moza bint Nasser. Under her guidance and at her request, US consultancy RAND Corporation in 2003 established itself in the state and set to work analysing the existing educational system from top to bottom. RAND's research methodology, conclusions, options, and suggestions have been exhaustively documented at each stage, and reveal a fascinating story of bold but ultimately unsuccessful attempts to transform the education landscape in Qatar.[26]

The overhaul began with the premise that 'the leadership of the Arabian Gulf nation of Qatar sees education as the key to Qatar's economic and social progress.'[27] The report further notes that the changes had been motivated by long-standing beliefs that existing educational structures were not up to the task of providing a twenty-first-century education. RAND came in, examined existing educational structures, and proposed various options for reform. Presented with these choices, Hamad bin Khalifah and Moza bint Nasser chose the most extreme option, involving 'system-wide structural change.'[28] Such profound changes in education form a key part of Qatar National Vision 2030, a clear articulation of the goals that Qatar is striving to attain, and which underpins much of the economic diversification inherent in the work of Moza bint Nasser's Qatar Foundation (QF).[29]

Although RAND also contributed to an overhaul of practices at Qatar University, it is Qatar's other higher education policies that are more noteworthy.[30] Beginning in 1998 with Virginia Commonwealth University, followed by Weill Cornell Medical College in 2002, Texas A&M University in 2003, Carnegie Mellon University in 2004, Georgetown School of Foreign Service in 2005, Northwestern University in 2008, and University College London (UCL) in 2012, leading foreign higher educational institutions were established in the Education City project in northern Doha. Degrees are now available in a range of subjects at both undergraduate and masters level. HEC Paris also offers professional MBAs under the QF umbrella.

Moza bint Nasser, who is also a UNESCO Special Envoy for Basic and Higher Education, frequently describes education as being of central importance, whether externally as a 'tool for peace' or internationally to boost dialogue and mutual understanding. A (now former) Qatar-based ambassador, meanwhile, has described education in Qatar as undergoing a 'silent revolution.'[31] For the small numbers of Qataris who attend Education City, the experience is typically positive. They receive a world-class education and are highly prized students who are practically guaranteed the pick of jobs in the Qatari workforce.

However, some Qataris fear the implications of these new educational programmes, and this has led to a backlash against Education City. Interviews reveal a certain amount of animosity or at least discomfort with practices and curricula at the institutions. For example, some Qatari students highlighted the mixed teaching and socialising in Education City as a source of disquiet.[32] Equally, the sheer cost of the initiative infuriates others, with many believing that Qatar University does not receive its fair share. One Gulf-based think tank conducted a study into the actual costs per student and, more interestingly, per Qatari student at Education City until 2012. To provide a sense of the high cost of attending Education City institutions, it was estimated that, per Qatari student at Texas A&M operating expenses per year in 2011 were $291,888, compared with just $72,189 in the US.[33]

Whether fiscally, culturally, or pedagogically-motivated, a wide range of complaints frequently appear in both Arabic and English-language media in Doha. Some focus on perceived discrepancies in spending on Education City as opposed Qatar University, with a comparison between lavish US-inspired graduation ceremonies in Education City and more demure ceremonies at Qatar University becoming a lightening-rod for criticism.[34] Another more fundamental thrust of complaints lodged against the educational reforms charges—quite rightly—that they have failed. Qatar's educational attainment is basically as poor now as it was at the beginning of the reform process, as PISA international student assessments statistically prove.[35]

Criticism is also often directed at Qatar University's administration and the former president Professor Sheikha Al Misnad.[36] A notable example of this was an outpouring of abuse following the dissemination of a speech by Sheikha Al Misnad at a Canadian university, where she discussed—too flippantly as far as many Qataris were concerned—the difficulties she faced when starting at Qatar University. Specifically, her remarks about how she had to expel thousands of students whose grades were impossibly low or who were taking years to complete their degrees attracted significant anger, much of which was marshalled by the Twitter hashtag which translates as 'resign and apologise, [Sheikha] Al Misnad, [this is the] right/demand of Qatari people.'[37]

Many of these criticisms are unfair. Qatar University is generally well-funded, and although Education City boasts beautiful, state-of-the-art campuses while much of Qatar University is located in 1980s buildings inevitably leading to unfortunate comparisons. But even this critique is increasingly invalid given the scale of huge improvements and new buildings being erected on the Qatar University campus. Furthermore, Sheikha Al Misnad was only ever seeking to raise standards at Qatar University, which inevitably meant that failing students could not continue and grade entrance requirements were raised.

Nevertheless, Qatar's elite is aware of these growing concerns. In 2012, an edict from Moza bint Nasser, that is widely believed to have come directly from then Crown Prince Tamim bin Hamad, changed the language of instruction in key courses at Qatar University from English to Arabic (in International Studies and Management, for example). The decision was taken with no discussion with the management of Qatar University or even Sheikha Al Misnad herself. It also went directly against Qatar National Vision 2030 in that it limited Qatar University's ability to produce English-educated Qataris for the local work-force, which will increasingly call for English-speaking, reading, and writing abilities as a core skill. Moreover, on a practical level, announcing the change in February 2012 and expecting the university to teach the courses in Arabic by autumn the same year was demanding the impossible. Not only did Qatar University not have the staff to do this, but the entire curriculum had to be changed—particularly in a subject such as International Affairs where there is no critical mass of translated works. It is entirely sensible for the only national university to teach its programmes in the native language. However, for this decision to be taken so abruptly caused havoc for students who had prepared for years for study in one language, only to have to then work in another.

Part of the motivation for the decision was to make it easier for Qataris who lacked the English-language proficiency levels to enter Qatar University. Although the decision will inevitably lower standards (as well as weaker students filling courses, there simply are not enough suitably qualified Arabic-speaking lecturers and professors to teach the subjects), this will sate some local criticism that the Qatari elite is too focused on supporting the foreign educational establishments.

Funding and forming a local narrative

One of the tactical reasons why the new Qatari elite has pursued MICE industries so rigorously is that they are expected to form a plank of Qatar's future post-hydrocarbon economy. A desire to counter post-oil and gas economic concerns is nothing new, and Gulf elites have enunciated economic diversification as a goal since the 1960s. However, such drives have generally been unsuccessful.[38] With copious hydrocarbon reserves and no immediate need to engage seriously in diversification, states such as Qatar, Kuwait, and Saudi Arabia have broadly avoided the difficult decisions that need to be made.[39]

Part of the way in which the MICE industries are expected to contribute to economic diversification is through job creation. Values and expectations that have been established in recent decades mean that Qataris will not engage in menial or labour-intensive work in the near future, and clerical industries represent a more plausible option. Similarly, a Qatar-based ambassador noted that the focus on clerical and (certain) hospitality-based jobs is more suitable in the Qatari context for women.[40]

Some of the inspiration to bolster Qatar's domestic economy and 'future-proof' it has come from following examples abroad. In particular, Singapore is known to have been something of a model for Qatar, particularly in the economic realm, achieving prominence and prosperity despite a dearth of domestic resources.[41] Aside from inspiration from successful city-states around the world, the QF's decision to build the QNCC and that of the Tourism Authority to construct its own separate world-class conference centre highlight the importance of personal politics. Qatari society in a business context is beset with 'Chinese walls' between personal fiefdoms. Sheikha Moza bint Nasser and her QF, and Hamad bin Jassim with his diverse interests in business including (formerly) the Tourism Authority, have been two notable fiefdoms in recent Qatari history.

Large vanity projects are no strangers to the Gulf, and the power of individuals in Qatar is significant. As a result, hosting such events could stem from a Sheikh's (or Sheikha's) whimsical desire to 'play host.' Similarly, it would be difficult to provide an economic case for why a small state such as Qatar should require two enormous convention centres. Nevertheless, even if the underlying reasons for pursuing MICE industries so vigorously are informed to a degree by optimism, the overall impression is that such initiatives are attempts at economic diversification more than whimsical, personally-led activities, given the pipeline of planning underpinning the push (namely the MICE education initiatives in the QF).

The fiefdoms have differing goals and targets, and the QF is increasingly focusing on social and education projects. As such, while personal politics may militate against sharing a convention centre, if these entities can—theoretically—specialise in their own sectors to a sufficiently high degree, each can pursue MICE industries tailored to their own specific focus.

Equally, with Qatar's sporting aspirations, gas-fuelled growth has been essential in allowing these policies to be pursued with such vigour. Otherwise, extensive interviews in Doha with former and current ambassadors, senior advisers to members of the elite, academics, and those working specifically in the sporting field highlight the importance of individuals in Qatar's engagement with sport.[42] The fact that both Hamad bin Khalifah and Tamim bin Hamad are sports fanatics—as benign as it may sound—is an important reason why Qatar has become such a hub for sport. Although members of the elite may want to host sporting events because of their own personal desire to see such events come to Qatar, a number of corollaries benefit the wider nation. Using sport to bolster a national identity is a much discussed trope in the literature and has been applied to case studies ranging from Northern Ireland to Hungary.[43]

Given that Qatar is a young state without many distinguishing features, particularly in the regional context, sport is part of the emerging tapestry giving Qatar its own unique character. Indeed, in the UNESCO-published *International Social Sciences Journal*, Geoffrey Caldwell notes that 'sporting success in international sport [can be used] as an internal and external validation of that system's worth…[a] drive for international sporting success may be a testament to the insecurity of a country's identity.[44] Such a conceptualisation fits well with the Qatari example. Not only have Hamad bin Khalifah and Tamim bin Hamad used sport 'as the vehicle par excellence' for promoting their leadership, but, by virtue of the world-class sporting events that Qatar is hosting, they are endowing Qatar with a global status compared with its previous almost complete lack of presence on the international stage.[45]

Aside from the issue of national identity, discussed below, providing sporting infrastructure is a domestically popular move. One former ambassador notes that Hamad bin Khalifah's use of sport in the form of constructing sports facilities was one of the key ways in which he increased his popularity in Qatar in the 1980s and built up his own constituency.[46] Similarly, on winning the right to host the 2022 World Cup, it is interesting to note that Hamad bin Khalifah took a slow procession down the Corniche in Doha amid celebrating Qataris of all generations, explicitly linking himself with the remarkable achievement.

The vast increase in the amount of sport on the Qatari calendar is also of potentially critical importance given epidemic levels of obesity in the country. The World Health Organisation has stated that 74 per cent of Qatari men and 70 per cent of Qatari woman are overweight, while other surveys have suggested that almost 50 per cent of adults and 33 per cent of children are obese.[47] In their efforts to combat growing obesity in Qatari society, the government have established a national obesity centre.[48] Similarly, 'National Sports Day'—a mandated national holiday—was inaugurated in 2012 by the then Crown Prince Tamim bin Hamad to encourage Qataris to exercise. Whatever professional-level sport can do to encourage Qatar's increasingly overweight youth in particular to take up a sport would have to be a good thing, particularly if the burgeoning epidemic of type-2 diabetes incapacitates increasing numbers of Qataris at a time when there are so few of them to staff the Qatari economy. Many of these ideas referring specifically to the sporting benefits for Qataris themselves, and Qatar more generally, are contained in the Qatar Olympic Committee Strategic Plan.[49]

Nonneman's framework dictates that, for domestic determinants of foreign policy, it is important to consider 'domestic survival' as a key instigator of policy. Although sport or art purchases cannot be linked to existential concerns, such cultural gambits should be considered part of wider policies with broader aims that contribute to assuaging Qatar's core security concerns, albeit in tangential ways.

Many of these cultural policies are a key part of Qatar's desire to mark itself out as a unique and unusual country engaged in overtly developmental actions. Although there are reasons to do this in respect of an international and regional audience, so too is it important to burnish a clear, positive, and unique image—or brand—of Qatar for Qataris. With a limited history on which to draw, and surrounded by other states with overwhelmingly similar identities, Qatar needs to carve out a niche for itself. Moreover, creating a distinct, attractive brand around Qatar—otherwise known as place or country branding—is all the more important, given the wider context of the general thrust of globalisation as Cerny notes.

> Today...national boundaries are under siege at myriad of levels—from civil wars and economic transnationalization, from cultural exclusivity and religious revivals, and from political disillusion and institutional decay (and reinvention).[50]

Gulf states are particularly vulnerable to the homogenising powers of globalisation because they are, in the words of Cerny, archetypal 'postmodern' states. His theory revolves around the emergence of so-called 'competition states,' by which he is referring to states so actively seeking to augment their business credentials and business ties throughout the world (as Qatar certainly is doing) that 'today's state constitutes the main agency of the process of globalization.' States undertake this push for economic gain and to remain relevant to their people, Cerny notes. Yet, by seeking to relentlessly attract a variety of economic activity to fulfil the needs of domestic constituents, states foist a paradox on themselves. By undertaking such business-savvy, business-attracting actions, the very process 'hinders the capacity of state institutions to embody the kind of communal solidarity or *Gemeinschaft* which gave the modern nation-state its deeper legitimacy, institutionalised power, and social embeddedness.'[51] This is where state branding is so critical.

Against this doubly homogenising backdrop, branding in the domestic context is crucial for a state to maintain a sense of individuality. The domestic importance of country branding is well-noted in the literature. As previously noted, Van Ham among others argues that 'internally, they [states] are making their citizens feel better and more confident about themselves by giving them both power and identity.'[52] The pressing need to establish a unique brand for Qatar for Qataris themselves to latch on to is, therefore, evident. Mediation and sport, as already noted, contribute to the Qatari brand, as do the various cultural initiatives.

At this point, discussion must inevitably turn to Benedict Anderson, one of the most influential authors on the topic of nationalism and its origins in the post-colonial world. Anderson argues that nations are 'imagined' communities:

> [They are] *imagined* because the members of even the smallest nation will never know most of their fellow-members, meet them, or even hear of them, yet in the minds of each lives the image of their communion...Communities are to be distinguished, not by their falsity/genuineness, but by the style in which they are imagined.[53]

Along with a census and a map, museums form the third spoke of the key 'agencies for culturing "the public" and for "thinking" nation-states', as Macdonald puts it.[54] Macdonald also notes that not all museums 'were an expressive site and agency of some of these new ways of thinking and of public culturing.' Nor is this role confined to museums, with other public institutions helping to foster and inculcate new norms of identity.[55]

In the case of Qatar, the art museums established by the new elite, along with the film festival and the cultural village hub of Katara (which hosts numerous art galleries and small museums, as well as a huge open-air amphitheatre hosting visiting theatre and opera) are a part of establishing, inculcating, and propagating a worldly, culturally sophisticated, and internationally oriented brand. It is not crucial from Anderson's perspective that the museums are full of national artefacts charting the nation's history.

> The idea of 'having a culture' has become crucial to nationalise and politicise ethnic discourse: it is taken as a mark of being a *bona fide* 'people' who should also have rights of at least some degree of self-governance...For nations, culture is their means of such expression: it is the outward sign of distinctive 'inner depths.'

> This did not necessarily mean that all that was on show had necessarily to be 'of the nation', though 'national' artefacts and art works were an important strand. Just 'having a museum' was itself a performative utterance of having an identity.[56]

By expending so much time and money on explicitly fostering and advertising the fact that Qatar 'has a culture', the state is asserting its legitimacy as a bona fide nation.[57] J E Peterson sees this assertion of legitimacy—stemming not only from cultural heritage but also from Qatar's brand creation as a whole—as assuring 'the legitimacy of the micro-state...[which] in turn leads to the single most important factor: increased awareness of and legitimacy accruing to Qatar—in domestic and external terms—[which enhances] the prospects for the state's survival.'[58]

Both the tactical use of culture to augment the Qatari brand and the strategic use of a brand are resolutely elite-led ventures. In particular, Al Mayassa bint Hamad is personally in charge of museums, art, and cinema initiatives in Qatar, serving as the public figurehead and chair of the Qatar Museums Authority, the Doha Film Institute, and various other cultural and charitable organisations.

As Nonneman notes, the policy-making elite is of particular relevance in the Middle East because it often has unusual influence and freedom of action. This is particularly true of Qatar, a small country with a small native population that the ruling family has historically dominated. It is therefore plausible to suggest that the personal whims and desires of one of the most important Al Thanis may be enacted on a state level, and that these figures may use their power, influence, and financial might to pursue personal policies on a larger political scale. This is potentially all the more true in respect of more 'ethereal' policy spheres such as art and culture, where there is more room for personal subjectivity to play a part. Indeed, *The Economist* haughtily warned Al Mayassa that she would have to make sure that, 'to be more than a rich girl's plaything', the Qatar Museums Authority would have to 'do better than put expensive foreign baubles on display in her homeland.'[59]

However, Al Mayassa has firmly sought to couch the various cultural initiatives within a much wider thrust of Qatari policy. Her speeches and remarks in respect of why she is emerging as such a leading figure in the art world and so assiduous a promoter of other cultural activities in Qatar fit the strategic thrust of many Qatari policies. For example, in her 2012 speech at the TEDx Forum explaining her rationale behind the cultural policies and museums that she oversees, Al Mayassa discussed the place of culture and art acting as a tool to smooth the transition between the globalised, homogenising world, and the domestic necessities of retaining a sense of identity. She favourably quotes Richard Wilk and his notion of 'globalizing the local and localizing the global.'[60]

Al Mayassa also notes that there is a certain 'security' in having a local identity, an interesting turn of phrase alluding to the challenges that Qatar faces in terms of establishing its sense of self and the important role that her cultural projects play in this. Echoing Macdonald, she notes that 'art becomes a very important part of our national identity...[the] social and political impact of an artist on his nation's development of cultural developing is very important.'

The personal role of Moza bint Nasser, the former emir's consort, in the pursuit of improving Qatar's education standards also cannot be overestimated. There is little doubt that, without her personal desire, prominent position, and sheer force of will, RAND would not have undertaken its key initial evaluation of Qatar's education system and overhaul. In the same manner, only someone as powerful as Moza could have secured the billions of dollars required to establish so many foreign universities in Education City.

Carving a regional niche

There are many facets and levels of regional competition. States can compete in the cultural, political, economic, or sporting spheres, and can do so for reasons including personal elite rivalries, a need to establish a competitive edge, or a need to carve a niche vis-à-vis regional and international competitors. All of these concerns and drivers are present to some degree in Qatar's decisions to vigorously pursue 'softer' policies as a part of an overall strategy to establish a new brand for the country.

At the core of these accentuated regional rivalries, as previously noted, is the issue of the smaller Gulf states' homogeneity. For most of the Arabian Peninsula's history, there have been no clearly demarcated dividing lines between tribal-political entities, as Brauer notes:

> [I]t is not unjust to conclude that [medieval Muslim] geographers...recognized the existence of political boundaries in the sense that as one progressed in a direction away from the centre of a state, one would sooner or later pass from one sovereignty to another or that one's taxes would flow to different places on either side of such a division. Yet, clearly in the minds of these cartographers such boundaries were constituted not as sharply defined boundary lines but rather as transition zones of uncertain sovereignty between two states.[61]

Historically resonant borders, as demarcated by a river or mountain range for example, are but one way in which a community can begin to coalesce against another community across the dividing line. However, the Arabian Peninsula largely lacks such physical features, particularly in the case of Qatar, the UAE, and Kuwait. While not fatal to nation-forming, it makes it more difficult, particularly in a context in which roaming, tribal dynamics have been a way of life.

Aside from providing states with specific issues, as in the case of the Bidoon in Kuwait or the Al Murrah in Qatar, pressure to establish a border where none previously existed means that there needs to be a reason to separate state

A from state B.[62] However, this is difficult in a context in which religion, culture, political dynamics, social milieus, familial links, histories, economic practices, and tribal structures are all similar. Needless to say, there are differences, such as those between port cities and those further inland, or between settled (*hadar*) and roaming (*bedouin*) populations. But, overall, there are more features of commonality than difference.

One area in which distinctions can be made is in terms of ruling elites. The fact that Kuwait is synonymous with the Al Sabah and Qatar with the Al Thani contributes to each state's implicit drive to differentiate itself. However, the tribal dynamic cuts both ways, as Wilkinson notes:

> Even today the formal state divisions, which are largely the heritage of the British presence, are still permeated by tribal, clan and family relations, whilst membership and affiliation to commercial, linguistic, religious and ethnic groupings and networks cut across borders and are often still of greater significance than state citizenship.[63]

The tribe is a competitor for loyalty to the state, and its links span the region. Tribes and families are spread throughout the Gulf Co-operation Council (GCC) area, and there are Al Rumaihis, Al Najjars, and Al Ghanims in each Gulf state.[64] The tribe is also a social unit that has commanded some form of loyalty for hundreds of years. By contrast, these new states have barely been in existence for more than a few generations, but demand the ultimate loyalty of their citizens over the tribe. This is a difficult sell, and one that needs to be explicitly worked on.

Equally in the Gulf context, Islam is a pan-state phenomenon that demands devotion and is a rival to the state for loyalty. This represents a significant challenge for any state, let alone newly emerging ones. Making this concern all the more acute for the smaller Gulf states is the fact that Saudi Arabia is the central state in Islam. The kingdom dominates the region, not only by virtue of its sheer size, but also because of its long-established, religiously-based credentials.

In short, the history of the specific region in terms of geography, people, and society provides two interrelated problems for a modern state. Firstly, a pervasive homogeneity means that each state must fight vigorously if it wants to differentiate itself and vie for recognition. Secondly, the region's nature and history provides several strong competitors for the loyalty of the people, with Islam (personified in the state of Saudi Arabia), tribal, and pan-Arab dynamics all having varying degrees of influence over a citizen's loyalties. Developing the MICE sector, in addition to sporting and cultural endeavours, forms part of Qatar's tactical answers to these strategic issues.

As Peterson rightly notes, 'Few countries have taken the lessons and importance of branding to heart more thoroughly than Qatar has in recent years.'[65] Peterson discusses the importance of hosting key events such as the WTO 'Doha Round' in November 2001, the Organisation of Islamic Conference summit in March 2003, and the Second South Summit of the Group of 77 in June 2005. He also notes the importance of sports in contributing to Qatar's emerging brand. Securing the right to host the 2022 FIFA World Cup is the crown jewel in this respect, and is arguably the single most prominent act that Qatar has undertaken in terms of publicising its brand. Indeed, the sporting and MICE sector examples help to significantly, if not exponentially, boost Qatar's brand recognition world-wide. There are several key benefits to this, including that increased recognition is critical to competing for greater foreign direct investment (FDI). The literature discusses at length the recent growth in place-branding in the context of obtaining greater FDI,[66] and the personal context, for example, is crucial:

> It [is] clear that the decision maker's personal views of target countries, and related influences from personal contacts with competitors, customers, suppliers, distributors, and others, play a pivotal role in the target country selections...research has found that the images that executives hold of various countries are significantly different from objective descriptors of these countries, and yet influences their actions.[67]

The authors proceed to quote a study of US business leaders relying on their perceptions of countries in South-east Asia in terms of their decision whether to invest there or not. Another long-term study found that 'subjective considerations by executives involved play a major role in investment decisions.'[68] With personal impressions being so important, Qatar's explicit focus on the luxury tourism sector and lavish MICE Industry events—whisking delegates from business class travel with Qatar Airways to a luxury five-star hotel, and on to world-class conference buildings—is a (potentially) savvy business-orientated policy, though questions concerned with cost-benefit analysis persist. Similarly, by making Qatar known as a state that actively supports leading sports and cultural events, the state is endeavouring to create an attractive and familiar image for the country.

Boosting Qatar's international profile in this way using sporting and MICE events is frequently commented upon. As one sports media professional put it, '[Qatar] is putting itself on the map...Its hosting of major sporting events is also a significant endorsement of a country's emergence, its credibility, its infrastructure, and of it being a destination in its own right.'[69] Academic sources echo this thrust, with Campbell referring to Qatar carving 'a global niche through hosting world sporting events.'[70] Amara views Qatar's various sporting ventures as a way to 'modernise through sport,' and as a way of assuring national prestige through sporting success.[71] Equally, through textual analysis of statements from official Qatari organs including the (former) crown prince's office, Amara suggests that it can be used 'externally for establishing Qatar as a leading country, and thus not a periphery of Saudi Arabia.'[72]

From the author's perspective, it was interesting to note how perceptions of Qatar have evolved in recent years. On leaving for Doha initially in 2007, few friends in the UK knew of the state. However, when returning in late 2009, Qatar was suddenly 'that place England played Brazil [at football],' while Qatar today is most certainly 'that place that will host the World Cup in 2022.' Media scrutiny of Qatar's World Cup bidding process has only heightened Qatar's prominence, albeit for negative reasons. This needs to be factored into Qatar's decision-making process in its responses to the accusations, and will be directly addressed in Chapter 10.

As well as being a savvy strategy to carve out a place for Qatar as a destination with unique attractions, regional competition as a spur to action is an impossible factor to ignore. In terms of the tourism industry, Dubai has sought mass-market tourism appeal, while Qatar has concentrated on high-spending MICE visitors. A US embassy cable quoted former acting director-general of the Qatar Tourism Authority Jan Poul De Boer explicitly discussing Qatar's strategy as opposed to a 'Dubai strategy.' Rather than a mass-market approach, Qatar has pursued 'a niche market for educational, medical, and sports tourism along with the existing meetings, incentives, conventions and expo travellers market.'[73] Such a repudiation of Dubai's strategy stems not only from a rejection of its fundamental model, but also from the sensitivities of Qatar's leadership in respect of overt Westernisation.[74]

Equally, it can seem at times that the states are too rich to be concerned with the costs of duplication, and can be driven by deep and often personal elite-to-elite desires to compete. The duplication of cultural and educational strategies in Abu Dhabi and Doha (the Sorbonne, New York University and the Guggenheim as opposed to Education City and the Museum of Islamic Art) is informed by the regional context and regional competition. Certainly, each fits into wider domestic strategies. However, while difficult to quantify, it is impossible to ignore country-to-country, elite-to-elite rivalry and competition.

Carving an international niche

Outside the regional context, the key determinants of such policies relate to deep, systemic changes in the international system that have diluted the grip of traditional states on the levers of the world economy. In her seminal article in *Foreign Affairs*, Matthews described this in terms of an issue of relative decline:

> The most powerful engine of change in the relative decline of states and the rise of non-state actors is the computer and telecommunications revolution...Widely accessible and affordable technology has broken governments' monopoly on the collection and management of large amounts of information and deprived governments of the deference they enjoyed because of it. In every sphere of activity, instantaneous access to information and the ability to put it to use multiplies the number of players who matter and reduces the number who command great authority.[75]

Writings such as this (particularly in the 1990s) discussing how globalisation will 'erode national boundaries' were in vogue for a time, and while the rhetoric can go too far, few would deny that what one may describe as globalisation has diluted the reach and power of states.[76] Moreover, for a small state seeking to emerge in its own right in the early 1990s, and under a new leadership with a fundamentally different idea of how to conceptualise the Qatari state, these new challenges were doubly as daunting.

A potential answer to this conundrum lies in the post-modern conception of state branding. Specifically in terms of globalisation in a branding context, along the lines of Cerny as outlined previously, Olins discusses the internationalisation of commerce. He notes that, while having numerous positive impacts, this has also resulted in 'a very harsh and turbulent commercial environment [in which] the nation that makes itself the most attractive wins the prizes—others suffer.'[77] Van Ham continues on this theme:

> Globalization and the harmonizing effects of European integration put further pressures on territorial entities to develop, manage, and leverage their brand equity. To stand out from the crowd and capture significant mind share and market share, place branding has become essential.
>
> ...
>
> One has to recognise that the unbranded state has a difficult time attracting economic and political attention. Why would we invest in or visit a country we do not know, and why would we pay attention to its political and strategic demands if we have no clue what the country is all about and why we should care?[78]

For Van Ham's concerns with the 'harmonizing effects of European integration,' read in the Qatari context—as dealt with above—issues stemming from regional homogeneity. However, Aronczyk elevates these concerns to the international level:

> Nation branding is currently justified among state and corporate actors as a necessary corrective to the waning importance of the nation-state in the context of glo-

balized economic, political, and cultural exchange. Nationally imagined identity is compromised by a number of indigenous and exogenous factors: the spectre of cultural homogeneity or, conversely, hyper-hybridity; stronger allegiances at the subnational, supranational or transnational levels...and widening networks of mobility, media and migration. In this context, corporate branding is a demonstrably effective way to assign unique identification by consciously highlighting certain meanings and myths while ignoring others. It is increasingly adopted by governments as a means to promote national identity while encouraging the economic benefits necessary to compete in a modern globalized world.[79]

Qatar's MICE industries, along with the explicit promotion of sport and Qatar's cultural ambitions, are key plinths of Qatar's emerging state brand. They have the publicity element crucial to branding, and carry positive, new, trans-cultural messages that attest to Qatar's modern appeal. Another way to conceive of the international sphere is in terms of Qatar's evident desire to join the mainstream international consensus. By hosting sporting and other key events, the state is asserting both its right and also its legitimacy to act as a traditional state, a small point but nevertheless worth making against Qatar's backdrop of overarching Saudi power and concerns over its independence. In a wider esoteric sense, however, one can also see 'the Asian Games as an opportunity for Qatar to reiterate its adherence to the universal values of democracy, solidarity and human rights.'[80]

There are further tactical issues to consider at the international level in the educational sphere. In the original plan for Education City, it was assumed that the venture would be populated by British universities, given historic Anglo-Qatari relations.[81] However, no British university could be persuaded to engage with the venture, leaving Qatar to turn to the US, where there was no shortage of candidates. The fact that Qatar now has US institutions at the heart of its society is a significant factor intimately tying the US to the state, and sends a deep signal to both the US and the world of Qatar's intentions. It implicitly shows that Qatar's orientation is towards a Western-centric curriculum, pedagogy, and ethos, firmly situating it on a path that Western states can understand and of which they approve, a potentially important point given the depth of misunderstanding and mistrust that has consumed Western-Arab and Muslim relations since September 2001. Or at the very least, it provides Qatar's leadership with a form of ammunition to use to face its critics in Europe and the US. This is precisely the kind of notion that Qatar needs to be promoting to a greater extent in Western media, given that the state has been increasingly castigated as a form of Islamist and at times terrorist-supporting state.

Overall, the central driving goal of these branding policies, with their cultural, sporting, educational and business-orientated facets, is to contribute to diversifying Qatar's economy and facilitating the transition to a post-hydrocarbon economy. This will depend on skills that a traditional Gulf education system does not provide (for example, professional use of the English language, analysis and critical thinking skills). Such concerns have been at the heart of Qatar National Vision 2030 and the state's educational drive since 1995. Although it is possible to recognise the importance of developing such educational skills and business-related attributes and facilities in a *prima facie* way, one can equally point to their importance empirically.

As noted in the introduction to this book, Kotler et al in their study of the importance of country branding—after much hypothesising and subsequent testing—discerned ten key concerns for companies seeking new locations for their business:

- Local labour market
- Access to customer and supplier markets
- Availability of development site facilities and infrastructure
- Transportation
- Education and training opportunities
- Quality of life
- Business climate
- Access to research and development (R&D) facilities
- Capital availability
- Taxes and regulation [clarity][82]

If these issues are of interest to potential businesses, by definition existing businesses desire them too. The brand that Qatar is so assiduously creating, primarily though not exclusively through its cultural, sporting, MICE and educational projects, speaks directly to several of these concerns. A suitable local labour market refers to a local labour force that is educated to work, the central goal of the QF. Further education and training opportunities, and the creation of a research and design location (Qatar Science and Technology Park (QSTP)), are also crucial to the QF's mission. Equally, concerns over quality of life and even an improvement in the business climate are answered to varying degrees by Qatar's cultural and MICE industry policies.

In this way, these cultural, sporting, and educational policies, far from being perennially relegated to the ethereal world of branding and popularity, can be seen as direct tactical answers to key business-related questions, and designed to make Qatar a more viable alternative for businesses.

9

QATAR AND THE ARAB SPRING

FROM ARBITRATOR TO ACTOR TO ACTIVIST

The wave of protests stemming from the self-immolation of Tunisian street vendor Mohammed Bouazizi on 17 December 2010 constitutes one of the most tumultuous periods in modern Arab history. The Arab spring, as it came to be widely known, fomented protests that unseated dictators who had been in power for decades and sparked civil wars. The only state in the entire Arab world where the Arab spring had practically no direct domestic ramifications was Qatar. However, the uprisings had important effects on the state's foreign policy, providing its leadership with the opportunity to engage in a new set of policies.

Broadly speaking, Qatar went from being an arbitrator to an actor, and from actor to activist with occasional arbitrational tendencies, a progression that fundamentally changed the basic orientation of its foreign policy. The state moved from being a state that assiduously attempted to foster an air of neutrality about its actions (for example, with its mediation or relations with Iran and Israel), to one that firmly chose sides. This meant that, for a period, it became a more important regional actor exerting a direct influence on events. However, the costs of reneging on its previously neutral status would soon increase significantly.[1]

As well as Qatar's elite directing its policies, the very mechanics of policy-making and policy implementation exerted an influence over whom Qatar dealt with. In short, institutional inability to diversify the types of clients with which Qatar dealt contributed to the emergence of a particular atmosphere backing the state's support for Islamist groups. This reputation and modus operandi became a focus of ire for Gulf Co-operation Council (GCC) states that fundamentally opposed this kind of policy. A combination of the salacious nature of the intrinsic story (a small, rich, World Cup-hosting state supporting Islamists) and active encouragement of such stories by other GCC states' lobbying groups, resulted in a tsunami of negative media coverage for Qatar particularly in 2013 and 2014. In this sense, the Arab spring deeply affected the state.

The following section outlines the more important aspects of Qatar's actions during the uprisings by focusing on levers of power in the state. Specifically, it seeks to understand how the Qatari elite sought to act and shape events through television network Al Jazeera, by using a form of cheque-book diplomacy, and by leveraging personal elite connections and a host of other personal ties, often with Islamists who had been resident in Doha. It is preferable to discuss Qatar's actions in the Arab spring via specific levers of power rather than on a country-by-country basis, because this provides a better pan-regional perspective for comparative purposes. Similarly, this section is not designed to provide a compendium of every Qatari action in the Arab spring, but rather to focus on areas in which Qatar exerted greater authority and influence. This allows for an evaluation of the salient facts without digging through a state-by-state narrative for details.

After Qatar's actions in the Arab Spring have been discussed, subsequent sections focus on explaining the policy logic according to the underlying motives for its actions as well as the twin factors that shaped the policy creation and execution. Also analysed and critiqued are the widely misconstrued reasons for Qatar's actions in the Arab Spring. Lastly, given the seriousness of the charges relating to Qatar being an extremist-supporting state, these accusations are examined directly.

The revolution will be televised

Never a stranger to controversy, Al Jazeera often became the story itself during the Arab spring, at least to some in the Arab world, because it played an important role in the emerging uprisings. However, it is difficult to specifically discern, let alone empirically justify, just how influential Al Jazeera's role was. The network's initial role in Tunisia was of immediate importance. After all, it was the video of Bouazizi's mother's protest at the site where her son had killed himself that was uploaded to social media and then 'broadcast by Al Jazeera, reaching hundreds of thousands of people overseas', that proved to be a key catalyst of the Arab spring.[2]

Al Jazeera at this point was banned from Tunisia, and the innovative use of social media feeds and other unconventional sources such as mobile phone footage came to characterise the network's flexible and ultimately highly effective approach.[3] Zayed prophetically quotes Rami Khouri, the highly respected journalist and author, noting that the events Al Jazeera played a key part in precipitating in Tunisia and elsewhere 'marks the maturity of Jazeera television as a political force that can play a role in changing political orders.'[4]

Al Jazeera covered the unfolding events in Tunisia persistently. It also used small clips—which it inserted into its news credits several times per day—to keep tensions high, and to remind viewers of the passions that had been enflamed. One example noted by Marzouki refers to a short clip of a man on the central thoroughfare in the Tunisian capital Tunis, in which he can be heard shouting 'Ben Ali fled—the Tunisian people is free! The Tunisian people will not die! The Tunisian people is sacred! [sic]', which was shown on the news opening credits.[5] Marzouki also characterises the relationship between Al Jazeera and the Tunisian demonstrators as a 'love affairs of sorts' in which a 'robust interaction developed: the network used images of Tunisians to promote its coverage and protesters carried signs reading "Thank you, Al Jazeera"'.[6]

Al Jazeera's coverage was also widely viewed as highly influential in Egypt's January 2011 uprising. Part of the reason why the network's role has been so heralded is that the contrast between its coverage and that of traditional domestic television news stations was so great.[7]

> While Al Jazeera was showing hundreds of thousands of people calling for the end of the regime, Egyptian TV showed humdrum scenes of traffic quietly passing by; when Al Jazeera reported hundreds of people queuing for bread and petrol, Egyptian TV showed happy shoppers with full fridges using footage filmed at an unknown time in the past.[8]

The influence of Al Jazeera's coverage was highlighted by the extraordinary lengths to which the Egyptian government went to shut down its coverage, as Miles catalogues:

> On Jan. 27 Al Jazeera Mubasher, the network's live channel, was dropped by the government-run satellite transmission company, Nilesat. On Jan. 30, outgoing Egyptian Information Minister Anas al-Fiqi ordered the offices of all Al Jazeera bureaus in Egypt to be shut down and the accreditation of all network journalists to be revoked. At the height of the protests, Nilesat broke its contractual agreement

with the network and stopped transmitting the signal of Al Jazeera's Arabic channel—which meant viewers outside Egypt could only follow the channel on satellites not controlled by the Egyptian authorities.

...

The next day, six Al Jazeera English journalists were briefly detained and then released, their camera equipment confiscated by the Egyptian military. On Feb. 3, two unnamed Al Jazeera English journalists were attacked by Mubarak supporters; three more were detained. On Feb. 4, Al Jazeera's Cairo office was stormed and vandalized by pro-Mubarak supporters. Equipment was set on fire and the Cairo bureau chief and an Al Jazeera correspondent were arrested. Two days later, the Egyptian military detained another correspondent, Ayman Mohyeldin; he was released after nine hours in custody. The Al Jazeera website has also been under relentless cyber-attack since the onset of the uprising.[9]

Nevertheless, while Al Jazeera's effect should not be overestimated, the network for a time enjoyed something of a 'CNN moment,' a sense that it had provided transformative and hugely influential coverage that earned it plaudits and qualitatively separated it from the competition.[10]

However, there was an increasing backlash against what some viewed as Al Jazeera's slavish and uncritical reporting of the Muslim Brotherhood, reflecting the Qatari government's priorities.[11] The replacement of long-serving director Wadah Khanfar with a member of the Qatari royal family in September 2011 further stoked accusations that the channel increasingly reflected official thinking.

Days after Egyptian president Hosni Mubarak had left office, Al Jazeera launched *Al Jazeera Mubasher Misr* (Al Jazeera Egypt Live/Direct). Sultan Al Qassemi, an Emirati social media and cultural commentator, refers to *Mubasher Misr* as a part of Al Jazeera's unrelenting pro-Muslim Brotherhood coverage in Egypt in particular.[12] Although his tone is consistently critical of what he views as this emerging slant, Al Qassemi provides evidence to back up his claims. Aside from *Mubasher Misr* following Egyptian politics twenty-four hours per day from a mostly Muslim Brotherhood angle, he charges that Qatar's close relationship with the Muslim Brotherhood leadership in Egypt allowed senior members from the movement to appear on Al Jazeera several times, including Deputy Supreme Guide Khairat El Shater; General Guide Mohammed Badie; and Mohammed Morsi himself.[13] Equally, as noted previously, Yusuf Al Qaradawi, arguably the Arab world's most influential theologian, has close ties to the Muslim Brotherhood and presented a programme on Al Jazeera for some time. Al Qassemi contends that the overarching tone of coverage on Al Jazeera Arabic was manifestly deferential and uncritical of the Muslim Brotherhood as a whole. Al Jazeera's coverage of the post-Morsi Egyptian government has also been critical.

Any one of these facets could potentially be dismissed. For example, it should not be that surprising that senior members of a popular political party would want to be interviewed on a popular television network, or that Al Jazeera, hungry for ratings, would want to televise interviews with such individuals. However, taken in the round, Al Qassemi's strident criticism represents a reasonable critique, and supports wider academic and social media opinion as to Al Jazeera's changing, pro-Muslim Brotherhood tone.[14]

There are clearly examples in Al Jazeera's history of the Qatari government directly altering its editorial line. Most notably, the network's editorial line towards Saudi Arabia was amended in 2008 to facilitate a rapprochement between the kingdom and Qatar.[15] After Saudi Arabia, the UAE, and Bahrain withdrew their ambassadors from Doha in early 2014, calls by regional states for Al Jazeera's coverage to be toned down threatened to further circumscribe its editorial line.

However, these examples of interference are the exception rather than the rule, and it would be too simplistic to suggest that Al Jazeera is merely a tool of Qatari foreign policy. While there certainly is alignment, a generation of Arab reporters who grew up under dictatorial regimes of varying degrees do not need to be told to cover a spate of uprisings exuberantly.

Aref Hijjawi, a former director at Al Jazeera Arabic, broadly agrees that the network's coverage has a somewhat pro-Islamist bent. However, he offers a persuasive, rounded explanation of its orientation. He begins an article for the Heinrich Böll Foundation discussing the notion of neutrality and objectivity, maintaining that 'if a person did not favor one of the two sides: Hosni Mubarak, or the crowds in Tahrir Square for example, he would be confused at best, at worst psychologically ill.'[16] He then invokes the basic dynamics of the newsroom, of exiled Tunisians covering their own state's uprising, and of the everyday realities of people 'impassioned about Arab and Islamic issues' working and producing television coverage.[17] Indeed, he gives an impression of a natural evolution of an innate 'pro-Islamic' sentiment, and fundamentally views Al Jazeera as a mirror on wider Arab society.[18] In a sense then, Al Jazeera moved swiftly from arbitrating, showing both sides of the argument as it did for a few months in Syria and a few days in Egypt, to becoming an actor, taking part in the revolution, to an activist increasingly supporting one side.

Certainly, the Egyptian government under President Abdel Fatah El Sisi would agree with this characterisation, as it showed with the arrest and subsequent prosecution of several Al Jazeera journalists in December 2013 on a range of trumped-up charges.[19] The trial was an embarrassment for the Egyptian state and a patent travesty of justice.[20] Even Sisi himself 'regrets' the trial and imprisoning of the journalists. Not only did it damage Egypt's reputation, but it further strained bilateral relations with Qatar.[21]

However contrived or natural Al Jazeera's coverage was, the end result has been a significant loss of trust and viewers.[22] To a degree, this was inevitable. Al Jazeera had 'first mover' advantage when it entered the modern media era in the Arab world, and competition would inevitably eat away at its initial market share over time. Yet there is a sense that there is more to its loss of viewers and trust than simply market forces readdressing an imbalance. As with Qatar as a whole, which has abandoned any notion of being a neutral regional actor, so too Al Jazeera became distractingly synonymous with support for groups or movements such as the Muslim Brotherhood.

Even as regional pressure on Qatar grew to curtail its affiliations with the Muslim Brotherhood and it exiled (broadly by mutual consent) key Muslim Brotherhood figures, Al Jazeera still resolutely stood, tinged with its Muslim Brotherhood-supporting tone. If it was merely a case of changing its editorial line, the network in all likelihood would have changed its tack. However, it is not that simple. Bureaucracies have a strength and a resilience of their own. The reason that Hamad bin Khalifah Al Thani established supreme councils alongside existing ministries was that he did not believe he could enact meaningful change through existing ministries. Consequently, he bypassed them entirely, at the cost of creating a duplicate system.

Tamim bin Hamad has experienced the same problems with Al Jazeera; the network's culture and staff cannot be changed overnight. This is one rationale for underwriting the launch of a new London-based media venture called *Al Arab Al Jadeed* ('The New Arab'). The idea being to start afresh with a new news organisation, which would not be challenged by old working practices and one that did not suffer from a reputational hangover.

Chequebook diplomacy

From the spring of 2011 onwards, Qatar stepped up its role in Libya across the political, financial, and military spectrums as protests erupted across the country.[23] Diplomatically, it was the first Arab state to recognise the emerging Transitional National Council (TNC) leadership only days after France had led the way, while then Qatari foreign minister Hamad bin Jassim Al Thani played a crucial role in engineering 'Libya's suspension from the Arab League and subsequently secured a unanimous vote of support in favour of the No Fly Zone (NFZ).'[24] In terms of trade and finance, Qatar supported selected rebel groups with money and goods, ranging from cooking oil to (tons of) weapons to trading oil on behalf of rebel groups to circumvent sanctions.[25] Crucially, along with the UAE, Qatar also gave the NATO alliance the political cover it needed by joining in patrolling the NFZ over Libya. To do this, it sent six Mirage fighter-jets—accounting for the majority of its operational fast-jet capacity[26]—3,000 miles to Libya, a move without precedent in Qatar's history.[27] Towards the end of the campaign, as more of the country fell outside Gaddafi's control, Qatar became bolder and inserted elements of its special forces to help train and co-ordinate rebels, as well as flying some groups to Doha for training.[28] Never before had the state taken such direct and combative action to unseat a regional leader. Indeed, in the case of Libya, it moved straight to the role of actor and activist, with almost no attempt at arbitration at all.

In Egypt, Qatar scarcely engaged in cheque-book diplomacy ahead of President Hosni Mubarak's ousting, but this modus operandi was clearly evident in its subsequent attempts to prop up the President Mohammed Morsi regime. In August 2012, Qatar provided $2.5 billion of deposits to the Egyptian Central Bank and another $2.5 billion deposit in January 2013, alongside a grant of $500 million.[29] On 10 April 2013, Qatar provided a further $3 billion in the form of a purchase of Egyptian bonds, and agreed to supply the state with liquefied natural gas (LNG) during the hot summer months.[30] Five Qatari LNG cargoes covered the summer-time deficit in the Egyptian domestic gas market.[31] These cargoes were also meant to form part of a larger deal, under which an estimated further 18–24 cargoes would be provided over the subsequent eighteen months.[32] Wider Qatari promises of investment included an estimated $8 billion for a port project and $10 billion for a resort project in the north of the country. Furthermore, while Qatar did not want—as claimed—to acquire the Suez Canal or the Pyramids (former Qatari foreign minister Hamad bin Jassim denied the claims, both of which are intrinsically ludicrous)—suggestions were tabled in respect of Qatar investing $10 billion in the wider Suez Canal regeneration project.[33] All in all, Qatar's investment and aid to Egypt theoretically amounted to around $40 billion.

However, most of these investments, opportunities, and agreements disintegrated after the coup that ousted Morsi in July 2013. The new Egyptian government, flush with financial support from the UAE and Saudi Arabia in particular, no longer immediately needed Qatar's financial largesse. A demonstrable snubbing of Qatar began in earnest, with Egypt returning $2 billion to the state in September 2013 and two lots of $500 million in November and December 2013. Other proposed investments withered, LNG discussions stalled, and Egypt withdrew its ambassador from Doha and joined (if not led) a regional chorus calling for the Muslim Brotherhood to be banned and demanded the extradition of now-Qatari citizen Yusuf Al Qaradawi.[34]

Although Qatar provided a greater financial stimulus to Egypt than any other Arab Spring country, there have been intense rumours surrounding its financial support for key actors in post (and pre) revolutionary Tunisia. However, the closest anyone has come to providing proof of a quasi-funding link has been the Tunisian Court of Auditors, which raised questions over the provenance of political party Ennahda's funding in August 2012.[35]

Aside from this inference of underhand government-to-government support, billions of dollars of wider Qatari investment have unquestionably been channelled into the Tunisian economy since the Arab spring. Initially, Qatar pledged loans of $500 million, an amount matched by Turkey but more than the EU and the US combined, which was subsequently increased to $1 billion.[36] The state also invested several billion dollars in the Tunisian telecommunications, banking, tourism and hydrocarbon sectors, as well as promising 20,000 jobs for Tunisians in Qatar. Some Qatari backers also apparently sought to buy out one of the new, popular Tunisian newspapers—*Attounisia*—that was established following the fall of former president Zine El Abidine Ben Ali.[37]

In Syria, meanwhile, Qatar soon became one of the central champions of change after initial efforts to persuade President Bashar Al Assad's regime to moderate its position failed. Once again using its role as the then head of the Arab League, Qatar sought to isolate and co-ordinate the overthrow of Al Assad's regime. Qatari prime minister and foreign minister Hamad bin Jassim led the Syria committee in the Arab League, and engineered the 'startling' suspension of Syria's Arab League membership in November 2011 with the promise of subsequent economic sanctions.[38] Qatar led diplomatic activities, including hosting key conferences to marshal support against the Syrian regime, and handed the Syrian embassy in Doha over to main opposition group the Syrian National Council (SNC) in February 2013.

Although Qatar did not support rebels in Syria as comprehensively as their counterparts in Libya, in 2012 and 2013 the state was still viewed as being at the forefront of international efforts to oust Al Assad and corral support for the opposition. While confirmed details are inevitably sparse, particularly those relating to the first eighteen months after the state realised that that Al Assad could not be reasoned with, Qatar supplied—at the very least—significant non-military support, as well as light weaponry and manpads (man-portable air defence systems) to a range of generally moderate groups.[39]

Personal relationships and Islamist connections

To engage in chequebook diplomacy or otherwise invest money in the hope of influencing people or parties, or assuring wider outcomes, relationships need to be developed. While typically far more difficult to accurately discern than often alluded to by the media, it is important to at least plot out what is known about the relations in which Qatar has engaged in the wider region.

Tunisia offers a clear example of a particular partner or group of people with whom Qatar is widely assumed to have intimate relations. According to the logic of 'we know it happens, but there is no proof', Qatar is widely believed to favour and even support Rashid Ghannouchi's Ennahda party.[40] However, if publications are sufficiently cavalier to outright assert that these supposed links are matters of fact, lawyers extract grovelling apologies, as the UK's *Independent* newspaper found to its cost in August 2012.[41]

Nevertheless, there are many important personal links and shared histories between Qatar and senior Ennahda members and other key Tunisian politicians. Ennahda's founder, Rashid Ghannouchi, has been a frequent visitor to Doha over the years (which have included audiences with Yusuf Al Qaradawi), and he has been a regular on Al Jazeera.[42] Indeed, his appearances on Al Jazeera alongside opposition figures such as Moncef Marzouki (Tunisia's president from December 2011 to December 2014) in 2000 and 2001 prompted the recall of Tunisia's ambassador to Qatar.[43] Some even predicted a lucrative retirement for Ghannouchi in Doha, effectively taking over from Qaradawi as Al Jazeera's resident popular Islamist theologian of choice.[44]

Adding fuel to the fire, Ghannouchi stated in an interview with *Al Arab* newspaper after the Tunisia uprising that Qatar was a 'partner' in Tunisia's revolution, not least because of Al Jazeera's coverage. Equally, other Ennahda members caused a storm by suggesting that the (now former) Qatari Emir Hamad bin Khalifah attend the opening of the new Tunisian National Constituent Assembly in 2011. Meanwhile, Ghannouchi's son-in-law Rafik Abdessalem, after working as head of research at the Al Jazeera studies centre in Doha, became Tunisia's foreign minister, further cementing ties between the two countries.

In terms of Qatar's interactions in Libya during the country's uprising, there is a readily identifiable Doha-based connection. Dr Ali Al Sallabi was an influential Libyan cleric despite living in exile in Doha for more than a decade. His father was also one of the founding members of the Muslim Brotherhood in Benghazi, while Al Sallabi (the younger) 'was seen as an ideological guide for the movement.'[45] Ali's brother Ismael, meanwhile, led a Qatar-backed militia that received hundreds of millions of dollars in support from Qatar,'[46] while one of the most prominent rebel commanders, Abdulkarim Belhaj, was also strongly associated with Ali Al Sallabi.[47] This is no casual link. Belhaj and Ismael's *khatiba* (militia) was supplied directly because of its links to Al Sallabi, who was given an audience almost exclusively because he happened to be present in Qatar, a clear case of availability over preference (or 'more by accident than by design' as Ulrichsen puts it).[48] Nor was Belhaj reticent about highlighting his links to Qatar: his political party, Al Watan, used Qatar's colours on its campaign material. In an era in which fear of perfidious foreign influence was rising, this was a recipe for disaster and Al Watan's popularity duly slumped in elections in mid 2012.[49]

Qatar also has a range of contacts that are often affiliated or otherwise closely related to the Muslim Brotherhood. As noted earlier, Al Qaradawi, the influential Islamist theologian closely associated with the Muslim Brotherhood, has been based in Qatar since 1961. Initially, he oversaw Islamic education in the state, while he has also been a regular fixture on local television since the 1970s. From the late 1950s, there was a steady influx of Muslim Brotherhood exiles (or those with associated sympathies) to the Gulf states, including Qatar. Figures such as Abdul Badi Saqr, Ezzeddin Ibrahim, Ahmed Al Assal, AbdelMoaz Al Sattar, and Dr Kemal Al Naji came to occupy important positions throughout the nascent Qatari bureaucracy. Although they hardly used Qatar as a 'pulpit' for the Muslim Brotherhood, their presence speaks to the ebb and flow of both people and ideas in and out of the state.[50]

In Qatar, relatively prominent Muslim Brotherhood members have run influential centres, such as Hisham Mursi (Al Qaradawi's son-in-law)'s 'Academy of Change'—an NGO teaching non-violent protest, much to the consternation of many regional elites.[51] Meanwhile, Al Jazeera's staff, both rank-and-file and those in the most senior positions (for example, Wadah Khanfar and the aforementioned Rafiq Abdul-Salem)[52] are widely assumed to have connections to or sympathy with the Muslim Brotherhood.[53]

Nevertheless, Qatar is diverse, and former Arab-Israeli Knesset (Israeli parliament) member Azmi Bishara is widely viewed as having been an important link for the state in its Arab spring activities in the Levant region. Since arriving in Doha, Bishara has been a 'near permanent' presence on Al Jazeera. He has also established a think tank (the Arab Centre for Policy Studies), been a key mentor and adviser to crown prince and then Emir Tamim bin Hamad, consolidated his place in Doha by evolving his think tank into a government-backed, full-fledged university, and been the creator and editor-in-chief of Qatar's new online print and television media foray, *Al Arab Al Jadeed*.[54] However, while his influence is clearly significant, he is far from an Islamist. Rather, Bishara is a dyed-in-the-wool pan-Arabist, a Christian Palestinian who has served in the Israeli parliament. Similarly, Qatar's bureaucracies are not staffed solely by former Muslim Brotherhood members; ardent Palestinian nationalists have played key roles too, including Mahmoud Abbas, Hani Hassan, and Kamal Adwan.[55]

The Qatari state by no means operates solely by building relationships with sub-state actors. Indeed, the personal friendships between the leaders of Qatar and Syria (and those of their families) is well-documented.[56] These close friendships, and doubtless some political calculation (Syria is an important ally of Iran, with whom Qatar has long sought to bolster relations), meant that when protests erupted in Syria in March 2011, Hamad bin Khalifah sent his Prime Minister and Foreign Minister Hamad bin Jassim to Damascus in early April 2011 with a message of support and solidarity.[57] Although there is no evidence of any formal arbitration between the Assad government and the protesters, despite an escalating crackdown by the Syrian regime, Hamad bin Khalifah for months attempted to calm the situation.[58] However, with increasing brutality reflecting Assad's ignorance of any semblance of compromise, Qatar withdrew its ambassador from Damascus on 18 July 2011 and switched to seeking Assad's removal.[59] As such, its role as an arbitrator during the Arab spring lasted for only a few months in the Syrian context, and never in a formal setting. As Bishara put it, Assad could have remained in power if he had reformed, but 'the regime chose not to change, and so the people will change it'.[60]

The first key body that Qatar sought to support financially and politically in Syria was the Syrian National Council, an organisation that the Muslim Brotherhood came to increasingly dominate.[61] Figures such as Mustafa Al Sabbagh, a Syrian with close associations in Doha and the Syrian National Coalition's former secretary, and Ghassan Hitto, the first prime minister of the interim Syrian National Coalition government, are widely viewed as being 'Qatar's men.'[62] Otherwise, this dynamic is typically framed as Qatar supporting particularly Muslim Brotherhood actors in these types of Syrian coalitions.[63] However, Qatar is not immune to being influenced; for example, it followed the US plan to subsume the Syrian National Council into a new, more inclusive entity, the National Coalition for Revolutionary Forces, in November 2012.[64]

Aside from this political support, Qatar has ploughed millions of dollars into supporting several militia groups in Syria financially, with humanitarian supplies, and with (on the whole) light weaponry. As far as can be determined, it has tended to support groups associated with the Muslim Brotherhood. Qatar is long believed to have a close association with Liwaa Al Tawhid (the Tawhid Brigade) in and around the northern Syrian city of Aleppo, many of whose members have reportedly been trained in Qatar.[65] Another group tenuously linked to the Muslim Brotherhood and with connections to Qatar (and the US, before its dissolution in March 2015) was Harakat Hazm (Steadfast Movement).[66] However, Qatar is not solely wedded to groups associated with the Muslim Brotherhood. The Syrian conflict is dynamic, and a constantly shifting mosaic of groups, and associations. Just as during the Arab spring as a whole, Qatar's support evolved in Syria. Aside from its move from quasi-arbitrator to actor as the death toll increased and Assad remained in power, both factors emphasising the complete failure of those seeking his ousting, Qatar became even more of an activist seeking his removal from power.

Tenuous but apparent associations and links to other more extreme groups appeared. For example, Ahrar Al Sham ('Men of the Sham [the Levant region]') is a more extreme splinter group of Al Qaida in Syria that has reputedly received support from Qatar and Turkey.[67] Before a bomb attack in September 2014 killed its entire leadership, leader Hassan Abboud on 8 June 2013 appeared on Al Jazeera Arabic to spread the message of the growing efficiency of the group, which *Foreign Affairs* described as 'an Al Qaida-linked group worth befriending.'[68] Similarly, as the struggle became increasingly intractable, a critical mass of evidence began to emerge as 2013 progressed suggesting increasing contact between Qatar and another Al Qaida affiliate, Jabhat Al Nusra (the Victory Front).[69]

Jabhat Al Nusra committed its first terrorist attack on 6 January 2012 and officially announced its existence by taking responsibility for the attack on 24 January 2012.[70] It was formed as a Syria-focused group to consolidate dozens of the estimated 1,000 militant groups that had sprung up across the country.[71] Members tended to be drawn from networks of militants that had fought with Al Qaida in Iraq (AQI).[72] Led by Abu Muhammad Al Jolani, the group's goals are confined to replacing Assad and forming a Sharia (Islamic law)-governed caliphate across the country.[73] Although linked to Islamic State (IS), Jabhat Al Nusra maintains its independence and has overtly sought to create an image for itself as rejecting the logic of attacking the 'far enemy' (Western countries) in favour of focusing on the 'near enemy' (authoritarian regimes in the Middle East and, in its case, Syria).[74] Similarly, although its ranks are by no means purely staffed by Syrians, Jabhat Al Nusra is seen as far more Syrian-dominated and focused than a group such as IS, which is infamous for having foreign fighters.[75] Lastly, it is important to note that Jabhat Al Nusra has been frequently referred to as the most effective force fighting against Assad, particularly after it changed its tactics from merely suicide bombings to taking on Assad's forces more directly.[76]

The links between Qatar and Jabhat Al Nusra became apparent particularly from late 2013 onwards. In particular, the state developed a relationship with the group under which it could extract concessions when it came to securing the release of hostages. In March 2014, 13 Greek Orthodox nuns and 3 aides were released as a result of Qatari negotiations (with the payment of an alleged $16 million ransom and the release of 153 Syrian prisoners from Syrian prisons);[77] US journalist Theo Curtis was released from Jabhat Al Nusra captivity in August 2014;[78] nine Lebanese men were released in October 2014 following Qatari intervention;[79] and 45 kidnapped Fijian soldiers were released in early September 2014, also as a result of Qatar's involvement.[80] The link between Qatar and Jabhat Al Nusra became even clearer with interviews on Al Jazeera with Al Jolani in 2014 and 2015 that could not have taken place without some official connivance.[81]

How Qatar secured the release of these hostages is unknown. The state's foreign minister flatly denied that Qatar had paid a ransom for the Fijian hostages, and said that the Qatari state did not 'believe in paying ransoms... [this only] fuels [conflicts]'.[82] Israeli media (perhaps unsurprisingly) reported that Qatar had paid $25 million to secure the release of the Fijian hostages, while US officials insisted that they asked Qatar not to pay any money to secure Curtis's release.[83] If Qatar does not pay for the release of hostages, this begs the question of how it persuades these groups to give them up.

All politics is domestic

In terms of Qatar's policies during the Arab spring as a whole, a recurring criticism has been that the state has supported the formation of democracy abroad to stave off engaging in democratic practices domestically.[84] However, this kind of proposition does not stand up to much scrutiny. Simply put, there is no widespread push for democracy in Qatar. Occasionally, a small group of Qatari intellectuals will tentatively state that Qataris would like more influence on domestic policy,[85] but such notions remain niche. As surveys have shown, 'in the six tumultuous months spanning December 2010 and June 2011, support for democracy and interest in political participation has dropped markedly among Qatari citizens.'[86] This conclusion will come as no surprise to anyone who has spent years researching, studying, conducting interviews, and working in Qatar, where the overwhelming reaction to questions of democratic development in the state is one of apathy. Between the chaos of the Arab spring and the sclerotic economic development of Kuwait, the Gulf state with by far the most advanced democratic system, democracy is simply not deeply sought in Qatar. Consequently, the notion that Qatar's elite is seeking to foment democracy abroad to stave off implementing it domestically is not credible. While Facebook pages established during the Arab spring dedicated to 'revolution in Qatar' organised protests in Doha, not a single person (bar the author) turned up to see what 'the opposition' in Qatar looked like.[87]

Although Qatar's leadership did not undertake its actions in the Arab spring out of fear of its own people, to a degree it took action because of them in a different context. Only on a small handful of occasions in Qatar's history has the state taken on anything approaching a leadership role in the Middle East. All of these examples occurred under Hamad bin Khalifah and typically revolved around mediation, with the Lebanese example in 2008 particularly prominent. During the Arab spring, however, Qatar took its prominence to a new level. Not only was it at the very forefront of championing the cause of Arabs on the street, with Al Jazeera fuelling the uprisings, but it was also among the first countries to actively participate and overthrow rulers such as widely despised Libyan leader Gaddafi. As noted when discussing motives for Qatar's forays into mediation, this kind of positive, prominent role is often well-received by Qataris.[88]

Hamad the revolutionary

When seeking to discern factors influencing foreign policy formation in the Gulf states emanating from the domestic arena, the leadership's conception of its role is important. In the Qatari context, and in terms of the state's Arab spring policies, this notion can be whittled down to the views and proclivities of just a few individuals, with former Emir Hamad bin Khalifah a particularly influential figure.[89]

Hamad has long viewed himself as something of a revolutionary who repeatedly overturned the status quo in Qatar. Internally, he revolutionised the Qatari education system by importing a US model and ending the teaching in Arabic of key subjects at school-level (though this was later reversed). In foreign affairs, when the opportunity of the Arab spring presented itself, he took it to support ongoing uprisings. Hamad's particular background is hard to ignore, in terms of where he grew up and with whom, and his subsequent penchant for decisive and unusually bold actions.

Hamad bin Khalifah's mother, Aisha bint Hamad Al Attiyah, died in childbirth (or at least while Hamad was very young) and he was raised by Aisha's full brother, (his uncle) Ali bin Hamad bin Abdullah Al Attiyah. The Al Thani and Al Attiyah families have enjoyed a close relationship since the late nineteenth century. Sections of the Al Attiyah were particularly influential as certain members became important advisers to and supporters of various Al Thani leaders, leading the Al Attiyah to receive a limited government stipend (as many Al Thanis do to this day) in 1978.[90]

Hamad bin Khalifah deepened this relationship even further. He grew up with Hamad bin Ali Al Attiyah, whom he made his chief of defence staff on coming to power in 1995. Another close Al Attiyah friend from childhood, Abdullah bin Hamad Al Attiyah, played the central role in the formation of Qatar's liquefied natural gas industry from the early 1990s onwards.[91] Other key influences on Hamad bin Khalifah include his most prominent wife, Moza bint Nasser Al Misnad, and his confidant and political right-hand-man, Hamad bin Jassim Al Thani.

As a result, two of Hamad bin Khalifah's four closest advisers (Abdullah Al Attiyah and Moza bint Nasser, both of whom he had known since his youth) were the children of leading Qatari revolutionaries of the 1960s. Their fathers—Nasser Al Misnad and Hamad bin Abdullah Al Attiyah—led pan-Arabism-inspired protests across the country, and were arrested and exiled, with the two men even spending time in prison together.[92]

It is hard to ignore the parallels between the fathers of Hamad bin Khalifah's two closest advisers and his own subsequent policies. The 1960s revolutionaries took advantage of emerging and unifying regional currents of dissent—pan-Arabism—to agitate for change. For years, speculation in Qatar held that Hamad bin Khalifah was something of an Arab nationalist himself.[93] His appointment of Bishara—the ardent Arab nationalist and former member of the Israeli parliament—as an adviser both to himself and his son, Tamim bin Hamad, hints at some substance to this claim. However, whether or not this is the case is largely irrelevant, given that Arab nationalism has all but disappeared; it certainly does not command the loyalties of tens of thousands of Arabs across the region. In lieu of pan-Arabism, Hamad bin Khalifah took advantage of the regional current of dissent that emerged in the form of the Arab spring, namely moderate Islamism. In a sense, this was used as the modern proxy for the pan-Arabism of yesteryear, a pragmatic, uniting concept enlisted to agitate for change.

Brotherhood path dependency

Whatever his rationale, Hamad bin Khalifah used moderate Islamism to project Qatar's power and influence, particularly during the initial period of the Arab spring. Indeed, he had little option if Qatar was to play a significant role. The state is a young country that has managed modern bureaucracies for only a generation, while its foreign ministry remains a work in progress—anything approaching a critical mass of trained, professional staff capable of fulfilling the traditional tasks of such a ministry has yet to emerge. The notion of the Qatari embassy in Cairo or Tunis reporting evolving events, developing contacts with key figures, or providing the Doha elite with analysis of events is fanciful. This is not the function of Qatari embassies (or not yet at any rate). Politics, particularly in the Arab world and even more so in Qatar's case, is directly conducted by the minister or the emir himself, with negligible intervention by or advice from the embassies in question.

As such, Hamad bin Khalifah and Hamad bin Jassim, the key architects of Qatar's Arab spring policies, were left to their own devices in respect of the regional uprisings and how to react to them, save for informal advice from confidants and whomever they called on to discuss the topic. Neither was provided with institutional support, as one may assume, from the foreign ministry or an external security service agency, which Qatar does not possess.[94] In practical terms, in respect of establishing contacts with individuals on the ground in Arab spring states, Hamad bin Khalifah and his organs of government had to fall back on what was available. In essence, this meant using the number of exiles who had accumulated in Qatar over the years, many of whom were linked to the Muslim Brotherhood or other associated Islamist groups.

The importance of Muslim Brotherhood exiles in Doha and Al Jazeera Arabic staff, who inevitably included a number of questioning, networking, media-savvy Arabs with religious convictions, should not be underestimated.

Other links, such as those with Ali Al Sallabi (discussed above) were equally as important. In addition, Muslim Brotherhood networks throughout the region are substantial. Overall, it would perhaps be judicious to paraphrase Anderson; for 'Egyptian Facebook campaigners' being a 'modern incarnation of Arab nationalist networks whose broadsheets disseminated strategies for civil disobedience throughout the region in the years after World War 1,' read 'Muslim Brotherhood networks.'[95]

However, Qatar's links were not exclusively to Islamists or those affiliated with the Muslim Brotherhood. Although both Sallabis are linked to the movement, a more accurate reading of the disparate groups highlights that they are not one and the same. Indeed, when Ali Al Sallabi attempted to unite with the 'official' Libyan Muslim Brotherhood group, his overture was rejected.[96] Moreover, another conduit for Qatar's support was a Sufi, Aref Ali Al Nayed, an important middle-man for a time at least, before he turned against Qatar's policies. Qatar has also worked with the secular Mahmud Shammam, who in 2011 was chosen to head the new Libyan television station broadcast from Doha. Support for those not linked to the Al Sallabi network took the form of the funnelling of thousands of tons of weapons through Misratan networks.[97]

Pragmatism is the key concept here. Although Qatar is frequently portrayed as a state that perennially seeks to support the Muslim Brotherhood, its relations are far more practical than such assertions assume and infer. There is certainly no ideological affinity between Qataris and the Muslim Brotherhood. Qatar officially follows the Salafi, Wahhabi creed of Islam: the Fanar Centre, the state's central Islamic educational outreach institution, takes an unabashedly Wahhabi tone, while the national mosque was named the Muhammad Ibn Abdul Al Wahhab mosque in late 2011. However, just as Qatar is shoring up its regional Salafi-Wahhabi roots in Saudi Arabia with the naming of the state mosque, so too—in addition to the practicalities of using Qatar-based Muslim Brotherhood members during the Arab spring—is Qatar attempting to firm up a wider Muslim Brotherhood constituency through these channels.

Context, media interpretation, and Machiavellian scheming

The aforementioned logic suggesting that Qatar's foreign policy during the Arab Spring was shaped by the basic realities of the informal contacts that the state's elite could muster is persuasive, but is only part of the answer. Qatar's leadership was not merely a passive actor directed by circumstance, it had multiple concurrent and wider goals in mind.

However, fathoming these plans is not straight-forward. The leadership rarely—if ever—speaks candidly in public, and in such a closed, small circle as exists at the top of Qatar's elite, there are few policy advisers or other interlocutors to reliably explain the state's policy. Despite Qatar's love of the limelight, it is curiously reticent to talk about its own actions.

In this void of information, journalists inevitably grope in the dark for 'the answer' as to why Qatar became as involved as it did in the Arab spring. There was a palpable sense of excitement in early 2011 when journalists eagerly called around experts in Doha to confirm whether or not Moza bint Nasser Al Misnad had been exiled in Benghazi with her father when she was younger, and had perhaps even studied at university there.[98] Although there was little evidence on which to base this conclusion (only the loosest notion that her father had business associates there),[99] this snippet of information promised a neat, clean answer to the conundrum, the logic being that Moza bint Nasser had a personal attachment to Benghazi and Libya, and consequently persuaded her husband, the emir, to act.

Qatar is also often described as seeking to fill a 'regional void' with its actions in the first few years of the Arab Spring.[100] This idea conceives of a rudderless Arab world with a Baghdad decimated by war, Cairo decaying under an introspective dictator and then beset by revolution, and Riyadh having no dynamism with its septuagenarian, octogenarian, and nonagenarian leadership.[101] Another great cliché frames Qatar's actions as a part of a confrontational, regional chess game, pitting proxy against proxy in a struggle for wider regional influence.[102]

The first theory speaks to a perennially crucial aspect that underpins many of Qatar's international forays—that of the importance of a pliant international atmosphere allowing Qatar to act. Similarly, other prosaic but crucial issues allowed Qatar to engage in the Arab spring. Without the sheer scale of the uprisings that disrupted the status quo in Arab politics, the Arab League would have been unlikely to have supported NATO-led action against a fellow Arab state. Furthermore, without the Arab League sanctioning such action, Qatar and the UAE would have found it more difficult to act as they did. Qatar, which has no history of aggressive 'regime-change' policies, would not have sent planes and supported the removal of Gaddafi as stridently without this overarching narrative.

Indeed, it took the Arab spring, one of the most powerful revolutionary movements to sweep the Arab world, to provide the prompt and opportunity for Qatar to change some of its central foreign policy tenets. As various studies of Qatari mediation argue, the notion of relative neutrality was of central importance, as it often is with less powerful mediators.[103] Yet with its actions in Libya and then Syria, any notion that Qatar is a 'neutral' state has vanished. From now on, the state will be viewed as a state with definite interests that it supports. Otherwise, only a state as fundamentally secure as Qatar could send the majority of its operational fast-jet force thousands of miles across the region, leaving its capital city effectively unguarded by the Qatari Air Force (or at best guarded by a skeleton force). However, these points are fundamentally contextual and do not speak directly to the impetus for Qatar acting in and of itself.

The second theory, regarding proxy conflicts, is logical and provides some answers for newspaper editors as to why Qatar sought to involve itself. This notion—namely the idea of nefarious Qatari leaders playing chess with their proxies against Saudi Arabia and other regional states—offers one possible interpretation as to why Qatar and Saudi Arabia supported different sides in the Syrian conflict.[104] However, this is arguably too journalistic and Machiavellian, and does not ring true. While certainly possible, given the freedom of action that Qatar's leadership enjoys, the theory's tenor does not fit comfortably with Qatar's policies overall. Equally, these differences in terms of support are more likely simply to be the result of each side's contacts. As noted previously, Qatar's ability to actively seek out new, preferred actors is more limited because of its lack of intelligence or other foreign assets.

For example, in the search for a more scheming account to explain Qatar's motivation, the notion that the state's intervention in Syria formed part of a wider, proxy-force-imbued geopolitical narrative undercutting a key plinth of Iranian foreign policy, is (at least) a logical suggestion. The theory here is that, from a realpolitik Sunni Muslim perspective, driving a mortal wedge between Iran and its quasi-client state Syria would be beneficial.[105] And it is certainly true that Qatar has been trying as hard as any regional state to undercut the rule of Assad in Syria, which certainly contradicts Iranian interests.

However, the notion that Qatar is engaging in an aggressive policy aimed at undermining Iran is not persuasive. Such a nakedly aggressive policy towards the Islamic republic has never been a trait of Qatar's foreign policy. In recent decades, Qatar has in fact consistently sought to improve its relations with Iran, despite a range of tactical and strategic differences. As Chapter 5 discusses in more detail, opening amicable dialogues, seeking to entangle Iran in trade relations, supporting key Iranian allies financially and with diplomatic protection, and undermining Iran's international isolation have been consistent Qatari policies. Qatar has done this out of a combination of fear but also a pragmatic assessment of its local reality. Chief among these concerns is the two states' shared gas field. Qatar's continued economic success and development depends on the continued and safe extraction, processing, and shipping of gas from the North Field. This is the central vulnerability in Qatar's national infrastructure much of which is contiguous with its Iranian border. It is therefore of little surprise that Qatar felt engagement to be a better strategy than confrontation.

Although Qatar's policies militate against Iranian interests, the state's significant efforts since the late 1980s to show that it is not unduly antagonistic towards the Islamic republic and that it is not seeking to force the regime in Tehran into a corner suggest that this is not one of Qatar's aims. Without any reason to suppose that the threat from Iran has diminished—Qatar remains as vulnerable and as secure as it ever has in respect of the Islamic republic—Qatar's leadership clearly feel that the state has built up a sufficiently positive relationship with Iran and that this most crucial of security-orientated bilateral relationships can survive pointed differences over the issue of Syria. As such, a clichéd, proxy conflict-type explanation simply does not work in this case.

The politics of reciprocity

The concept of reciprocity in academic literature is often defined in two ways—specific and diffuse reciprocity. The former includes examples such as arms treaties between the US and the USSR, whereby one state removed 20 ballistic missiles from active service and the other reciprocated. The latter has no such clear-cut or immediate returns in mind. As Keohane puts it, 'a contribution to the lifeboat service in the United Kingdom or to the Wilderness Society in the United States will not increase one's own chances of being rescued at sea or enjoying public wilderness.'[106]

Similarly, Qatar could have had only modest expectations of any immediate, tangible benefit accruing from supporting the Arab spring uprisings. The theoretical concept of Qatar playing a positive role in support of the evident popular yearning for freedom by hundreds of thousand Arabs is a sensible conclusion in the abstract, boosting Qatar's soft power. However, tying down such a notion is difficult.

Supporting what appeared to be a widespread, democratic yearning for change held the promise of replacing corrupt, nepotistic, and often repressive Arab regimes with a more representative form of government. Such a transition must be seen as a progressive, unambiguously positive act from anything approaching a liberal perspective, and being intimately associated with this transformation has benefits all of its own. Much of the new Qatari elite's plans during the late twentieth and early twenty-first centuries revolved around creating and spreading a modern, positive brand for the state. In this sense, Qatar's role in the Arab spring fits with its overall thrust. The logic behind wanting to augment a widespread positive image for a state is dealt with in particular in Chapter 8, and revolves around burnishing a state's wider brand image, which is so important in an ever more homogenised Gulf and a globalised world, particularly in the perennial struggle for foreign direct investment and human capital.

Moreover, at least at the beginning of the Arab spring, Qatar successfully positioned itself as a full-blooded champion of the individual, effectively supporting what often appeared to be a majority of people seeking social and political change. The Arab spring itself heralded a quantum leap in the importance of 'the individual' in the Arab context. The act and relative (initial) success of the uprisings demonstrated a significant increase in the agency of individuals in an autocratic region which tended to ignore individual rights and freedoms. In a situation where the individual has increased agency or, for a time at least, is actually an important actor, Qatar—as a country that sought to provide assistance in the uprisings—was well-placed to benefit.[107] Attempting to court constituencies, foster influence, and build relations with what at the time appeared to be an emerging, powerful grouping of people is a sensible ploy for any state. But for a state such as Qatar, which has been as concerned with as large and dominating a state as Saudi Arabia for as long as it has, such a ploy is savvy if not necessary. Indeed, Qatar's Arab spring support can be seen as just the latest policy designed to cement its independence from Saudi Arabia by creating constituencies of support further afield.

In the early days of the uprisings, Qatar unambiguously sought to support the majority of Arabs who appeared to be revolting across regional states. Its means often included channelling support through Islamist groups but, as noted previously, this is likely to have been a function of necessity as much as preference. Attempting to support a wave of rising popular sentiment, most notably with Al Jazeera championing the uprisings, is an understandable ploy. Facing no threat of a revolt at home, Qatar's leadership was entirely unencumbered by any notion that it could be stoking a revolutionary problem for itself. This kind of freedom makes Qatar unusual—if not entirely unique—in the Middle East.

As with other 'diffuse' aspects of reciprocity, it is often difficult to tell how the 'favour' gets returned. However, this does not stop people supporting the lifeboat service in the UK or the Wilderness Society in the US, to use Keohane's example, and it did not stop Qatar acting so forcefully during the Arab spring. The theory does dictate that reciprocity is only possible 'when some norms of obligation exist: that is, when international regimes are relatively strong.'[108] But this approach implicitly revolves around a rational actor approach of leaders in bureaucracies weighing decisions and acting on considered, aggregated judgement. Such an approach does not sufficiently cover the quirks of Qatar's leadership, in which the emir's place is so privileged, and the state overall so fiscally and physically secure that decisions that may be far more contentious or costly elsewhere can be taken relatively easily.

Even though the emir's power in Qatar could clearly result in policies with little identifiable pay-off and which resemble an altruistic act, reciprocity, in its technical definition, should not 'necessarily embody ethical principles that override self-interest.'[109] Nor can Qatar's policies purely be seen as the result of path dependency. Qatar has its own priorities and, like every other state, seeks to maximise the benefits available from any given situation. Indeed, Qatar's relations in the Arab spring should be seen as aimed at aiding the translation of Qatar's financial wealth, political clout, and media projection into other commodities in the world of diplomacy and politics.

The example of Qatar's support for Egypt highlights some of the more direct instances of 'diffuse reciprocity.' With its tens of billions of dollars of investment, Qatar achieved a privileged place in Egyptian domestic and foreign relations. There are suggestions that the state also sought economic benefits such as an advantageous tax regime, as it enjoys in France, or first choice on viable investment opportunities.[110] Specifically, Qatar would have gained from the cancellation of a 10% capital gains tax on the $2 billion acquisition of the Egyptian Bank National Société Générale, which was finally acquired in March 2013.[111]

Qatar also sought political advantages. Its previous diplomatic relationship with Egypt had been difficult, and WikiLeaks documents revealed the extent of troughs in relations. A conversation between former Egyptian Foreign Minister Ahmed Aboul Gheit and former Deputy Head of the Egyptian mission in Qatar Adham Naguib was relayed to the US Embassy's Political and Economic Officer Stephen Rice. In the conversation, Aboul Gheit insisted that Egypt would 'thwart every single initiative Qatar proposes [sic]' during its presidency of the Arab League.[112] Without such a flagrantly antagonistic government in Egypt, Qatar could have expected more co-operation with its regional policies, whether in multilateral forums such as the Arab League or on a more specific basis, such as continuing Qatari mediation and other political efforts in Sudan.

Throwing its support behind the Muslim Brotherhood in Egypt and elsewhere in the region at the time seemed like a sensible decision born of realpolitik. Given the large numbers of individuals nominally affiliated with the Muslim Brotherhood, and the fact that the movement has been a bona fide organisation for almost a century, the movement had finally demonstrated its capacity to organise and mobilise support. Crucially, there was little alternative. There was no similarly cohesive grouping of any other constituency, be it youth actors, secular supporters, or anyone of any other political or social stripe.

Understanding Qatar's 'extremist turn'

Without getting bogged down in the nuance and debate over methodological definitions of what constitutes a moderate and an extremist in the context of the fluid Syrian civil war, a broad consensus has emerged.[113] Groups such as the Free Syrian Army are overall seen as classic 'moderate' actors. Some of the groups cobbled together under the banner of the Islamic Front as of November 2013 were generally more extreme.[114] As noted above, Qatar is widely viewed as supporting one such 'moderate' group, the Tawhid Brigade. Further towards the end of the spectrum are groups that are almost unequivocally viewed as extremist, Al Qaida type groups, including Jabhat Al Nusra and Ahrar Al Sham.

Although it would be disingenuous to assert that Qatar actively supports groups such as Jabhat Al Nusra with finance or weapons (there is no available open-source evidence to support such a notion), it would equally be wrong to ignore the few instances that point to some form of relationship. The first thing to note about any such relationship between Qatar and groups such as Jabhat Al Nusra is how unlikely bedfellows the two are. From the wholesale change of its education system to a US-aligned model, including initially removing of Arabic as a key teaching language, to the almost unique prominence of Qatari women compared with their regional counterparts, to Qatar's evident desire to establish modern, pragmatic relations with all actors from Israel to Iran, the entire tenor of Qatar under Hamad bin Khalifah, which has continued under his son Tamim bin Hamad, contradicts the notion of Qatar as a terrorist-supporting state.

These tenuous links, as described in detail below in the section on personal relationships and Islamist connections, understandably snag the media's attention and have led (equally understandably, given much of the media's inability to sufficiently contextualise or investigate topics) to a barrage of criticism, particularly in 2014, that Qatar was a terrorist-supporting state. Exacerbating this theme is the role of a few apparently important individual Qatari terrorist financiers and their often unfettered comings and goings, along with lax anti-terrorist financing laws, further creating the impression of Qatar as actively supporting such nefarious actors and activities.[115]

Assuming that there has been no profound, schizophrenic volte-face by the Qatari elite and that its previously enlightened and modern policies were not some kind of a Machiavellian diversion from their deep-seated, extremist inner-beliefs—which any sane analyst would surely have to agree with—the answer as to why Qatar has some relationship with extremists must lie else-where. Two factors are particularly important in understanding these kinds of Qatari relationships.

Firstly, contrary to the clichéd trope of Qatar's foreign policy as being fiendishly complex or incomprehensible, in reality it can be rather straightfor-ward. The state's leadership for many years has said that Qatar is seeking Assad's removal in Syria. It tried to accomplish this diplomatically through the Arab League, corralling international pressure, and through its own actions, seeking to lead a vanguard against the regime (for example, closing its embassy in Damascus soon after the outbreak of conflict and being the first Arab state to open a Syrian National Coalition embassy). When this approach failed, the state began to seek a military solution. Supporting the Free Syrian Army and other relatively moderate groups, Qatar was first among international states to provide both military and non-military assistance. However, this ploy also failed. As a result, driven by necessity and by the logic of an ever more extreme conflict needing a more extreme actor, Qatar appeared to increase its support for groups that subsequently came under the umbrella of the Islamic Front. No evidence has yet been uncovered to suggest that Qatar has actively sought to send weapons to Jabhat Al Nusra, though in the chaotic mess that is Syria, some doubtless leaked away. Nevertheless, Qatar recognises the a priori utility and reality of actors such as Jabhat Al Nusra, and is likely to reconcile its interaction on these twin bases.

The key point here is the importance of the domestic Qatari context in facilitating this kind of policy. There are no formal lobbying groups, lawyers within the foreign ministry, influential independent experts in government with influence, vociferous media outlets acting as a watchdog, or other domes-tic actors to question the wisdom of such actions. The emir and foreign minister keep their own counsel and are not 'advised' on an identifiable basis by any one group, save for their ad hoc close advisory circle. In short, there is no one in Doha available to point out (or at least question) the short-sightedness of this policy, or that it will lead to a media-led evisceration of Qatar. Although the emir's latitude in making decisions should not be overestimated—he certainly consults key advisers and ministers, and faces institutional intransigence—there is no meaningful formal body to critique policy before it has been made.

Indeed, many of the ransom deals that Qatar has arranged appear to have been conducted without a direct cash payment. The only other plausible commodity that Qatar has is some form of quasi-political understanding to support Jabhat Al Nusra's interests in some way. Occasional snippets of speeches by Qatar's foreign minister hint at such rationales. In November 2014, speaking at the Italian Air Force Academy, Dr Khalid Al Attiyah noted that Qatar's goal was to 'encourage productive communication channels through moderate mediators with various groups that have been in isolation, and instead focused on violence.'[116]

This notion of having moderate mediators in contact with extremists has long been evident in Qatar's foreign policy. The state's wider foreign policy strategies have clearly involved efforts to speak to all sides in a given conflict, no matter how potentially unpalatable they may be. Although undoubtedly extreme, Jabhat Al Nusra is a nationalist-focused group that is specifically concerned with Syria, and does not have grand, entirely irreconcilable designs on attacking some 'far enemy.' While it should remain only speculation in lieu of detailed evidence, Qatar may at some stage have designs on attempting to establish contacts now to bring Jabhat Al Nusra into the political fold in future. The state would be far from the first state to engage with a terrorist organisation to curb its excesses and involve it in a political process, the Irish Republican Army (IRA) and the British government being a classic example. The first step towards such a plan would be to attempt to bring groups such as Jabhat Al Nusra 'in from the cold' to make them more palatable. Multiple interviews with Jabhat Al Nusra's leader on Al Jazeera are an obvious way of attempting to achieve such a goal.

Secondly, but intimately linked to the first point, it is crucial to remember how Qatar's intrinsic lack of human capital and experience curtails its ability to chop and change alliances. The actors with whom Qatar deals—as a result of whatever kaleidoscopic melange of Al Jazeera associates, acquaintances, and business partners of the elite who happened to be elevated in the first place—

are hard to replace. Although one should not eulogise the foreign services or intelligence outfits of other states, Qatar has even fewer options. A lack of alternatives, coupled with an unusual emphasis on the importance of personal contacts in the Arab world, means that Qatar doubles down on its contacts time and time again.

As the Syrian civil war progressed, more moderate groups became increasingly marginalised and lost influence.[117] Fighters who had previously belonged to more moderate groups often 'fled to better armed and more effective groups because of necessity', and even 'on several occasions, entire factions became more extreme to ensure a share of foreign funding.'[118] Qatar, as a state seeking influence to remove Assad from power, is consequently likely to engage with more extreme groups on two levels. Firstly, if the elite in Doha wants to help or seek to control an effective opposition to Assad in some small way, it is behoved to support the more extreme groups in some fashion. Secondly, regardless of any such strategic notion, those groups or individuals with whom Qatar has had contact inexorably gravitated to the more extreme end of the jihadi spectrum as the wider conflict became more brutal. Although Qatar of course did not have to maintain these contacts, it did if it wanted to maintain any influence.

10

QATAR UNDER EMIR TAMIM BIN HAMAD

The trilingual, thirty-three-year-old Crown Prince Tamim bin Hamad Al Thani became emir of Qatar on 25 June 2013 when his father and Emir, Hamad bin Khalifah Al Thani, voluntarily abdicated. There is no compelling explanation backed up by evidence to explain why Hamad bin Khalifah decided to step down. Some accounts suggest that he wanted to demonstrate that succession was not to be feared, a salient lesson in the Arab world and particularly in the midst of the Arab spring, with regional leaders clinging on to power to the detriment of their state and people.[1] Others suggest that he abdicated because of ill-health.[2] Hamad bin Khalifah's first kidney operation was in 1997 and he is believed to have undergone a second operation in the 2010s. It is clear that he lost a significant amount of weight from 2012 onwards, which could point to health concerns.[3] The nature of the kidney condition indicates an ongoing or at least recurring acute medical condition spanning a significant length of time. The first operation in 1997 spurred him to appoint his first Crown Prince, Jassim bin Hamad Al Thani, while the second, along with subsequent health concerns, may have prompted him to consider his position more fundamentally.[4]

In thinking carefully about his legacy in the event of his death, Hamad bin Khalifah would have had visions of his son and crown prince taking power at the same time as Hamad bin Jassim Al Thani, his dominant foreign minister and prime minister, was still in the prime of life (fifty-four). This may not have been a palatable proposition.[5] Hamad bin Jassim would still have been the most important voice for Qatar, the director of foreign policy; critically important internally as prime minister; and Qatar's dominant businessman, in charge of the nation's airline and directing its sovereign wealth fund. Although Hamad bin Jassim would have been unlikely to make a play for the position of emir, Tamim bin Hamad's freedom of action could have been significantly restricted.

Either way, Hamad bin Khalifah resigned and Tamim bin Hamad came to power amid a widespread cabinet change. In total, ten ministers were replaced and five retained their portfolios, while six new ministries were created or reformed. The key conclusion to be drawn from the reshuffle was a keen emphasis on competence and hard work, to the detriment of the 'business as usual', lackadaisical approach that had characterised traditional cabinets in Qatar (and elsewhere in the Gulf).[6] The new emphasis on discipline was personified in the new Prime Minister and Minister of the Interior, Abdullah bin Nasser Al Thani, who enjoys an unparalleled reputation in Qatar as an assiduous, hard-working taskmaster.[7]

However, aside from these structural changes, Qatar to no one's surprise did not change significantly in the first year of Tamim bin Hamad's rule. Indeed, any form of sharp change of direction would have been unlikely. Firstly, his father, Hamad bin Khalifah, while not interfering in any discernible way in Qatari politics, was still present in Doha, while his mother, Moza bint Nasser Al Misnad, was still the powerful chairwoman of the Qatar Foundation (QF). Furthermore, had Tamim bin Hamad been minded to change his father's policies and unpick his legacy, Hamad bin Khalifah may not have abdicated in his favour so willingly, particularly as he was under no pressure to step aside.

Nevertheless, Qatar has evolved under Tamim bin Hamad's leadership, as this chapter details. After placing his first months in power in the context of a relentless media barrage, as well as severe setbacks on the international front ('An "annus horribilis"' and 'No such thing as bad publicity?') it focuses on the tone of changes as suggested by the new emir himself ('An internal focus'). The new emir's speeches and deeds are used to examine his record, and it transpires that in his first years in power he was largely focused on internal issues. The move from the prime minister also holding the foreign affairs portfolio to the prime minister also being the minister of the interior nicely sums up this change. However, whatever plans Tamim bin Hamad may have had were derailed. Stemming from a combination of happenstance, the evolution of international conflicts, and regional leaders seeking to take advantage of his youth and inexperience, Qatar was besieged by hostile diplomatic pressure and even more hostile media coverage. Finally, consideration will be given to whether something is emerging that could be described as a 'Tamimi approach' which hints at Qatar's future direction of travel under its young, new emir.

An 'annus horribilis'

Between a steep escalation in attacks by the media and plummeting regional relations, Tamim bin Hamad's first year in power was something of an annus horriblis. After barely a week in office, Egypt's Muslim Brotherhood president and close Qatar ally Mohammed Morsi was removed from power in a military coup in July 2013.[8] As a result, a central plinth of Qatar's Arab spring foreign policy dissolved. Elsewhere in the region, as Al Qassemi notes, particularly where Qatar's interests coincided with co-ordination with moderate Islamist forces linked to the Muslim Brotherhood (as in Tunisia, Libya, and Syria), Qatar's interests were set back.[9]

The single biggest challenge came from Qatar's contiguous neighbours in the Gulf. Angry at Qatar's foreign policy of supporting Islamists around the region and sensing a golden opportunity to change its policies following the 33-year old Tamim bin Hamad's ascent to the throne, Saudi Arabia, the UAE, and Bahrain removed their ambassadors from Doha in March 2014.[10] Although Saudi Arabia had previously removed its ambassador from Doha between 2002 and 2008, the co-ordinated action in 2014 was new and worrying. The move caught the Qatari elite by surprise and there was widespread fear of further escalation. Suggestions that Saudi Arabia would close its airspace to Qatari planes, that an imminent Qatar Airways deal with Saudi Arabia would be cancelled, or that the border between Qatar and Saudi Arabia would be closed were all leaked to Arab newspapers.[11] The last threat in particular was particularly salient. Not only had Saudi Arabia used such a tactic before (in a dispute with the UAE in 2009)[12] but Qatar is also highly dependent on its border with Saudi Arabia, which is its only land border. Cross-border trade accounts for 23 per cent of imports by value and is particularly important for Doha's construction industry, providing 30 per cent of cement and stone, 27 per cent of iron and steel, and 92 per cent of aluminium imports.[13] While such an escalation might seem far-fetched in hindsight, the fact that the three ambassadors were withdrawn in the first place was deeply surprising too. Either way, this situation presented a challenge to the new administration, which took it seriously, putting Qatar's armed forces on alert immediately following the ambassador's withdrawal.

The triumvirate tabled a variety of demands. They demanded that Qatar abandon its policy of supporting the Muslim Brotherhood, stop naturalising other Gulf Co-operation Council (GCC) citizens, curtail Al Jazeera's 'hostile' coverage of President Ali Abdel Fatah El Sisi's new regime in Egypt, and more generally rein in its role as a regional 'renegade' and toe the GCC line.

Whatever the initial reaction within the Qatari Emiri Diwan, Qatar's reaction in public appeared calm, mature, and statesman-like. The state did not react in kind to any of the threats or accusations, but rather worked with more amenable elements of the Saudi and Emirati governments to resolve the situation. After nine months of discussions, Qatar agreed not to naturalise GCC citizens and made vague concessions regarding the importance of not interfering in other states, as well as doubtless making other concessions in private.[14] Most notably, several members of the Muslim Brotherhood, some of whom had fled Egypt in the wake of the Sisi coup and others who had been at least partly resident in Doha for some time, were asked to leave the country or otherwise not allowed to return.[15] Such individuals included Muslim Brotherhood Secretary-General Mahmoud Hussein; Amr Darrag, a former cabinet minister in the Morsi government and an important member of the Muslim Brotherhood's political wing, the Freedom and Justice Party (FJP); Wagdi Ghoneim, a controversial Islamist preacher; Essam Telima, a former office manager for the widely-known Islamist cleric Yusuf Al Qaradawi; Hamza Zawbaa, an FJP spokesman; Gamal Abdel Sattar, a prominent professor at Al Azhar University in Cairo and a leader of the National Alliance party; and Ashraf Badr Eddin, a senior Muslim Brotherhood leader who fled Egypt after the Sisi coup.[16]

Such concessions, in conjunction with contemporaneous regional fears revolving around the escalating conflict in Yemen, were sufficient to secure the return of the three GCC ambassadors to Qatar on 17 November 2014 in preparation for Qatar's hosting of the annual GCC summit the following month. The individuals left Qatar agreeably and without recrimination, often thanking Qatar for its support, though the fact remains that the actions of the UAE and Saudi Arabia forced this change.[17] However, while this represented something of a tactical victory for the triumvirate, there have been no signs since that Qatar has fundamentally altered its strategic policies. Some of the 'exiled' members returned to Qatar briefly 'to sort out paperwork', hardly indicative of a strict Qatari deportation order.[18] Al Jazeera Arabic has broadly yet to change its tone and remains cool at best to the Sisi regime (if, according to one regional commentator, there has been some de-escalation in its pointed rhetoric).[19] Qatar still hosts Egyptian exiles, as illustrated by the publication in a Qatari newspaper of a full-page interview with wanted Egyptian Salafist

Asim Abdul Majid the day before the ambassadors' return was announced. Also, Tareq Al Zumr, a leader of the political faction of terrorist group Gamaa Al Islamiyya, continues to live in Doha and contributes sporadically to Al Jazeera.[20] The diplomatic relationship between Egypt and Qatar also remains prickly: on 1 December 2014, Qatar's ambassador to Cairo refused to submit to a security inspection at Cairo's airport and take off his shoes.[21] Meanwhile, Qatar fast-tracked the application for citizenship of Rashid Mohammed Rashid, a man wanted in Egypt on charges of large-scale corruption and now working for Moza bint Nasser in Qatar.[22]

Qatar in all likelihood will repair (on the surface at least) its relations with Egypt, if only to placate Saudi Arabia, the fundamental driver of the wider reconciliation. However, it will also continue to pursue its foreign policy interests via its collection of exiles based in Doha, many of whom are Islamists of one variety or another, even if this has been complicated and will need to be done more quietly in future.[23] Not only is this kind of policy historical in nature, but Qatar will also be loath to abandon allies with whom it has developed a working relationship, to say nothing of in whom it has invested hundreds of millions of dollars. Equally, given the limited nature of Qatar's foreign ministry and other assets of its government, it would be difficult to 'switch' its alliances even if it wanted to. A fundamental change is possible, but Qatar will have to be put under concerted pressure for an extended period that would be likely to have to include extreme measures such as a border blockade. Qatar's offer to mediate between the Egyptian government and the Muslim Brotherhood in August 2015 reinforced the idea of Qatar biding its time until it can resume, presumably more quietly, its support for the Muslim Brotherhood.[24]

As for Tamim bin Hamad's other bête noire, media criticism is by no means a new phenomenon. However, it has ratcheted up since Qatar won the right to host the 2022 FIFA World Cup, which took the spotlight on the country to an entirely new level. At a glance, Figure 5 shows not only the increase in searches for the word 'Qatar,' but also a huge spike in interest in Qatar at the end of 2010 and the beginning of 2011, when the tournament was awarded to the state. Given that interest drives content to a large degree and while a crude measurement, the upward slope and spike are sure indicators of an increased media focus on Qatar.

'World Cup' criticism revolves around two topics: migrant worker rights and a concerted campaign, led mostly by British media, to uncover the corruption they are convinced won Qatar the right to host the tournament. The situation for migrant workers in the state is plainly deplorable, as several reports by

Figure 4: Google Trends Search for 'Qatar' 2004–2014

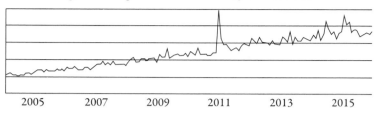

2005   2007   2009   2011   2013   2015

Source: Information from Google Trends search for 'Qatar' conducted on 10 December 2015.

Human Rights Watch and Amnesty International have made clear.[25] Whatever laws are in place are weakly enforced and employers feel they can act with impunity. The core of Qatar's problem—its *kafala* system of labour, under which employees are locked into contracts with employers via their sponsorship arrangement—is popular domestically, with nearly 90 per cent of Qataris not wanting to see the system weakened and 30 per cent wanting employers' rights strengthened.[26] Although occasional thoughtless apologia suggest that this is perpetuated because of a Qatari desire to retain some 'stability [lest] cultural values be undermined', in essence it is about finance.[27] Modern working contracts would be more expensive and give Qataris less control over their sponsees. In the face of such deep-seated local feeling, it is unsurprising that the government's actions have been slow and ineffectual.

In response to increased criticism, the government has mooted that things will change, though this is not the first time such utterances have been made. The National Human Rights Committee was established in 2002, and promises of changes or consultations have been forthcoming ever since.[28] Vaunted new laws and the imposition of fines or even prison sentences for certain offences are welcome, but will take a long time to have an effect. Nevertheless, while workers in Qatar have some rights and they may well accrue greater protections, employers' rights are likely to remain paramount.

Qatar has been beset by negative media coverage in respect of the 2022 FIFA World Cup itself. Mohammed bin Hammam, the Qatari former president of the Asian Football Federation, resigned his position in 2011 and was banned from football for life by FIFA, the sport's overarching controlling body, amid mounting corruption scandals.[29] A cache of millions of Qatar 2022 emails also contained hints that Qatari officials had used gifts and hospitality with abandon to curry favour.[30] The story was broken by the

Sunday Times newspaper in the UK, where such Qatar 2022 stories are popular and perennially negative.[31] Indeed, the British press at times appears indignant that Qatar was awarded the right to host the 2022 World Cup in the first place.

This is not to say that there is no logic to their anger. England was not awarded the right to host the 2018 World Cup despite putting together one of the strongest bids with the least risk and the joint highest potential revenues.[32] By contrast, FIFA itself adjudged Qatar to pose a potential health risk to players, given summer temperatures in Doha, and considered it 'high' risk overall.[33] Moreover, by choosing Qatar and Russia (for the 2018 World Cup), FIFA later stated that it had wanted to take the World Cup to new markets and locations. There is nothing wrong with this. However, if FIFA held such views, it was unfair to let countries such as England—namely established footballing nations—bid for a World Cup they evidently had little chance of winning. Crucially, for those in the UK or Europe, the Qatar World Cup will be a very different World Cup. Germany in 2006 and Brazil in 2014 are the archetypal examples of football-loving countries hosting huge, successful tournaments. By contrast, a Qatari World Cup, with little footballing heritage and mired in scandal does not set the pulses of football traditionalists racing.

In addition to deeply negative media coverage of workers' rights and the World Cup, as the Arab spring progressed and initial optimism was confronted by an ever more brutal civil war in Syria and reversals elsewhere, Qatar came under an increasingly withering media spotlight. In particular, the state's policies of channelling support along typically moderate Islamist lines was criticised.[34] The imprisoning of Al Jazeera journalists in Egypt on the most spurious of charges and the banning of Al Jazeera in Iraq in April 2013 and in Egypt in September 2014 were physical manifestations of a wider backlash against the network specifically and the Qatari state more generally.[35]

Late 2014 also saw a rash of articles deeply critical of Qatar's perceived support for or active facilitation of militants and terrorists, particularly in Syria.[36] An investigative piece by Glenn Greenwald put forward a compelling case suggesting that the influence of lobbying companies with ties to Israel and the UAE in Washington and New York had played a role in propelling some of the negative stories about Qatar.[37] Meanwhile, *Private Eye*, the British satirical-investigative magazine, commented on an extraordinary series of negative articles in *The Daily Telegraph* throughout the autumn and winter of 2014. Certainly, there is a genuine thirst for salacious Qatar-focused articles that newspapers would want to cover, but *The Daily Telegraph's* dogged coverage has been curious. Ben

Rumsby's dozens of articles on World Cup issues, Robert Mendick's focus ('Terror financiers are living freely in Qatar, US discloses', 'Qatar must lose World Cup over terror links', 'Qatar's moneymen behind the kidnappers'), Andrew Gilligan's transparent distrust of Qatar ('Britain has sold its soul with the Qatari deal', 'Ministers' family ties to terror', 'The Club Med for Terrorists', 'UK extremists linked to Qatar World Cup bid') alongside other articles with titles such as 'How Qatar funds extremists across the Middle East' and 'Whose side is Qatar really on in the war against Islamic State?', all in the space of a few months, suggest that something else may be at play. *Private Eye* comments that the proprietors of *The Daily Telegraph*, the Barclay brothers, have been locked in a battle with members of the Qatari elite over acquisitions of London hotels.[38] Although no causative link between the elite-level issues and subsequent *Telegraph* coverage can be made, the link is suggestive. Whether contrived or more organic, these issues for Qatar are negative externalities of the state's desire for international prominence.

No such thing as bad publicity?

While negative publicity surrounding Qatar has clearly increased, there is less of a consensus as to whether this actually matters or not. Rhetoric aside, there have as yet been no serious consequences for the state. Nevertheless, media hysteria surrounding Qatar has created a climate of mistrust of the state that is affecting, at the very least, domestic politics in key allies.

For example, there is a curiously vivid dislike of Qatar in France's popular press that is also evidenced by a veritable cottage industry of non-academic books lambasting the state. 'Le Qatar-bashing' has fostered an atmosphere in which articles with little authority or evidence portray Qatar as, for example, directly supporting Al Qaida in Mali.[39] This was one of many stories that contributed to hysteria in 2013 when Qatar sought to invest €50 million in Paris's dilapidated, Muslim-dominated suburbs in a venture that was part-investment, part an act of corporate social reasonability.[40] Utterly bemused by the popular reaction in France, which charged Qatar with seeking to spread some form of Islamist ideology, the investment was put on hold and reassessed. There should be concerns for Qatar's elite that, in Paris or London, such a reaction might affect a more traditional investment opportunity or otherwise undercut diplomatic relations.

Elsewhere, a growing number of relatively senior government ministers and officials have openly criticised Qatar. Germany's minister of development in

August 2014 claimed that Qatar was a key sponsor and supporter of Islamic State (IS),[41] while, during Prime Minister's Questions in the British parliament, Member of Parliament (MP) Steve Barclay asked Prime Minister David Cameron whether he agreed that Qatar was 'a permissive jurisdiction for terrorist financing.'[42] Another MP, Steve Rotherham, asked a British Foreign and Commonwealth Office (FCO) minister whether Qatar was failing to pay the bills of British companies working on the 2022 World Cup project because it was sending money to IS.[43] Similarly, *Military Times* in the US suggested that some US lawmakers were discussing the 'feasibility of moving the [US military] base' from Qatar, while Qatar has openly been accused of supporting terrorism in some Congressional hearings.[44] One NATO member state has also seriously considered officially designating Qatar as a state sponsor of terrorism. In short, the 'near misses' for Qatar are increasing.

Certainly, it is true that these issues are mostly the ramblings of ill-informed parliamentarians, and that those in power in the UK, Germany, and the US understand Qatar's usefulness in the region and the truth that, overall, 'cock-up rather than conspiracy' is likely to underlie the state's inept counter-terror legislation. However, Qatar would be foolish to ignore these warning signs. These states are, after all, democracies and domestic pressure can, theoretically at least, play a role in the state's wider foreign policies. Moreover, airstrikes against Islamic State targets in northern Iraq in late 2014 in which most air assets were mobilised from a temporary base in the UAE hint that, as crucial as the Al Udeid base in Qatar is, it is not the only option for the US and other international allies.[45]

An internal focus

In his first few years as emir, Tamim bin Hamad has given a number of content-heavy (as opposed to merely rhetorical) speeches, usually on the opening of parliament (the *Majlis Al-Shura*). In terms of external relations, Tamim bin Hamad has declared that Qatar's foreign policy will remain steadfastly independent and that he will follow a thread apparent since Jassim bin Mohammed Al Thani's day, namely Qatar acting as a 'Kaaba of the dispossessed.'[46] This is an interesting aside from Tamim bin Hamad, for it is the first time in modern Qatari history that the tactic of hosting a variety of exiles has been suggested to be something approaching an active policy of state.

But arguably the most prominent focus of his speeches has been Qatari domestic issues, and in particular fiscal and economic matters. Indeed, one theme emerges quite clearly from the speeches given by Tamim bin Hamad on assuming power and at the opening of the Majlis Al Shura in 2013, 2014, and 2015. Time and again Tamim bin Hamad has highlighted the necessity of financial prudence at both the state and the individual level, and sometimes in remarkably taboo-breaking language that suggests that the sentiments are more than mere stump-speech rhetoric.[47]

In November 2015, in the wake of the oil price crash that challenged the Qatari economy, Tamim bin Hamad suggested that this period of economic tightening could be an opportunity to correct 'negative phenomena' that had come about thanks to Qatar's meteoric economic rise.[48] He encouraged Qataris to 'band together in the face of challenges', to neither panic nor succumb to 'self-delusion', expecting somehow the fiscal situation to improve by itself.[49] Most notably, he warned Qatari citizens that there would be changes from their previous 'dependency on the state to provide for everything'—an attitude that 'reduces the motivation of individuals to take initiatives and be progressive.'[50]

In a Qatari context, this is relatively revolutionary rhetoric. It is particularly challenging because one of the key assumptions of the Qatari political compact is the cliché of 'no taxation for no representation.' Yet it looks here like Tamim bin Hamad is practically warning Qataris about changes to one half of this agreement. Interestingly, figures suggest that in the 2014–2015 financial year wages and salaries in the public sector (where the vast majority of Qataris work: only 12,000 Qataris work in the entire private sector)[51] fell for the first time in a decade.[52] The fall was not huge—only 2.7 per cent—but given that wages are one of the central ways that states in the Gulf region redistribute wealth, it is a telling development, particularly after 60 per cent and 120 per cent pay rises in 2011. Moreover, the GCC states announced in December 2015 after years of consultation that there were meaningful plans to introduce a region-wide VAT tax.[53] While such plans had been discussed for a decade or more, the alarming nature of the oil price crash and the lack of expectations that it will rebound quickly gives this policy a reasonable chance of coming into effect.

Indeed, it is these kinds of external pressures that have forced Tamim bin Hamad's hand. From 2012, the Qatari government, in common with a number of international institutions, expected oil prices to fall, which they subsequently did.[54] But no one expected the drop to be quite as precipitous as it was. For Qatar, the value of its exports fell by 41.7 per cent between July 2014 and July 2015.[55] Given that more than 90 per cent of Qatar's government revenues comes from 'activities tied to the energy sector',[56] the US-based financial services corporation Citi forecast Qatari government revenues to decline by up to one third in 2015.[57] Tamim bin Hamad's conservative fiscal approach reflects both the reality of lower revenues and the expectation that they may take some time to rebound.

Thus far, most energy market-focused commentators, institutions, and analysts suggest that in the absence of a black swan event such as another war in the Gulf region that would prompt a spike in oil prices, they will only recover slowly.[58] Given that the gas price follows the oil price (albeit in a delayed fashion), the fiscal horizon for Qatar looks challenging, if not daunting. Indeed, the resilience of the lower oil price stems from an unfortunate conflation of demand and supply-driven problems, none of which looks set to alter particularly quickly.[59]

Changes on the supply side will affect Qatar more than most oil producing nations. The days of Qatar's dominance of the LNG industry are dwindling. Australia currently supplies approximately 33 million cubic metres (mcm) of LNG and has invested over $200 million in order to add another 60 mcm of capacity by 2018.[60] It is expected to overtake Qatar's number one position as an LNG supplier by the end of the decade. Elsewhere, the US has, thanks to the shale gas revolution that it led, become the world's largest natural gas producer.[61] Though it remains to be seen how the high cost-base US shale gas producers fare with low oil prices, billions of dollars being invested in LNG exporting infrastructure and deals are being signed.[62] But the competition does not stop there. Tanzania, Mozambique, Israel, Egypt, not to mention established gas giants Russia and Iran, with the promise of dwindling sanctions, all have plans at various stages of development to enter (or grow their presence in) the LNG market.[63] Not all of these gas developments will come to fruition, but it looks a certainty that overall there will be a significant amount of new LNG supply entering the market in the coming decade.

This might not be a problem but for serious questions as to the level of energy demand in the coming years. China's startling economic growth of over 10 per cent a year for much of the 2000s was the central driver of world energy demand. But no more. Expected Chinese economic growth of 5–7 per cent is still impressive, but with the current and near-term forecasted state of the world economy, it is difficult to see how the overall drop in Chinese demand could be made up elsewhere.

Facing such a bearish fiscal future, Tamim bin Hamad's exhortations to thriftiness make sense. Nevertheless, the concept of demanding more from citizens while the state gives less could be seen as Tamim bin Hamad grasping the 'third rail' of politics in the Gulf states. Though this may be rhetorically true—one might expect citizens to react negatively to a unilateral reorganisation of the ruling bargain to their fiscal detriment—Tamim bin Hamad has been clever about how he has approached the whole situation. Not only did he concentrate on fiscal issues in his speech, but he also emphasised the importance of urging Qatar's youth to contribute more to society.[64] This is a savvy angle and plays well in a society with wider fears as to the veritable corruption—'negative phenomena' in Tamim bin Hamad's words—of Qatari youth thanks to the great wealth that the state has accrued. In such a context, by leading policies that seek to repair or gird Qatari society against both fiscal and moral threats, Tamim bin Hamad strikes a deeply resonant chord.

Moreover, several other Tamimi policies can be seen as directly focused on similar concerns. As previously noted, Tamim bin Hamad led the change in the language of instruction at Qatar University for some subjects from English to Arabic in February 2012. This reinforced his role defending indigenous Qatari culture against foreign ideas, concepts, and languages. In a similar fashion, Tamim bin Hamad's policy that introduced a short stint (three to four months, depending on the level of education) of military service for Qatari men aged between eighteen and thirty-five was also a populist policy. This policy spoke directly to fears as to the loss of identity and discipline in Qatar's youth.

Otherwise, Tamim bin Hamad focused on the Qatari military far more than his father. The fact that Qatar is unusually secretive about its defence spending means that it is hard to accurately assess relative growth in this area,[65] but sharp increases in spending under Tamim bin Hamad have been self-evident. Before coming to power, Tamim bin Hamad was a (or in all likelihood 'the') central decision-maker in respect of matters concerning the armed forces,[66] overseeing the purchase of German Leopard 2A7 tanks and German artillery for an estimated $2.47 billion.[67] He has also overseen the procurement of AH-64 Apache Attack Helicopters, additional Patriot Missile defence systems, air surveillance radar systems, fast boats, refuelling air tankers, NH90 military helicopters, and AWACS air-craft, while also establishing a new military staff college that will eventually become a fully-fledged defence academy.[68] All told, expenditure on these initiatives has been estimated at $23 billion, comfortably outstripping any Qatari procurement in recent decades.[69]

This defence spending and the desire to establish a military staff college to improve the professionalism of and training opportunities for the Qatari military—in essence, to make the military better—fit a wider pattern that has been evident in Qatar under Tamim bin Hamad, and a greater focus on the armed forces is not necessarily surprising. The state's armed forces to a large extent, and unusually so in the Gulf, have been marginalised and ignored in recent Qatari history. While the UAE has purchased more than 100 high-end US fast-jets and Saudi Arabia has continued to plough tens of billions of dollars into military complexes in the UK, the US, and France in particular, Qatar's business in such markets has been conspicuous by its absence. The state's fast-jet capability, often seen as the pinnacle of a military's capability, hails from the late 1990s and, despite being upgraded over time, the platform is of an older generation. Qatar has more recently bought heavy-lift aircraft from the US, but most of its land forces equipment is antiquated. The navy is also curiously underpowered considering the importance of Qatar's shoreline for its LNG and oil industries.

While Hamad bin Khalifah prioritised education and foreign relations, Tamim bin Hamad is reverting to more of a norm, focusing on the military to a greater degree. Indeed, this is arguably the best interpretation of the 120 per cent pay increase for the Qatari armed forces. This was not done because of Arab spring-inspired fears of a mutinous military, but rather to give the forces more prestige after years of effective marginalisation.

A Tamimi approach?

Tamim bin Hamad's overtly internal focus during his first eighteen months in power was unsurprising. Although there was nothing approaching a challenger for the succession, a new leader first and foremost resorting to shoring up his domestic popularity is not unusual, and Tamim bin Hamad did this in spades. The wage increase was a simple but effective tool towards this end, as was the promotion of Arabic at Qatar University and the introduction of military service, both of which hit a 'sweet-spot' of growing concern among Qataris over the perceived erosion of their cultural identity. Evidently Tamim is a leader with his finger on the Qatari pulse.

Expanding the state's military capabilities is also rarely likely to be unpopular, particularly in a volatile region such as the Gulf. Moreover, Qatar's experience in Libya of providing the NATO coalition (alongside the UAE in Operation Unified Protector) with political cover was enlightening for the state. In reality, the Qatari fast-jets that were used in the Libya operations were of limited value in and of themselves; or at least did not provide any military capabilities that the coalition did not already possess. Nevertheless, the concept of Qatar being a force multiplier, even with its small military, was introduced to the lexicon of Qatari leaders. This type of role, namely one in which Qatar provides crucial aid to a Western-led coalition on a matter of grave international importance, is exactly the type of niche role that Qatar has long sought to cultivate. Ramping up the state's military professionalism and training (with its new staff college taught by King's College London in Doha, based on the UK Defence Academy model), as well as giving the military the up-to-date equipment that it requires, is a necessary prerequisite for Qatar to play this type of role again in future.

Qatar subsequently built on its niche role in Unified Protector. From autumn 2014, Qatar joined the airstrike campaign against IS in Iraq. Though its role was mostly logistical, Qatar's fast jets flew some active sorties too.[70] Also in the Saudi Arabian and UAE-led military operations—Decisive Storm—against the Houthis in Yemen, Qatar has played an active—albeit relatively small—role. Qatari planes were used in concert with their GCC allies attacking Houthi targets, and reports indicate that Qatar even deployed 1000 troops to Yemen.[71] In reality, the Qatari deployment was likely far smaller (the suggested numbers would equate to the Qataris deploying around 10 per cent of their entire Armed Forces), but any troops on the ground is an assertive step for Qatar.

There are signs, therefore, that Qatar's leadership wants to move from a merely rhetorical or a niche role to a meaningful, active one. Qatar's heavy lift capacity (thanks to its C-17 and C-130J cargo planes) gives it genuine capability that even the UK and Germany have failed to show in recent years.[72] Similarly, the purchase of two A330 multi-role tanker transport air-to-air refuelling aircraft directly points to the state's continuing desire to engage in expeditionary, out-of-region operations. Simply put, Qatar does not need such tanker aircraft to defend its sovereignty alone. Not only is the state relatively small, but its current generation of fast-jets has ample range, not to mention the ability to support additional fuel tanks, doubly negating the necessity of air-to-air refuelling unless Qatar has far wider aspirations. Nevertheless, although this burgeoning capability points to an aspiration to, at the very least, have the capacity to either join larger coalitions further afield or project power unilaterally, Tamim bin Hamad's approach to foreign policy is more conservative than this might suggest.

Under Tamim bin Hamad's leadership, Qatar has become largely reactive in foreign affairs, without the expansive desire that was evident previously. Qatar's joining in with the military coalitions against IS and the Houthis needs to be contextualised. These missions were not undertaken necessarily because Qatar was exhibiting an overtly expeditionary streak under Tamim bin Hamad's leadership. Instead, an important factor underpinning why Qatar involved itself in these actions is because it had little choice in the matter. On both occasions there was strong political pressure for Qatar to join in. Against IS, Qatar needed to counter the narrative that it was funding the likes of IS. And against the Houthis there is a real sense that Qatar was forced to prove that it was aligned sufficiently with its GCC allies by attacking the group with which it used to have amicable relations.

Elsewhere in terms of its foreign policy, Qatar is simply maintaining its alliances. This applies to its relationships with main Palestinian Islamist movement Hamas and key rebel groups in Syria. The state certainly exploits its tenuous contacts in Syria or with the Afghan Taliban when the opportunity arises to secure the release of hostages. However, unlike Hamad bin Khalifah's initial forays in the Arab spring, which qualitatively and quantitatively changed Qatari foreign policy, there has been little sign yet that Tamim bin Hamad is seeking a new front, a new set of actors, or a new set of problems for Qatar to tackle.

This is perhaps unsurprising. The ease with which Qatar operated during the early days of the Arab spring has dissipated. In place of a relative unity of purpose among revolutionaries in Libya or a small-scale uprising in Syria, chaos now reigns in both locations, if to differing degrees. Moreover, there is little evidence that Tamim bin Hamad is fundamentally actively interested in foreign policy. Even before he came to the throne, he was powerful in Qatar. Although Hamad bin Jassim was a domineering foreign minister, there can be little doubt that Tamim bin Hamad could and would have taken hold of a foreign policy issued had he felt inclined to do so.

However, there are scarcely any examples of Tamim bin Hamad being overly concerned with foreign policy. There is scant evidence for him starting any peace initiatives, dealing with ongoing Qatari mediation efforts, founding philanthropic international organisations, or leading foreign portfolios. Aside from occasionally leading Qatari delegations, something that fell squarely within his remit as crown prince, or being involved in the burgeoning Syria campaign, the one example of Tamim bin Hamad taking an important foreign role has been resetting the relationship between Saudi Arabia and Qatar alongside former Saudi Crown Prince Nayef bin Abdul-Aziz Al Saud in 2008.[73] However, this was notable precisely because it was such an atypical role for Tamim bin Hamad.

Without evidence of any great proclivity to engage with foreign policy during his initial period in power, it is tempting to conclude that Qatar under

Tamim bin Hamad will follow a particular pattern, namely reaffirming and strengthening existing alliances where possible and reacting when presented with opportunities, or otherwise demurely maintaining wider relations and focusing on domestic politics.

Certainly, there are other reasons for Qatar's relatively quiescent approach to foreign policy in the early period of Tamim bin Hamad's rule. Not only has Qatar come under extraordinary media scrutiny, but regional neighbours have also put significant pressure on the state to stop 'meddling' abroad. This, and an understandable internal focus during his first months in power, may exacerbate any such appearance of Qatar having a 'calm' foreign policy. Similarly, a more fiscally conservative climate in Qatar could also be expected to contribute to a curtailing of foreign policy initiatives. In other words, the reactive, opportunistic sense that has been emerging in Qatari foreign policy will be reinforced as opposed to the grand, expensive initiatives of the Hamad bin Khalifah era.

Domestically, if the budget becomes increasingly strained, the exigency of the World Cup 2022 spending will mean that savings will need to be found elsewhere. Education City, the amalgam of Western universities, consists of an expensive set of institutions. Just as in the UK or the US, these top-level universities are relatively elitist; a student typically needs to have gone to a Qatari private international school to have a good chance of being admitted to, for example, Georgetown University or Texas A&M University in Doha, despite their significant outreach initiatives. This, combined with perceived vast differences in spending on these foreign universities compared with that on Qatar University (which found an unfortunate comparison between the state-of-the-art campuses in Education City and its decrepit 1980s campus) makes the Western universities unpopular. Others dislike the mixed-sex environments and the fundamental notion of Western universities being based in Qatar at all. These campuses are feeling the fiscal pinch already as the Qatar Foundation, their overarching body, seeks to cut their budgets.

In short, Education City is a relatively unpopular, expensive addition to the Doha skyline. Furthermore, despite having the personal support of its chairwoman, Moza bint Nasser, a number of whose children sit on the board, she will not be there forever. Although there is little prospect that the concept as a whole will be abandoned, the departure of some universities who disagree with cost savings imposed on them is likely. This Tamim bin Hamad-led policy is, once again, relatively popular and is seen as the emir being in touch with ordinary Qataris, clamping down on financial extravagance led by expensive foreign institutions.

This type of issue goes to the heart of the kind of state that Tamim bin Hamad wants to oversee. For example, Education City is crucial to Qatar National Vision 2030 and efforts to diversify the economy by creating an internationally-focused knowledge economy. Such efforts are difficult to promote because they require meaningful buy-in from the population, the adherence to foreign curricula, and the promotion of the English language. A change of mentality and working practices are also part and parcel of such a change, and have unsurprisingly been resisted. The question is whether Tamim bin Hamad will stick with the often unpopular decisions that lie at the core of the QF project that are arguably necessary to derive wider economic benefit. Put another way, will he persist with Education City and continue to push for Qataris to enter the private sector and leave comfortable public-sector jobs? Or will he break from some of his positive, early rhetoric and continue the traditional Gulf model of everlasting subsidies, growing inefficiencies, and overbearing cradle-to-grave state support?

Early on, Tamim bin Hamad took a paternal, munificent approach, with wage increases and the token policy of national service for younger Qataris pandering to wider public opinion. But his rhetoric has increased in recent years suggesting that he might actually take meaningful action. The mooted introduction of VAT across the GCC would be a significant step forwards. But the broad history of modern Gulf politics is against him. The dominant tenor of regional politics has long been one of indulgence in the form of subsidies and cloyingly populist policies from the governments of energy-rich states. That said, Tamim bin Hamad has two of the most revolutionary parents in modern Gulf history; if any leader in the region was to implement the necessary reforms, Tamim is as good a candidate as any.

11

SECURING THE GLOBAL AMBITIONS
OF A CITY STATE

The Qatari state changed more under Emir Hamad bin Khalifah Al Thani (r. 1995–2013) than it had under any previous leader. Even though his predecessors had founded and developed the state, and oversaw its transition to independence, none of these events changed much in reality. The day after the British anointed Mohammed Al Thani as leader in 1868, the proto-state of Qatar remained a conglomeration of underdeveloped villages loosely agreeing to his rule, but still largely at the mercy of regional avarice. Decades after his death and the rule of his son, Jassim bin Mohammed Al Thani (r. 1878–1913), who is credited with playing a decisive role in the state's formation, Qatar was but a slightly more developed collection of undeveloped villages loosely agreeing to his rule, but still largely at the mercy of regional avarice. Even independence did not change much, and certainly not for Ahmed bin Ali Al Thani (r. 1960–1972), Qatar's first independent emir, who did not even return to Doha for his installation ceremony, choosing instead to remain in Geneva.

Hamad bin Khalifah enacted profound changes to fundamentally alter the international perception of Qatar as well as the day-to-day life of Qatari citizens. The overarching aim of his new policies was to secure the soaring ambitions he held for the Qatari city-state to answer perennial security-related questions, as well as newly arising domestic, regional, and international challenges.

An appreciation of Qatar's history highlights that, while there are recurring traits in the key policies of the Hamad bin Khalifah era, most policies were quantitatively and qualitatively different from their predecessors. In explaining the genesis of these new and different answers to often familiar problems, context is crucial.

The first section of this conclusion highlights the persistent strategic concerns that typically stem directly from the regional environment—while a country can change many things, its location is not one of them. Hamad bin Khalifah's approach to these issues differed from that of his father, the previous emir, in that he sought to balance Qatar's interests against Saudi Arabia's overbearing influence. This approach is relatively consistent with the historical tenor of Qatar's regional relations, even if Hamad bin Khalifah, as so often, took things to the extreme by also assiduously courting closer relations with, for example, Iran. The newer concerns of Hamad bin Khalifah's age are then noted. The dogged pursuit of monetising Qatar's huge gas field opened up a variety of options for Qatar's leaders as the state's balance sheet improved with liquefied natural gas (LNG) sales. Equally, the rising importance of the shared gas field with Iran created a new vulnerability for Qatar and called for close relations with the Islamic republic. Otherwise, the basic proclivities of Hamad bin Khalifah, who sought to foster a largely benevolent, progressive autocracy in Qatar, saw him court public opinion and reinforce Qatar's national identity through a variety of externally-facing policies. His basic preference for supporting pan-regional movements also saw him throw Qatar's weight behind broadly Islamist actors when presented with the opportunity that the Arab spring uprisings provided.

The second section brings together core reasons as to how and why Qatar engaged in such new, ahistorical policies, by focusing on how the power of personality is constrained by the international context in which it operates. The final section draws together conclusions from the Hamad and Tamim eras to assess the strength and resilience of the fundamental pillars of the Qatari state.

Old and new concerns

A Saudi threat

Qatar's history has long been punctuated by challenges emanating from modern-day Saudi Arabia. Over the centuries, this has taken the form of marauding Wahhabi-inspired raids; the manipulation of Qatari tribes against the leadership in Doha; the payment of a tribute to the founder of modern Saudi Arabia, 'Ibn Saud', to stay his hand; geologists working for Saudi Arabian state-owned oil company Aramco scouting for oil wells in the Qatari Peninsula; border skirmishes; and the sporadic withdrawal of Saudi ambassadors to increase diplomatic pressure on Qatar.

Highlighting the importance of the leader's personal inclinations, the personal affinity of Khalifah bin Hamad Al Thani with Saudi Arabia's rulers saw a discernible improvement in bilateral relations against the backdrop of a mutually-agreed security-focused understanding. This was something of an ahistorical policy, given that Qatar's default position had been far from acquiescent and typically involved attempts to reduce the state's dependence on Saudi Arabia (as Chapter 1 discusses extensively), something for which there is negligible evidence of Khalifah bin Hamad attempting to do. Under his leadership, not only did Qatar devoutly follow Saudi Arabia throughout the 1970s and 1980s, but the relationship also reinforced Riyadh's intrinsic belief in its role as the dominant 'father figure' in the Arabian Peninsula and a consequently small role for Qatar.

Against this backdrop, as well as a regional culture of deferring to elders and deep conservatism reflected in glacially slow political change, the emergence of the new Qatari elite was jarring. Slowly taking power from the mid 1980s, the young elite wanted to change tack significantly, something that found no favour in Riyadh. Going beyond the regional détente of the time, Qatar sought to normalise relations with Iran and entered negotiations with Israel. Although these relations to a large degree were undertaken with the aim of engaging the US, they fitted snugly with Qatar's subsequent orientation and indicated a growing independence from Riyadh. Indeed, the symbolism of these two new sets of relations is important. For a country that had been largely unknown and that mostly subsumed any vestiges of its own independent international personality under Saudi Arabia's auspices, such policies handmaidened the emergence of an independent Qatari character.

In the face of rapidly deteriorating relations and increasing border tensions with Saudi Arabia, as Hamad bin Khalifah himself noted, Qatar had no choice but to seek new protective arrangements. Just as his predecessors had throughout the eighteenth and nineteenth centuries, when faced with escalating tensions that could not be controlled, external security agreements were sought. In this case, it was not with the Sultan of Muscat, the Al Khalifah in Bahrain, the Ottomans, or the British, but rather with the new global superpower, the US. Although deteriorating relations with Saudi Arabia were not the only reason Qatar sought an improved, security-focused relationship with Washington, they were of paramount immediate importance. The deterrence that Qatar derived from the US bases in Qatar was important, but in lieu of explicit contractual protective defensive promises from the US, subsequent defence-focused agreements with the UK and France were a sensible ploy. By mirroring the tenor of historic relations in seeking to relieve Qatar's dependence on any one guarantor and seeking as much autonomy as possible from regional powers such as Saudi Arabia, Hamad bin Khalifah's policies represented a reversion to the Qatari norm.

Although US agreements and bases were in place (and expanding), Saudi Arabia continued to loom large over Qatar and bilateral relations deteriorated with border conflicts in the early 1990s, stifling Saudi policies (such as blocking Qatari regional gas expansion plans), and the 1995 coup and subsequent counter coups that Riyadh allegedly supported. Qatar's desire to further differentiate itself on the international stage can in part be seen as a reaction to Saudi Arabia's regional overbearance and belligerence. Establishing and propagating a progressive and popular brand using sport; the meetings, incentives, conferences and exhibitions (MICE) industry and high-profile cultural initiatives increased rapidly as Qatar's finances allowed. Had Hamad bin Khalifah followed Saudi Arabia's line, he would never have entrusted control of the Qatar Foundation, the multi-billion-dollar engine of social and educational change in Qatar, to his wife; enfranchised women; or conducted a television interview with his wife by his side. That these policies were so antithetical to anything that Saudi Arabia could have produced is a part of the reason they were pursued.

Al Jazeera was another key part of this drive. Not only did the network publicise Qatar effectively, but it was also a potential mechanism for the state to alert the wider region if Saudi belligerence continued. Outflanked on key fronts (financially, politically, and militarily), creating Al Jazeera was a savvy, asymmetric policy to exponentially increase one arm of Qatar's defences. Whether this was purely in terms of deterrence or for more active defence by stirring up controversy about Saudi Arabia (or any other state), establishing the network was a shrewd move that gave Qatar an outsized ability to hit back. Later on, during the Arab spring, the network provided yet another means for Qatar to exert an influence vastly greater than could be assumed of a small, Gulf state with an indigenous population of less than 300,000.

Finally, a direct consequence of Saudi Arabia blocking any putative intra-Gulf Co-operation Council (GCC) gas pipeline network was that Qatar was forced to pursue extra-GCC gas schemes, namely LNG. Although the move reflected the new elite's ideas about securing wider relationships and would have been undertaken in any event, that it was undertaken so early was a direct corollary of Saudi Arabian obstructionism.

Regional dynamics

No discussion of Qatar and its regional influences can pass without a strong emphasis on Iraq's invasion of Kuwait in 1990. Comparisons between Qatar and Kuwait in terms of size, orientation, power, location, intrinsic vulnerability, and wealth have been repeatedly made in this book for good reason. The invasion of Kuwait shocked the region and amounted to confirmation that 'black swan' events can and do happen. Following the destruction wreaked by Iraqi forces in Kuwait, it was obligatory for Qatar to secure wider security-focused agreements.

Regional competition from similar city states such as Manama, Dubai, and Abu Dhabi has also been a discernible driver of Qatari policy. Aside from perennial elite competition and the desire among royals who have known each other for decades to 'out-do' each other, having an edge or particular niche is key in an era when all states are vying to diversify their economies and attract talent and investment. In this context, it is possible to see various Qatari policies forming, spreading, and embedding a brand for the state. This brand is primarily designed to boost Qatar's visibility as an attractive state for international business against the backdrop of the Gulf states' relative homogeneity. Although differences may be obvious to a Qatari or Emirati, they may not necessarily be so to Europe-based decision-makers, who may struggle to tell Doha apart from Abu Dhabi. Whatever Qatar can do to differentiate itself positively from its regional rivals, through creating and spreading a unique brand, is an understandable and necessary ploy.

Remembering that, for Nye, soft power emanates from espoused values, such as the promotion of Al Jazeera and modern education, Qatari mediation efforts have also contributed to the state's brand by creating a positive image of Qatar as a state pursuing dialogue and peace. However, such efforts can also be seen as a tactical policy to calm tensions in areas of critical interest to Qatar. For example, although Qatari mediation efforts in Yemen were ultimately unsuccessful, the fact that the state extensively sought to intervene and calm the situation can be seen straightforwardly as a self-interested attempt to boost Qatar's immediate security arena. Equally, considering widespread perceptions of Iran's influence in Yemen, a Qatari desire to prevent the state from imploding and allowing Iran-backed forces to exploit the ensuing instability would also be logical. Similar considerations can be seen to be at play in respect of Qatar's mediation in the Darfur conflict in western Sudan. Aside from notions of Qatar seeking to build relations with a view to future agribusiness opportunities in the 'breadbasket of Africa,' the intervention can be seen as part of plans to retain influence with the Sudanese government as Iran sought to boost ties in the region.

The North Field

Although the North Field made Qatar the richest country on earth per capita, its vulnerability to Iran inevitably increased as its dependence on the field grew. This dynamic mandated a new approach, and it is no coincidence that Qatar improved its relations with Iran at the same time as it was corralling interest and investment in the North Field project. Qatar could not just hope that Iran would chose not to interfere, and it could certainly not persist with the sporadically aggressive anti-Iran policies that its GCC neighbours had pursued in the 1980s. Numerous bilateral visits, a deal to pipe water, and subsequent examples of Qatar's atypical desire as a Sunni GCC state to occasionally protect Iranian interests and boost relations with the Islamic republic, are primarily consequences of Qatar's development of the North Field.

Although Qatar wanted to improve relations with Iran, it did not do so naively. Aware of Kuwait's experience of attempting to placate an irascible larger neighbour on its border (Iraq) with neither a meaningful indigenous military capability nor the ability to rely on the moribund GCC Peninsula Shield, Qatar was forced to seek external security-focused agreements. Not only were these crucial in boosting international confidence in financing the LNG projects, but Qatar needed a hard security element (e.g. the US base near Doha) if it was not to remain vulnerable to Iran. Claiming (as Iraq had done with Kuwait) that Qatar was 'stealing its resources' would have been a plausible charge for Iran to make, given the contiguous border and comparatively quick rate at which Qatar would extract the gas with Western technology compared with Iran's older, less efficient equipment.

Once the field's basic security was secured, accruing a diverse array of international alliances and trading partners not only made sense commercially, but it was also the epitome of the post-Cold War neoliberal ethos, tying Qatar into world trade. A certain security comes with such interconnectedness in direct ways—by integrating Qatar into the energy mix of so many important states, the state explicitly tied its customers into its own security dynamics.

A post-hydrocarbon future

Frequently and unambiguously referred to by Qatar's elite, enshrined in Qatar Vision 2030, explicitly found in the deep changes wrought across the education system, embodied in Education City, and an implicit thread running throughout many of Qatar's newer policies, striving to create a knowledge-based economy and commerce-based post-hydrocarbon future is a central goal of the Qatari state.

Although economic diversification has nominally been a concern of the Qatari elite for several decades, and various downstream industrial plants have been constructed towards this end, the progress made by Hamad bin Khalifah's predecessors was meagre. This was partly because his predecessors had nothing like the financial surplus to enact expensive policies aimed at securing the state's post-hydrocarbon future. Equally, the specific influence of Hamad bin Khalifah and his close allies was crucial. The central driving force behind pursuing this goal came from an elite a generation younger than most of its peers across the Middle East when it came to power. Within this elite was the powerful guiding force of Moza bint Nasser Al Misnad, who had the latitude and trust of the emir, the financial backing of LNG, and a relatively acquiescent domestic social milieu—initially at least—to push through her radical educational vision.

The project to underpin Qatar's future economy is a constant cycle of self-reinforcing industries and strategies. These can be best understood as disparate policies coming together to create and propagate a central business-savvy, progressive, and attractive brand for Qatar. Developing the MICE industry directly seeks to bolster economic diversification to initiate a self-sustaining new sector of the economy, while also leading the international push to boost Qatar's international image. A significant focus on sport and cultural events forms part of the same package, with the aim of boosting Qatar's attractiveness to foreign visitors and businesses alike. Meanwhile, Education City is intended to feed top graduates into Qatar's nascent industries or into research at the QF Science and Technology Park (QSTP), which is itself explicitly designed to attract foreign research and design. Qatar's investments often have an element of human resource-building about them. Investments in top-flight companies can come with an agreement to open a regional headquarters in Doha or an office in the Qatar Financial Centre (QFC). This contributes to creating a critical mass in finance in the state, which it is hoped will eventually act as a self-sustaining part of Qatar's economic diversification and further boost the state's brand as a regional hub for commerce.

All politics is domestic

Various new policies in Qatar can be readily interpreted as playing to a domestic audience, such as the promotion of sport and culture, and the founding of world-class education institutions in Doha. At times, Qatar has also been popular abroad, as demonstrated in Beirut in 2008 and, more recently, in Benghazi in 2011, when people waved Qatari flags to thank the state for its support. Such examples play well in Doha, with Qataris pleased that their country for the first time is developing a good reputation in certain quarters of the wider Middle East and North Africa region. Despite some grumbling over the money spent on these foreign adventures or 'Western' influence, particularly in the educational sphere, nothing approaching a widespread movement critical of Hamad bin Khalifah emerged.

Increasing media attacks, the nigh-on vilification of Qatar, particularly in Egypt following the overthrow of Muslim Brotherhood president Mohammed Morsi, and the unusual pressure put on Qatar by its Gulf allies to alter its foreign policies were an externality of Qatar's adventurism. Judging by spats between Qataris and Emiratis on social media, such pressure has only increased the 'rally around the flag' mentality in the state. Indeed, Qataris closed ranks, and while many may not agree with the state's overt support for the Muslim Brotherhood, any disagreement with the policy was overridden by the affront caused by Qatar being attacked and pressured. Counterintuitively, then, these kinds of externalities are not as domestically damaging as might be assumed.

In terms of Qatar's foreign policies resonating positively at home, there have also been more subtle effects to note, particularly in terms of country branding. Qatar struggles to positively differentiate itself from its regional neighbours because of two key factors. Firstly, it lacks the typical building-blocks of statehood (for example, a 'romantic' struggle for independence or unique characteristics of the state), and is very similar to other regional states in respect of factors such as language, culture, traditions and societal formation. Secondly, these issues are compounded by the homogenising globalised forces of international finance and commerce, the increased ease and frequency of travel, and an exponential increase in communication technologies. Moreover, Qatar's efforts to harness these globalising forces and forge an explicitly international reputation for its finance, aviation, education, research, sport, and culture sectors, have exacerbated these issues. In other words, the very act of competing in the aforementioned sectors may be a savvy economic policy, but the process has had its drawbacks.

A huge influx of foreigners, a direct corollary of Qatar's pursuit of its central place in these global industries, is the clearest example of the effect that this 'chase' has had on Qatar. Qataris are a minority in their own homeland, while English is the language of business. These factors, and others like them, challenge Qatar's identity. As Cerny notes, the desire to compete internationally and all that that entails undermines the creation of a particular and unique *Gemeinschaft*, further hampering efforts to create and maintain a unique national identity. Some of the answers to these issues are answered, at least in part, by Qatar's country brand, which seeks to resonate both internally and externally. This is not to say that Qataris did not know who they were or how they differed from Emiratis, for example, before country branding efforts were undertaken. Rather, in this era of rapid change, the mechanics of the 'invention of tradition' have come to the fore, as Hobsbawm notes.

> We should expect it [the invention of tradition] to occur more frequently when a rapid transformation of society weakens or destroys the social patterns for which 'old' traditions had been designed, producing new ones to which they were not applicable, or when such traditions and their institutional carriers and promulgators no longer prove sufficiently adaptable and flexible, or are otherwise eliminated.[1]

It is normal for national identity to evolve in the face of such pressures. The understanding of what it means to be Qatari is being consistently fleshed out, and the differences extenuated with the adoption of newer policies. Branding is a central tool that the Qatari state has used to create, tweak, and embed an evolving national identity. For example, Qatar's National Day was switched from a low-key celebration on 3 September to a no-expense-spared jamboree on 18 December. While the former date marked independence from the British in 1971 and was celebrated annually until 2007, 18 December celebrates the uniting of tribes behind Jassim bin Mohammed Al Thani, the leader on whom Qatar's elite has alighted as the state's seminal historical figure, a move Hobsbawm would readily recognise.

One of Tamim bin Hamad's first policies could be seen as playing directly into these kinds of narratives and concerns. The period of mandatory military service for Qatari men focused in particular on imbuing young men with a sense of national unity and camaraderie amid fears that Qataris were losing the essence of what it meant to be Qatari.

The Arab Spring

Never before has Qatar sought to unseat regional leaders or so overtly support one side in a given conflict or post-conflict situation. However, although the state's tactics have changed, its strategic aims have not. Before the Arab spring, Qatari foreign policy was fundamentally aimed at making the state as vital to as wide an array of important actors as possible. This was precisely the aim of Qatar's policies during the Arab spring.

Despite sporadic instances of positive relations with former Libyan ruler Colonel Muammar Al Gaddafi, such as facilitating the release of Bulgarian nurses accused of spreading AIDS in Libya in 2007 or that of Abdelbaset Al Megrahi, the man imprisoned as a result of his role in the bombing of Pan Am Flight 103 over the Scottish town of Lockerbie in 2009, relations with Libya were fundamentally brittle. Indeed, when a leader as unstable and undiplomatic as Gaddafi was in power, the foundation for a serious, long-term relationship was not present. In Egypt, animosity towards Qatar ran deeper. Partly this stemmed from then President Hosni Mubarak's dislike of Al Jazeera, but more importantly Mubarak resented Qatar's attempts to intervene in Darfur, an area that Egypt firmly considered to be its 'back yard.' While there was something of a rapprochement just before the start of the Arab spring, it is hard to imagine a Mubarak-led Egypt ever being a solid, dependable ally for Qatar.

Egypt is of central importance in the Arab world and the Arab spring presented an opportunity for Qatar to remake its relationship with Cairo. Primarily using its contacts with and support for the Muslim Brotherhood, the state immediately put itself first in line to financially and rhetorically aid the new Mohammed Morsi-led government in Cairo. In the same way that it had sought to actively engage and make itself important to the US (bases), the UK (gas trade and investment), France (investment and trade), Germany (investment), China (energy trade), Japan (energy trade), and South Korea (energy trade), Qatar sought to do the same in Egypt.

The principle of reciprocity is an important component in establishing these relationships. In a low-probability, high-impact eventuality (for example, natural disaster, industrial accident or war), Qatar will feel that it can call on its allies to offer support. This was clearly expressed by Hamad bin Jassim Al Thani when speaking to a visiting US dignitary. After being thanked for Qatar's $100 million donation in the aftermath of Hurricane Katrina in the US, Hamad bin Jassim replied that 'we may have our own Katrina someday.'[2] Whether this potential future support is rhetorical, material, military, political, or diplomatic, for a small state in a perilous region, Qatar can never have enough potential avenues of support. Taking the example of Iranian aggression, Qatar's array of international allies potentially provide it with additional anti-mining capability (from Western allies), economic pressure (from key consumers of Iran's oil and gas, Japan and China), supporting votes in forums such as the UN Security Council or the Arab League, or, at one time at least, the rhetorical solidarity of the Muslim Brotherhood across the region.

Specifically in terms of its 'new' relationship with Egypt, Qatar positioned itself to reap economic benefits in the new Egypt. Aside from being rewarded with tax breaks, Qatar hoped that its weekly interaction with Egypt's elite would provide it with an advantage in respect of any prime investment opportunities, and allow it to drive a hard bargain. Politically and diplomatically, aside from counting on Morsi's support in regional forums, Qatar hoped for Egyptian support for its policies in Darfur and the Gaza Strip.

Although Qatar planned to strengthen its geopolitical position with active support during the Arab spring, it would be remiss to omit the personal element influencing Qatar's policies during the regional uprisings. More than most Arab countries, Qatar is run in a personalised manner and the emir's decision is final and uncontested, and the evidence of Hamad bin Khalifah's two decades in power highlights his role as the archetypal benevolent dictator. Benevolent in that part of the rationale for undertaking various policies can be described as enlightened (for example, educational improvement along Western lines, the ending of press censorship, the promotion of significant state-run charities, the desire to offer mediation services), and dictatorial in that the Qatari parliament had no meaningful powers.

This is not to say that Qatar's record is perfect. From the Qatari poet imprisoned in 2012 for little more than writing and spreading offensive poems about Hamad bin Khalifah and his family, to noble initiatives that were started (notably the Doha Centre for Media Freedom) but subsequently failed to live up to their promise, to the murky issue of Qatar's support of different Islamist groups in the region, there are causes for concern. It would be foolish to suggest that Qatar operated an altruistic policy during the Arab spring (or in other such instances), because numerous other political motivations were at play. However, it would equally be wrong to ignore the progressive tenor of many, if not most of Qatar's policies, which appear to have been strongly informed by the personal politics of those in power.

Qatar's policy towards Syria since the start of the Arab spring offers more evidence of the importance of personal politics in the state. Given Syria's importance as an ally to Iran, Qatari efforts to oust President Bashar Al Assad are likely to have played poorly in Tehran, with Iran's leaders viewing such moves as evidence of Qatar subscribing to the Sunni GCC mentality of attempting to undermine Iran's security whenever possible. Just as Qatar refrained from acting in Bahrain for fear of antagonising Saudi Arabia, so too it would have been natural to have expected the state to do the same in Syria to maintain good relations with Iran.

Empirically speaking, the threat that Iran poses to Qatar has not changed—Tehran still has the Islamic Revolutionary Guard Corps and the ability to severely impinge on Qatar should it choose to do so. For its part, Qatar's deterrence in terms of US and other Western allies are significant, while the state's own domestic defences, notably its National Security Shield are—while new and untested—potentially effective. Nevertheless, given Iran's asymmetric threat, Qatar's complete lack of strategic depth and the fact that the state's economic future is invested in a small number of locations (notably its gas-processing city, Ras Laffan), Iran remains a threat. As such, Qatar's intervention in Syria was surprising. The key factor in its decision must have been either that Hamad bin Khalifah did not believe that Iran posed a credible threat to Qatar, or that he had sufficient confidence in his long-term relationship with Tehran to undercut Iran's key ally without serious repercussions. Equally, he may have felt that the political and humanitarian concerns that the Syrian conflict had thrown up were so acute, or that Assad's shunning of his personal advice had been unforgivable, that taking action justified the risk. Whatever the specific reason, the personal element appears to have been unusually important in Qatar's policy towards Syria.

Cometh the hour, cometh the man?

In terms of understanding Qatar's overall orientation since the late 1980s, the fact that Hamad bin Khalifah had more than two decades in office to stamp his personality on the state is an important but not decisive factor. Length alone cannot explain the pervasive nature of his influence, and Hamad bin Khalifah's twenty-three years in power in fact mirrored the average length of rule in Qatar. Three previous rulers had led the country for longer, but failed to 'convert' length of service into more significant change.

The new, innovative, and ahistorical policies that the new Qatari elite undertook reflected a broader array of factors, though two particular issues resurfaced time and again as playing central roles. These were the enduring importance of the ruling elite and how key contextual factors directly shaped, supported or obstructed their proclivities.

Cometh the hour: the determining nature of context

While all leaders are constrained in the pursuit of their policies by a range of factors, Qatar is more constrained than most. In particular, the young, underdeveloped nature of the state's bureaucracies severely impinges on their effectiveness. This means that the types of services that, for example, a more established foreign ministry might offer—such as breadth of analysis of actors, contacts, and expertise in advising and checking the power of the executive—is not present in Qatar. As a result, policy execution becomes particularly ad hoc.

As dynamic and innovative as Hamad bin Khalifah and his coterie of advisers were, they could never have had as much of an impact without a heady confluence of domestic, regional, and international factors that were unique to Qatar, as well as the precise moment in history that facilitated the elite and allowed Qatar to engage. Factors shaping the art of the possible in respect of Qatar's policies ranged from prosaic financial concerns to macro-regional changes, shifts in international relationships, and the emergence of new technologies, discourses, and opportunities.

Aside from the sheer fortune of possessing such a large gas field, Qatar needed the LNG market to be receptive to its overtures for finance in the late 1980s and early 1990s. The state also benefitted from a blank international slate that gave it unusual freedom of action: Qatar in the 1990s and 2000s was often seen as a largely honest broker without predetermined interests or a history of belligerence. When the state was undoing its reputation as a 'neutral' arbiter during the Arab spring, its actions were facilitated by its historic policy of hosting exiles, many of whom became key conduits for information and for channelling support.

Aside from these Qatar-centric opportunities, timing is also crucial in explaining Qatar's shifting priorities. The ending of the Iran-Iraq war, the swift US-led reaction to the invasion of Kuwait in 1990, and the subsequent stationing of US troops in the Gulf allowed investment in Qatar to be contemplated and insurance premiums to be lowered. For Qatar, the invasion of Kuwait recast its own predicament, and galvanised existing desires to reorient its foreign relations. The end of the Cold War, meanwhile, unshackled small states from the polarising doctrine of superpower alignment or non-alignment.

Moreover, the end of the Cold War sparked latent conflicts around the world and created a target-rich environment for now more unencumbered small states that were inclined to act as mediators. The euphoria that characterised the immediate post-Cold War period, the presumed triumph of capitalism, and the surge in popularity of neoliberal institutionalism, particularly in terms of collective security and notions of reciprocity, greased the wheels for Qatar's emergence on to the international stage. Notions deeply associated with this era—collective defence, the prominence of international trade, a desire to broaden diplomatic contacts and dialogue—run through Qatar's subsequent international relations, and remain a consistent feature of the ruling elite's policies. Specifically delineating the lines of causation and correlation—whether the elite was already so minded or whether it was persuaded to adopt some of these key notions—is difficult to say, but the similarities between Qatar's shifting approaches and the new era's features are undeniable.

Cometh the man: an unusually influential elite

A state's policies often stem from a push by the elite that is then filtered through factors that determine the art of the possible. In Qatar's case, however, the elite's preferences are of central importance. The elite in Doha is unusually unhindered in decision-making, particularly in respect of external matters. Although informal pressures exist in Qatar (amorphous public pressure on domestic issues such as education is relatively significant and effective in altering policy) and the freedom of action of Qatar's leaders should not be over-emphasised, there is a demonstrable lack of lobbying groups and other formal (or informal) constituencies to impinge on the elite's prerogative to rule. A combination of societal conservatism, improving socioeconomic conditions, trust in the leadership, and an ability to affect domestic policy when enough Qataris are sufficiently roused, means that the elite retains relative freedom of action. Practically speaking, Qatar's leadership seldom outlines its broader vision or discusses what it does, meaning that there is little for any group in Doha to firmly grasp on to to lobby against. For example, there has been no opportunity for any group to consider or react to a government white paper outlining its strategic and tactical goals in the Arab spring.

Although the importance of elite politics in the Gulf is far from new, it introduces an element of uncertainty into this dynamic. While all Qatari leaders have reacted to many of the same sets of issues, they have done so with different intrinsic proclivities and preferences. Few would disagree that the elite that took over from the late 1980s onwards was quite unique. Qatar is not the only small, rich country in the Gulf, and various other leaders could theoretically have engaged in the same types of policies as Hamad bin Khalifah. Yet nowhere is there as systematic and as progressive a set of policies as in Qatar. These policies did not originate organically from the Qatari milieu, but rather closely reflect the interests of the elite.

As noted above, the personal element was of particular importance in Qatar during the Arab spring. The politics of Hamad bin Khalifah's familial milieu and key allies with whom he grew up uncannily resemble the overarching tenor of his policies. More generally, the intrinsic orientation of the emir and his key advisers (either inward or outward-looking), their innate approach to contemporary concerns such as modernisation (whether it should be resisted or embraced), and their conception of their country's future (as a local, regional and/or international power) was always going to play a role.

Securing Qatar's global ambitions

Age-old problems stemming primarily from Qatar's immediate surrounding region continue to vex the state's leaders as they did centuries ago. The answer of former leaders—seeking external 'guarantors' and developing ways to diversify Qatar's dependence on them—is still broadly pursued today. However, infinitely greater domestic financial capacity and an unusually progressive leadership since 1995 have produced atypical and innovative solutions to Qatar's concerns, and combined with a profoundly new international system characterised by different limits and norms. Qatar's prodigious financial power is impressive, as is its ever-growing diplomatic influence. However, money can only buy so much influence, while the state's frenetic diplomatic activity in recent decades has yet to be institutionalised.

The personalised nature of politics in Qatar is both a blessing and a curse. Quick to make decisions and establish relations with the world's political and financial elite, shrewd negotiation can secure strategic relationships and gilt-edged opportunities for Qatar. However, it can equally mean that Qatar's relations are unusually tied specifically to certain leaders or certain groups. For example, Qatar struggled to restart relations with President Francois Hollande of France after having had unusually close relations with his predecessor, Nicolas Sarkozy.[3]

Another issue is the detrimental degree to which decisions are made only at the very highest levels of the Qatari elite. This means that Qatar's policy is worryingly dependent on two or three individuals, giving the state little strategic depth or institutional back-up capability. The personalised nature of politics marginalises the structures in place to inform and support decision-making. This cycle is exacerbated by Qatar's youth as a country, which means it has only had a meaningful bureaucracy for a generation, while its educational system has been mediocre at best. Every ministry and company suffers from a chronic shortage of talented, hard-working Qataris. This is the result of having such a small population, a lack of motivation stemming from the pay disparities between sectors that plague all the Gulf states, and the knock-on effects of the generous cradle-to-grave Qatari welfare state.

But these issues have been Tamim bin Hamad's initial focus, with a real, zealous attempt to slim down and professionalise ministries to make the Qatari state more efficient. In a curious irony, this was also one of Hamad bin Khalifah's first focuses in the late 1980s. He succeeded in making some ministries work as he wanted them to, but only by duplicating them and having them run as personal fiefdoms.

Consider Qatar's decision to actively support the ousting of Gaddafi, which represented an entirely new policy direction. While the Libyan revolution initially proceeded relatively swiftly and painlessly, this was far from certain at the beginning. Also, from Qatar's own perspective, intervening in Libya was a risky move. Gaddafi was one of the world's most unpredictable leaders, with a history of directly supporting terrorism, seeking weapons of mass destruction, and he had huge funds at his disposal. It is little wonder that Qataris in Spain during the early months of the Libyan uprising insisted to all who asked that they were Omani, for fear of some form of Gaddafi-sponsored reprisal.

A wide range of ambassadors and diplomats in Doha concur that there is no evidence that the Qatari authorities undertook a systematic, rigorous, and meticulous risk assessment of their policy. Moreover, had a ministry undertaken such a study, it is difficult to imagine that it would have presented findings critical of the emir's decision to intervene. Doubtless the pros and cons of aiding anti-Gaddafi forces were discussed at length in the emir's majlis and with key government contacts, but such a process is far from systematic. This kind of an ad hoc approach is one thing when Qatar is operating in the Gulf or otherwise on matters of lesser importance, but quite another in respect of ousting violent dictators such as Gaddafi.

Given the lack of evidence of a rigorous risk assessment when undertaking such potentially dangerous policies, it is prudent to ask whether Qatar's history of relying on external powers for its security has removed an element of caution from the elite's calculations. Now more than ever, with the greatest military power in history encamped in Qatar, the elite must guard against a complacency that could—again—overly embolden policy without careful consideration of the potential consequences of its actions, out of a belief that its US relations will perennially tacitly defend the Qatari state.

Similarly, it is easy for Qatar's elite to support a range of actors, including Islamists, when the state is resolutely secure. The strongest socio-economic bargain on earth shared by a tiny population, a strong conservative culture, and societal pressure combine to provide the elite with no discernible internal opposition. Under such conditions, it is easy to state that, for example, previously marginalised Islamists should be given a voice and integrated into political systems when Qatar itself will not be directly affected by such advice. By mistake, therefore, Qatar has been—albeit to different degrees—complicating the security arena for other Arab states. The regional isolation and pressure that Qatar suffered at the hands of its GCC allies from 2014 onwards amounted to these states reminding Qatar just how much its policies were affecting their own security considerations. Tamim bin Hamad, who dealt with these repercussions left over by his father's policies, will certainly want to maintain his independence, but has shown no signs thus far of a personal desire to advocate anything like as strongly Qatar's pointed pro-Brotherhood (or moderate Islamist more generally) stance.

Nevertheless, such pivotal decisions as those that Qatar made during the Arab spring are unlikely to resurface. Not only was the Arab spring a deeply unusual phenomenon, but neither the Qatari elite nor anyone else expects Qatar to continue to lead the Middle East's reaction to events. Already, key regional players such as Saudi Arabia and Egypt are attempting to reassert themselves and dominate the political landscape, which they can easily do by virtue of their natural disposition, importance, and influence.

Qatar needs to concentrate on sustainable areas of policy in which it has a comparative advantage. The various fonts of its soft power—ranging from Al Jazeera, to cultural and sporting policies, to education initiatives and MICE industry promotion—are as forward-thinking, economically-focused, and as sophisticated an answer (or at least a potential answer) as any regional state has found to the diverse and pressing problems of modernity. The goals that these tactics aim for are enshrined in Qatar's wider 2030 National Vision.

Qatar can never hope to compete on traditional metrics of power because it lacks the capacity. However, if it can continue to develop its foundations of higher education in particular, it could position itself as the 'US of the Gulf,' a veritable hoover for and font of regional educational excellence, training future elites for decades to come. Such a notion is not so far-fetched, and the plans and projects that Qatar currently has in place have few peers throughout the Middle East.

However, such policies need to be actively nurtured, carefully thought through, and supported. It is far from clear presently whether Tamim bin Hamad truly buys into the QF and Education City ideology. The budget cuts that he has overseen across the economy have fallen particularly hard on

Education City. His strict pruning of their budgets could be a public opinion-driven corrective to the perceived years of overspending by the universities, exacerbated by wider budgetary pressures. But if Education City is to prosper and to play its central part in fostering a Qatari knowledge economy, Tamim bin Hamad will have to invest some political capital in it at some stage and defend it as a concept from criticism, and support this forward-looking venture.

External criticism is problematic given how much time and effort the Qatari state has spent in establishing and propagating a brand that was designed to be attractive not only to business elites, but also to a wider pool of potential human capital to staff its economy. Crucially, Qatar is not engaging in this fight for resources alone, but is in deep regional competition. If job offers or investment opportunities appear in Doha or Dubai, and there is little to choose between the two, it can only be surmised that Qatar, as a state with a burgeoning media reputation as some kind of 'terrorist financier-state', will lose out. This is more than a cosmetic problem and a response needs to be marshalled effectively to counter such criticisms.[4]

It is a similar story with Al Jazeera. Qatar's role in promoting freedom of expression and freedom of the press, as personified by Al Jazeera, was—while imperfect—an immensely powerful tool that widely and effectively built a positive reputation for the state. However, while Al Jazeera has always had its detractors, its actions in the Arab spring have meant that it is no longer just governments complaining about the television network but also a growing number of ordinary people. Increasingly seen as a 'stooge' of the Qatari government's support for the Muslim Brotherhood and amid increasing competition, Al Jazeera's reputation is suffering, as are its viewing figures.

This is a part of a wider problem for Qatar, in that the state needs to better express its policies and goals. Qatar is not a slavish, ideological supporter of the Muslim Brotherhood, and it needs to actively divest itself of this label by overtly seeking greater balance in respect of those that it supports. Although Qatar has built up support among Muslim Brotherhood elites and those often linked to them, not only is this relationship actively problematic for the state, but this is an intrinsically fickle group: beyond finance and shaky notions of reciprocity, there is no reason why 'the Brotherhood' should continue to support Qatar. The relationship is not based on deep cultural, political, or religious links, but rather a temporary alignment of politics, financial convenience, and some shared history of support.

This is not to say that Qatar either could or should divest itself of these links. However, the state needs to revert to the central feature of its foreign policy that has been evident since the late eighteenth century, namely balance. From the Utub paying a tribute to the Persians to protect them from the Sultan of Muscat in 1799, to Ahmed bin Ali Al Thani refusing to acquiesce to flyovers by the UK's Royal Air Force in the 1960s lest it give the impression of Qatar being overly dependent on the British, to supporting Israel and Hamas at the same time as supporting the US and Iran, Qatar has always sought balance.

In the 2000s, Al Jazeera was in its pomp, large-scale Qatari mediation forays were underway, relations with Israel were ongoing, ties with Iran showed fitful promise, and Qatar was speaking with all actors while favouring none. The state was viewed as an enemy to no one, and as a small state with a dynamic, progressive, and inclusive vision of its place in the region. It was because of these types of relationships that Qatar was truly diversifying its dependencies. Qatar's continued integration into the energy nexus of an increasing array of international states, its increasing financial penetration across the world's key capitals, and its brand gaining increasing traction in business communities and populations alike, were all positive signs of progress. Only by following this inoffensive path can Qatar assuage its core concerns.

Moreover, only by following such a trajectory can Qatar ever hope to escape the gilded cage of its quasi-protective relationships. If the state's history proves anything, it is that such relationships always end: the US will leave at some stage. If Qatar is to avoid continually transitioning from one quasi-guarantor to another, it cannot be a divisive state. Rather, facilitated by its popular brand, it must be able to rely on an ever thickening web of international relations, trade agreements, and financial deals uniquely provided by Qatar that make many of the most important international states dependent on its continued prosperity.

NOTES

INTRODUCTION

1. Anthony Shadid, 'Qatar Wields an Outsized Influence in Arab Politics', *The New York Times*, 14 November 2011; Steven Goff, 'Qatar Gets 2022 World Cup over U.S.; Russia Beats out England for 2018 Event', *The Washington Post*, 8 March 2013, 3 December 2010; Hugh Eakin, 'The Strange Power of Qatar', *New York Review of Books*, 28 October 2011; Maike Currie, 'The Case for Qatar', *Investors Chronicle*, 11 April 2011; Cameron Barr, 'Qatar Stands by US as War Looms', *The Christian Science Monitor*, 10 December 2002; David Conn, 'How Qatar Became a Football Force', *The Guardian*, 18 November 2013; Diana Untermeyer, 'Racing Horses Towards Modernity in Qatar', *Huffington Post*, 15 February 2012; Alex Duff, 'Fifa's Blatter Says Summer Qatar World Cup a "Mistake"', Bloomberg, 16 May 2014; Tatum Collins and Paul Solman, 'What Can the Middle East Learn from What's Happening in Qatar?', *PBS Newshour*, 28 June 2013; Blake Hounshell, 'The Qatar Bubble', *Foreign Policy*, 23 April 2012; Abigail Hauslohner, 'Qatar Loses Clout Amid Fading Arab Spring', *The Washington Post*, 13 November 2013; Helia Ebrahimi, 'Qatar's UK Ambitions Could Mean Billions More in Investment', *The Daily Telegraph*, 14 March 2013.

2. Anthony Shadid, 'Qatar's Capital Glitters Like a World City, but Few Feel at Home', *The New York Times*, 29 November 2011; Larry Luxner, 'Qatar's Prosperity as High as Its Geopolitical Ambitions', *The Washington Diplomat*, 2 October 2012; Jeffrey Fleishman and Noha El Hennawy, 'Qatar's Ambitions Roil Middle East', *Los Angeles Times*, 21 April 2009; Jenny Southan, 'Doha's Ambition', *Business Traveller*, 20 August 2010; Matthew Teller, 'Has Wealth Made Qatar Happy?', BBC, 28 April 2014.

3. For a better-than-average look at Qatar's role in the Arab Spring see: Kristian Coates Ulrichsen, 'Qatar and the Arab Spring: Policy Drivers and Regional Implications', *Carnegie Endowment for International Peace*, September 2014; Kristian Coates Ulrichsen, *Qatar and the Arab Spring*, London: Hurst & Co., 2014; Mehdi Hasan,

'Voice of the Arab Spring', *New Statesman*, 7 December 2011; Aryn Baker, 'Bahrain's Voiceless: How Al-Jazeera's Coverage of the Arab Spring Is Uneven', *Time*, 24 May 2011. For the best encapsulation of Qatar's problems as the Arab spring developed see: Elizabeth Dickinson, 'The Case against Qatar', *Foreign Policy*, 30 September 2013; Aryn Baker, 'Qatar Haunted by Its Decision to Back the Arab Spring's Islamists', *Time*, 26 September 2013; David D Kirkpatrick, 'Qatar's Support of Islamists Alienates Allies Near and Far', *The New York Times*, 7 September 2014; David D Kirkpatrick, 'Muslim Brotherhood Says Qatar Ousted Its Members', *The New York Times*, 13 September 2014.

4. Yadullah Ijtehadi, 'Qatar's Global Rise', *Gulf Business*, 21 November 2011; Brandon Friedman, 'Qatar: Security Amid Instability', *The Jewish Policy Centre: inFocus* V, 4 (Winter 2011); Kessler Oren, 'Qatar Punches Above Its Diplomatic Weight', *The Jerusalem Post*, 3 August 2012; Elizabeth Dickinson, 'Qatar Punches Above Its Weight', *The National*, 26 September 2012; David Rosenberg, 'Qatar Punches Above Its Weight', *The Jerusalem Post*, 18 January 2012; Michael Young, 'Pragmatic Diplomacy Enables Qatar to Punch Above Weight', *The National*, 24 November 2011; Dominic Moran, 'New Qatari PM, Diplomatic "Maverick"', *International Relations and Security Network (ISN)*, 6 April 2007; David B Roberts, 'Punching above Its Weight', *Foreign Policy*, 12 April 2011; Robert Siegel, 'How Tiny Qatar "Punches above Its Weight"', *NPR*, 23 December 2013.

5. 'Pygmy with the Punch of a Giant', *The Economist*, 5 November 2011; 'Too Rich for Its Own Good', *The Economist*, 7 June 2014; 'Qatar: A Bouncy Bantam', *The Economist*, 7 September 2006; 'Flying-Carpet Diplomacy', *The Economist*, 18 February 2012.

6. Robert F Worth, 'Qatar, Playing All Sides, Is a Non Stop Mediator', *The New York Times*, 9 July 2008. Hugh Eakin, 'The Strange Power of Qatar', October 2011.

7. 'Key Population Indicators (2011)', *Central Department of Statistics and Information*, last accessed 26 August 2012; 'Population, Total (1981–2011)', in *Data*, World Bank, last accessed 26 August 2012; The figure for Qatar's native population used here (275,000) stems from commonly accepted extrapolations of the emirate's population in lieu of available statistics from the Qatari Statistics Authority (the organisation has the statistics but considers this particular statistic a secret).

8. I.e. Iran's 'volunteer' paramilitary forces.

9. Figures taken from *The Military Balance 2014* (International Institute for Strategic Studies), Glasgow: Routledge, 2014 (Chapter 7); Anthony H Cordesman and Khalid Al Rodhan, *The Gulf Military Forces in an Era of Asymmetric War, Volume 1*, Westport, CT: Praeger Security International, 2007, p. 148. Anthony Toth, 'Qatar', in *Persian Gulf States: Country Studies*, ed. Helen Chapin Metz, Washington DC: U.S. Government Printing Office, 1994, p. 151.

10. Operation Cast Lead is the Israeli name for the three week military operation also

known as the Gaza War at the end of 2008. The Israelis launched the offensive, they declared, to stop random rocket fire emanating from the Gaza Strip into Israel. The results of this short, sharp offensive were felt disproportionately harshly by civilians. Estimates vary as to the eventual direct death toll. The UN Office for the Coordination of Humanitarian Affairs found that 1383 Palestinians including 333 children died during the offensive, 'a significant proportion' of whom were civilians. Added to the ongoing outrage in the Arab world as to Israel's existing blockade of Gaza, this conflict stoked tensions to such a degree that Qatar was forced to close the Israeli trade office in Doha. See also 'Locked In: The Humanitarian Impact of Two Years of Blockade on the Gaza Strip', in *Special Focus* (United Nations Office for the Coordination of Humanitarian Affairs Occupied Palestinian Territory, August 2009), p. 3.

11. Gerd Nonneman, 'The Three Environments of Middle East Foreign Policy Making and Relations with Europe', in *Analyzing Middle East Foreign Policies*, Abingdon, UK: Routledge, 2005, p. 19.

12. 'World Economic Outlook Database', *World Economic and Financial Surveys*, International Monetary Fund, April 2015.

13. Particularly as Qatar became an oil exporter from 1949, the demands and black-mailing tactics of the wider Al Thani family became a source of almost paralysing difficulty for Qatar's leaders. See Mehran Kamrava, 'Royal Factionalism and Political Liberalization in Qatar', *Middle East Journal* 62, 3 (Summer 2009), pp. 411–14; Richard Harlakenden Sanger, *The Arabian Peninsula*, Oxford University Press, 1954, p. 124; Penelope Tuson, ed., *Report of Visit to Qatar: Persian Gulf Residency, Bahrain to Foreign Office, London—18th August 1949*, Records of Qatar: Primary Documents 1820–1960: Volume 6: 1935–1949 (Slough: Archive Editions, 1991), p. 644.

14. Jill Crystal, *Oil and Politics in the Gulf: Rulers and Merchants in Kuwait and Qatar*, Cambridge: Cambridge University Press, 1995, pp. 156–7, 163.

15. See Jennifer Lambert, 'Political Reform in Qatar: Participation, Legitimacy, and Security', *Journal Essay; Middle East Policy Council*.

16. Mehran Kamrava, in 'Royal Factionalism and Political Liberalization in Qatar', writes interestingly about modern political factionalism in Qatar. However, while such factionalism is certainly present, it still does not compare to the levels of open subversion seen historically.

17. Although Hamad bin Khalifah's exposure to the crisis sparked by Iraq's invasion of Kuwait in 1990 was to catalyse his policy preferences and provide him with a spur to action, the broad thrust of his policy outlook was evident prior to this change.

18. Michael Willis and Nizar Messari, 'Analyzing Moroccan Foreign Policy and Relations with Europe', in *Analyzing Middle East Foreign Policies*, Abingdon, UK: Routledge, 2005, p. 47.

19. Gerd Nonneman, ed., *Analyzing Middle East Foreign Policies: A Conceptual Framework*, Abingdon, UK: Routledge, 2005, p. 12.

20. J Stephen Hoadley, 'Small States as Aid Donors', *International Organization* 34, 1 (1980), p. 124.

21. Miriam Fendius Elman, 'The Foreign Policies of Small States: Challenging Neorealism in Its Own Backyard', *British Journal of Political Science* 25, 2 (1995) and Andrew F Cooper and Bessma Momani, 'Qatar and Expanded Contours of Small State Diplomacy', in ISA Conference, New Orleans, February 2010.

22. Peter Van Ham, 'The Rise of the Brand State: The Postmodern Politics of Image and Reputation', *Foreign Affairs*, September–October 2001.

23. Terence Shrimp, Saeed Saimee, and Thomas Madden, 'Countries and Their Products: A Cognitive Structure Perspective', *Journal of the Academy of Marketing Science* 21, 4 (1993).

24. A general growing appreciation of the need to recognise such topics is evident from the increase in academic attention to the topic in papers and articles, including a special journal edition of *Brand Management* focusing specifically on such concerns in April 2002. One of the articles in the issue conducts an inventory and taxonomy of the research into this concept to ascertain the 'state of the art'; quite clearly there is significant research being undertaken on this issue Nicolas Papadopoulos and Louise Heslop, 'Country Equity and Country Branding: Problems and Prospects', *Brand Management* 9, 4–5 (2002) and Nadia Kaneva, 'Nation Branding: Towards an Agenda for Critical Research', *International Journal of Communication* 5 (2011), p. 117.

25. Van Ham, 'The Rise of the Brand State: The Postmodern Politics of Image and Reputation'.

26. Wally Olins, 'Branding the Nation—the Historical Context', *Journal of Brand Management* 9, 4–5 (2002), p. 242, quoted in Peter Van Ham, 'Place Branding: The State of the Art', *The Annals of the American Academy of Political and Social Science* 616, 1 (2008), p. 9.

27. Ibid.

28. Phillip Kotler and David Gertner, 'Country as Brand, Product, and Beyond: A Place Marketing and Brand Management Perspective', *Brand Management* 9, 4–5, April 2002, p. 249.

29. Van Ham, 'Place Branding: The State of the Art', p. 3.

30. Kotler and Gertner, 'Country as Brand, Product, and Beyond: A Place Marketing and Brand Management Perspective', p. 251.

31. Phillip Kotler, Donald Haider, and Irving Rein, *Marketing Places: Attracting Investment, Industry, and Tourism to Cities, States, and Nations*, Free Press, 1993, p. 232, quoted in Kotler and Gertner, 'Country as Brand, Product, and Beyond: A Place Marketing and Brand Management Perspective', p. 257.

32. Olins, 'Branding the Nation—the Historical Context', p. 246.

33. Fiona Gilmore, 'A Country-Can It Be Repositioned? Spain—The Success Story of Country Branding', *Brand Management* 9, 4–5 (2002), p. 282.

34. Shannon Mattern, 'Font of a Nation: Creating a National Graphic Identity for Qatar', *Public Culture* 20, 3 (2008), p. 480.

35. Joseph S. Nye, *The Future of Power*, Philadelphia, PA: Public Affairs, 2011, p. 81.

36. Ibid., p. 84.

37. Joseph S. Nye, *Soft Power: The Means to Success in World Politics*, New York: Public Affairs, 2004, p. 33; Carol Atkinson, 'Does Soft Power Matter? A Comparative Analysis of Student Exchange Programs 1980–2006', *Foreign Policy Analysis* 6, 1 (2010).

38. Mahfoud Amara, '2006 Qatar Asian Games: A "Modernization" Project from Above?', in Fan Hong (ed.) *Sport, Nationalism and Orientalism*, Abingdon: Routledge, 2007, p. 507.

39. Eakin, 'The Strange Power of Qatar'; Lawrence Rubin, 'A Typology of Soft Powers in Middle East Politics', Working Paper, Dubai: The Dubai Initiative, December 2010; Bill Law, 'Jazz, the Sound of Soft Power in the Desert', BBC News, 20 January 2013; George Abraham, 'Qatar Is a Diplomatic Heavy-Hitter', Al Jazeera, 21 July 2008.

1. QATAR IN HISTORICAL CONTEXT

1. The better books include: Mehran Kamrava, *Qatar: Small State, Big Politics*, Ithaca: Cornell University Press, 2013; Ulrichsen, *Qatar and the Arab Spring*; Matthew Gray, *Qatar: Politics and the Challenges of Development*, Lynne Rienner Publishers, 2013; Christian Chesnot and Georges Malbrunot, *Qatar: Les Secrets Du Coffre-Fort*, Neuilly-sur-Seine: Michel Lafon, 2013.

2. Zamil Muhammad Al-Rashid, *Saudi Relations with Eastern Arabia and Oman, 1800–1870*, London; Luzac, 1981, p. 34.

3. The Ottomans were active on the Arabian Peninsula in the sixteenth and seventeenth centuries. Although there is evidence of plans to send representatives to extend their control to the Qatari Peninsula, what historical evidence there is suggests that this never transpired. Kursun Zekeriya, *The Ottomans in Qatar: A History of Anglo-Ottoman Conflicts in the Persian Gulf*, Studies on Ottoman Diplomatic History, Istanbul: Isis Press, 2002, p. 34.

4. Habibur Rahman, *The Emergence of Qatar*, London: Keegan Paul Ltd, 2005, pp.103–107; Frederick F. Anscombe, *The Ottoman Gulf: The Creation of Kuwait, Saudi Arabia, and Qatar*, New York: Columbia University Press, 1997, p. 49; and Kursun, *The Ottomans in Qatar*, pp. 142–143.

5. Kursun, *The Ottomans in Qatar*, p. 143.

6. Anscombe, *The Ottoman Gulf*, p. 56.

7. Rosemarie Said Zahlan, *The Creation of Qatar*, London, New York: Croom Helm 1979, p. 60.

8. Charles W. Hamilton, *Americans and Oil in the Middle East*, Houston, Tex.: Gulf Pub. Co., 1962, p. 100.

9. Alexander Melamid, 'Political Geography of Trucial 'Oman and Qatar', *Geographical Review* 43, 2 (1953), p. 202.

10. Michael Field, *The Merchants: The Big Business Families of Saudi Arabia and the Gulf States*, Woodstock, NY: The Overlook Press, 1985, p. 210.

11. Zahlan, *The Creation of Qatar*, p. 96; Field, *The Merchants: The Big Business Families of Saudi Arabia and the Gulf States*, p. 210

12. Penelope Tuson, ed., 'Report on Qatar: Political Agency, Doha to Political Resident, Bahrain—28 December 1958', Records of Qatar: Primary Documents 1820–1960: Volume 7: 1949–1960 (Slough: Archive Editions, 1991), p. 519.

13. Bernard A Burrows, 'Annual Report 1955', Foreign Office Annual Reports from Arabia 1930–1960', Chippenham: Archive Editions, 1993, p. 171.

14. 'Annual Report 1956', Foreign Office Annual Reports from Arabia 1930–1960, Chippenham: Archive Editions, 1993, p. 257.

15. Michael Field, 'Tree of the Al Attiyah', *Arabian Charts* (v.1)

16. Ibid.

17. Frank Stoakes, 'Social and Political Change in the Third World', in Derek Hopwood, *ed., The Arabian Peninsula: Society and Politics*, London: Allen and Unwin, 1972, p. 197.

18. Anita L.P. Burdett, ed. 'British Resident E.F. Henderson, Doha, to Jl Beaven Arabian Department, FCO London', 'Qatar Internal' 21 February 1972, vol. IV: 1970–1971, Records of Qatar 1966–1971 (Slough, U.K.: Archive Editions Limited, 2006), p. 724; British Resident E.F. Henderson, Doha, to Arabian Department, FCO London, 'Priority, Cypher Cat A', vol. IV: 1970–1971, Records of Qatar 1966–1971 (Slough, U.K.: Archive Editions Limited, 2006).

19. Quoted in Crystal, *Oil and Politics in the Gulf: Rulers and Merchants in Kuwait and Qatar*, p. 155.

20. Ibid., pp. 156–157.

21. Ibid., p. 163.

22. 'State of Qatar', *The Times*, 15 May 1972.

23. 'Diplomatic Relations with Finland to Be Established', Cairo MENA 1974; 'First Senegalese Ambassador', Paris AFP 1974; 'Diplomatic Ties Established with Trinidad, Tobago', Cairo MENA 1974l 'Arafat Meets with Amir in Ad-Dawhah', Cairo MENA, 1974; 'As-Sadat Stops over at Ad-Dawhah for Talks', Cairo MENA, 1974; 'Gabonese Foreign Minister Arrives for Visit', Cairo MENA, 1974; 'Diplomatic Relations Established with Brazil', Cairo MENA, 20 May 1974; 'First Moroccan Ambassador', Qatar Domestic Service, 14 October 1974; 'Qatar, Burundi Establish Diplomatic Relations', Cairo MENA, 4 November 1974; 'Mali President Arrives for State Visit', Cairo MENA, 5 May 1975; 'Swiss Ambassador's Credentials', Doha, 12 June 1975; 'Diplomatic Relations with Malta', Doha, QNA

20 June 1975; 'Ambassador to Belgium', Doha QNA, 19 July 1975; 'Shaykh Receives Dprk's Chon Myong-Su', Pyongyang KCNA, 22 August 1975; 'Uganda President Amin Arrives on Visit', Doha QNA, 20 October 1975; 'Cabinet Decides to Recognize Comoros Islands', Doha QNA, 28 January 1976; 'Syrian President Al-Asad in Ad-Dawhah for Talks', Damascus Domestic Service 1974; 'Congolese Minister Concludes 3-Day Visit', Doha QNA, 9 March 1976; 'Diplomatic Relations with Indonesia', Doha QNA, 12 June 1975.

24. '2 Million Dollars Given to Mali as Grant in Aid', Doha QNA, 9 March 1976; 'Contributions to Unesco', Doha QNA, 9 July 1975.

25. Kohei Hashimoto, Jareer Elass, and Stacy Eller, 'Liquefied Natural Gas from Qatar: The Qatargas Project', Geopolitics of Gas Working Paper Series, Stanford: Baker Institute Energy Forum, Rice University, December 2004, p. 8.

26. Ibid., p. 9.

27. Julian Walker, 'Qatar: Annual Review for 1986', ed., Middle East Department, Foreign and Commonwealth Office, London: FCO, 4 January 1987, p. 12.

28. Patrick Nixon, 'Qatar: Annual Review for 1987', ed. Middle East Department, Foreign and Commonwealth Office, London: FCO, 30 December 1988.

29. 'Qatar: Annual Review for 1988', ed. Middle East Department, Foreign and Commonwealth Office, London: FCO, 31 December 1988.

30. Gulf States Qatar, Oxresearch Daily Brief Service, 19 September 1989.

31. 'Ruler Replaced Seven in Major Qatar Cabinet Reshuffle', Reuters, 18 July 1989.

32. Graham Boyce, 'Qatar: Annual Review for 1990', ed. Middle East Department, Foreign and Commonwealth Office, London: FCO, 7 January 1991.

33. 'Qatar: Annual Review for 1992', ed. Middle East Department, Foreign and Commonwealth Office, London: FCO, 12 January 1993.

34. Anthony H. Cordesman, *Bahrain, Oman, Qatar, and the UAE: Challenges of Security*, CSIS Middle East Dynamic Net Assessment, Boulder, CO.: Westview, 1997, p. 223.

35. 'Qatar: Political Modernisation', *Oxford Analytics Daily Brief Service*, 3 July 1998.

36. David Wright, 'Qatar: Annual Review for 1997', ed. Middle East Department, Foreign and Commonwealth Office, London: FCO.

37. Andrew Rathmell and Kirsten Schulze, 'Political Reform in the Gulf: The Case of Qatar', *Middle Eastern Studies*, 36, 4 (2000), p. 53.

38. Lambert, 'Political Reform in Qatar: Participation, Legitimacy, and Security'.

39. Ibid.

40. Ibid.

41. Uzi Rabi, 'Qatar's Relations with Israel: Challenging Arab and Gulf Norms', *The Middle East Journal*, 63, 3 (2009).

42. 'Qatar Gives $50m to Palestinians', BBC News, 17 April 2006.

43. 'Qatar Said to Give $50m in Aid to Hamas-Led Government', *Haaretz*, 17 April 2006.

44. Herb Keinon, 'FM Rebuffs Qatari Hamas Mediation Offer', *The Jerusalem Post*, 13 February 2006.

45. For a more detailed look at Qatar's gas ventures, see Chapter 3; Jamie Smyth, 'LNG Boom Fuels Australia Export Ambitions', *Financial Times*, 2 October 2014.

46. Nye, *Soft Power: The Means to Success in World Politics*, p. 6.

47. This is not to say that the effects of Qatar's sporting promotion have been universally positive. There is a negative discourse to be addressed regarding, for example, Qatar's hosting of the 2022 World Cup, either from disgruntled (often Western journalists) who do not approve of the World Cup going to Qatar, or from the human-rights angle in terms of the rights of workers building the stadia. Both issues are addressed in Chapter 10, which focuses on Tamim bin Hamad's first years in office, when such criticisms came particularly to the fore.

48. Margaret Coker, Sam Dagher, and Charles Levinson, 'Tiny Kingdom's Huge Role in Libya Draws Concern', *The Wall Street Journal*, 17 October 2011.

49. 'Qatari Emir: Govt Can No Longer "Provide for Everything"', *Al Arabiya News*, 3 November 2015.

50. Francis Warden, 'Historical Sketch of the Uttoobee Tribe of Arabs (Bahrein) from the Year 1716 to the Year 1817', *Selections from the Records of the Bombay Government*, Bombay; London, 1856, p. 366, in Penelope Tuson, *Records of Qatar: Primary Documents 1820–1960* (Slough: Archive Editions, 1991), p. 8.

51. Al-Rashid, *Saudi Relations with Eastern Arabia and Oman, 1800–1870*, p. 39.

52. John Gordon Lorimer, *Gazetteer of the Persian Gulf, 'Oman, and Central Arabia*, Volume 1, Part 1, Calcutta: Superintendent Government Printing, India, 1915, p. 789.

53. Ibid, p. 790; Warden, 'Historical Sketch of the Uttoobee Tribe of Arabs (Bahrein) from the Year 1716 to the Year 1817', p. 368; Tuson, *Records of Qatar: Primary Documents 1820–1960*, p. 10.

54. Yousof Ibrahim Abdulla, *A Study of Qatari-British Relations, 1914–1945*, Doha: Orient Publishing & Translation, 1981, p. 16.

55. George Rentz, *Oman and the South-Eastern Shore of Arabia*, Reading: Ithaca, 1997, p. 178; James E. Onley, 'The Politics of Protection in the Gulf: The Arab Rulers and the British Resident in the Nineteenth Century', *New Arabian Studies*, eds B Pridham, J Smart and G Rex Smith, Exeter: University of Exeter Press, 2004, p. 55.

56. 'The Politics of Protection in the Gulf: The Arab Rulers and the British Resident in the Nineteenth Century', pp. 55–56.

57. Zahlan, *The Creation of Qatar*, p. 65.

58. Patrick Nixon, 'Qatar: Valedictory Annual Review for 1989', ed. Middle East Department, Foreign and Commonwealth Office, London: FCO, 22 January 1990.

59. Ibid.

60. 'Qatar: Annual Review for 1988'.

61. Boyce, 'Qatar: Annual Review for 1990'.

62. Jeremy M Sharp, 'Qatar: Background and U.S. Relations', in *CRS Report for Congress*, Washington DC: Congressional Research Service, 17 March 2004, p. 8.

63. Clyde Haberman, 'Israel Seeks Deal with Qatar on Gas', *The New York Times*, 29 October 1993; 'Qatar, Israel Discuss Aviation Pact', *United Press International*, 18 November 1995.

64. Al-Rashid, *Saudi Relations with Eastern Arabia and Oman, 1800–1870*, p. 37.

65. Lorimer, *Gazetteer of the Persian Gulf, 'Oman, and Central Arabia*, Volume 1, Part 1, p. 789; Al-Rashid, *Saudi Relations with Eastern Arabia and Oman, 1800–1870*, p. 39.

66. Warden, 'Historical Sketch of the Uttoobee Tribe of Arabs (Bahrein) from the Year 1716 to the Year 1817', p. 368, in Tuson, *Records of Qatar: Primary Documents 1820–1960*, p. 10.

67. Zahlan, *The Creation of Qatar*, p. 54.

68. Ibn Saud quoted in Jacob Goldberg, *The Foreign Policy of Saudi Arabia: The Formative Years, 1902–1918*, Harvard Middle Eastern Studies, Cambridge, Mass: Harvard University Press, 1986, p. 66.

69. Ibid., p. 67.

70. Field, *The Merchants: The Big Business Families of Saudi Arabia and the Gulf States*, p 196.

71. Jawad Salim Al-Arayed, *A Line in the Sea: The Qatar Versus Bahrain Border Dispute in the World Court*, Berkeley, California: North Atlantic, 2003, pp. 98–102. Although Al-Arayed clearly writes with an anti-Qatar bias, he is referring to verifiable instances in the examples used here.

72. Ibid., p. 100.

73. Crystal, *Oil and Politics in the Gulf: Rulers and Merchants in Kuwait and Qatar*, p. 115.

74. Stephen Hemsley Longrigg, 'Oil in the Middle East—Second Edition [with Maps]', pp. xiii, 401, Oxford University Press: London, 1961, p. 228.

75. J B Kelly, *Eastern Arabian Frontiers*, London: Frederick A Praeger, 1964, p. 243.

76. Ibid., pp. 171–2.

77. Kamal was an Egyptian lawyer who was of central importance in Qatar until the late-1980s. Educated in Egypt he had the trust of Khalifah and was the driving force behind the day-to-day running of the emirate as he—and more or less only he—had the experience to do so.

78. Interview, Dr Birol Baskan, 13 May 2014.

79. J B Richards, 'British Residency Bahrain, Despatch No. 85, (17 July 1956, 17410/7/56)', ed. Anita L P Burdett, *Islamic Movements in the Arab World 1913–1966*, London: Cambridge Archive Editions, 1998, p. 170.

80. Interview with Qatari elite policy-maker, 6 November 2012.

81. Justin Dargin, 'Qatar's Natural Gas: The Foreign-Policy Driver', *Middle East Policy* 14, 3 (2007), p. 137; William B Quandt, *Saudi Arabia in the 1980s: Foreign Policy, Security and Oil*, Washington DC: The Brookings Institution, 1981, pp. 24–25.

82. Helen Chapin Metz, ed. *Persian Gulf States: Country Studies*, 3rd Edition, Area Handbook Series, Washington DC: US Government Printing Office, 1994, p. 192.

83. Sarah Searight, 'Special Report on Qatar (3): This Proud Aloof Nation', *The Times*, 12 November 1985.

84. 'The Bahrain-Qatar Border Dispute: The World Court Decision, Part 1', *The Estimate*, 23 March 2001. Metz, *Persian Gulf States: Country Studies*, p. 192.

85. Ramin Seddiq, 'Border Disputes on the Arabian Peninsula', *Policy Watch*, The Washington Institute for Near East Policy, 2001.

86. Robert Litwak, *Sources of Inter-State Conflict, Security in the Persian Gulf*, Montclair, NJ: Rowman & Littlefield Inc., 1981, p. 52.

87. J. B. Kelly, 'Saudi Arabia and the Gulf States', *Critical Choices for Americans*, Lexington, MA: D.C. Heath, 1976, p. 449; Litwak, *Sources of Inter-State Conflict*, p. 52.

88. Colin Brant, 'Valedictory from Qatar: A Land of Promise', ed. Middle East Department, Foreign and Commonwealth Office, London: FCO, 9 July 1981, pp. 2–3; Litwak, *Sources of Inter-State Conflict*

89. 'Saudi Troops Attack Border Post; 2 Killed', Paris AFP, FBIS-NES-92–191, 30 September 1992.

90. Gregory Gause III, *Oil Monarchies*, New York: Council on Foreign Relations, 1994, p. 131; 'Gulf Security Force Withdrawn', Paris AFP, FBIS-NES-92–193, 5 October 1992.

91. Cordesman, *Bahrain, Oman, Qatar, and the UAE: Challenges of Security*, p. 222; Gwenn Okruhlik and Patrick J Conge, 'The Politics of Border Disputes on the Arabian Peninsula', *International Journal* 54, 230 (1999), p. 236.

92. 'The Politics of Border Disputes on the Arabian Peninsula', p. 235.

93. Daniel Pipes, 'Interview with Hamad Bin Jassim Bin Jabr Al Thani', *Middle East Quarterly*, December 1996.

94. Mary Anne Weaver, 'Qatar: Revolution from the Top Down', *National Geographic Magazine*, March 2003.

95. 'Qatar Investment Authority, Part One: History and Structure', *Cablegate*, 23 July 2008.

96. Robert F Worth, 'Al Jazeera No Longer Nips at Saudis', *The New York Times*, 4 January 2008.

97. Rahman, *The Emergence of Qatar*, p. 21.

98. Lorimer, *Gazetteer of the Persian Gulf, 'Oman, and Central Arabia*, Volume 1, Part 1, p. 796.

99. Ibid., p. 795.

100. Ibid., pp. 786–787; Rahman, *The Emergence of Qatar*, pp. 42, 47.

101. Zahlan, *The Creation of Qatar*, pp. 36–37.

102. Rentz, *Oman and the South-Eastern Shore of Arabia*, p. 174.

103. Zahlan, *The Creation of Qatar*, p. 36; Rentz, *Oman and the South-Eastern Shore of Arabia*, p. 48.

104. Rahman, *The Emergence of Qatar*, p. 48.

105. See David B Roberts, 'Qatar and the Muslim Brotherhood: Pragmatism or Preference?', *Middle East Policy* 21, 3 (2014).

106. Ibid.

107. Ibid.

108. 'Qatar Emir to Change Style but Keep Policy', GulfNews.com, 27 June 2013.

2. CLOSE RELATIONS WITH THE US

1. Kenneth Katzman, 'Oman: Reform, Security, and U.S. Policy', *CRS Report for Congress*, Congressional Research Service, 27 December 2013, p. 9.

2. Youssef Ibrahim, 'U.S. Quietly Gets Gulf States' Aid Against Iranians', *The New York Times* 10 October 1987.

3. Ibid.

4. Elaine Sciolino, 'Qatar Rejects U.S. Demand for Return of Illicit Stingers', *New York Times* (28th June 1988).

5. John H Cushman, 'U.S. Says Qatar Has Stinger, Raising Fear of Missile Spread', *The New York Times*, 1 April 1988.

6. Michael Wines and Doyle McManus, 'Gulf State of Qatar Gets Stinger Missiles', *Los Angeles Times*, 31 March 1988.

7. 'US Seeks Return of Qatar's Stingers', *Janes Defence Weekly*, 6 August 1988.

8. 'Gulf State of Qatar Gets Stinger Missiles'.

9. 'Qatar Opens Diplomatic Relations with China', Reuters, 9 July 1988; 'Talks with Qatar Suspended', *The New York Times*, 28 July 1988.

10. 'Shaikh Ahmed Al Thani to Visit the Soviet Union', *Middle East Economic Digest*, 16 September 1988.

11. Patrick Tyler, 'US Drawn into Gulf Dispute', *Washington Post*, 6 October 1988.

12. 'Qatar Upgrades PLO Office to Embassy', Reuters, 7 January 1989; 'Qatar Sets up Full Ties with Yugoslavia', Reuters, 24 August 1989; 'Cuba and Qatar Establish Diplomatic Relations', Reuters, 14 December 1989.

13. 'The GCC: Regional Stabilizer', *Jane's Defence Weekly*, 31 March 1990.

14. 'Qatar Approves Deployment of Friendly Forces', Reuters, 27 August 1990.

15. Bob Hepburn, 'Canadians in Qatar Officially Don't Exist', *Toronto Star*, 7 October 1990; Judith Miller, 'Stand-Off in the Gulf', *The New York Times*, 25 December 1990.

16. 'Mirages to Qatar', *Jane's Defence Weekly*, 13 October 1990.

17. While the British did not have a military base in Doha (though the RAF had land-

ing rights), the noted presence of a British Agent in Doha was a clear sign not only of the British presence, but also of deeper agreements and relations stemming from his presence.

18. Sharp, 'Qatar: Background and U.S. Relations', p. 8.

19. Angus Hindley, 'Early Embrace Leads to Deep Relationship', *Middle East Economic Digest*, 17 February 1997.

20. Kedar Sharma, 'U.S., French Advance Qatar Wargames—Diplomats', Reuters, 27 February 1996.

21. 'US Marines Storm Qatar Beach in Military Exercises', ibid, 18 March 1996.

22. 'US Air Force Begins Joint Exercises in Qatar', Reuters, 3 July 1996.

23. 'US-Qatar Navies End Joint Military Exercises', Reuters, 17 December 1996

24. 'Qatar Boycotts Gulf Arab War Games', Reuters, 5 March 1996.

25. Christopher M Blanchard, 'Qatar: Background and U.S. Relations', *Congressional Research Service*, 10 October 2007, p. 10. Al-Udeid is sometimes referred to as 'Camp Andy', which technically refers to the large tent/semi-permanent building complex within Udeid named after Master Sergeant Evander Earl 'Andy' Andrews, who died in an accident on 2 October 2001 and is thought to have been the first US fatality during Operation Enduring Freedom.

26. Eric Schmitt, 'Pentagon Construction Boom Beefs up Mideast Air Base', *The New York Times*, 18 September 2005; Collins and Solman, 'What Can the Middle East Learn from What's Happening in Qatar?', *PBS Newshour*, 28 June 2013.

27. Michael R Gordon and Eric Schmitt, 'Aftereffects: Bases; US Will Move Air Operations to Qatar', *The New York Times*, 28 April 2003.

28. 'Often the GCC Maverick, Qatar Gives "Assured Access" to the US Military', *Gulf States Newsletter*, 28 November 2003.

29. Weaver, 'Qatar: Revolution from the Top Dow; Are We Ready?, Q&A with Rear Admiral Stephen H Baker, *CDI Terrorism Project*, 12 September 2002.

30. Michael DeLong and Noah Lukeman, *Inside Centcom: The Unvarnished Truth About the Wars in Afghanistan and Iraq*, Washington DC: Regnery Pub, 2004, p. 91.

31. David Lepeska, 'US Envoy Looks Back to Qatar's Future', *The National*, 11 December 2009.

32. Adam Entous and Julian E Barnes, 'Pentagon Bulks up Defences in the Gulf', *The Wall Street Journal*, 17 July 2012.

33. 'Report on Allied Contributions to the Common Defense', US Department of Defense, March 2001. Unfortunately, the reports were discontinued after 2004.

34. See Gause III, *Oil Monarchies*, p. 119, and the subsequent chapter for a discussion of the security and foreign policy concerns for Gulf states, particularly in terms of innate factors in their militating against the effectiveness of indigenous Gulf defence.

35. See earlier discussion of the 1965 border settlement and Khalifah bin Hamad's role in it.

36. Talal Salman, 'An Old Dialogue with the Emir of Qatar in the Context Of: Israel Being a Gatekeeper of Arab Affiliation with Washington', *As Safir*, 21 October 2009.

37. For an encapsulation of US interests and concerns in the Gulf particularly vis-à-vis the Soviet Union see Shahram Chubin, 'US Security Interests in the Persian Gulf in the 1980s', *Daedalus* 109, 4 (Fall 1980), and S A Yetiv, 'How the Soviet Military Intervention in Afghanistan Improved the US Strategic Position in the Persian Gulf', *Asian Affairs* 17, 2 (Summer 1990).

38. Zalmay Khalilzad, 'The United States and the Persian Gulf: Preventing Regional Hegemony', *Survival* 27, 2 (1995), p. 96.

39. Joe Stork and Martha Wenger, 'The US in the Persian Gulf: From Rapid Deployment to Massive Deployment', *Middle East Report*, 168 (January–February 1991), p. 23.

40. Ibid, p. 24.

41. Gause III, *Oil Monarchies*, p. 122.

42. Yetiv, 'How the Soviet Military Intervention in Afghanistan Improved the US Strategic Position in the Persian Gulf', p. 67.

43. Stork and Wenger, 'The US in the Persian Gulf: From Rapid Deployment to Massive Deployment', p. 25.

3. GAS POLICIES

1. 'Persian Gulf: Qatar: Use of Natural Gas', *Middle East Economic Digest*, 2 November 1960; 'Japanese Participate in LNG Development', *Middle East Economic Digest*, 31 January 1975.

2. Birnur Buzcu-Guven, Robert Harriss, and Donald Hertzmark, 'Gas Flaring and Venting: Extent, Impacts, and Remedies', *Energy Market Consequences of an Emerging US Carbon Management Policy*, Houston, TX: James A Baker III Institute for Public Policy, Rice University, September 2010, p. 8. For an example of unfulfilled early gas delivery ideas see 'Liquid Gas Project', *Middle East Economic Digest*, 19 March 1971.

3. Justin Dargin, 'The Dolphin Project: The Development of a Gulf Gas Initiative', Oxford: Oxford Institute for Energy Studies, 2008, p. 15.

4. Ragaei El Mallakh, *Qatar: Development of an Oil Economy*; London: Croom Helm, 1979, p. 38; Justin Dargin, 'The Gas Revolution in Qatar', *Natural Gas Markets in the Middle East and North Africa*, ed. Bassam Fattouh and Jonathan Stern, Oxford: Oxford University Press, 2011, p. 322.

5. John Whelan, 'Qatar Fire', *Middle East Economic Digest*, 15 April 1977; 'The 100 Largest Losses 1972–2001', Marsh Risk Consulting Practice, February 2003; Samuel H Williamson, 'Seven Ways to Compute the Relative Value of a U.S. Dollar Amount, 1774 to Present', *MeasuringWorth* (2015); For pictures of the devastation caused by the explosion, see 'Umm Said Lpg Plant Disaster 03–04–77', *Scribd*.

6. Quoted in Dargin, 'The Gas Revolution in Qatar', p. 322.

7. Whelan, 'Qatar Fire'.

8. El Mallakh, *Qatar: Development of an Oil Economy*, p. 37.

9. Hashimoto, Elass, and Eller, 'Liquefied Natural Gas from Qatar: The Qatargas Project', p. 1.

10. 'Qatar: In Brief', *Middle East Economic Digest*, 18 June 1976; 'Gulf States: Q.P.C's Liquid Gas Project', *Middle East Economic Digest*, 19 March 1971.

11. John Whelan, 'Qatar: Cutbacks in Spending Masks Big Chances for Contractors', *Middle East Economic Digest*, 22 June 1978.

12. Henry T Azzam, *The Arab World Facing the Challenge of the New Millennium*, London: I.B. Tauris, 2002, p. 192.

13. 'Qatar Predicts Wider Budget Deficit in 1988/89', Reuters, 17 February 1988.

14. Dargin, 'The Gas Revolution in Qatar', p. 327; Hashimoto, Elass, and Eller, 'Liquefied Natural Gas from Qatar: The Qatargas Project', p. 15.

15. Dargin, 'The Gas Revolution in Qatar', p. 330.

16. 'The Dolphin Project: The Development of a Gulf Gas Initiative', p. 18.

17. Ibid, pp. 28–31.

18. Hashimoto, Elass, and Eller, 'Liquefied Natural Gas from Qatar: The Qatargas Project', p. 20.

19. Ibid, p. 21.

20. Ibid, pp. 2 and 11.

21. 'Natural Gas Information', *IEA Statistics*, Paris: OECD, 2000; 'Natural Gas Information', *IEA Statistics*, Paris: OECD, 2005); 'Natural Gas Information', *IEA Statistics*, Paris: OECD, 2012.

22. Ibid, p. 247.

23. David B Roberts, 'Qatar and Japan: A Marriage of Convenience?', *Kyoto-Durham Symposium* (Kyoto, Japan 2012), p. 8.

24. 'BP Statistical Review of World Energy', London: British Petroleum (BP), June 2012, p. 4.

25. Dargin, 'The Dolphin Project: The Development of a Gulf Gas Initiative', p. 34.

26. Ibid, p. 38.

27. Ibid.

28. Abedlghani Henni, 'Dolphin Energy's CEO: We Supply 30% of the UAE's Gas Demand', *JPT Online*, 4 October 2012.

29. Dargin, 'The Dolphin Project: The Development of a Gulf Gas Initiative', p. 2.

30. Hashimoto, Elass, and Eller, 'Liquefied Natural Gas from Qatar: The Qatargas Project', p. 10.; Brant, 'Valedictory from Qatar: A Land of Promise', p. 3.

31. Hashimoto, Elass, and Eller, 'Liquefied Natural Gas from Qatar: The Qatargas Project', p. 10.

32. Ibid.

33. 'BP Statistical Review of World Energy', London: British Petroleum (BP), 2010.

34. *Government Cancels Debts for 10 Countries*, Paris AFP, FBIS-NES-90–195 on 1992–10–09, 7 October 2012.

35. Dargin, 'The Dolphin Project: The Development of a Gulf Gas Initiative', p. 21.

36. 'The Dolphin Project: The Development of a Gulf Gas Initiative', p. 2.

37. For a summary of the UAE's energy concerns see 'Addressing the UAE Natural Gas Crisis: Strategies for a Rational Energy Policy', *Policy Brief*, Dubai, UAE: The Dubai Initiative, Belfer Centre for Science and International Affairs, Harvard Kennedy School, August 2010.

38. Sara Hamdan, 'Gasoline Crisis in Emirates Brings Lines and Fears', *The New York Times*, 15 June 2011.

39. Dargin, 'The Gas Revolution in Qatar', p. 331. It must be remembered that a structural problem exists throughout the Gulf states in that domestic energy prices cannot realistically reflect the cost of production. As per the ruling bargain, subsidies are universal and citizens expect, if not demand, to pay either no charges for domestic energy supply (as in Qatar) or at least receive highly subsidised energy and fuel. This hamstrings GCC states and represents a significant additional cost for them to bear. Even the July 2015 removal of petrol subsidies, worth an estimated $7bn per year, will still leave around $22bn worth of state subsidies for energy. Simeon Kerr and Pilita Clark, 'UAE Drops Fuel Subsidies to Boost Finances and Cut Emissions', *The Financial Times*, 22 July 2015.

40. While Dolphin gas may make a profit, the opportunity cost is high. Significantly larger profits can be made by selling the gas via LNG to East Asia demand.

41. James T Jensen, 'The Development of a Global LNG Market', Oxford: Oxford Institute for Energy Studies, 2004, p. 8.

42. Ken Koyama, 'Growing Energy Demand in Asian Countries: Opportunities and Constraints for Gulf Energy Exporters', *Gulf Energy and the World: Challenges and Threats*, Abu Dhabi: The Emirates Centre for Strategic Studies and Research, 1997, pp. 45–46.

43. Ibid, p. 48.

44. Kang Wu and Jit Yang Lim, 'Supplying Asia-Pacific Oil Demand: Role of the Gulf', *Gulf Oil and Gas: Ensuring Economic Security*, Abu Dhabi: The Emirates Centre for Strategic Studies and Research, 2007, p. 255.

45. Koyama, 'Growing Energy Demand in Asian Countries: Opportunities and Constraints for Gulf Energy Exporters', p. 56; 'Japan's Uncertain Energy Prospects: The Problem of Import Dependence', *Energy Policy*, September 1974.

46. Don Hedley, *World Energy: The Facts and the Future* (London: Euromonitor Publications, 1986), p. 38.

47. 'Natural Gas Information', *IEA Statistics*, Paris: OECD, 2001; Koyama, 'Growing Energy Demand in Asian Countries: Opportunities and Constraints for Gulf Energy Exporters', p. 57.

48. 'Natural Gas Information'.

49. O'Brien quoted in Clair Apodaca, 'Global Economic Patterns and Personal Integrity Rights after the Cold War', *International Studies Quarterly* 45 (2001), p. 587.

50. Cindy Hurst, 'Liquified Natural Gas: The Next Prize?', *Energy Security Challenges for the 21st Century*, ed. Gal Luft and Anne Korin, Santa Barbara, CA: ABC CLIO, 200), p. 279.

51. Fred C Bergsten, 'The World Economy after the Cold War', *Foreign Affairs* (Summer 1990), p. 96.

52. 'Natural Gas Information'; 'Growing Energy Demand in Asian Countries: Opportunities and Constraints for Gulf Energy Exporters', p. 57.

53. 'Qatar Considers Ways of Keeping Iranians Off Their Rigs', *Gulf States Newsletter*, 845, 16 January 2009.

54. 'Natural Gas Information', *IEA Statistics*, Paris: OECD, 2014, pp. 11–57.

4. INTERNATIONAL MEDIATION AND NEGOTIATION

1. For a brief sketch noting these issues see Hessa Bint Khaled Al Thani, 'Shaikh Ahmed Bin Ali Bin Abdullah Bin Qassim Al Thani: A New Perspective on Domestic and Foreign Relations', Qatar University, September 2014. *'Abdalmajid Shiki: Qatar Ra'at Mafawidaat Istqlal Al-Jazair* (Abdalmajid Shiki: Qatar Sponsored Algeria's Independence Negotiations)', *Al Arab*, 6 July 2008.

2. Although the Qatari interaction appears to be minor, these small gestures can be pivotally important.

3. Jacob Bercovitch, 'Introduction', *Studies in International Mediation*, eds Jacob Bercovitch and Jeffrey Z Rubin, Basingstoke: Palgrave MacMillan, 2002, p. 6, quoted in David B Roberts, 'Qatari Mediation', *Gulf Research Centre Conference*, Cambridge, UK 2010, p. 4.

4. Marieke Kleiboer, 'Understanding Success and Failure of International Mediation', *Journal of Conflict Resolution* 40, 2 (1996), p. 360, quoted in Roberts, 'Qatari Mediation', p. 4.

5. Facilitation is also known as communication, process mediation, and offering 'good offices' in the literature. Similarly, manipulation is also known as content mediation.

6. Bertram I Spector and Anna R Korula, 'Facilitative Mediation in International Disputes: From Research to Practical Application', Laxenburg: International Institution for Applied Systems Analysis, February 1992, p. 4.

7. Roberts, 'Qatari Mediation', pp. 4–5, quoting Spector and Korula, 'Facilitative Mediation in International Disputes: From Research to Practical Application', p. 4

8. For a good overview see Robert G Rabil, 'Lebanon at the Crossroads', *Open Democracy*, 5 June 2009.

9. Mehran Kamrava, 'Mediation and Qatari Foreign Policy', *Middle East Journal* 65, 4 (Autumn 2011), p. 548.

10. Caitlin B Doherty, 'Lebanon: Back from the Brink?', *The National Interest*, 27 May 2008; Daniel Steinvorth and Alexander Szandar, 'The Victors of Beirut: Hezbollah Triumphs in Lebanon', *Spiegel Online International*, 29 May 2008.

11. Interview: Senior Diplomat in Qatar, 17 March 2010.

12. Interview: Academic Practitioner, 28 March 2010.

13. Adam Goldman and Karen DeYoung, 'Qatar Played Now-Familiar Role in Helping to Broker U.S. Hostage's Release', *Washington Post*, 25 August 2014; Ernesto Londono, 'Taliban-Held U.S. Soldier Released in Exchange for Afghan Detainees', *Washington Post*, 1 June 2014.

14. Farnaz Fassihi and Nour Malas, 'Syria Rebels Free Iranians in Prisoner Swap', *The Wall Street Journal*, 9 January 2013.

15. 'Qatar Says It Mediated Release of Fiji Peacekeepers', *The Daily Star*, 12 September 2014.

16. Mohamed Baluwt, 'Rihlat Al-Raahibaat Min Yabrud Ila Al-Huriya ('The Journey of the Yabrud Nuns to Freedom')', *As Safir*, 3 October 2014.

17. 'Erdogan Steps in to Try and Mediate in Lebanese Hostage Crisis in Qatar', *An Nahar*, 15 September 2014.

18. Sami Aboudi, 'Yemen Kidnappers Free Swiss Woman after Qatari Mediation: Agency', Reuters, 28 February 2013.

19. Tajudin, 'After Mediation of Qatar, Eritrea Releases Djiboutian Soldier', *The Diplomat*, 19 September 2014.

20. Catherine Putz, 'Tajik Border Guards Held by Taliban to Be Released', *The Diplomat*, 16 June 2015.

21. Bercovitch, 'Introduction', p. 9, quoted in Roberts, 'Qatari Mediation', p. 8.

22. 'The Constitution', *Qatar Ministry of Foreign Affairs*.

23. Qatari press often comments favorably, as one might expect, when Qatari mediation efforts are successful. In addition, surveys indicate that, for example, 88 per cent of Qatari youths are pleased with their state's orientation and direction of travel, and that Qataris are more proud of their nationality than any other country in the world; 'Young Qataris More Proud of Their National Identity Than Ever Before: Survey', *Gulf Times*, 4 June 2013; Zack Beauchamp, 'Where People Really Love Their Countries—and Where They Kinda Don't', *Vox*, 18 May 2014.

24. 'Qatar Emir to Change Style but Keep Policy'.

25. Anders Gulbrandsen, *Bridging the Gulf: Qatari Business Diplomacy and Conflict Mediation*, Georgetown University, 2010.

26. Ibid, p. 51.

27. Ibid, pp. 40–75.

28. 'Outsourcing's Third Wave', *The Economist*, 21 May 2009.

29. Bassam Ramadan, 'Qatar Under Pressure Over Support for Brotherhood', *Al Monitor*, 23 April 2014.

30. Andrew England, 'Bashir Hailed in Qatar Despite Darfur Charges', *Financial Times*, 30 March 2009.

31. On this theme in the Sudanese example, see Sultan Barakat, 'Qatari Mediation: Between Ambition and Achievement', *Brookings Doha Center Analysis Paper*, Doha, Qatar: Brookings Doha Centre, November 2014, pp. 17–19.

32. See Kristian Coates Ulrichsen, 'The Gulf States and South-South Cooperation, 1961–1990: Contradictions and Commonalities', *BRISMES Annual Conference 2012* (LSE 2012).

33. Crystal, quoted in David B Roberts, 'Kuwait', in *Power and Politics in the Persian Gulf Monarchies*, ed. Christopher Davidson, London: Hurst & Co., 2011, p. 105.

34. Goldberg, *The Foreign Policy of Saudi Arabia: The Formative Years, 1902–1918*, p. 31.

35. Oman had much the same kinds of relations, though arguably not as extensive in the Levant.

36. I must thank Gerd Nonneman for framing this issue in this particular fashion at the Exeter Gulf Conference in 2010.

37. Rabi, 'Qatar's Relations with Israel: Challenging Arab and Gulf Norms', p. 454.

38. For example, 'Yemen's Houthis Hold Secret Meet with Iran', *Al Arabiyya*, 13 December 2009; David Schenker, 'Who's Behind the Houthis?', *The Weekly Standard*, Volume 15, 22 (22 February 2010); 'Houthis Receive Arms from Iran Via Eritrea', *Yemen Post*, 10 April 2010; Shaun Overton, 'Understanding the Second Houthi Rebellion in Yemen', *Terrorism Monitor*, The Jamestown Foundation, 17 June 2005; J E Peterson, 'The Al-Huthi Conflict in Yemen', *Arabian Peninsula Background Note* No. APBN-006 (August 2008).

39. Amir Taheri, 'Sudan: An Expanding Civil War with an Iran Connection', *The New York Times*, 9 April 1997.

40. Dan Williams, 'Sudan: A Front for Israel's Proxy War on Sinai Jihadis?', Reuters, 25 October 2012.

41. Although *Gulf News*'s debunking of the report was not particularly convincing, neither was the original report. Furthermore, given the US's presence in Djibouti and Ethiopia, it seems highly unlikely that a serious Iranian presence in Eritrea would remain unverified and not public to this day. Abdul Nabi Shaheen, 'Eritrea: In Pursuit of the Truth', *GulfNews.com*, 21 April 2012.

42. 'A Search for Allies in a Hostile World', *The Economist*, 4 February 2010; Jeffrey A Lefebvre, 'Iran in the Horn of Africa: Outflanking U.S. Allies', *Middle East Policy* XIX, 2 (Summer 2012).

43. 'Iran and Hamas Back Sudan's Bashir', *Al Jazeera*, 7 March 2009; 'Iran and Hamas Back Sudan's Bashir', *Al Jazeera*, 7 March 2009; Colum Lynch, 'U.N. Report Cites Outside Military Aid to Somalia's Islamic Forces', *Washington Post*, 15 November 2006; Lefebvre, 'Iran in the Horn of Africa: Outflanking U.S. Allies'.

44. Paul C Stern and Daniel Druckman, *International Conflict Resolution after the Cold War*, Washington DC; [United Kingdom]: National Academy Press, 2000, p. 1.

45. Quoted in Marcus Foster, 'Small States in Peacemaking Roles', *Jackson School Journal of International Studies* 1, 2 (Spring 2011), p. 24.

46. Ibid.

47. Muzaffer Ercan Yilmaz, '"The New World Order": An Outline of the Post-Cold War Era' *Alternatives: Turkish Journal of International Relations* 7, 4 (Winter 2008), p. 46.

48. 'You Are Either with Us or against Us', *CNN*, 6 November 2001.

49. Sophie Evans, 'Doha's Expanding Diplomatic Role', *Middle East Economic Digest* 53, 24 (2009).

50. Matthew Rosenberg, 'Taliban Opening Qatar Office, and Maybe Door to Talks', *The New York Times*, 3 January 2012.

51. Personal Interview: Qatar-Based European Diplomat, 6 April 2010; 'Taliban Shuts Doha HQ over "Broken Promises"', *Al Jazeera*, 9 July 2013.

5. TABOO INTERNATIONAL RELATIONS: ISRAEL, IRAN

1. Anthony H Cordesman, 'The Tanker War and the Lessons of Naval Conflict', *The Lessons of Modern War* II (1990), pp. 17–18.

2. 'Iranian Envoy, on Gulf Tour, Meets Qatari Emir', Reuters, 9 November 1988; 'Iranian Minister Holds Talks on Gulf in Qatar', Reuters, 1 June 1987; 'Iran's Foreign Minister Visits Oman, UAE, and Qatar', BBC Monitoring Service: Middle East, 14 April 1988.

3. 'Iran's Oil Minister to Tour Gulf for Qatar Gas Talks', Reuters, 9 January 1990; 'Iran Drafts Plan to Exploit Joint Gas Field with Qatar', Reuters, 12 November 1990.

4. 'Iran Starts Weekly Service to Qatar', *Lloyd's List International*, 3 January 1991.

5. Uzi Rabi, 'Qatar', *Middle East Contemporary Survey*, ed. Ami Ayalon, Boulder, Colorado: Westview Press, 1991, p. 607; 'Qatari Crown Prince Starts Four-Day Visit to Iran', Reuters, 7 November 1991.

6. Kamran Taremi, 'The Role of Water Exports in Iranian Foreign Policy Towards the GCC', *Iranian Studies* 28, 2 (June 2005), p. 323; 'Iran, Qatar Consider Huge Water Pipeline Project', Reuters, 11 November 1991.

7. 'Iran's Defence Minister Visiting Qatar', Reuters, 28 December 1991.

8. 'Iranian Vice-President Arrives in Qatar', Reuters, 5 May 1991; 'Qatari Interior Minister in Iran', Reuters, 10 May 1992; R K Ramazani, 'Iran's Foreign Policy: Both North and South', *The Middle East Journal* 46, 3 (Summer 1992), p. 401.

9. Patrick Wogan, 'Qatar: Annual Review for 1993', ed. Middle East Department, Foreign and Commonwealth Office, London: FCO, 12 January 1994.

10. Ramazani, 'Iran's Foreign Policy: Both North and South', p. 393.

11. *Iranian Protection Asked against Saudi 'Threats'*, Misr Al Fatah, Cairo: FBIS-NES-92-201 on 1992–10–16, 12 October 1992.

12. 'Qatar Approves Deployment of Friendly Forces'.
13. 'The GCC: Regional Stabilizer'.
14. 'Iran: A Need for Budget Cuts', *Stratfor Global Intelligence*, 13 April 2009.
15. 'Qatar Opens Diplomatic Relations with China'.
16. 'The GCC: Regional Stabilizer'.
17. 'Scenesetter for August 26 Centcom Component Commanders Conference', *Wikileaks*, 18 August 2008; 'Civilian Use of Al-Udeid Air Base in Qatar', *Wikileaks*, 21 December 2008.
18. Although this event was reported by Press TV, which takes a pro-Iran editorial line, it did actually happen; 'Iranian Warship, Destroyer Dock at Qatari Port', *Press TV*, 15 February 2010.
19. Joseph LeBaron, 'Subject: Scenesetter for Senator Kerry's Visit to Qatar', *Wikileaks*, 8 February 2010.
20. Ibid.
21. 'US Embassy Cables: Qatari Prime Minister: 'Iranians Lie to Us'', *The Guardian*, 28 November 2010.
22. Rabi, 'Qatar's Relations with Israel: Challenging Arab and Gulf Norms', p. 448.
23. Personal Interview: Israeli Diplomat, 11 August 2010.
24. Ibid.
25. Ibid.
26. 'Israel to Sever Ties with Qatar', *The Daily Star*, 26 August 2011.
27. 'Qatar Could Sever Ties with Israel If Part of Joint Arab Stance', *Cablegate*, Doha, Qatar: *Wikileaks*, 12 January 2009.
28. 'Address by FM Livni to the 8th Doha Forum on Democracy, Development, and Free Trade', *Israel Ministry of Foreign Affairs*, 14 April 2008.
29. 'Israel Rejects Qatar Diplomatic Overtures: Report', *Al Arabiyya*, 18 May 2010. Egypt played a blocking role in not allowing Qatar's goods into Gaza, which contributed to stymying the reopening of the office.
30. Raphael Ahren, 'Israel and the Gulf States: It's Complicated', *The Times of Israel*, 9 August 2013.
31. 'Qatar to Open Office in Gaza', *Jerusalem Post*, 31 July 1995.
32. 'Iran: A Need for Budget Cuts'.
33. These ages and birthdays are as accurate as possible, but the age of Gulf leaders often varies according to different sources.
34. CNN Interview quoted in Louay Bahry, 'Elections in Qatar: A Window of Democracy Opens in the Gulf', *Middle East Policy* VI, 4 (June 1999).
35. Danna Harman, 'Backstory: The Royal Couple That Put Qatar on the Map', *The Christian Science Monitor*, 5 March 2007.
36. While Saudi Arabia was also improving its relations with Iran in the early 1990s, this did not last long.
37. Gause III, *Oil Monarchies*, p. 134.

38. Ibid, pp. 134–135.

39. Searight, 'Special Report on Qatar (3): This Proud Aloof Nation'.

40. AP, 'Iran-Qatar Gas Field', *The New York Times*, 14 November 1990; 'Qatar National Bank Denies Investing in Iran Oilfield', Reuters, 4 October 2009.

41. 'Iran, Qatar, Russia Form Gas Alliance', *The Wall Street Journal*, 22 October 2008.

42. Kamrava, *Qatar: Small State, Big Politics*, pp. 72–78.

43. Joseph S Nye, 'What New World Order?', *Foreign Affairs*, 1 March 1992, p. 83.

44. 'After the War: The President; Transcript of President Bush's Address on End of the Gulf War', *New York Times*, 7 March 1991.

45. Efraim Karsh, 'Cold War, Post-Cold War: Does It Make a Difference for the Middle East?', *Review of International Studies*, 23 (1997), p. 271.

46. Francis Fukuyama, *The End of History and the Last Man*, London: Hamilton, 1992.

47. 'After the War: The President; Transcript of President Bush's Address on End of the Gulf War', p. 83.

48. Karsh, 'Cold War, Post-Cold War: Does It Make a Difference for the Middle East?', p. 271.

49. Philip G Cerny, 'Plurilateralism: Structural Differentiation and Functional Conflict in the Post-Cold War World Order', *Millennium—Journal of International Studies* 22, 27 (1993), p. 31.

50. For a detailed explanation of these issues in the context of the end of the Cold War, see Ibid, pp. 32–35.

51. Ibid, p. 28.

52. Salman, 'An Old Dialogue with the Emir of Qatar in the Context Of: Israel Being a Gatekeeper of Arab Affiliation with Washington'.

6. INTERNATIONAL INVESTMENTS

1. 'Qatar Investment Authority, Part One: History and Structure'.

2. David French, 'Emir Appoints New CEO at Qatar Investment Authority', Reuters, 3 December 2014.

3. 'France Scores Big', *Financial Times*, 20 July 2012.

4. Kartikay Mehrotra, 'Bharti Gets $1.26 Billion Investment from Qatar Foundation', Bloomberg, 3 May 2013.

5. 'Enabling Growth: Looking Overseas to Invest in the Oil, Gas, and Power Segments', Oxford Business Group.

6. 'Funds Investment', General Retirement & Social Insurance Authority, 29 July 2015; Stephen Burgen, 'Qatar's Armed Forces Pay €78.5m for Barcelona's Renaissance Hotel', *The Guardian*, 31 January 2014.

7. Andy Sharman, 'British Land's "Super-Prime" Mayfair Penthouse Breaks Sale Record', *Financial Times*, 22 September 2014.

8. Victoria Barbary, 'Sovereign Wealth Funds Don't buy Apartments. Read: "Middle Eastern Royal"': @EMInvestment', Twitter, 22 September 2014.

9. See for example Una Galani, 'Breakingviews: Qatar's Sovereign Funds: A Guide for the Perplexed', Reuters, 2 October 2012.

10. Benjamin J Cohen, 'Sovereign Wealth Funds and National Security: The Great Tradeoff', *Global & International Studies*; University of California, March 2009; William L Megginson, 'Determinants of Sovereign Wealth Fund Cross-Border Investments', *The Financial Review* 48 (2013).

11. Camilla Hall, 'New Qatar Emir Shakes up Sovereign Wealth Fund', *Financial Times*, 2 July 2013; Sami Nader, 'Emir Replaces Head of Qatar Investment Authority', *Al Monitor*, 12 July 2013.

12. Dinesh Nair, 'Exclusive: Qatar Bolstering Wealth Fund Team to Diversify Portfolio—Sources', Reuters, 2 September 2013.

13. Simeon Kerr, 'Qatar's Sovereign Wealth Fund Looks to Diversify in Asia and US', *Financial Times*, 18 June 2015.

14. Jake Spring, 'Qatar's Wealth Fund to Launch $10 Billion Investment Fund with China's Citic', Reuters, 4 November 2014.

15. For a detailed look at the relevance behind and logic of this initiative see 'The Chinese Remninbi Lands in Doha', *Economic Commentary*, 19 April 2015.

16. Amena Bakr, 'Qatar Launches First Chinese Yuan Clearing Hub in Middle East', Reuters, 14 April 2014.

17. For a range of estimates from SWF experts see: Bernado Bortolotti, Veljko Fotak, and William L Megginson, 'The Rise of Soveriegn Wealth Funds: Definition, Organization, and Governance', Universita Commerciale Luigi Bocconi: BAFFI Center on International Markets, Money and Regulation, 2014; 'Fund Rankings', *Sovereign Wealth Fund Institute*, June 2015; 'Fund Profiles', *Sovereign Wealth Center*, July 2015; Javier Santiso, 'Sovereign Wealth Funds', ESADE Business School and KPMG, 2014; Sven Behrendt, 'Sovereign Wealth Funds: Fiscal Buffers against the Deterioration of Oil Prices?', *Sovereign Wealth Funds Update Series*, GeoEconomica, January 2015.

18. Personal Correspondence: Patrick Flaherty, Sovereign Wealth Fund Researcher, 15 March 2013; Camilla Hall et al., 'Qatar: What's Next for the World's Most Aggressive Deal Hunter?', *Financial Times*, 4 July 2013.

19. Personal Correspondence: Patrick Flaherty, Sovereign Wealth Fund Researcher

20. For a brief examination of some of the costs of Qatari citizens for their government see Zahra R Babar, 'The Cost of Belonging: Citizenship Construction in the State of Qatar', *The Middle East Journal* 68, 3 (Summer 2014), p. 416.

21. Bortolotti, Fotak, and Megginson, 'The Rise of Soveriegn Wealth Funds: Definition, Organization, and Governance', p. 17.

22. Qatar is among the world's least transparent SWFs. Anne-Sylvaine Chassany, 'QIA Leads Fund Rankings for Missing Santiago Governance Standards', *Financial Times*, 27 October 2014.

23. Galani, 'Breakingviews: Qatar's Sovereign Funds: A Guide for the Perplexed'.

24. Wogan, 'Qatar: Annual Review for 1993'.

25. Gulbrandsen, 'Bridging the Gulf: Qatari Business Diplomacy and Conflict Mediation', pp. 15–19.

26. Hall et al, 'Qatar: What's Next for the World's Most Aggressive Deal Hunter?'.

27. For the full list of typologies, see Ashby H B Monk and Adam Dixon, 'Rethinking the Sovereign in Sovereign Wealth Funds', 3 August 2010.

28. Ibid, p. 13–14.

29. The figure for Qatari investment comes from a personal interview: Doha-Based British Embassy Official, 20 February 2013.

30. Regan Doherty and Dinesh Nair, 'Analysis—Qatar Swf's Hefty Appetite Draws Global Players', Reuters, 3 March 2011.

31. Richard Levick, 'Game-Changer: Qatar Plays Historic Role in Glencore's Bid for Xstrata', Forbes, 12 September 2012.

32. Cassell Bryan-Low, 'UK Boosts Support to Opposition Military', The Wall Street Journal, 6 March 2013. Geraldine Amiel and Laurence Norman, 'France Urges EU to End Arms Embargo on Syria', The Wall Street Journal, 14 March 2013.

33. Christopher Davidson, After the Sheikhs: The Coming Collapse of the Gulf Monarchies, London: Hurst & Co., 2012. In particular, see section on strategic investments in the West.

34. Richard Norton-Taylor, 'Defence Chief Signals Major UK Military Presence in Gulf', The Guardian, 18 December 2012.

35. 'UK to Establish £15m Permanent Mid East Military Base', BBC News, 6 December 2014. For a wider look at the notion of the UK's 'return' to the Gulf region, see David B Roberts, 'British National Interest in the Gulf: Rediscovering a Role?', International Affairs 90, 3 (2014).

36. Rupert Neate, 'Qatar Nurtures Its City Assets: From the Shard to Glencore Shares', The Guardian, 27 June 2012.

37. Scott Sayare, 'Qatar Is Becoming a Player in French Sports', The New York Times, 26 October 2012.

38. 'Continuity Trumps Change on Hollande's Qatar Visit', France 24, 22 June 2013.

39. David Conn, 'Qatar Cash Is Stirring French Football Revolution at Paris St Germain', The Guardian, 22 November 2011.

40. John Lichfield, 'Nicholas Sarkozy "Colluded" to Get Qatar 2022 World Cup', The Independent, 29 January 2013.

41. Oliver Kay, 'Qatar Vote a French Plot, Says Blatter', The Times, 29 October 2015.

42. Rob Draper, 'Backed by Qatar's Billions, Sarkozy's Brokerage and Beckham's Glamour, Paris St Germain Are Forging the New French Revolution', Mail on Sunday, 30 March 2013.

43. Tom Bill, 'Qatar Top Sovereign Europe Property Buyer with Six Weeks Gas Cash', Reuters, 17 August 2012.

44. 'China Grants Qatar Fund Qfii Licence: Report'.

45. Harry Papachristou and Ingrid Melander, 'Qatar Signs Deal to Invest up to $5bn in Greece', Reuters, 24 September 2010; Courtney Trenwith, 'Qatar to Invest $10bn in Malaysia—Report', *ArabianBusiness.com*, 30 January 2013.

46. Personal Interview: Qatar-Based European Diplomat.

7. AL JAZEERA—1996–2011

1. Louay Bahry, 'The New Arab Media Phenomenon: Qatar's Al-Jazeera', *Middle East Policy* 8, 2 (2001), p. 89.

2. Larry Pintak, *The New Arab Journalist: Mission and Identity in a Time of Turmoil*, Kindle edition, London: I. B. Tauris, 2011, Chapter 1.

3. Bahry, 'The New Arab Media Phenomenon: Qatar's Al-Jazeera', p. 91.

4. Shawn Powers and Eytan Gilboa, 'The Public Diplomacy of Al Jazeera', *New Media and the New Middle East*, ed. Philip M Seib, Basingstoke: Palgrave Macmillan, 2007, p. 55.

5. Bahry, 'The New Arab Media Phenomenon: Qatar's Al-Jazeera', p. 90.

6. Scott Bridges, *18 Days: Al Jazeera English and the Egyptian Revolution*, Kindle edition, Braddon, Australia: Editia, 2013, Introduction.

7. El Mustapha Lahlai, *Contemporary Arab Broadcast Media*, Edinburgh: Edinburgh University Press, 2011, p. 80.

8. Larissa Bender, 'Al Jazeera—the Enigma from Qatar', *Qantara.de*, 6 November 2006; Al Jazeera's Brand Name News', *Foreign Policy*, 18 April 2005.

9. Mohammed El Nawawy and Adel Iskander, *Al-Jazeera: How the Free Arab News Network Scooped the World and Changed the Middle East*, First edition; hardback edition, Cambridge, MA: Westview, 2002, p. 122.

10. Hugh Miles, *Al-Jazeera: How Arab TV News Challenged the World*, London: Abacus, 2006, p. 31.

11. See Hugh Miles' excellent book for a more in-depth look at this episode; Ibid, p. 32.

12. Bahry, 'The New Arab Media Phenomenon: Qatar's Al-Jazeera', p. 90.

13. Miles, *Al-Jazeera: How Arab TV News Challenged the World*, p. 35.

14. Ibid., p. 36.

15. Steve Clarke, 'Al Jazeera Wins Rts Award', *Variety*, 23 February 2012; Marwan M Kraidy, 'Al Jazeera and Al Jazeera English: A Comparative Institutional Analysis', in *Annenberg School for Communication Departmental Papers*, Philadelphia: University of Pennsylvania, 2008), p. 25.

16. This kind of characterisation can be found not only in the literature, but also by briefly sampling the two channels' products. For an interesting read on the differences between the channels, see Bridges, *18 Days: Al Jazeera English and the Egyptian Revolution*, Chapter 1; Sherry Ricchiardi, 'The Al Jazeera Effect', *American Journalism Review*, March–April 2011.

17. While a few documentaries, such as Al Jazeera English's 'Shouting in the Dark,' an exposé focusing on Bahrain, have caused friction, such instances are simply not rated as that important by Arab governments. Their core concern is not with Al Jazeera pushing its propaganda (as they would see it) towards the international audience, but rather towards an Arab audience.

18. Bahry, 'The New Arab Media Phenomenon: Qatar's Al-Jazeera', p. 92.

19. Quoted in Ricchiardi, 'The Al Jazeera Effect'.

20. Alexander Smoltczyk, 'The Voice of Egypt's Muslim Brotherhood', *Spiegel Online International*, 15 February 2011.

21. Bahry, 'The New Arab Media Phenomenon: Qatar's Al-Jazeera', p. 95; Miles, *Al-Jazeera: How Arab TV News Challenged the World*, p. 67; Field, 'Tree of the Al Attiyah', p. 8

22. Bahry, 'The New Arab Media Phenomenon: Qatar's Al-Jazeera', p. 95.

23. For a brief snapshot of the criticism of al Jazeera see: Jonathan S Tobin, 'The Al Jazeera Liberal', *Commentary*, 1 April 2013; Oren Kessler, 'The Two Faces of Al Jazeera', *The Middle East Quarterly* XIX, 1 (Winter 2012).

24. Sam Thielman, 'Some Advertisers View Al Jazeera America as Too Risky, Conservative Clients Are Balking', *Adweek*, 18 August 2013.

25. Jeanie Poggi, 'Al Jazeera America at Six Months: Some New Advertisers, Few Viewers,' *Advertising Age*, 4 March 2014.

26. Laura M James, 'Whose Voice? Nasser, the Arabs, and 'Sawt Al-Arab'', *Transnational Broadcasting Studies* 16 (2006).

27. For a brief discussion of al Jazeera and Sawt al-Arab in terms of their similarities and differences, see Morten Valbjorn and Andre Bank, 'The New Arab Cold War: Rediscovering the Arab Dimension of Middle East Regional Politics', *Review of International Studies* (2011).

28. Personal Interview: Dr Steven Wright, Qatar University, 6 February 2013.

29. Pippa Norris, 'The Restless Searchlight: Network News Framing of the Post-Cold War World', *Political Communication* 12 (1995), p. 358.

30. Ibid, pp. 358–359.

31. Ibid, p. 358.

32. Sofiane Sahraoui and Mohamed Zayani, *The Culture of Al Jazeera: Inside an Arab Media Giant*, Jefferson, NC: McFarland & Company Inc, 2007; For a broad discussion of the emerging Middle Eastern media landscape, see Annabelle Sreberny-Mohammadi, 'The Media and Democratization in the Middle East: The Strange Case of Television', *Democratization* 5, 2 (1998), and Marc Lynch, *Voices of the New Arab Public*, New York, NY: Columbia University Press, 2006.

33. Eytan Gilboa, 'Global Television News and Foreign Policy: Debating the CNN Effect', *International Studies Perspectives* 6 (2005), p. 335.

8. SOFT POWER POLICIES: MICE, SPORT, CULTURE, AND EDUCATION

1. Meredith Lawrence and Vivienne McCabe, 'Managing Conference in Regional Areas: A Practical Evaluation in Conference Management', *International Journal of Contemporary Hospitality Management* 14, 4 (2001), p. 204.

2. Larry Dwyer and Peter Forsyth, 'Economic Measures of Tourism Yield: What Markets to Target?', *International Journal of Tourism Research* 10 (2008), p. 155.

3. Nina Mistilis and Larry Dwyer, 'Tourism Gateways and Regional Economies: The Distributional Impacts of Mice', Ibid 1 (1999), p. 441.

4. Jack Carlsen, 'A Review of Mice Industry Evaluation and Research in Asia and Australia 1988–1998', *Journal of Convention & Exhibition Management* 1, 4 (1999), p. 52.

5. The Leadership in Energy and Environment Design (LEED) is an independent programme established by the US Green Building Council; '"Gold Certification" for Convention Centre', *Gulf Times*, 10 May 2012.

6. 'Qatar National Convention Centre Records Robust Growth', *Breaking Travel*, 21 May 2012.

7. Thanks to Kristian Ulrichsen for pointing this out.

8. Dominic Ellis, 'Qatar's Conference Scene Is About to Change Beyond All Recognition...', *Middle East MICE & Events*, 30 June 2011.

9. Luis Henrique Rolim Silva, 'The Establishment of the Qatar National Olympic Committee: Building the National Sport Identity', *The International Journal of the History of Sport* 31, 3 (2014), pp. 307–308.

10. Ibid, pp. 308–315.

11. Christopher Clarey, 'Qatar Makes a Move to Be a "Sports Capital"', *The New York Times*, 17 October 1993.

12. Andrew England, 'Qatar Pursues Sporting Goals with African Aid', *Financial Times*, 21 August 2009.

13. Amy Yee, 'Qatar Sets Scene for Film Industry', *Financial Times*, 11 February 2009.

14. Larry Rother, 'Mixing Oil and Hollywood: Tribeca Festival Expands to the Persian Gulf', *The New York Times*, 23 October 2009.

15. Daniel Bardsley, 'Qatar Aims to Build Film Industry', *The National*, 21 August 2009.

16. '"Made in Qatar" Showcase at 2012 Doha Tribeca Film Festival', *AMEInfo.com*, 23 October 2012.

17. Victoria Scott, 'Dfi Postpones New Film Festival after Laying Off Dozens of Employees', *Doha News*, 12 January 2014.

18. Georgina Adam, 'Fireworks as Qatar Steals the Show', *Financial Times*, 29 November 2008.

19. Georgina Adam and Simeon Kerr, 'Saud Bin Mohammed Bin Ali Al-Thani, Collector, 1966–2014', *Financial Times*, 14 November 2014; Rob Sharp, 'Qatar Hero? The Sheikh Who Shook up the Art World', *The Independent*, 29 June 2011.

20. Tahira Yaqoob, 'Can Billion-Dollar Investment Put Qatar on the Cultural Map?', ibid, 20 October 2012; Alexandra Peers, 'Qatar Purchases Cezannes *the Card Players* for More Than $250 Million, Highest Price Ever for a Work of Art', *Vanity Fair*, 2 February 2012.

21. Sharp, 'Qatar Hero? The Sheikh Who Shook up the Art World'.

22. Georgina Adam and Charlotte Burns, 'Qatar Revealed as the World's Biggest Contemporary Art Buyer', *The Art Newspaper*, 7 July 2011.

23. 'Sotheby's Exhibition at Katara', *Gulf Times*, 22 October 2012.

24. 'Qatar's Culture Queen', *The Economist*, 31 May 2012.

25. Jessica Holland, 'Qatari Royal Family Sponsors Damien Hirst Retrospective at Tate Modern', *The National*, 5 April 2012.

26. Certain facets of the RAND-led programme have been successful, but many of the key changes instigated by the firm were opposed by the Qatari public and subsequently reversed. See Gail L Zellman et al, 'Implementation of the K-12 Education Reform in Qatar's Schools', in *RAND Qatar Policy Institute*, Santa Monica, CA: RAND, 2009; Gail L Zellman et al, 'Education for a New Era: Design and Implementation of K-12 Education Reform in Qatar', ibid (2007).

27. Gail L Zellman et al, 'Implementation of the K-12 Education Reform in Qatar's Schools', ibid (2009), p. iii.

28. Ibid.

29. 'Qatar National Vision 2030', Doha, Qatar: General Secreteriat for Development Planning, July 2008.

30. Joy S Moini et al, 'The Reform of Qatar University', Santa Monica, CA: RAND, 2009.

31. Personal Interview: Qatar-Based South American Ambassador, 21 March 2010; 'Frost over the World: HH Sheikha Mozah', *Al Jazeera*, 19 January 2010.

32. Personal Interview: Qatar-Based Focus Group, 25 March 2010.

33. The detailed blog post was posted on 8 December 2012 but removed soon after. The post was taken down, the author noted, because of a certain unhappiness in the Qatar Foundation hierarchy that these figures had been published.

34. 'Comparisons between Education City, Qatar University Spark Controversy', *Doha News*, 17 May 2012; 'Qatar Varsity Students Vent Ire on Twitter', *The Peninsula*, 17 May 2012.

35. Jehanzeb R Cheema, 'The Migrant Effect: An Evaluation of Native Academic Performance in Qatar', *Research in Education* 91 (May 2014).

36. Rabia bin Sabah Al-Kuwari, *'Hal Tuhib Reyaah Al-Tughrayyr Ala Idara Jaamiaah Qatr Al-Wataniyah?'* (Are the Winds of Change Blowing on the Management at Qatar University?)', *Al Sharq*, 1 January 2014; *'Jaamiaah Qatr Thaat Al-Hisaanah* (Qatar University [the University of] Immunity!)', *Al Watan*, 30 April 2014.

37. Abdulrahman al-Qathani, *'Khutabki…Asaaa L'naa* (Your Speech Offended Us)', ibid, 27 November 2013. 'Al-Jaamiah Tutrud 1849 Taalinaan Qatariyan Bikhutah

Tatwyr 2004 (The University Has Expelled 1849 Qatari Students [According to] the 2004 Development Plan)', *Al Arab*, 25 September 2012.

38. For an overview of the successes and failures of diversification in the region, see Martin Hvidt, 'Economic Diversification in GCC Countries: Past Record and Future Trends', *Kuwait Programme on Development, Governance and Globalisation in the Gulf States*, London: London School of Economics, January 2013. Personal Interview: Qatar-Based European Ambassador, 3 March 2010.

39. Amid the wider oil price crash in 2015, there are now rumours that the GCC states may introduce VAT. This would be a positive step, but it is the sort of measure that has often been mooted yet delayed. Moreover, it is far from the root and branch change that the GCC states require to meaningfully transition to a post-hydrocarbon economy. 'GCC Moves Closer to Value-Added Tax', *Arab News*, 8 December 2015.

40. Personal Interview: Qatar-Based European Ambassador, 3 March 2010.

41. 'Qatar Looks East to Singapore as a Model for Security and Economic Development', *Cablegate*, Doha, Qatar: *Wikileaks*, 17 December 2007.

42. Interview with Qatari Elite Policy-Maker; Personal Interview: Qatar-Based European Ambassador, 7 March 2010; Personal Interview: Qatar-Based European Diplomat, 16 March 2010; Personal Interview: Qatari Government Adviser, 22 October 2012; Regan Doherty, 'Qatar Bets on Future as Sports Mecca', Reuters, 7 September 2011.

43. Alan Bairner, 'Political Unionism and Sporting Nationalism', *Identities: Global Studies in Culture and Power* 10, 4 (2003); Tamas Doczi, 'Gold Fever: Sport and National Identity—the Hungarian Case', *International Review for the Sociology of Sport* 47 (February 2011). For a wider examination of this topic, see Alan Tomlinson and Christopher Young, *National Identity and Global Sports Events: Culture, Politics, and Spectacle*, Albany, NY: State University of New York Press, 2006.

44. Geoffrey Caldwell, 'International Sport and National Identity', *International Social Science Journal* XXXIV, 2 (1982).

45. Amara, '2006 Qatar Asian Games: A "Modernization" Project from Above?', p. 503.

46. Personal Interview: Former Ambassador to Qatar, 30 November 2010.

47. Connor Bell, 'Obesity: A Big Problem for Fast Growing Qatar', *Al Jazeera*, 25 July 2012; Haley Sweetland Edwards, 'The Richest, Fattest Nation on Earth (It's Not the United States)', *The Atlantic*, 16 November 2011.

48. Fazeena Saleem, 'HMC to Set Up National Obesity Centre' The Peninsula (Qatar).

49. 'Sports Sector Strategy (2011–2016)', Doha, Qatar: Qatar Olympic Committee, July 2011.

50. Philip G Cerny, 'Paradoxes of the Competition State: The Dynamics of Political Globalization', *Government and Opposition* 32, 2 (April 1997), p. 252.

51. Ibid, p. 251, quoted in Van Ham, 'Place Branding: The State of the Art', p. 6.

52. 'Place Branding: The State of the Art', p. 6.

53. Benedict Anderson, *Imagined Communities*, London: Verso, 2006 (revised edition), pp. 6–7.

54. Sharon J Macdonald, 'Museums, National, Postnational and Transcultural Identities', *Museum and Society* 1, 1 (2003), p. 2.

55. Ibid.

56. Ibid., pp. 2–3

57. This is not meant to be a value judgement but rather a practical assessment. Simply put, Qatar just does not have a long history from which the typical tangible evidence of long-term civilisation remains (for example, in the form of documents, pottery or ancient cities). This discrepancy is all the more stark when compared with Iran, Bahrain (or Dilmun, as part of it was known), Oman, or Saudi Arabia's two holy sites of Mecca and Medina.

58. J E Peterson, 'Qatar and the World: Branding for a Micro-State', *The Middle East Journal* 60 (2006), p. 748.

59. 'Qatar's Culture Queen'

60. TED Talks, 'Sheikha Al Mayassa: Globlizing the Local, Localizing the Global', *TED Talks Director*, YouTube, 8 February 2012.

61. Ralph W. Brauer, 'Boundaries and Frontiers in Medieval Muslim Geography', *Transactions of the American Philosophical Society* 85, 6 (1995), p. 5.

62. The Bidoon issue in Kuwait is complex and cannot be solely reduced to emerging borders, but this factor nevertheless played a central role. In the Qatari context, the Al Murrah tribe has been the source of numerous problems. The Al Murrah traditionally (but today uncomfortably) straddle the border between Qatar and Saudi Arabia. Saudi Arabian Al Murrah were accused of supporting an alleged Saudi Arabian counter coup attempt in Qatar in 1996. Arrested, sentenced to death but never executed, many of the Al Murrah were released in 2010 and flew immediately to Saudi Arabia for an audience with the then king Abdullah. Habib Toumi, 'Saudi Prisoners Release from Qatar Jail Eases Relations', *Gulf News*, 27 May 2010.

63. Papadopoulos and Heslop, 'Country Equity and Country Branding: Problems and Prospects', p. 29.

64. For various examples of this see Field, *The Merchants: The Big Business Families of Saudi Arabia and the Gulf States.*

65. Peterson, 'Qatar and the World: Branding for a Micro-State', p. 746.

66. See Papadopoulos and Heslop, 'Country Equity and Country Branding: Problems and Prospects'.

67. Ibid., p. 304.

68. Ibid.

69. Elizabeth Bains, 'Qatar's Quest for Sporting Glory', *Middle East Economic Digest*, 12 June 2009.

70. Rook Campbell, 'Staging Globalization for National Projects: Global Sport

Markets and Elite Athletic Transnational Labour in Qatar', *International Review for the Sociology of Sport* 46, 45 (July 2010).

71. Amara, '2006 Qatar Asian Games: A "Modernization" Project from Above?', pp. 503–504.

72. Ibid, p. 506.

73. 'Subject: Qatar Establishing a Tourism Niche', *Cablegate*, Doha, Qatar: *Wikileaks*, 26 February 2007.

74. 'Jan Poul De Boer: Qatar Is Not Another Dubai', *Travel Daily News*, 20 October 2007; Benjamin Barthe, 'Gloom Grips Qatar's Arab Riviera after Alcohol Ban', *The Guardian* (21 February 2012).

75. Jessica T Matthews, 'Power Shifts', *Foreign Affairs* 76, 1 (January/February 1997), p. 51.

76. Anne-Marie Slaughter, 'The Real New World Order', Ibid, 5 (1997), p. 192.

77. Olins, 'Branding the Nation—the Historical Context', p. 246.

78. Van Ham, 'Place Branding: The State of the Art', pp. 4 and 6.

79. Melissa Aronczyk, '"Living the Brand": Nationality, Globality and the Identity Strategies of Nation Branding Consultants', *International Journal of Communication* 2 (2008), p. 43.

80. Amara summing up some of the repeated goals of Qatari desirable outcomes for the 2006 Games. Amara, '2006 Qatar Asian Games: A "Modernization" Project from Above?', p. 507.

81. Personal Interview: Former Ambassador to Qatar.

82. Kotler, Haider, and Rein, *Marketing Places: Attracting Investment, Industry, and Tourism to Cities, States, and Nations*, p. 232. Quoted in Kotler and Gertner, 'Country as Brand, Product, and Beyond: A Place Marketing and Brand Management Perspective', p. 257.

9. QATAR AND THE ARAB SPRING: FROM ARBITRATOR TO ACTOR TO ACTIVIST

1. Elizabeth Dickinson, 'Qatar's Role as Peace Broker at Risk in Syria', *The National*, 24 September 2012.

2. Mohamed A El Khawas, 'Tunisia's Jasmine Revolution: Causes and Impact', *Mediterranean Quarterly* 23, 4 (Fall 2012), p. 9.

3. Dina Zayed, 'Feature: Al Jazeera TV Makes Waves with Tunisia Coverage', Reuters, 21 January 2011; Larry Pintak, 'The Al Jazeera Revolution', *Foreign Policy*, 2 February 2011; Aref Hijjawi, 'The Role of Al Jazeera (Arabic) in the Arab Revolts of 2011', *Heinrich Böll Foundation*.

4. Zayed, 'Feature: Al Jazeera TV Makes Waves with Tunisia Coverage'.

5. Nadia Marzouki, 'From People to Citizens in Tunisia', *Middle East Report* 273 (Winter 2014).

6. Ibid.

7. Andrew Hammond, 'Analysis—Egypt's Al Jazeera Bans Channel's Key Role', *Reuters*, 30 June 2011.

8. Hugh Miles, 'The Al Jazeera Effect', *Foreign Policy*, 9 February 2011.

9. Ibid.

10. John Plunkett and Josh Halliday, 'Al-Jazeera's Coverage of Egypt Protests May Hasten Revolution in World News', *The Guardian*, 7 February 2011. For a discussion of al-Jazeera in a theoretical comparison to CNN et al, see Tal Samuel-Azran, 'Al-Jazeera, Qatar, and New Tactics in State-Sponsored Media Diplomacy', *American Behavioral Scientist* 57, 9 (2013).

11. Michael Peel, 'Al Jazeera Coverage Raises Tough Questions', *Financial Times*, 4 January 2013; Alain Gresh, 'Gulf Cools Towards Muslim Brothers', *Le Monde Diplomatique*, November 2012.

12. Sultan al-Qassemi, 'Morsi's Win Is Al Jazeera's Loss', *Al Monitor*, 1 July 2012.

13. Ibid.

14. Although caution should be exercised when citing self-referential articles or those purely from a media organisations potentially hostile to Al Jazeera's agenda, the network's pro-Brotherhood bias is widely noted. Ahmed Magdy Youssef, 'On Al Jazeera's Lopsided Coverage of Egypt', *Open Democracy*, 2 August 2013; Ayman Sharaf, 'Al Jazeera Staff Resign after "Biased" Egypt Coverage', *GulfNews.com*, 8 July 2013; 'Must Do Better', *The Economist*, 12 January 2013; Gregg Carlstrom, 'Why Egypt Hates Al Jazeera', *Foreign Policy*, 19 February 2014; Mohammed Abdel Rahman, 'Egypt: Al Jazeera's Cameras Blind to Revolutionaries', *Al Akhbar*, 6 December 2012.

15. Samuel-Azran, 'Al-Jazeera, Qatar, and New Tactics in State-Sponsored Media Diplomacy'.

16. Hijjawi, 'The Role of Al Jazeera (Arabic) in the Arab Revolts of 2011'.

17. Ibid, p. 70.

18. Ibid, pp. 70–71. For the single best encapsulation of the evolving mind-set prevalent within Al Jazeera and the Arab media scene more widely, see Pintak, *The New Arab Journalist: Mission and Identity in a Time of Turmoil*. The introduction and chapters 4 ('Islam, nationalism and the media') and 6 ('Arab journalism in context') are particularly relevant to this discussion.

19. 'Egypt Crisis: Al Jazeera Journalists Arrested in Cairo', BBC News, 30 December 2013.

20. To grasp the absurdity of the trial, the evidence, and the conviction, see Patrick Kingsley, 'Six Flaws in the Case against Three Jailed Al-Jazeera Journalists', *The Guardian*, 24 June 2014; Mohammed Salem, 'What Egypt Lost in the Al Jazeera Trial', *Al Monitor*, 26 August 2014.

21. AFP, 'Egypt's President Sisi "Regrets" Jailing Al-Jazeera Journalists', *The Daily Telegraph*, 7 July 2014.

22. 'Must Do Better'.

23. For an article summing up Qatar's actions in Libya and the reasons behind it see David B Roberts, 'Behind Qatar's Intervention in Libya', *Foreign Affairs*, 28 September 2011.

24. Ulrichsen, *Qatar and the Arab Spring*, p. 124.

25. Peter Cole and Umar Khan, 'The Fall of Tripoli: Part 1', in *The Libyan Revolution and Its Aftermath*, ed. Peter Cole and Brian McQuinn, London: Hurst & Co, 2015, p. 44.

26. Qatar has twelve Mirage jets in total. However, as a rule with such high-end machinery there is almost never a time when all of them are working at the same time. Add to this Qatar's poor reputation in terms of repair and continual main-tenance of its military equipment, and the state's remaining fighter jet capacity to protect the homeland during the Libyan campaign was negligible.

27. It should be noted that Qatari troops were involved in the Gulf War in a set-piece battle under US supervision, though its air force has never undertaken such an action. Indeed, the novelty of the action was illustrated by the fact that Qatari pilots had never practiced air-to-air refuelling until they had to do so *en route* to bases in the Mediterranean.

28. Coker, Dagher, and Levinson, 'Tiny Kingdom's Huge Role in Libya Draws Concern'.

29. The Associated Press, 'Qatar Doubles Aid to Egypt', *The New York Times*, 8 January 2013.

30. 'Qatar Country Report', *EIU Country Report*, London: Economist Intelligence Unit, April 2013.

31. 'Qatar Gas Swap Deal with Egypt Collapses', *Gulf States Newsletter*, September 2013.

32. Oleg Vukmanovic, 'Qatar's LNG Gift to Egypt to Find Foreign Firms', Reuters, 12 July 2013.

33. '*Raiis Wuzara Qatr: Misr Akbar Min an Tishtryha Wa Lam Naard Taajyr Al-Ahramaat Aw Al Qanaat (*Qatar's Prime Minister: Egypt Is Bigger Than We Could Afford [Sic]. We Did Not [Try to] Hire the Pyramids or the [Suez] Channel)', *Al Misry Al Youm*, 27 March 2013; Mohamed Hesham Abey, '*Misr: Istithmaaraat Qatariyah Tulamis Qanaat Al Suez* (Egypt: Qatari Investment Touches the Suez Canal)', *As Safir*, 18 January 2013; 'Qatar Country Report', *EIU Country Report*, London: Economist Intelligence Unit, July 2013; Dana El Baltaji, 'Qatar Bankrolls Muslim Brothers as U.A.E. Jails Them', Bloomberg, 11 December 2012; AbdulRahman Al Rashed, '*Min Harrods Ila Al-Ahramaat!* (from Harrods to the Pyramids!)', *Al Sharq Al Awsat*, 2 March 2013.

34. Maggie Fick, 'Egypt Summons Qatar's Chargé D'affaires Over Egyptian Cleric', Reuters, 4 February 2014.

35. An Nahda is often elided to Ennahda. Kristina Kausch, '"Foreign Funding" in Post-Revolution Tunisia', 2013.

36. 'Country Report: Tunisia', *Country Report*, London: Economist Intelligence Unit,

October 2011; 'Country Report: Tunisia', *Country Report*, London: Economist Intelligence Unit, April 2012.

37. Jihen Laghmari, 'Qatar Giving Tunisia $1bn Loan, May Provide Jobs', Bloomberg, 26 April 2012, and 'La chaîne tunisienne privée Attounissia va être rachetée par un groupe du Qatar', *Kapitalis*.

38. Guido Steinberg, 'Qatar and the Arab Spring', German Institute for International and Security Affairs, SWP Berlin, February 2012, p. 6.

39. Coker, Dagher, and Levinson, 'Tiny Kingdom's Huge Role in Libya Draws Concern'.

40. Kausch, '"Foreign Funding" in Post-Revolution Tunisia'.

41. 'Rachid Ghannouchi', *The Independent*, 9 October 2012.

42. Sana Ajmi, 'Rached Ghannouchi Visits Qatar', All Africa News [BBC Monitoring], 5 January 2012.

43. 'Tunisia Reportedly Recalls Its Ambassador in Qatar after TV Programme', Zeitouna [BBC Monitoring], 9 March 2001.

44. 'Qatar Refinery Play Highlights Tunisian Agenda', *Gulf States Newsletter* 36, 924, May 2012.

45. Cole and Khan, 'The Fall of Tripoli: Part 1', p. 68.

46. Qatar and Libya Open a New Geopolitical Axis in North Africa', *Gulf States Newsletter* 35, 907, 2 September 2011; Cole and Khan, 'The Fall of Tripoli: Part 1', p. 70–72.

47. Peter Beaumont, 'Qatar Accused of Interfering in Libyan Affairs', *The Guardian*, 4 October 2011. 'Pygmy with the Punch of a Giant'; Tony Karon, 'Does Qatar Share the West's Agenda in Libya', *Time*, 5 October 2011.

48. Ulrichsen, *Qatar and the Arab Spring*, p. 78.

49. Al Monitor, 'Islamists Suffer Major Defeat in Libya's Early Election Results', *Al Monitor*, 12 October 2012. See 'Popular Distrust May Derail Al-Thani's North African Ambitions', *Gulf States Newsletter* (July 2012) for a wider look at this issue.

50. See Roberts, 'Qatar and the Muslim Brotherhood: Pragmatism or Preference?'.

51. Ahmed Azem, 'Qatar's Ties with the Muslim Brotherhood Affect Entire Region', *The National*, 18 May 2012.

52. Ian Black, 'Al Jazeera Boss Wadah Khanfar Steps Down to Be Replaced by Qatari Royal', *The Guardian*, 20 September 2011; Layla Al-Shoumari, 'Muslim Brotherhood Paves Way for Qatar's Ascent', *Al Akhbar*, 12 April 2013.

53. Marc Lynch, 'Al Jazeera Challenges: Pass the Salt', *Abu Aardvark Blog*, 29 June 2007; Al-Shoumari, 'Muslim Brotherhood Paves Way for Qatar's Ascent'.

54. Salah Awudah Al Din, 'Sudanese Writer Accuses Al Jazeera of Selectivity in Covering Arab Revolutions', Al Sahafah [BBC Monitoring], 17 March 2011 [18 March 2011]; Ian Black, 'Qatar's Youthful New Ruler Signals Continuity for Maverick Gulf State', *The Guardian*, 27 June 2013.

55. Roberts, 'Qatar and the Muslim Brotherhood: Pragmatism or Preference?', p. 87.

56. The extent of the relationship between the ruling families became clearer when a trove of emails of Assad and his wife were leaked to *The Guardian* newspaper. See, for example, Alastair Macdonald, 'Friendship Soured: How Assads "Laughed" at Ally', Reuters, 16 March 2012.

57. 'President Al-Assad Receives Letter from Emir of Qatar Affirming His Country's Support for Syrian Leadership's Effort to Foil Attempts at Undermining Syria's Security and Stability', *Tishreen*, 3 March 2011.

58. For a comprehensive explanation of Qatar's early involvement in Syria, see Ulrichsen, *Qatar and the Arab Spring*, pp. 131–133.

59. 'Qatari Ambassador Closes Embassy, Leaves Damascus', *France 24*, 18 July 2011; Ian Black, 'Qatar Breaks Arab Ranks over Syria', *The Guardian*, 21 July 2011.

60. Roula Khalaf and Abigail Fielding-Smith, 'How Qatar Seized Control of the Syrian Revolution', *Financial Times*, 17 May 2013.

61. Emile Hokayem, 'Syria's Uprising and the Fracturing of the Levant', Abingdon: Routledge for the International Institute for Strategic Studies, 2013. See Chapter 2 in particular, on the rise of the opposition. Phil Sands, 'GCC Rift Could Trigger New Power Struggle in Syrian Opposition', *The National*, 10 March 2014.

62. 'Qatar Trumps Saudi Arabia on Syrian Opposition Leader', *Al Monitor*, 21 March 2013; Mohammed Ballout, 'Syrian Opposition Attempts Consolidation', ibid, 11 May 2013.

63. Hassan Hassan, 'Saudis Overtaking Qatar in Sponsoring Syrian Rebels', *The National*, 15 May 2013; Ballout, 'Syrian Opposition Attempts Consolidation'.

64. Babak Dehghanpisheh, 'Syrian Opposition Group Strike Reorganization Deal', *The Washington Post*, 11 November 2012.

65. Amena Bakr, 'In Qatar Desert, Syrian Opposition Mourns Fallen Commander', Reuters, 21 November 2013; 'Qatar Pares Support for Islamists but Careful to Preserve Ties', Reuters, 2 November 2014; Khalaf and Fielding-Smith, 'How Qatar Seized Control of the Syrian Revolution'; Jeffry White, 'Rebels Worth Supporting: Syria's Harakat Hazm', 28 April 2014; Suhaib Anjarini, 'Harakat Hazm: America's New Favorite Jihadist Group', *Al Akhbar*, 22 May 2014.

66. Liz Sly, 'US-Backed Syria Rebels Routed by Fighters Linked to Al Qaeda', *Washington Post*, 2 November 2014.

67. Aron Lund, 'Syria's Ahrar Al-Sham Leadership Wiped out in Bombing', 9 September 2014.

68. 'Competition among Islamists', *The Economist*, 18 July 2013; 'Syria's Ahrar Al-Sham Leadership Wiped out in Bombing'; Michael Doran, William McCants, and Clint Watts, 'The Good and Bad of Ahrar Al-Sham', *Foreign Affairs*, 23 January 2014.

69. Although there are concerns that some of these articles alleging close Qatari relations with extreme groups were prompted by lobbying groups seeking to tarnish Qatar's record, there are a reasonable amount of concerns voiced overall to warrant at least discussing the issues. Kirkpatrick, 'Qatar's Support of Islamists

Alienates Allies Near and Far'; Fehim Tastekin, 'Saudi Arabia and Qatar Vie for Influence in Syria', *Al Monitor*, 17 April 2013. For one of the better articles in *The Daily Telegraph*, see: David Blair and Richard Spencer, 'How Qatar Is Funding the Rise of Islamist Extremists', *The Daily Telegraph*, 20 September 2014; Taimur Khan, 'Hostage Release Highlights Two-Sides of Qatar's Foreign Policy', *The National*, 26 August 2014.

70. 'Analysis: Syria's Insurgent Landscape', IHS Aerospace, Defence, & Security, September 2013; Ruth Sherlock, 'Inside Jabhat Al Nusra—the Most Extreme Wing of Syria's Struggle', *The Daily Telegraph*, 2 December 2012.

71. 'Analysis: Syria's Insurgent Landscape'.

72. 'Jabhat Al Nusra', Quilliam Foundation; 'Jabhat Al Nusra', *Mapping Militant Organizations*, Stanford University.

73. 'Jabhat Al Nusra'; Sarah Birke, 'How Al-Qaeda Changed the Syrian War', *The New York Review of Books (Blog)*; Raffaello Pantucci, 'The Al-Nusra Front "Merger": Underscoring the Growing Regionalisation of Al-Qa'ida', 15 April 2013.

74. Sherlock, 'Inside Jabhat Al Nusra—the Most Extreme Wing of Syria's Struggle'; Pantucci, 'The Al-Nusra Front "Merger": Underscoring the Growing Regionalisation of Al-Qa'ida'; Birke, 'How Al-Qaeda Changed the Syrian War'.

75. 'How Al-Qaeda Changed the Syrian War'.

76. Charles Lister, 'The "Real" Jabhat Al-Nusra Appears to Be Emerging', *The Huffington Post*, 8 July 2014.

77. Mohammed Ballout, 'How the Maaloula Nuns Were Freed', *Al Monitor*, 11 March 2014; 'Qatari Mediation Succeeds in Releasing Maaloula Nuns', *Qatar Ministry of Foreign Affairs*, 1 September 2014.

78. Goldman and DeYoung, 'Qatar Played Now-Familiar Role in Helping to Broker U.S. Hostage's Release'.

79. Hashem Osserian, 'Isis, Nusra Front Hand Demands to Qatari Mediators', *Daily Star*, 6 September 2014; Jack Moore, 'Lebanon: Nusra Front Release Army Soldier after Qatar Negotiations', *International Business Times*, 1 October 2014; 'Freed Lebanese Hostages Arrive in Beirut', *Al Jazeera*, 20 October 2013.

80. AFP, 'Qatar Says It Mediated Release of Fiji Peacekeepers', *Daily Star*, 12 September 2014.

81. 'Al-Jazeera Interview with Nusra Leader Draws Criticism', *Middle East Online*, 28 May 2015.

82. 'Dr Khalid Bin Mohammed Al Attiyah: Qatari Foreign Policy Today: Challenges and Opportunities', *Princeton University, YouTube.com*, 3 October 2014, c.1:03.

83. Peter Baker, 'U.S. Says It Told Qatar Not to Pay a Ransom', *The New York Times*, 25 August 2014; 'Report: UN Had Qatar Pay Off Al-Qaida Fighters for Release of Fiji Peacekeepers', *Haaretz*, 11 October 2014.

84. This argument is referred to in various opinion pieces and articles including Francine Kiefer, 'Qatar: The Small Arab Monarchy with the Loud Democratic

Voice', *The Christian Science Monitor*, 27 May 2011; Justin Gengler, 'Qatar's Ambivalent Democratization', *Foreign Policy*, 1 November 2011.

85. This happened in 1991, and more recently Dr Ali Al Kuwari edited a book in Qatar on this topic: Ali Khalifah Al Kuwari, ed. *Al Shaab Yureed Al-Islah Fee Qatar Aydan [the People Want Reform in Qatar Too]*, Beirut: The Knoweldge Forum, 2012. Dr Al Kuwari has written extensively on this topic, including articles such as '*Haalah Al Dimokratiyah Fee Qatr* [the State of Democracy in Qatar]'.

86. Gengler, 'Qatar's Ambivalent Democratization'. For more detail see 'The Political Costs of Qatar's Western Orientation', *Middle East Policy* XIX, 4 (Winter 2012).

87. David B Roberts, 'News from Qatar Protest', *TheGulfBlog.com*, 16 March 2011. Many such Facebook pages are simply individuals from around the MENA region calling for revolution in hope rather than in expectation 'The 2011 Qatar Revolution: Revolution against Hamad Bin Khalifah and Al Jazeera', *Facebook*— https://www.facebook.com/the.Qatar.revolution.2011/timeline.

88. The increasing backlash against Qatar that gathered intensity throughout 2014 will be discussed later on.

89. GSN, 'Qatar and Libya Open a New Geopolitical Axis in North Africa'.

90. Field, 'Tree of the Al Attiyah'; 'Tree of the Al Thani', *Arabian Charts* (v.10).

91. This relationship is frequently alluded to, including by Mehran Kamrava in his latest book on Qatar.

92. Louay Bahry, 'Qatar: Democratic Reforms and Global Status', *Governance in the Middle East and North Africa*, ed. Abbas Kadhim, New York: Routledge, 2013, p. 258.

93. Shibley Telhami, 'Behind the Abdication of Qatar's Emir', Reuters, 26 June 2013; Michael Stephens, 'Shuttle Diplomacy: Qatar Playing Politics in Palestine', *Open Democracy*, 29 October 2012.

94. Qatar does not have an organisation such as the CIA or MI6. The closest equivalent that it possesses are small elements of the military intelligence apparatus that sporadically operate internationally on a case-by-case basis.

95. Lisa Anderson, 'Demystifying the Arab Spring', *Foreign Affairs* 90, 3 (May–June 2011).

96. Omar Ashour, 'Libyan Islamists Unpacked', *Policy Briefing*, Brookings Doha Center, May 2012, p. 4; Frédéric Pons, 'Tripoli Sous La Loi Des "Katibas"', *Valeurs Actuelles*, 12 January 2012.

97. Cole and Khan, 'The Fall of Tripoli: Part 1', p. 73.

98. I received dozens of phone-calls about this matter in early 2011 as the rumour of such a perfect 'answer' swept around journalists in the region.

99. Roula Khalaf and Simeon Kerr, 'Sheikha Moza, Matriarch of the Modern Gulf', *Financial Times*, 28 June 2013.

100. For a wider explanation of this issue as it pertains to Qatar, see one of the central arguments running through Kamrava, *Qatar: Small State, Big Politics*, pp. 10–11.

101. Roula Khalaf, 'Qatar Steps in to Fill Regional Void', *Financial Times*, 30 November 2011.

102. Rania Abouzeid, 'Syria's Secular and Islamist Rebels: Who Are the Saudis and the Qataris Arming?', *Time*, 18 September 2012; 'Saudi Arabia and Qatar Fight for Influence', *Huffington Post*, 22 August 2013.

103. Roberts, 'Qatari Mediation', p. 21; Kamrava, 'Mediation and Qatari Foreign Policy', p. 543.

104. David B Ottaway, 'The Saudi-Qatari Clash over Syria', *The National Interest*, 2 July 2013; Khaled Yacoub Oweis, 'Saudi-Qatari Rivalry Divides Syrian Opposition', Reuters, 15 January 2014.

105. This kind of logic is explored from the Saudi Arabian perspective in Banedetta Berti and Yoel Guzansky, 'The Syrian Crisis and the Saudi-Iranian Rivalry', *Foreign Policy Research Institute*, October 2012.

106. Robert O Keohane, 'Reciprocity in International Relations', *International Organization* 40, 1 (Winter 1986), p. 20.

107. For discussion on the wider aspects of the Arab Spring and the increase in individual agency, see Andreas Krieg, 'Individual Security and Small State Security', *Gulf Research Centre*, Cambridge, UK, July 2014.

108. Keohane, 'Reciprocity in International Relations', p. 25.

109. Ibid., p. 21.

110. In France, Qatar enjoys a tax break on property acquisition and sales, saving institutional investors and Qatari individuals alike hundreds of millions of Euros in tax. Lionel Laurent, 'Special Report—in France, a Tax-Free Property Empire', Reuters, 8 September 2013; Suggestions as to potential tax breaks in a 'new' Egypt centred around commercial investments and raising the limits allowed by foreigners to invest; Mohammed Ammar, '*Hilal: 'Diar' Tashtiry 30 Miliyoon Metr Marbaa Lil'istithmaar Al Aaaqaary* [Hilal: 'Diar' to Buy 30 Million Square Metres of Real Estate [as] Investment]', *Al Arab*, 18 January 2013; Mohammed Hisham Abeih, 'Qatar to Invest in Suez Canal', *Al Monitor*, 19 January 2013.

111. 'Egypt Country Report', *Country Report*, London: Economist Intelligence Unit, May 2013, p. 20.

112. 'Egypt Country Report', *Country Report*, London: Economist Intelligence Unit, May 2013, p. 20.

113. 'Egyptian Dcm: Cairo to Thwart Any Qatari Initiative', *Wikileaks*, 28 January 2010. Omar Kaddour, 'Is There a Moderate Syrian Opposition?', *Al Monitor*, 23 September 2014.

114. Aron Lund, 'The Politics of the Islamic Front, Part 1: Structure and Support', *Carnegie Endowment for International Peace*, 14 January 2014.

115. For the most comprehensive report summarising Qatar's nefarious links see Dickinson, 'The Case against Qatar'.

116. 'Qatar's Foreign Policy Focuses on Promoting Communication: FM', *Gulf Times*, 17 November 2014.

117. 'Rebels V Rebels', *The Economist*, 21 November 2013; Deborah Amos, 'Who Are the Syrian Rebels?', *NPR*, 9 September 2013.

118. '*Lakin Haqqaan: Man Hiya Al Maaridah Al Souriyah Al Maatadila?* [But Really: Who Is the Moderate Syrian Opposition?]', *Al Hayat*, 21 September 2014.

10. QATAR UNDER EMIR TAMIM BIN HAMAD

1. Elizabeth Dickinson, 'Qatar Succession: Seven Minutes When Power Changed Hands', *The National*, 26 June 2013; Roula Khalaf, 'Abdication of Qatar' Ruler Avoids Risky Elections', *Financial Times*, 25 June 2013.

2. Kamal Fayad, 'Will Qatar's Emir Abdicate in August?', *Al Monitor*, 11 June 2013.

3. Khalaf, 'Abdication of Qatar' Ruler Avoids Risky Elections'; 'All in the Family: The Changing of the Guard in Qatar', *The Institute for National Security Studies*, 2 July 2013.

4. 'Qatar Country Report', p. 24.

5. 'Abdication of Qatar's Ruler Avoids Risky Elections.'

6. 'Qatar Country Report', p. 24.

7. Ibid.

8. David Kirkpatrick, 'Army Ousts Egypt's President; Morsi Is Taken into Military Custody', *The New York Times* 3 July 2013.

9. Sultan al-Qassemi, 'Qatar's Annus Horribilis', *Al Monitor*, 26 June 2014.

10. For one of the better summaries of this issue from a Qatar-expert see Jamal D Abdullah, '*Azmah Suhab Al Sufara Min Al Dawah: Al Bwaaath Wa Al Tduayaat* [Crisis Withdrawal of Ambassadors from Doha: Motives and Implications]', *Al Jazeera Centre for Studies*, 24 March 2014.

11. Simeon Kerr, 'Qatar Prepares for Sanctions If Brotherhood Dispute Escalates', *Financial Times*, 14 March 2014.

12. 'Saudi and UAE Border in Dispute over ID Cards', Reuters, 23 August 2009.

13. 'Qatar Risks Major Economic Fallout from Gulf Dispute', *Oxford Analytica Daily Brief*, 25 March 2014.

14. 'Qatar Pledges to End Naturalisation of GCC Citizens: Report', *GulfNews.com*, 16 August 2014; Hassan Hassan, 'Making Qatar an Offer It Can't Refuse', *Foreign Policy*, 22 April 2014.

15. There is some discrepancy between those who lived in Qatar and then left (Telima, Ghoneim, Zobaa) and the others, who lived predominantly in Turkey and could not return to Qatar.

16. 'The Brotherhood Disapora', *MadaMasr*, 30 September 2014; Amany Maged, 'Shown the Red Card', *Al Ahram Weekly*, 17 September 2014; Patrick Kingsley, 'Qatar Asks Senior Muslim Brotherhood Leaders to Leave Country', *The Guardian*, 13 September 2014; Louise Loveluck, 'Qatar Asks Muslim Brotherhood Members to Leave Country', *The Daily Telegraph*, 13 September 2014.

17. 'Amr Darrag: Number of Fjp, Muslim Brotherhood Leaders Leave Qatar', *IkhwanWeb*, 13 September 2014.

18. 'The Brotherhood Disapora'.

19. See the comments of Khaled Batarfi in 'Putting the GCC House in Order', *Inside Story: Al Jazeera*, 8 December 2014.

20. AbdulMajid Qatub, '*Asim Abdulmajid: 28 Nowfember Sayushaahid Tahwilaan Nuwaayan Fee Huwiya Al Thawra Al Misriyah* [Asim Abdulmajid: 28 November Will See a Qualitative Shift in the Identity of the Egyptian Revolution]', *Al Sharq*, 16 November 2014.

21. Hassan Hussein, '*Al Watan' Tanashr Tufaseel Tafteesh Safeer Qatr Fee Mataar Al Qaahirah: Rafad Khalaa Al Hithaa* ['Al Watan' Publishes Details of the Inspection of the Qatari Ambassador at Cairo Airport: Refused to Take Off His Shoes]', *El Watan News*, 1 December 2014.

22. Thanks to Kristian Ulrichsen for pointing out this interesting snippet. Ahmed Abdullah, '*Mustanad Yuthbt Husool Rashid Mohammed Rashid Ala Al Jinsiyah Al Qatariyah (Soorah)* [Proof That Rashid Mohammed Rashid Has Obtained Qatari Nationality (Picture)]', *Al Misry Al Youm*, 24 October 2014.

23. For an excellent article on the utility of Qatar for the Muslim Brotherhood, see Abigail Hauslohner, 'Egypt's Muslim Brotherhood Finds Havens Abroad', *Washington Post*, 6 November 2013.

24. Ashraf Abd Al Hameed, 'Egypt Rejects Qatari Mediation to Reconcile with Brotherhood', *Al Arabiyya*, 9 August 2015.

25. 'The Dark Side of Migration', London: Amnesty International, 2013; 'Building a Better World Cup', Human Rights Watch, 12 June 2012.

26. Richard Morin, 'Indentured Servitude in the Persian Gulf', *The New York Times*, 12 April 2013.

27. Teller, 'Has Wealth Made Qatar Happy?'

28. 'Al Mahmoud Reviews Human Rights Situation in Qatar', *National Human Rights Committee*, 9 February 2010; Mohammed Saeed M El Tayeb, 'The Qatari National Human Rights Committee: A Search for Evaluation', *Asia Pacific Human Rights Information Centre* 47, March 2007; 'Degree Law No. (38) of 2002 on the Setting up of the National Human Rights Committee', *National Human Rights Committee*.

29. Rob Hughes, 'Bin Hammam Is Latest Fifa Official to Go, but Cloud Remains', *The New York Times*, 24 July 2011.

30. Jonathan Calvert and Heidi Blake, 'Plot to buy the World Cup', *The Sunday Times*, 1 June 2014.

31. The briefest reading of the *Sunday Times* and *The Times* archives will highlight the tone of their coverage of the Qatar 2022 World Cup.

32. David Bond, 'England 2018 World Cup Bid Viewed as "Low Risk"', BBC Sport, 16 November 2010.

33. Tariq Panja, 'Qatar Is Only "High Risk" Candidate among Nine Bidders to Host World Cup', Bloomberg, 18 November 2010.

34. Amena Bakr, 'Defiant Al Jazeera Faces Conservative Backlash after Arab Spring', Reuters, 2 July 2014.

35. 'Iraq Bans Al-Jazeera and Nine Other TV Channels over "Sectarian Bias"', *The Guardian*, 29 April 2013; 'Egypt State Council Bans Al Jazeera, Rabaa on Nilesat', *Ahram Online*, 3 September 2014.

36. See for example: Jack Keane and Daniella Pletka, 'An American-Led Coalition Can Defeat Isis', *The Wall Street Journal*, 24 August 2014; Kirkpatrick, 'Qatar's Support of Islamists Alienates Allies Near and Far'; 'Pro-Israel Groups to Rally against Qatar's Financing of Terror', *Haaretz*, 18 September 2014; Ron Prosor, 'Club Med for Terrorists', *The New York Times*, 24 August 2014.

37. Glenn Greenwald, 'How Former Treasury Officials and the UAE Are Manipulating American Journalists', *The Intercept*, 25 September 2014. See also Rori Donaghy, 'UAE and Qatar: Public Relations Warfare', *Middle East Eye*, 30 October 2014.

38. 'Qatar Build-Up', *Private Eye*, 1379, 14–27 November 2014.

39. I examined this curious issue here: David B Roberts, 'Is Qatar Sponsoring Al Qa'ida in Mali', *RUSI*, 7 February 2013.

40. 'Qatar's Flowering Relationship with Paris', *Financial Times*, 1 November 2012.

41. Gunther Lachmann, Tim Rohn, and Daniel Wetzel, 'Wie Katars Reichtum Den Terrorverdacht Überstrahlt', *Die Welt*, 17 September 2014.

42. 'Steve Barclay: Ministers Must Not Pursue Trade with Qatar at Any Price', *The Daily Telegraph*, 2 November 2014.

43. Marc Waddington, 'Fears Liverpool Firms' Qatar World Cup Payments Funding Isis Terror', *Liverpool Echo*, 29 October 2014.

44. Robert Burns and Adam Schreck, 'Tiny Qatar Plays Outsized Role in U.S. War Strategy', *Military Times*, 15 September 2014; Julian Pecquet, 'Congress Goes after "Frenemies" Turkey, Qatar', *Al Monitor*, 9 September 2014.

45. Rajiv Chandrasekaran, 'In the UAE, the United States Has a Quiet, Potent Ally Nicknamed "Little Sparta"', *Washington Post*, 9 November 2014.

46. 'HH the Emir Patronizes Opening of Advisory Council's 43rd Ordinary Session', *QNA*, 11 November 2014.

47. 'Emir Sheikh Tamim's New Appointments', *Gulf States Newsletter*, 950, 4 July 2013; 'HH the Emir Patronizes Opening of Advisory Council's 43rd Ordinary Session'.

48. 'New Budget to Focus on Efficiency in Spending', *Gulf Times*, 4 November 2015.

49. 'HH the Emir Inaugurates Advisory Council 44th Ordinary Session', *Qatar News Agency*, 3 November 2015.

50. 'New Budget to Focus on Efficiency in Spending'.

51. Satish Kanady, 'Only 12,000 Qataris Working in Private Sector: IMF', *The Peninsula*, 6 September 2015.

52. 'Qatar Economic Outlook 2015–2017', Doha: Ministry of Development Plainning and Statistics, June 2015, p. 27.

53. 'Gulf States Agree to Push Value-Added Tax Project with Oil Low', *Al Arabiyya*, 10 May 2015.

54. 'Qatar Economic Outlook 2012–2013 Update', in *Qatar Economic Outlook*, Doha, Qatar: General Secreteriat for Development Planning, 2012, pp. 14–15.

55. AFP, 'Qatar Exports Plunge over 40 Pct in Year', *France 24*, 30 August 2015.

56. Nicolas Parasie, 'Qatar Risks Budget Deficit in 2016 Due to Low Oil Prices, IMF Says', *The Wall Street Journal* 2 April 2015.

57. Simeon Kerr, 'World Cup Woes Add to Qatar Business Jitters', *Financial Times*, 28 June 2015.

58. 'Annual Energy Outlook 2015 with Projections to 2040', US Energy Information Administration, April 2015; Gregori Kantchev, 'Oil Price Forecast to Stay Below $60 through Next Year', *Wall Street Journal*, 23 September 2015.

59. For a more in-depth examination of the future of Qatar's energy outlook see David B Roberts, 'Qatar Coming to Grips with New Realities of Global Energy Markets', in *Issue Paper*, Washington DC: Arab Gulf States Institute Washington, 13 November 2015.

60. David Ledesma, 'The Future of Australian LNG Exports', The Oxford Institute for Energy Studies, September 2014, p. 17.

61. Christine Buurma and Chou Hui Hong, 'U.S. Gas Boom Turns Global as LNG Exports to Shake up Market', Bloomberg, 1 October 2014. For the most detailed report focusing on the effect on Qatar of the US shale gas revolution, see Bassam Fattouh, Howard V Rogers, and Peter Stewart, 'The US Shale Gas Revolutions and Its Impact on Qatar's Position in Gas Markets', Center on Global Energy Policy, Columbia University, March 2015.

62. Alexis Crow, 'Falling Oil Prices Reveal America's Fracking Trap—and Saudi Arabia's Continued Energy Dominance', *Huffington Post*, 1 April 2015; Howard V Rogers, 'The Impact of Lower Gas and Oil Prices on Global Gas and LNG Markets', The Oxford Institute for Energy Studies, July 2015, p. 47.

63. Ronke Luke, 'Which East African Nation Will Win the LNG Race?', OilPrice.com, 27 May 2015; Allison Good, 'Israel's Big Moment: Sealing Gas Deals with Jordan and Egypt', *The National Interest*, 29 May 2015; Crispian Balmer and Stephen Jewkes, 'Update 2—Italy's ENI Makes Mega Gas Discovery Off Egyptian Coast', Reuters, 30 August 2015; 'Russian LNG: A Five Year Window and It's Closing', *Natural Gas Europe* (20 April 2015); Jack Farchy, 'Gazprom Considers Shelving Vladivostok LNG Project', *Financial Times*, 20 October 2014.

64. 'Al'amir: Qatar La Tubna Doon Al Shabab. Wa Al Mawatnah Maswwlyah [the Emir: Qatar Cannot Be Built without [Its] Youth and Citizenship responsibility', *Al Raya*, 4 November 2015.

65. *The Military Balance 2014*, p. 302.

66. As directly noted by Hamad bin Khalifah in his interview with the *Financial Times*. Martin Dickson and Roula Khalaf, 'Interview Transcript: Qatar's Sheikh Hamad', *Financial Times*, 24 October 2010.

67. *The Military Balance 2014*, p. 353

68. 'Qatar Goes on Spending Spree', IHS Jane's 360, 7 May 2014.

69. Ibid.

70. Rajiv Chandrasekaran, 'Airstrikes in Syria against Islamic State Bring Together Persian Gulf Nations at Odds', *Washington Post* 23 September 2014; Ali Unal, 'Qatar Deploys Warplanes to Turkish Air Base', *Daily Sabah* 4 September 2015; Jason Szep, 'Qatar, a Partner in U.S. Airstrikes, Says Syrian Regime Main Problem', Reuters, 4 September 2014.

71. 'UAE, Kuwait, Bahrain, Qatar, Jordan Deploy Warplanes against Houthis', *Al Arabiyya*, 26 March 2015; Khaled Abdullah, 'Qatar Sends 1,000 Ground Troops to Yemen Conflict: Al Jazeera', Reuters, 7 September 2015.

72. Tony Paterson, 'German Soldiers "Stranded" in Afghanistan as More Planes Breakdown', *The Daily Telegraph*, 1 October 2014; 'David Cameron Praises C17 Plane Just Moments before It Breaks Down', Ibid, 14 January 2013.

73. 'Saudis in Border Deal with Qatar', BBC News, 17 December 2008.

11. SECURING THE GLOBAL AMBITIONS OF A CITY STATE

1. Eric Hobsbawm and Terence Ranger, *The Invention of Tradition*, Cambridge: Cambridge University Press, 2010, pp. 4–5.

2. Personal Correspondence: Patrick Flaherty, Sovereign Wealth Fund Researcher.

3. Virginie Robert, 'La France Pour Une Relation Plus "Normale" Avec Le Qatar', *Les Echos*, 21 June 2013; Georges Malbrunot, 'France-Qatar: Refroidissement Durant La Visite De François Hollande', *Le Figaro*, 3 July 2013.

4. Qatar has hired a London-based PR agency to boost the capacity within Doha to counter the wider array of pernicious news stories ranged against the state. But the results as yet are meagre. Rory Jones, 'Qatar Moves to Craft a New Global Image', *Wall Street Journal*, 8 July 2015.

BIBLIOGRAPHY

'2 Million Dollars Given to Mali as Grant in Aid', *Doha QNA*, 9 March 1976, C2. FBIS-MEA-76–047.

'The 100 Largest Losses 1972–2001', Marsh Risk Consulting Practice, February 2003.

'The 2011 Qatar Revolution: Revolution against Hamad Bin Khalifah and Al Jazeera', *Facebook*, https://www.facebook.com/the.Qatar.revolution.2011/timeline '*Abdal-majid Shiki: Qatar Ra'at Mafawidaat Istqlal Al-Jazair* (Abdalmajid Shiki: Qatar Sponsored Algeria's Independence Negotiations)', *Al Arab*, 6 July 2008.

Abdel Rahman, Mohammed, 'Egypt: Al Jazeera's Cameras Blind to Revolutionaries', *Al Akhbar*, 6 December 2012, http://english.al-akhbar.com/node/14266.

Abdulla, Yousof Ibrahim, *A Study of Qatari-British Relations, 1914–1945*, Doha: Orient Publishing & Translation, 1981.

Abdullah, Ahmed, '*Mustanad Yuthbt Husool Rashid Mohammed Rashid Ala Al Jinsiyah Al Qatariyah (Soorah)* [Proof That Rashid Mohammed Rashid Has Obtained Qatari Nationality (Picture)]', *Al Misry Al Youm*, 24 October 2014, http://www.almasryalyoum.com/news/details/554308#.

Abdullah, Jamal D, '*Azmah Suhab Al Sufara Min Al Dawah: Al Bwaaath Wa Al Tduayaat* [Crisis Withdrawal of Ambassadors from Doha: Motives and Implications]', *Al Jazeera Centre for Studies*, 24 March 2014, http://studies.aljazeera.net/reports/2014/03/201432413826345572.htm.

Abeih, Mohammed Hisham, 'Qatar to Invest in Suez Canal', *Al Monitor*, 19 January 2013, http://www.al-monitor.com/pulse/business/2013/01/qatar-plans-to-invest-in-suez-canal.html.

Abey, Mohamed Hesham, '*Misr: Istithmaaraat Qatariyah Tulamis Qanaat Al Suez* (Egypt: Qatari Investment Touches the Suez Canal)', *As Safir*, 18 January 2013, http://m.assafir.com/content/1358472666557122600/first.

Aboudi, Sami, 'Yemen Kidnappers Free Swiss Woman after Qatari Mediation: Agency', Reuters, 28 February 2013, http://www.reuters.com/article/2013/02/28/us-yemen-hostage-swiss-idUSBRE91R07J20130228.

Abouzeid, Rania, 'Syria's Secular and Islamist Rebels: Who Are the Saudis and the Qataris Arming?', *Time Magazine*, 18 September 2012, http://www.ft.com/intl/cms/s/2/f2d9bbc8-bdbc-11e2–890a-00144feab7de.html#axzz2UlqxXisB.

Abraham, George, 'Qatar Is a Diplomatic Heavy-Hitter', *Al Jazeera*, 21 July 2008, http://www.aljazeera.com/focus/2008/07/200872164735567644.html.

Adam, Georgina, 'Fireworks as Qatar Steals the Show', *Financial Times*, 29 November 2008.

Adam, Georgina, and Charlotte Burns. 'Qatar Revealed as the World's Biggest Contemporary Art Buyer', *The Art Newspaper*, 7 July 2011, http://www.theartnewspaper.com/articles/Qatar+revealed+as+the+world%E2%80%9 9s+biggest+contemporary+art+buyer/24185.

Adam, Georgina, and Simeon Kerr, 'Saud Bin Mohammed Bin Ali Al-Thani, Collector, 1966–2014', *Financial Times*, 14 November 2014.

'Address by FM Livni to the 8th Doha Forum on Democracy, Development, and Free Trade.' *Israel Ministry of Foreign Affairs*, 14 April 2008, http://www.mfa.gov.il/MFA/About+the+Ministry/Foreign+Minister+Livni/Speeches+ interviews/Address+by+FM+Livni+to+the+Doha+Conference+14-Apr-2008.htm' AFP: Egypt's President Sisi 'Regrets' Jailing Al-Jazeera Journalists', *The Daily Telegraph*, 7 July 2014.

'After the War: The President; Transcript of President Bush's Address on End of the Gulf War', *New York Times*, 7 March 1991.

Ahren, Raphael, 'Israel and the Gulf States: It's Complicated', *The Times of Israel*, 9 August 2013, http://www.timesofisrael.com/israel-and-the-gulf-states-its-complicated/.

Ajmi, Sana, 'Rached Ghannouchi Visits Qatar', *All Africa News [BBC Monitoring]*, 5 January 2012.

'*Al-Jaamiah Tutrud 1849 Taalinaan Qatariyan Bikhutah Tatwyr* 2004' ('The University Has Expelled 1849 Qatari Students [according to] the 2004 Development Plan)', *Al Arab*, 25 September 2012.

'Al-Jazeera Interview with Nusra Leader Draws Criticism', *Middle East Online*, 28 May 2015, http://www.middle-east-online.com/english/?id=71534.

Al-Kuwari, Ali Khalifah, eds, *Al Shaab Yureed Al-Islah Fee Qatar Aydan [The People Want Reform in Qatar Too]*, Beirut: The Knoweldge Forum, 2012.

Al-Kuwari, Rabia bin Sabah, '*Hal Tuhib Reyaah Al-Tughrayyr Ala Idara Jaamiaah Qatr Al-Wataniyah?* (Are the Winds of Change Blowing on the Management at Qatar University?)', *Al Sharq*, 1 January 2014.

Al-Qathani, Abdulrahman, '*Khutabki...Asaaa L'naa* (Your Speech Offended Us).' *Al Watan*, 27 November 2013.

Al-Rashid, Zamil Muhammad, *Saudi Relations with Eastern Arabia and Oman, 1800–1870*, London: Luzac, 1981.

Al-Shoumari, Layla, 'Muslim Brotherhood Paves Way for Qatar's Ascent', *Al Akhbar*, 12 April 2013, http://english.al-akhbar.com/node/15508.

BIBLIOGRAPHY

Al Arayed, Jawad Salim, *A Line in the Sea: The Qatar Versus Bahrain Border Dispute in the World Court*, Berkeley, California: North Atlantic, 2003.

Al Hameed, Ashraf Abd, 'Egypt Rejects Qatari Mediation to Reconcile with Brotherhood', *Al Arabiyya*, 9 August 2015, http://english.alarabiya.net/en/News/middle-east/2015/08/09/Egypt-rejects-Qatari-mediation-to-reconcile-with-MB-.html.

'Al Jazeera's Brand Name News', *Foreign Policy*, 18 April 2005, http://www.foreign-policy.com/articles/2005/04/17/al_jazeeras_brand_name_news

'Al Mahmoud Reviews Human Rights Situation in Qatar', *National Human Rights Committee*,9February2010,http://www.nhrc-qa.org/en/h-e-al-mahmoud-reviews-human-rights-situation-in-qatar/.

Al Qassemi, Sultan, 'Morsi's Win Is Al Jazeera's Loss', *Al Monitor*, 1 July 2012, http://www.al-monitor.com/pulse/originals/2012/al-monitor/morsys-win-is-al-jazeeras-loss.html#.

Al Rashed, AbdulRahman, '*Min Harrods Ila Al-Ahramaat!* (from Harrods to the Pyramids!)', *Al Sharq Al Awsat*, 2 March 2013, http://classic.aawsat.com/leader.asp?section=3&issueno=12513&article=719325#.VJ TsEF4Cot.

Al Thani, Hessa Bint Khaled, 'Shaikh Ahmed Bin Ali Bin Abdullah Bin Qassim Al Thani: A New Perspective on Domestic and Foreign Relations', Qatar University, September 2014.

'*Al Tufaasyl Al Kaamlah Lil'nithaam Al Khidmaat Al Wataniyah* [Full Details of the National Service Programme]', *Al Rays*, 20 February 2014.

'All in the Family: The Changing of the Guard in Qatar', *The Institute for National Security Studies*, 2 July 2013, http://www.inss.org.il/index.aspx?id=4538& articleid=5147.

Amara, Mahfoud. '2006 Qatar Asian Games: A "Modernization" Project from Above?', In *Sport, Nationalism and Orientalism*, ed. Fan Hong. Abingdon: Routledge, 2007.

'Ambassador to Belgium', *Doha QNA*, 19 July 1975, C4.FBIS-MEA-75–141 Amiel, Geraldine, and Laurence Norman, 'France Urges EU to End Arms Embargo on Syria', *The Wall Street Journal*, 14 March 2013.

Ammar, Mohammed, '*Hilal: 'Diar' Tashtiry 30 Miliyoon Metr Marbaa Lil'istithmaar Al Aaaqaary* [Hilal: 'Diar' to Buy 30 Million Square Metres of Real Estate [as] Investment]', *Al Arab*, 18 January 2013.

Amos, Deborah, 'Who Are the Syrian Rebels?', *NPR*, 9 September 2013, http://www.npr.org/blogs/parallels/2013/09/09/220638228/who-are-the-syrian-rebels

'Amr Darrag: Number of Fjp, Muslim Brotherhood Leaders Leave Qatar', *IkhwanWeb* (13 September 2014), http://www.ikhwanweb.com/article.php?id=31803

'Analysis: Syria's Insurgent Landscape', IHS Aerospace, Defence, & Security, September 2013.

Anderson, Benedict, *Imagined Communities*, London: Verso, 2006 (revised edition) Anderson, Lisa, 'Demystifying the Arab Spring.' *Foreign Affairs* 90, 3 (2011).

Anjarini, Suhaib, 'Harakat Hazm: America's New Favorite Jihadist Group', *Al Akhbar*, 22 May 2014, http://english.al-akhbar.com/node/19874.

Anscombe, Frederick F, *The Ottoman Gulf: The Creation of Kuwait, Saudi Arabia, and Qatar*, New York; Chichester: Columbia University Press, 1997.

'AP. 'Iran-Qatar Gas Field.' *New York Times*, 14 November 1990, http://www.nytimes.com/1990/11/14/business/iran-qatar-gas-field.html.

Apodaca, Clair, 'Global Economic Patterns and Personal Integrity Rights after the Cold War.' *International Studies Quarterly* 45 (2001).

''Arafat Meets with Amir in Ad-Dawhah', *Cairo MENA*, 1974, Page B1.FBIS-MEA-74–042, DAILY REPORT. MIDDLE EAST & AFRICA.

'Are We Ready? Q&A with Rear Admiral Stephen H Baker', *CDI Terrorism Project*, 12 September 2002.

Aronczyk, Melissa, '"Living the Brand": Nationality, Globality and the Identity Strategies of Nation Branding Consultants', *International Journal of Communication* 2 (2008).

'As-Sadat Stops over at Ad-Dawhah for Talks,' *Cairo MENA*, 1974, Page B2.FBIS-MEA-74–039, DAILY REPORT. MIDDLE EAST & AFRICA.

Ashour, Omar, 'Libyan Islamists Unpacked', *Policy Briefing*, Brookings Doha Center, May 2012.

Atkinson, Carol, 'Does Soft Power Matter? A Comparative Analysis of Student Exchange Programs 1980–2006', *Foreign Policy Analysis* 6, 1 (2010).

Awudah Al Din, Salah, 'Sudanese Writer Accuses Al Jazeera of Selectivity in Covering Arab Revolutions'. *Al Sahafah [BBC Monitoring]*, 17 March 2011 [18 March 2011].

Azem, Ahmed, 'Qatar's Ties with the Muslim Brotherhood Affect Entire Region', *The National*, 18 May 2012.

Azzam, Henry T, *The Arab World Facing the Challenge of the New Millennium*, London: I.B. Tauris, 2002.

Babar, Zahra R, 'The Cost of Belonging: Citizenship Construction in the State of Qatar', *The Middle East Journal* 68, 3 (Summer 2014).

'The Bahrain-Qatar Border Dispute: The World Court Decision, Part 1', *The Estimate*, 23 March 2001.

Bahry, Louay, 'Elections in Qatar: A Window of Democracy Opens in the Gulf', *Middle East Policy* VI, 4 (June 1999).

——— 'The New Arab Media Phenomenon: Qatar's Al-Jazeera.' *Middle East Policy* 8, 2 (2001).

——— 'Qatar: Democratic Reforms and Global Status.' *Governance in the Middle East and North Africa*, ed. Abbas Kadhim, New York: Routledge, 2013.

Bains, Elizabeth, 'Qatar's Quest for Sporting Glory', *Middle East Economic Digest*, 12 June 2009.

Bairner, Alan, 'Political Unionism and Sporting Nationalism', *Identities: Global Studies in Culture and Power* 10, 4 (2003).

BIBLIOGRAPHY

Baker, Aryn, 'Bahrain's Voiceless: How Al-Jazeera's Coverage of the Arab Spring Is Uneven', *Time*, 24 May 2011, http://world.time.com/2011/05/24/bahrains-voiceless-how-al-jazeeras-coverage-of-the-arab-spring-is-uneven/.

———— 'Qatar Haunted by Its Decision to Back the Arab Spring's Islamists', *Time*, 26 September 2013, http://world.time.com/2013/09/26/qatar-haunted-by-its-decision-to-back-the-arab-springs-islamists/.

Baker, Peter, 'U.S. Says It Told Qatar Not to Pay a Ransom', *The New York Times*, 25 August 2014.

Bakr, Amena, 'Defiant Al Jazeera Faces Conservative Backlash after Arab Spring', Reuters, 2 July 2014, http://www.reuters.com/article/2014/07/02/us-qatar-jazeera-media-idUSKBN0F70F120140702.

———— 'In Qatar Desert, Syrian Opposition Mourns Fallen Commander', Reuters, 21 November 2013, http://www.reuters.com/article/2013/11/21/us-syria-qatar-desert-idUSBRE9AK0E520131121.

———— 'Qatar Launches First Chinese Yuan Clearing Hub in Middle East', Reuters, 14 April 2014, http://www.reuters.com/article/2015/04/14/qatar-china-yuan-idUS L5N0XB2D220150414.

———— 'Qatar Pares Support for Islamists but Careful to Preserve Ties', Reuters, 2 November 2014, http://www.reuters.com/article/2014/11/02/us-mideast-crisis-qatar-insight-idUSKBN0IM07B20141102.

Ballout, Mohammed, 'How the Maaloula Nuns Were Freed', *Al Monitor*, 11 March 2014, http://www.al-monitor.com/pulse/security/2014/03/syria-nuns-maaloula-released.html#.

———— 'Syrian Opposition Attempts Consolidation', *Al Monitor*, 11 May 2013, http://www.al-monitor.com/pulse/politics/2013/05/syrian-opposition-tries-to-consolidate.html.

Baluwt, Mohamed, '*Rihlat Al-Raahibaat Min Yabrud Ila Al-Huriya* (the Journey of the Yabrud Nuns to Freedom)', *As Safir*, 3 October 2014, http://assafir.com/Article/1/341366.

Barakat, Sultan, 'Qatari Mediation: Between Ambition and Achievement', *Brookings Doha Center Analysis Paper*. Doha, Qatar: Brookings Doha Centre, November 2014.

Barbary, Victoria, 'Sovereign Wealth Funds Don't buy Apartments. Read: 'Middle Eastern Royal: On.Ft.Com/1occ5ap Via @Ft.' *Twitter* (22 September 2014), https://twitter.com/EMInvestment/status/513988666440437760.

Barclay, Steve, 'Steve Barclay: Ministers Must Not Pursue Trade with Qatar at Any Price', *The Daily Telegraph*, 2 November 2014.

Bardsley, Daniel, 'Qatar Aims to Build Film Industry', *The National*, 21 August 2009

Barr, Cameron, 'Qatar Stands by US as War Looms', *The Christian Science Monitor*, 10 December 2002.

Barthe, Benjamin, 'Gloom Grips Qatar's Arab Riviera after Alcohol Ban', *The*

Guardian, 21 February 2012, http://www.guardian.co.uk/world/2012/feb/21/qatar-arab-riviera-gloom-alcohol-ban.

Beauchamp, Zack, 'Where People Really Love Their Countries—and Where They Kinda Don't', *Vox*, 18 May 2014, http://www.vox.com/2014/5/18/5724552/patriotism-pride-global-world.

Beaumont, Peter, 'Qatar Accused of Interfering in Libyan Affairs', *The Guardian*, 4 October 2011.

Behrendt, Sven, 'Sovereign Wealth Funds: Fiscal Buffers against the Deterioration of Oil Prices?', *Sovereign Wealth Funds Update Series*: GeoEconomica, January 2015.

Bell, Connor, 'Obesity: A Big Problem for Fast Growing Qatar', *Al Jazeera*, 25 July 2012 http://www.aljazeera.com/indepth/features/2012/07/2012722917422894.html.

Bender, Larissa, 'Al Jazeera—the Enigma from Qatar', *Qantara.de*, 6 November 2006 http://en.qantara.de/Al-Jazeera-The-Enigma-from-Qatar/7834c166/index.html.

Bercovitch, Jacob, 'Introduction', *Studies in International Mediation*, ed. Jacob Bercovitch and Jeffrey Z Rubin, Basingstoke; Palgrave MacMillan 2002.

Bergsten, Fred C, 'The World Economy after the Cold War', *Foreign Affairs* (Summer 1990).

Berti, Banedetta, and Yoel Guzansky, 'The Syrian Crisis and the Saudi-Iranian Rivalry', *Foreign Policy Research Institute*, October 2012, http://www.fpri.org/articles/2012/10/syrian-crisis-and-saudi-iranian-rivalry.

Bill, Tom, 'Qatar Top Sovereign Europe Property Buyer with Six Weeks Gas Cash', Reuters, 17 August 2012.

Birke, Sarah, 'How Al-Qaeda Changed the Syrian War', *The New York Review of Books (Blog)*. http://www.nybooks.com/blogs/nyrblog/2013/dec/27/how-al-qaeda-changed-syrian-war/.

Black, Ian, 'Al Jazeera Boss Wadah Khanfar Steps Down to Be Replaced by Qatari Royal', *The Guardian*, 20 September 2011.

——— 'Qatar's Youthful New Ruler Signals Continuity for Maverick Gulf State', *The Guardian*, 27 June 2013.

——— 'Qatar Breaks Arab Ranks over Syria', *The Guardian*, 21 July 2011 Blair, David, and Richard Spencer, 'How Qatar Is Funding the Rise of Islamist Extremists', *The Daily Telegraph*, 20 September 2014.

Blanchard, Christopher M, 'Qatar: Background and U.S. Relations', *Congressional Research Service*, 10 October 2007.

Bond, David, 'England 2018 World Cup Bid Viewed as 'Low Risk'', *BBC Sport*, 16 November 2010, http://news.bbc.co.uk/sport2/hi/football/9196434.stm.

Bortolotti, Bernado, Veljko Fotak, and William L Megginson, 'The Rise of Sovereign Wealth Funds: Definition, Organization, and Governance', Universita Commerciale Luigi Bocconi: BAFFI Center on International Markets, Money and Regulation, 2014.

Boyce, Graham, 'Qatar: Annual Review for 1990', ed. Middle East Department, Foreign and Commonwealth Office, London: FCO, 7 January 1991.

——— 'Qatar: Annual Review for 1992', ed. Middle East Department, Foreign and Commonwealth Office. London: FCO, 12 January 1993.

'BP Statistical Review of World Energy', London: British Petroleum (BP), 2010.

'BP Statistical Review of World Energy', London: British Petroleum (BP), June 2012 Brant, Colin, 'Valedictory from Qatar: A Land of Promise', ed. Middle East Department, Foreign and Commonwealth Office, London: FCO, 9 July 1981.

Brauer, Ralph W, 'Boundaries and Frontiers in Medieval Muslim Geography', *Transactions of the American Philosophical Society*, 85, 6 (1995).

Bridges, Scott. *18 Days: Al Jazeera English and the Egyptian Revolution* (Kindle edition), Braddon, Australia: Editia, 2013.

'The Brotherhood Disapora', *MadaMasr*, 30 September 2014, http://www.madamasr.com/sections/politics/brotherhood-diaspora.

Bryan-Low, Cassell, 'UK Boosts Support to Opposition Military', *The Wall Street Journal*, 6 March 2013.

'Building a Better World Cup', Human Rights Watch, 12 June 2012.

Burdett, Anita L P, ed. *British Resident Ef Henderson, Doha, to Arabian Department, FCO London, 'Priority, Cypher Cat A'*. Vol. IV: 1970–1971, Records of Qatar 1966–1971. Slough, UK: Archive Editions Limited, 2006.

——— ed. *British Resident Ef Henderson, Doha, to Jl Beaven Arabian Department, FCO London, 'Qatar Internal' 21 February 1972*. Vol. IV: 1970–1971, Records of Qatar 1966–1971. Slough, U.K.: Archive Editions Limited, 2006.

Burgen, Stephen, 'Qatar's Armed Forces Pay €78.5m for Barcelona's Renaissance Hotel', *The Guardian*, 31 January 2014.

Burns, Robert, and Adam Schreck, 'Tiny Qatar Plays Outsized Role in U.S. War Strategy', *Military Times*, 15 September 2014 http://www.militarytimes.com/article/20140915/NEWS08/309150052/Tiny-Qatar-plays-outsize-role-U-S-war-strategy.

Burrows, Bernard A, 'Annual Report 1955', *Foreign Office Annual Reports from Arabia 1930–1960*, Chippenham: Archive Editions, 1993.

——— 'Annual Report 1956', *Foreign Office Annual Reports from Arabia 1930–1960*, Chippenham: Archive Editions, 1993.

Buzcu-Guven, Birnur, Robert Harriss, and Donald Hertzmark, 'Gas Flaring and Venting: Extent, Impacts, and Remedies', *Energy Market Consequences of an Emerging US Carbon Management Policy*, Huston, TX: James A Baker III Institute for Public Policy, Rice University, September 2010.

'Cabinet Decides to Recognize Comoros Islands', *Doha QNA*, 28 January 1976, C1. FBIS-MEA-76-026.

Caldwell, Geoffrey, 'International Sport and National Identity', *International Social Science Journal* XXXIV, 2 (1982).

Calvert, Jonathan, and Heidi Blake, 'Plot to buy the World Cup', *The Sunday Times*, 1 June 2014.

Campbell, Rook, 'Staging Globalization for National Projects: Global Sport Markets and Elite Athletic Transnational Labour in Qatar', *International Review for the Sociology of Sport* 46, 45 (July 2010).

Carlsen, Jack, 'A Review of Mice Industry Evaluation and Research in Asia and Australia 1988–1998', *Journal of Convention & Exhibition Management* 1, 4 (1999).

Carlstrom, Gregg, 'Why Egypt Hates Al Jazeera', *Foreign Policy*, 19 February 2014 http://foreignpolicy.com/2014/02/19/why-egypt-hates-al-jazeera/.

Cerny, Philip G, 'Paradoxes of the Competition State: The Dynamics of Political Globalization', *Government and Opposition* 32, 2 (April 1997).

—— 'Plurilateralism: Structural Differentiation and Functional Conflict in the Post-Cold War World Order', *Millennium—Journal of International Studies* 22, 27 (1993).

Chandrasekaran, Rajiv, 'In the UAE, the United States Has a Quiet, Potent Ally Nicknamed "Little Sparta"', *The Washington Post*, 9 November 2014.

Chassany, Anne-Sylvaine, 'QIA Leads Fund Rankings for Missing Santiago Governance Standards', *Financial Times*, 27 October 2014.

Cheema, Jehanzeb R, 'The Migrant Effect: An Evaluation of Native Academic Performance in Qatar', *Research in Education* 91 (May 2014).

Chesnot, Christian, and Georges Malbrunot, *Qatar: Les Secrets Du Coffre-Fort*, Neuilly-sur-Seine: Michel Lafon, 2013.

'China Grants Qatar Fund Qfii Licence: Report', *MarketWatch*. http://www.market-watch.com/story/china-grants-qatar-fund-qfii-license-report-2012–10–07.

'The Chinese Remninbi Lands in Doha', *Economic Commentary*, 19 April 2015, http://www.qnb.com/cs/Satellite?blobcol=urldata&blobheader=application%2Fpdf&b lobkey=id&blobtable=MungoBlobs&blobwhere=1355517278795&ssbin ary=true.

Chubin, Shahram, 'US Security Interests in the Persian Gulf in the 1980s', *Daedalus* 109, 4 (Fall 1980).

'Civilian Use of Al-Udeid Air Base in Qatar', *Wikileaks*, 21 December 2008, https://wikileaks.org/plusd/cables/08DOHA882_a.html.

Clarey, Christopher, 'Qatar Makes a Move to Be a "Sports Capital"', *The New York Times*, 17 October 1993.

Clarke, Steve, 'Al Jazeera Wins Rts Award', *Variety*, 23 February 2012, http://www.variety.com/article/VR1118050636?refCatId=14.

Cohen, Benjamin J, 'Sovereign Wealth Funds and National Security: The Great Tradeoff', *Global & International Studies*; University of California, March 2009.

Coker, Margaret, Sam Dagher, and Charles Levinson, 'Tiny Kingdom's Huge Role in Libya Draws Concern', *The Wall Street Journal*, 17 October 2011, http://online.wsj.com/article/SB10001424052970204002304576627000922764650.ht ml.

Cole, Peter, and Umar Khan, 'The Fall of Tripoli: Part 1', in *The Libyan Revolution and Its Aftermath*, ed. Peter Cole and Brian McQuinn, London: Hurst & Co, 2015

Collins, Tatum, and Paul Solman, 'What Can the Middle East Learn from What's Happening in Qatar?', *PBS Newshour*, 28 June 2013, http://www.pbs.org/newshour/rundown/what-can-the-middle-east-learn-from-whats-happening-in-qatar/.

'Comparisons between Education City, Qatar University Spark Controversy', *Doha News*, 17 May 2012, http://dohanews.co/comparisons-between-education-city-qatar-university/.

'Competition among Islamists', *The Economist*, 18 July 2013.

'Congolese Minister Concludes 3-Day Visit', *Doha QNA*, 9 March 1976, C3. FBIS-MEA-75–050.

Conn, David, 'How Qatar Became a Football Force', *The Guardian*, 18 November 2013.

——— 'Qatar Cash Is Stirring French Football Revolution at Paris St Germain', *The Guardian*, 22 November 2011.

'The Constitution', *Qatar Ministry of Foreign Affairs*, http://english.mofa.gov.qa/details.cfm?id=80.

'Continuity Trumps Change on Hollande's Qatar Visit', *France 24*, 22 June 2013, http://www.france24.com/en/20130621-france-qatar-hollande-visit-continuity-trumps-change/.

'Contributions to Unesco', *Doha QNA*, 9 July 1975, C3.FBIS-MEA-75–132 Cooper, Andrew F, and Bessma Momani, 'Qatar and Expanded Contours of Small State Diplomacy', *ISA Conference*, New Orleans, February 2010.

Cordesman, Anthony H, *Bahrain, Oman, Qatar, and the UAE: Challenges of Security*, Csis Middle East Dynamic Net Assessment, Boulder, Colo.; Oxford: Westview, 1997.

——— 'The Tanker War and the Lessons of Naval Conflict', *The Lessons of Modern War* II (1990).

Cordesman, Anthony H, and Khalid Al Rodhan, 'The Gulf Military Forces in an Era of Asymmetric War, Volume 1', Westport, CT: Praeger Security International, 2007.

'Country Report: Tunisia', *Country Report*, London: Economist Intelligence Unit, April 2012.

'Country Report: Tunisia', *Country Report*, London: Economist Intelligence Unit, October 2011.

Crystal, Jill, *Oil and Politics in the Gulf: Rulers and Merchants in Kuwait and Qatar*, Cambridge: Cambridge University Press, 1995.

'Cuba and Qatar Establish Diplomatic Relations', Reuters, 14 December 1989 Currie, Maike, 'The Case for Qatar', *Investors Chronicle*, 11 April 2011.

Cushman, John H, 'U.S. Says Qatar Has Stinger, Raising Fear of Missile Spread', *The New York Times*, 1 April 1988.

Dargin, Justin, 'Addressing the UAE Natural Gas Crisis: Strategies for a Rational

Energy Policy', *Policy Brief*, Dubai, UAE: The Dubai Initiative; Belfer Centre for Science and International Affairs, Harvard Kennedy School, August 2010.

—— 'The Dolphin Project: The Development of a Gulf Gas Initiative', Oxford: Oxford Institute for Energy Studies, 2008.

—— 'The Gas Revolution in Qatar', *Natural Gas Markets in the Middle East and North Africa*, eds Bassam Fattouh and Jonathan Stern, Oxford: Oxford University Press, 2011.

Dargin, Justin 'Qatar's Natural Gas: The Foreign-Policy Driver', *Middle East Policy* 14, 3 (2007).

'The Dark Side of Migration', London: Amnesty International, 2013.

'David Cameron Praises C17 Plane Just Moments before It Breaks Down', *The Daily Telegraph*, 14 January 2013.

Davidson, Christopher, *After the Sheikhs: The Coming Collapse of the Gulf Monarchies*, London: Hurst & Co, 2012.

'Degree Law No. (38) of 2002 on the Setting up of the National Human Rights Committee', *National Human Rights Committee*, http://www.nhrc-qa.org/en/decree-law-no-38-of-2002-on-the-setting-up-of-the-national-human-rights-committee/

Dehghanpisheh, Babak, 'Syrian Opposition Group Strike Reorganization Deal', *The Washington Post*, 11 November 2012.

DeLong, Michael, and Noah Lukeman, *Inside Centcom: The Unvarnished Truth About the Wars in Afghanistan and Iraq* [in English], Washington, D.C: Regnery Pub, 2004.

Dickinson, Elizabeth, 'The Case against Qatar', *Foreign Policy*, 30 September 2013, http://www.foreignpolicy.com/articles/2014/09/30/the_case_against_qatar_funding_e xtremists_salafi_syria_uae_jihad_muslim_brotherhood_taliban.

—— 'Qatar's Role as Peace Broker at Risk in Syria', *The National*, 24 September 2012.

—— 'Qatar Punches Above Its Weight', *The National*, 26 September 2012.

—— 'Qatar Succession: Seven Minutes When Power Changed Hands', *The National*, 26 June 2013.

Dickson, Martin, and Roula Khalaf, 'Interview Transcript: Qatar's Sheikh Hamad, *Financial Times*, 24 October 2010, http://www.ft.com/intl/cms/s/0/9163abca-df97-11df-bed9-00144feabdc0.html#axzz2N97OFKcC.

'Diplomatic Relations Established with Brazil', *Cairo MENA*, 20 May 1974, C7. FBIS-MEA-74–100.

'Diplomatic Relations with Finland to Be Established', *Cairo MENA*, 1974, Page C2.FBIS-MEA-74–064, DAILY REPORT. MIDDLE EAST &NORTH AFRICA.

'Diplomatic Relations with Indonesia', *Doha QNA*, 12 June 1975, C2.FBIS-MEA-75–114.

'Diplomatic Relations with Malta', *Doha QNA*, 20 June 1975, C2.FBIS-MEA-75–120

'Diplomatic Ties Established with Trinidad, Tobago', *Cairo MENA*, 1974, Page B2.FBIS-MEA-74–051, DAILY REPORT. MIDDLE EAST & AFRICA.

Diyab, Halla, 'How Syria's Uprising Blurred Moderate, Extremist Lines', *Al Arabiyya*, 12 October 2014, http://english.alarabiya.net/en/views/news/middle-east/2014/10/12/How-the-Syrian-uprising-led-to-ISIS-rise-not-democracy-Part-2-.html.

Doczi, Tamas, 'Gold Fever: Sport and National Identity—the Hungarian Case', *International Review for the Sociology of Sport* 47 (February 2011).

Doherty, Caitlin B, 'Lebanon: Back from the Brink?', *The National Interest*, 27 May 2008 http://nationalinterest.org/article/lebanon-back-from-the-brink-2095.

Doherty, Regan, 'Qatar Bets on Future as Sports Mecca', *Reuters*, 7 September 2011, http://www.reuters.com/article/2011/09/07/us-qatar-sport-idUSTRE7863 E820110907.

Doherty, Regan, and Dinesh Nair, 'Analysis—Qatar Swf's Hefty Appetite Draws Global Players', *Reuters*, 3 March 2011, http://uk.reuters.com/article/2011/03/03/uk-qatar-fund-idUKTRE7223IH20110303.

Donaghy, Rori, 'UAE and Qatar: Public Relations Warfare', *Middle East Eye*, 30 October 2014, http://www.middleeasteye.net/in-depth/features/uae-and-qatar-public-relations-warfare-155477673.

Doran, Michael, William McCants, and Clint Watts, 'The Good and Bad of Ahrar Al-Sham', *Foreign Affairs*, 23 January 2014, http://www.foreignaffairs.com/articles/140680/michael-doran-william-mccants-and-clint-watts/the-good-and-bad-of-ahrar-al-sham.

'Dr Khalid Bin Mohammed Al Attiyah: Qatari Foreign Policy Today: Challenges and Opportunities', *Princeton University, YouTube.com*, 3 October 2014.

Draper, Rob, 'Backed by Qatar's Billions, Sarkozy's Brokerage and Beckham's Glamour, Paris St Germain Are Forging the New French Revolution', *The Mail on Sunday*, 30 March 2013.

Duff, Alex, 'Fifa's Blatter Says Summer Qatar World Cup a "Mistake"', *Bloomberg*, 16 May 2014, http://www.bloomberg.com/news/2014-05-16/fifa-s-blatter-says-summer-qatar-world-cup-a-mistake-1-.html.

Dwyer, Larry, and Peter Forsyth, 'Economic Measures of Tourism Yield: What Markets to Target?', *International Journal of Tourism Research* 10 (2008).

Eakin, Hugh, 'The Strange Power of Qatar', *New York Review of Books*, 28 October 2011.

Ebrahimi, Helia, 'Qatar's UK Ambitions Could Mean Billions More in Investment', *The Daily Telegraph*, 14 March 2013.

'Egypt Country Report', *EIU Country Report*, London: Economist Intelligence Unit, May 2013.

'Egypt Crisis: Al Jazeera Journalists Arrested in Cairo', *BBC News*, 30 December 2013 http://www.bbc.com/news/world-middle-east-25546389.

'Egypt State Council Bans Al Jazeera, Rabaa on Nilesat', *Ahram Online*, 3 September 2014, http://english.ahram.org.eg/NewsContent/1/64/109878/Egypt/Politics-/Egypt-State-Council-bans-Al-Jazeera,-Rabaa-on-Nile.aspx.

'Egyptian Dcm: Cairo to Thwart Any Qatari Initiative', *Wikileaks*, 28 January 2010, https://www.wikileaks.org/plusd/cables/10DOHA39_a.html.

El Baltaji, Dana. 'Qatar Bankrolls Muslim Brothers as U.A.E. Jails Them', *Bloomberg*, 11 December 2012, http://www.bloomberg.com/news/2012–12–10/qatar-bank-rolls-ascendant-muslim-brothers-as-u-a-e-jails-them.html.

El Khawas, Mohamed A, 'Tunisia's Jasmine Revolution: Causes and Impact', *Mediterranean Quarterly* 23, 4 (Fall 2012).

El Mallakh, Ragaei, *Qatar: Development of an Oil Economy*, London: Croom Helm, 1979.

El Nawawy, Mohammed, and Adel Iskander, *Al-Jazeera: How the Free Arab News Network Scooped the World and Changed the Middle East*, first edition; hardback, ed. Cambridge, MA: Westview, 2002.

El Tayeb, Mohammed Saeed M, 'The Qatari National Human Rights Committee: A Search for Evaluation', *Asia Pacific Human Rights Information Centre* 47 (March 2007).

Ellis, Dominic, 'Qatar's Conference Scent Is About to Change Beyond All Recognition...' *Middle East MICE & Events*, 30 June 2011.

Elman, Miriam Fendius, 'The Foreign Policies of Small States: Challenging Neorealism in Its Own Backyard', *British Journal of Political Science* 25, 2 (1995).

'Emir Sheikh Tamim's New Appointments', *Gulf States Newsletter*, 950, 4 July 2013.

'Enabling Growth: Looking Overseas to Invest in the Oil, Gas, and Power Segments', *OxfordBusinessGroup*,http://www.oxfordbusinessgroup.com/analysis/enabling-growth-looking-overseas-invest-oil-gas-and-power-segments.

England, Andrew, 'Bashir Hailed in Qatar Despite Darfur Charges', *Financial Times*, 30 March 2009.

——- 'Qatar Pursues Sporting Goals with African Aid', *Financial Times*, 21 August 2009.

Entous, Adam, and Julian E Barnes, 'Pentagon Bulks up Defences in the Gulf', *The Wall Street Journal*, 17 July 2012.

'Erdogan Steps in to Try and Mediate in Lebanese Hostage Crisis in Qatar', *An Nahar*, 15 September 2014, http://en.annahar.com/article/170948-erdogen-steps-in-to-try-and-mediate-in-lebanese-hostage-crisis-in-qatar.

Evans, Sophie, 'Doha's Expanding Diplomatic Role', *Middle East Economic Digest*, 53, 24 (2009): 30(2).

Fassihi, Farnaz, and Nour Malas, 'Syria Rebels Free Iranians in Prisoner Swap', *The Wall Street Journal*, 9 January 2013.

Fattouh, Bassam, Howard V Rogers, and Peter Stewart, 'The US Shale Gas Revolutions and Its Impact on Qatar's Position in Gas Markets', Center on Global Energy Policy, Columbia University, March 2015.

Fayad, Kamal, 'Will Qatar's Emir Abdicate in August?', *Al Monitor*, 11 June 2013, http://www.al-monitor.com/pulse/politics/2013/06/qatar-emir-abdicate-august. html.

Fick, Maggie, 'Egypt Summons Qatar's Charge D'affairs Over Egyptian Cleric', *Reuters*, 4 February 2014, http://www.reuters.com/article/2014/02/04/egypt-qatar-idUSL5N0L91SH20140204.

Field, Michael, *The Merchants: The Big Business Families of Saudi Arabia and the Gulf States*, Woodstock, NY: The Overlook Press, 1985.

——— 'Tree of the Al Attiyah', *Arabian Charts* (v.1), http://arabiancharts.wordpress. com/about/.

——— 'Tree of the Al Thani', *Arabian Charts* (v.10), http://arabiancharts.wordpress. com/about/.

'First Moroccan Ambassador' *Qatar Domestic Service*, 14 October 1974, C1. FBIS-MEA-74–217.

'First Senegalese Ambassador', *Paris AFP*, 1974, Page B1.FBIS-MEA-74–057, DAILY REPORT. MIDDLE EAST & AFRICA.

Fitzgerald, Mary, 'Libya's New Power Brokers?', *Foreign Policy*, 27 August 2014, http://foreignpolicy.com/2014/08/27/libyas-new-power-brokers/.

Fleishman, Jeffrey, and Noha El Hennawy, 'Qatar's Ambitions Roil Middle East', *Los Angeles Times*, 21 April 2009.

'Flying-Carpet Diplomacy', *The Economist*, 18 February 2012.

Foster, Marcus, 'Small States in Peacemaking Roles', *Jackson School Journal of International Studies* 1, 2 (Spring 2011).

'France Scores Big', *Financial Times*, 20 July 2012.

'Freed Lebanese Hostages Arrive in Beirut', *Al Jazeera*, 20 October 2013, http://www. aljazeera.com/news/middleeast/2013/10/freed-lebanese-hostages-arrive-bei-rut-20131019195217962484.html.

French, David, 'Emir Appoints New CEO at Qatar Investment Authority', *Reuters*, 3 December 2014, http://www.reuters.com/article/2014/12/03/qatar-investment-ceo-idUSL6N0TN3OJ20141203.

Friedman, Brandon, 'Qatar: Security Amid Instability', *The Jewish Policy Centre: inFocus* V, 4 (Winter 2011).

'Frost Over the World: HH Sheikha Mozah', *Al Jazeera*, 19 January 2010, http:// www.aljazeera.com/programmes/frostovertheworld/2010/01/201011613575214 7400.html.

Fukuyama, Francis, *The End of History and the Last Man*, London: Hamilton, 1992 'Fund Profiles', *Sovereign Wealth Center*, July 2015, http://www.sovereignwealth-center.com/fund-profiles.html.

'Fund Rankings', *Sovereign Wealth Fund Institute*, June 2015, http://www.swfinstitute. org/fund-rankings/.

'Funds Investment', *General Retirement & Social Insurance Authority*, 29 July 2015, http://www.grsia.gov.qa/english/Investment/Pages/default.aspx.

'Gabonese Foreign Minister Arrives for Visit', *Cairo MENA*, 1974, Page C1.FBIS-MEA-74–063, DAILY REPORT. Middle East & North Africa.

Galani, Una, 'Breakingviews: Qatar's Sovereign Funds: A Guide for the Perplexed', *Reuters*, 2 October 2012, http://in.reuters.com/article/2012/10/02/idINL3E8 L25ZB20121002.

Gause III, Gregory, *Oil Monarchies*, New York: Council on Foreign Relations, 1994 'The GCC: Regional Stabilizer', *Jane's Defence Weekly*, 31 March 1990.

Gengler, Justin, 'The Political Costs of Qatar's Western Orientation.', *Middle East Policy* XIX, 4 (Winter 2012).

—— 'Qatar's Ambivalent Democratization', *Foreign Policy*, 1 November 2011, http://mideast.foreignpolicy.com/posts/2011/11/01/qataris_lesson_in_revolution Gilboa, Eytan, 'Global Television News and Foreign Policy: Debating the CNN Effect', *International Studies Perspectives* 6 (2005).

Gilmore, Fiona, 'A Country Can It Be Repositioned? Spain—the Success Story of Country Branding', *Brand Management* 9, 4–5 (2002).

Goff, Steven, 'Qatar Gets 2022 World Cup over U.S.; Russia Beats out England for 2018 Event', *The Washington Post*, 8 March 2013.

"Gold Certification" for Convention Centre', *Gulf Times*, 10 May 2012, http://www.gulf-times.com/site/topics/article.asp?cu_no=2&item_no=506816&version=1&template_i d=36&parent_id=16.

Goldberg, Jacob, *The Foreign Policy of Saudi Arabia: The Formative Years, 1902–1918*, Harvard Middle Eastern Studies, Cambridge, Mass: Harvard University Press, 1986.

Goldman, Adam, and Karen DeYoung, 'Qatar Played Now-Familiar Role in Helping to Broker U.S. Hostage's Release', *The Washington Post*, 25 August 2014.

Gordon, Michael R, and Eric Schmitt, 'Aftereffects: Bases; US Will Move Air Operations to Qatar', *New York Times*, 28 April 2003.

'Government Cancels Debts for 10 Countries', Paris AFP, FBIS-NES-90–195 on 1992–10–09, 7 October 2012.

Gray, Matthew, *Qatar: Politics and the Challenges of Development*, Lynne Rienner Publishers, 2013.

Greenwald, Glenn, 'How Former Treasury Officials and the UAE Are Manipulating American Journalists', *The Intercept*, 25 September 2014, https://firstlook.org/theintercept/2014/09/25/uae-qatar-camstoll-group/.

Gresh, Alain, 'Gulf Cools Towards Muslim Brothers', *Le Monde Diplomatique*, November 2012, http://mondediplo.com/2012/11/02egypt.

—— 'Popular Distrust May Derail Al-Thani's North African Ambitions', *Gulf States Newsletter*, July 2012.

—— 'Qatar and Libya Open a New Geopolitical Axis in North Africa', *Gulf States Newsletter*, 2 September 2011.

Gulbrandsen, Anders, 'Bridging the Gulf: Qatari Business Diplomacy and Conflict Mediation', Georgetown University, 2010.

'Gulf Security Force Withdrawn', Paris AFP, FBIS-NES-92–193 on 1992–10–05, 5 October 1992.

'Gulf States Qatar', Oxresearch Daily Brief Service, 19 September 1989.

'Gulf States: Q.P.C's Liquid Gas Project', *Middle East Economic Digest*, 19 March 1971.

'*Haalah Al Dimokratiyah Fee Qatr* [the State of Democracy in Qatar]', http://arabs-fordemocracy.org/democracy/pages/view/pageId/460.

Haberman, Clyde. 'Israel Seeks Deal with Qatar on Gas', *New York Times*, 29 October 1993.

Hall, Camilla, 'New Qatar Emir Shakes up Sovereign Wealth Fund', *Financial Times*, 2 July 2013.

Hall, Camilla, Roula Khalaf, Lionel Barber, Patrick Jenkins, and Ed Hammond, 'Qatar: What's Next for the World's Most Aggressive Deal Hunter?', *Financial Times*, 4 July 2013.

Hamdan, Sara, 'Gasoline Crisis in Emirates Brings Lines and Fears', *The New York Times*, 15 June 2011.

Hamilton, Charles W, *Americans and Oil in the Middle East*, Houston, Tex.: Gulf Pub. Co., 1962.

Hammond, Andrew, 'Analysis—Egypt's Al Jazeera Bans Channel's Key Role', *Reuters*, 30 June 2011, http://www.reuters.com/article/2011/01/30/uk-egypt-aljazeera-idUKTRE70T2X220110130.

Harman, Danna, 'Backstory: The Royal Couple That Put Qatar on the Map', *The Christian Science Monitor*, 5 March 2007, http://www.csmonitor.com/2007/0305/p20s01-wome.html.

Harrabin, Roger, 'Gas-Fired Power Stations to Be Encouraged by Government', *BBC News*, 3 December 2012, http://www.bbc.co.uk/news/business-20577302.

Hasan, Mehdi, 'Voice of the Arab Spring', *New Statesman*, 7 December 2011.

Hashimoto, Kohei, Jareer Elass, and Stacy Eller, 'Liquefied Natural Gas from Qatar: The Qatargas Project', *Geopolitics of Gas Working Paper Series*, Stanford: Baker Institute Energy Forum, Rice University, December 2004.

Hassan, Hassan, 'Making Qatar an Offer It Can't Refuse', *Foreign Policy*, 22 April 2014, http://foreignpolicy.com/2014/04/22/making-qatar-an-offer-it-cant-refuse/.

——— 'Saudis Overtaking Qatar in Sponsoring Syrian Rebels', *The National*, 15 May 2013.

Hauslohner, Abigail, 'Egypt's Muslim Brotherhood Finds Havens Abroad', *The Washington Post*, 6 November 2013.

——— 'Qatar Loses Clout Amid Fading Arab Spring', *The Washington Post*, 13 November 2013.

Hedley, Don, *World Energy: The Facts and the Future*, London: Euromonitor Publications, 1986.

Henni, Abedlghani, 'Dolphin Energy's CEO: We Supply 30% of the UAE's Gas

Demand', *JPT Online*, 4 October 2012, http://www.jptonline.org/index.php?id= 2036 Hepburn, Bon, 'Canadians in Qatar Officially Don't Exist', *Toronto Star*, 7 October 1990.

'HH the Emir Patronizes Opening of Advisory Council's 43rd Ordinary Session', *QNA*, 11 November 2014, http://www.qna.org.qa/en-us/News/14111109530027/ HH-the-Emir-Patronizes-Opening-of-Advisory-Councils-43rd-Ordinary-Session.

Hijjawi, Aref, 'The Role of Al Jazeera (Arabic) in the Arab Revolts of 2011', *Heinrich Böll Foundation*, https://www.boell.de/sites/default/files/assets/boell.de/images/ download_de/Perspecti ves_02–10_Aref_Hijjawi.pdf.

Hindley, Angus, 'Early Embrace Leads to Deep Relationship', *Middle East Economic Digest*, 17 February 1997.

Hoadley, J. Stephen, 'Small States as Aid Donors', *International Organization* 34, 1 (1980).

Hobsbawm, Eric, and Terence Ranger, *The Invention of Tradition*, Cambridge: Cambridge University Press, 2010 (19th printing).

Hokayem, Emile. *Syria's Uprising and the Fracturing of the Levant* [in English]. Abingdon: Routledge for the International Institute for Strategic Studies, 2013.

Holland, Jessica, 'Qatari Royal Family Sponsors Damien Hirst Retrospective at Tate Modern', *The National*, 5 April 2012.

Hounshell, Blake, 'The Qatar Bubble', *Foreign Policy*, 23 April 2012, http://www.foreignpolicy.com/articles/2012/04/23/the_qatar_bubble.

—— 'The Revolution Will Soon Be Televised', *Foreign Policy*, 28 March 2011, http://www.foreignpolicy.com/articles/2011/03/28/the_revolution_will_soon_ be_televised.

'Houthis Receive Arms from Iran Via Eritrea', *Yemen Post*, 10 April 2010, http://www.yemenpost.net/Detail123456789.aspx?ID=3&SubID=1548.

Hughes, Rob, 'Bin Hammam Is Latest Fifa Official to Go, but Cloud Remains', *The New York Times*, 24 July 2011.

Hurst, Cindy, 'Liquified Natural Gas: The Next Prize?', *Energy Security Challenges for the 21st Century*, eds Gal Luft and Anne Korin, Santa Barbara, CA: ABC CLIO, 2009.

Hussein, Hassan, '*Al Watan' Tanashr Tufaseel Tafteesh Safeer Qatr Fee Mataar Al Qaahirah: Rafad Khalaa Al Hithaa* ['Al Watan' Publishes Details of the Inspection of the Qatari Ambassador at Cairo Airport: Refused to Take Off His Shoes]', *El Watan News*, 1 December 2014, http://www.elwatannews.com/news/details/ 609790.

Hvidt, Martin, 'Economic Diversification in GCC Countries: Past Record and Future Trends', *Kuwait Programme on Development, Governance and Globalisation in the Gulf States*, London: London School of Economics, January 2013.

Ibrahim, Youssef, 'U.S. Quietly Gets Gulf States' Aid against Iranians', *The New York Times*, 10 October 1987.

BIBLIOGRAPHY

Ijtehadi, Yadullah, 'Qatar's Global Rise', *Gulf Business*, 21 November 2011 Interview with Qatari Elite Policy Maker, 6 November 2012.

Interview, Academic Practitioner, 28 March 2010 Interview, Dr Birol Baskan, 13 May 2014.

Interview, Senior Diplomat in Qatar, 17 March 2010.

'Iran's Defence Minister Visiting Qatar', Reuters, 28 December 1991.

'Iran's Foreign Minister Visits Oman, UAE, and Qatar', *BBC Monitoring Service: Middle East*, 14 April 1988.

'Iran's Oil Minister to Tour Gulf for Qatar Gas Talks', Reuters, 9 January 1990 'Iran and Hamas Back Sudan's Bashir', *Al Jazeera*, 7 March 2009, http://english.aljazeera.net/news/africa/2009/03/200937132946576390.html.

'Iran Drafts Plan to Exploit Joint Gas Field with Qatar', Reuters, 12 November 1990.

'Iran Starts Weekly Service to Qatar', *Lloyd's List International*, 3 January 1991.

'Iran, Qatar Consider Huge Water Pipeline Project', Reuters, 11 November 1991.

'Iran, Qatar, Russia Form Gas Alliance', *Wall Street Journal*, 22 October 2008, http://online.wsj.com/article/SB122460817038154673.html.

'Iran: A Need for Budget Cuts', *Stratfor Global Intelligence*, 13 April 2009, http://www.stratfor.com/sample/analysis/iran-need-budget-cuts.

'Iranian Envoy, on Gulf Tour, Meets Qatari Emir', Reuters, 9 November 1988 'Iranian Minister Holds Talks on Gulf in Qatar', Reuters, 1 June 1987.

Iranian Protection Asked against Saudi 'Threats', Misr Al Fatah, Cairo: FBIS-NES-92–201 on 1992–10–16, 12 October 1992.

'Iranian Vice-President Arrives in Qatar', Reuters, 5 May 1991.

'Iranian Warship, Destroyer Dock at Qatari Port', *Press TV*, 15 February 2010 http://edition.presstv.ir/detail/118687.html.

'Iraq Bans Al-Jazeera and Nine Other TV Channels over 'Sectarian Bias'', *The Guardian*, 29 April 2013.

'Islamists Suffer Major Defeat in Libya's Early Election Results', *Al Monitor*, 12 October 2012, http://www.al-monitor.com/pulse/iw/politics/2012/07/libya-the-victory-of-jibrils-all.html#.

'Israel to Sever Ties with Qatar', *The Daily Star*, 26 August 2011, http://www.dailystar.com.lb/News/Middle-East/2011/Aug-26/Israel-to-sever-ties-with-Qatar.ashx#axzz1W7qMJ8Cy.

'*Jaamiaah Qatr Thaat Al-Hisaanah* (Qatar University [the University of] Immunity!)', *Al Watan*, 30 April 2014.

'Jabhat Al Nusra', *Mapping Militant Organizations*: Stanford University 'Jabhat Al Nusra', Quilliam Foundation.

James, Laura M, 'Whose Voice? Nasser, the Arabs, and "Sawt Al-Arab"', *Transnational Broadcasting Studies* 16 (2006).

'Jan Poul De Boer Qatar Is Not Another Dubai', *Travel Daily News*, 20 October 2007, http://www.traveldailynews.asia/columns/article/21366/jan-poul-de-boer-qatar.

'Japan's Uncertain Energy Prospects: The Problem of Import Dependence', *Energy Policy*, September 1974.

'Japanese Participate in LNG Development', *Middle East Economic Digest*, 31 January 1975.

Jensen, James T, 'The Development of a Global LNG Market', Oxford: Oxford Institute for Energy Studies, 2004.

Kaddour, Omar, 'Is There a Moderate Syrian Opposition?', *Al Monitor*, 23 September 2014, http://www.al-monitor.com/pulse/security/2014/09/syria-moderates-extremists-united-states-strikes.html#.

Kamrava, Mehran, 'Mediation and Qatari Foreign Policy', *Middle East Journal* 65, 4 (Autumn 2011).

—— *Qatar: Small State, Big Politics* [in English]. Ithaca: Cornell University Press, 2013.

—— 'Royal Factionalism and Political Liberalization in Qatar', *Middle East Journal* Vol. 62, 3 (Summer 2009).

Kaneva, Nadia, 'Nation Branding: Towards an Agenda for Critical Research', *International Journal of Communication* 5 (2011): 117–41.

Karon, Tony, 'Does Qatar Share the West's Agenda in Libya?', *Time*, 5 October 2011

Karsh, Efraim, 'Cold War, Post-Cold War: Does It Make a Difference for the Middle East?', *Review of International Studies* 23 (1997).

Katzman, Kenneth, 'Oman: Reform, Security, and U.S. Policy', *CRS Report for Congress*: Congressional Research Service, 27 December 2013.

Kausch, Kristina, '"Foreign Funding" in Post-Revolution Tunisia', (2013), http://www.fride.org/descarga/WP_Tunisia.pdf.

Keane, Jack, and Daniella Pletka, 'An American-Led Coalition Can Defeat Isis', *Wall Street Journal*, 24 August 2014.

Keinon, Herb, 'FM Rebuffs Qatari Hamas Mediation Offer', *The Jerusalem Post*, 13 February 2006, http://www.jpost.com/Israel/Article.aspx?id=13112.

Kelly, J. B. *Eastern Arabian Frontiers*, London: Frederick A Praeger, 1964.

—— 'Saudi Arabia and the Gulf States', *Critical Choices for Americans*. Lexington, MA: D.C. Heath, 1976.

Keohane, Robert O, 'Reciprocity in International Relations', *International Organization* 40, 1 (Winter 1986).

Kerr, Simeon, 'Qatar Prepares for Sanctions If Brotherhood Dispute Escalates', *Financial Times*, 14 March 2014.

—— 'Qatar's Sovereign Wealth Fund Looks to Diversify in Asia and US', *Financial Times*, 18 June 2015.

—— 'World Cup Woes Add to Qatar Business Jitters', *Financial Times*, 28 June 2015.

Kerr, Simeon, and Pilita Clark, 'UAE Drops Fuel Subsidies to Boost Finances and Cut Emissions', *Financial Times*, 22 July 2015.

Kessler, Oren, 'The Two Faces of Al Jazeera', *The Middle East Quarterly* XIX, 1 (Winter 2012).

'Key Population Indicators (2011)', *Central Department of Statistics and Information*, last accessed 26 August 2012.

Khalaf, Roula, 'Abdication of Qatar's Ruler Avoids Risky Elections', *Financial Times*, 25 June 2013.

——— 'Qatar Steps in to Fill Regional Void', *Financial Times*, 30 November 2011 Khalaf, Roula, and Abigail Fielding-Smith, 'How Qatar Seized Control of the Syrian Revolution', *Financial Times*, 17 May 2013.

Khalaf, Roula, and Simeon Kerr, 'Sheikha Moza, Matriarch of the Modern Gulf', *Financial Times*, 28 June 2013.

Khalilzad, Zalmay, 'The United States and the Persian Gulf: Preventing Regional Hegemony', *Survival* 27, 2 (1995).

Khan, Taimur, 'Hostage Release Highlights Two-Sides of Qatar's Foreign Policy', *The National*, 26 August 2014.

Kiefer, Francine, 'Qatar: The Small Arab Monarchy with the Loud Democratic Voice', *The Christian Science Monitor* (27 May 2011), http://www.bbc.co.uk/news/world-middle-east-20433145.

Kingsley, Patrick, 'Qatar Asks Senior Muslim Brotherhood Leaders to Leave Country', *The Guardian*, 13 September 2014.

——— 'Six Flaws in the Case against Three Jailed Al-Jazeera Journalists', *The Guardian*, 24 June 2014.

Kirkpatrick, David D, 'Army Ousts Egypt's President; Morsi Is Taken into Military Custody', *The New York Times*, 3 July 2013.

——— 'Qatar's Support of Islamists Alienates Allies Near and Far', *The New York Times*, 7 September 2014.

Kleiboer, Marieke, 'Understanding Success and Failure of International Mediation', *Journal of Conflict Resolution* 40, 2 (1 June 1996).

Kotler, Phillip, and David Gertner. 'Country as Brand, Product, and Beyond: A Place Marketing and Brand Management Perspective', *Brand Management* 9, 4–5 (April 2002).

Kotler, Phillip, Donald Haider, and Irving Rein, *Marketing Places: Attracting Investment, Industry, and Tourism to Cities, States, and Nations*, Free Press, 1993.

Koyama, Ken, 'Growing Energy Demand in Asian Countries: Opportunities and Constraints for Gulf Energy Exporters', *Gulf Energy and the World: Challenges and Threats*, Abu Dhabi: The Emirates Centre for Strategic Studies and Research, 1997.

Kraidy, Marwan M, 'Al Jazeera and Al Jazeera English: A Comparative Institutional Analysis', *Annenberg School for Communication Departmental Papers*, Philadelphia: University of Pennsylvania, 2008.

Krieg, Andreas, 'Individual Security and Small State Security', *Gulf Research Centre*, Cambridge, UK, July 2014.

Kursun, Zekeriya, *The Ottomans in Qatar: A History of Anglo-Ottoman Conflicts in the Persian Gulf*; Studies on Ottoman Diplomatic History, Istanbul: Isis Press, 2002 'La chaîne tunisienne privée Attounissia va être rachetée par un groupe du Qatar', *Kapitalis*, http://www.kapitalis.com/medias/15295-la-chaine-tunisienne-privee-attounissia-va-etre-rachetee-par-un-groupe-du-qatar.html.

Lachmann, Gunther, Tim Rohn, and Daniel Wetzel, 'Wie Katars Reichtum Den Terrorverdacht Überstrahlt', *Die Welt*, 17 September 2014, http://www.welt.de/politik/deutschland/article132359548/Wie-Katars-Reichtum-den-Terrorverdacht-ueberstrahlt.html.

Laghmari, Jihen. 'Qatar Giving Tunisia $1bn Loan, May Provide Jobs', *Bloomberg*, 26 April 2012, http://www.bloomberg.com/news/2012–04–26/qatar-giving-tunisia-1-billion-loan-may-provide-jobs.html.

Lahlai, El Mustapha, *Contemporary Arab Broadcast Media*, Edinburgh: Edinburgh University Press, 2011.

'Lakin Haqqaan: Man Hiya Al Maaridah Al Souriyah Al Maatadila? [But Really: Who Is the Moderate Syrian Opposition?]', *Al Hayat*, 21 September 2014, http://alhayat.com/Opinion/Writers/4687431/.

Lambert, Jennifer, 'Political Reform in Qatar: Participation, Legitimacy, and Security', *Journal Essay; Middle East Policy Council.*

Laurent, Lionel, 'Special Report—in France, a Tax-Free Property Empire', Reuters, 8 September 2013, http://uk.reuters.com/article/2013/09/08/uk-france-qatar-property-specialreport-idUKBRE98703D20130908.

Law, Bill, 'Jazz, the Sound of Soft Power in the Desert', *BBC News*, 20 January 2013, http://www.bbc.co.uk/news/world-middle-east-21077174.

Lawrence, Meredity, and Vivienne McCabe, 'Managing Conference in Regional Areas: A Practical Evaluation in Conference Management', *International Journal of Contemporary Hospitality Management* 14, 4 (2001).

LeBaron, Joseph, 'Subject: Scenesetter for Senator Kerry's Visit to Qatar', *Wikileaks*, 8 February 2010.

Lefebvre, Jeffrey A, 'Iran in the Horn of Africa: Outflanking U.S. Allies', *Middle East Policy* XIX, 2 (Summer 2012).

Lepeska, David, 'US Envoy Looks Back to Qatar's Future', *The National*, 11 December 2009.

Levick, Richard, 'Game-Changer: Qatar Plays Historic Role in Glencore's Bid for Xstrata', *Forbes*, 12 September 2012, http://www.forbes.com/sites/richardlevick/2012/09/12/game-changer-qatar-plays-historic-role-in-glencores-bid-for-xstrata/.

Lichfield, John, 'Nicholas Sarkozy "Colluded" to Get Qatar 2022 World Cup', *The Independent*, 29 January 2013.

'Liquid Gas Project', *Middle East Economic Digest*, 19 March 1971.

Lister, Charles, 'The "Real" Jabhat Al-Nusra Appears to Be Emerging', *The Huffington*

Post, 8 July 2014, http://www.huffingtonpost.com/charles-lister/the-real-jabhat-al-nusra_b_5658039.html.

Litwak, Robert, *Sources of Inter-State Conflict*. Security in the Persian Gulf, Montclair; NJ: Rowman & Littlefield Inc., 1981.

Londono, Ernesto, 'Taliban-Held U.S. Soldier Released in Exchange for Afghan Detainees', *The Washington Post*, 1 June 2014.

Longrigg, Stephen Hemsley, 'Oil in the Middle East...Second Edition [with Maps]', Oxford University Press: London, 1961.

Lorimer, John Gordon, *Gazetteer of the Persian Gulf, Oman, and Central Arabia*, Volume 1, Part 1, Calcutta: Superintendent Government Printing, India, 1915

Loveluck, Louise, 'Qatar Asks Muslim Brotherhood Members to Leave Country', *The Daily Telegraph*, 13 September 2014.

Lund, Aron, 'The Politics of the Islamic Front, Part 1: Structure and Support', *Carnegie Endowment for International Peace*, 14 January 2014, http://carnegieendowment.org/syriaincrisis/?fa=54183.

―― 'Syria's Ahrar Al-Sham Leadership Wiped out in Bombing', 9 September 2014, http://carnegieendowment.org/syriaincrisis/?fa=56581.

Luxner, Larry, 'Qatar's Prosperity as High as Its Geopolitical Ambitions', *The Washington Diplomat*, 2 October 2012, http://www.washdiplomat.com/index.php?option=com_content&view=article&id=85 74&Itemid=413.

Lynch, Colum, 'U.N. Report Cites Outside Military Aid to Somalia's Islamic Forces', *The Washington Post*, 15 November 2006.

Lynch, Marc, 'Al Jazeera Challenges: Pass the Salt', *Abu Aardvark Blog*, 29 June 2007, http://abuaardvark.typepad.com/abuaardvark/2007/06/al-jazeera-chal.html.

―― *Voices of the New Arab Public*, New York, NY: Columbia University Press, 2006.

Macdonald, Alastair, 'Friendship Soured: How Assads "Laughed" at Ally', Reuters, 16 March 2012, http://www.reuters.com/article/2012/03/16/syria-assads-email-idUSL5E8EG3NZ20120316.

Macdonald, Sharon J, 'Museums, National, Postnational and Transcultural Identities', *Museum and Society* 1, 1 (2003).

''Made in Qatar' Showcase at 2012 Doha Tribeca Film Festival', *AMEInfo.com*, 23 October 2012, http://www.ameinfo.com/largest-qatar-showcase-2012-doha-tribeca-316541.

Magdy Youssef, Ahmed, 'On Al Jazeera's Lopsided Coverage of Egypt', *Open Democracy*, 2 August 2013, https://www.opendemocracy.net/ahmed-magdy-youssef/on-al-jazeeras-lopsided-coverage-of-egypt.

Maged, Amany, 'Shown the Red Card', *Al Ahram Weekly*, 17 September 2014, http://weekly.ahram.org.eg/News/7284/17/Shown-the-red-card.aspx.

Malas, Nour, 'Qatar to Reap Rewards from Its Rebel Aid', *The Wall Street Journal*, 25 August 2011.

Malbrunot, Georges, 'France-Qatar: Refroidissement Durant La Visite De François Hollande', *Le Figaro*, 3 July 2013, http://blog.lefigaro.fr/malbrunot/2013/07/france-qatar-refroidissement-d.html.

'Mali President Arrives for State Visit', *Cairo MENA*, 5 May 1975, C5.FBIS-MEA-75–087.

Marzouki, Nadia, 'From People to Citizens in Tunisia', *Middle East Report* 273 (Winter 2014).

Mattern, Shannon, 'Font of a Nation: Creating a National Graphic Identity for Qatar', *Public Culture* 20, 3 (2008).

Matthews, Jessica T, 'Power Shifts', *Foreign Affairs* 76, 1 (January–February 1997) Megginson, William L, 'Determinants of Sovereign Wealth Fund Cross-Border Investments', *The Financial Review* 48 (2013).

Mehrotra, Kartikay, 'Bharti Gets $1.26 Billion Investment from Qatar Foundation', *Bloomberg*, 3 May 2013, http://www.bloomberg.com/news/2013–05–03/bharti-receives-1–26-billion-investment-from-qatar-foundation.html.

Melamid, Alexander, 'Political Geography of Trucial 'Oman and Qatar', *Geographical Review* 43, 2 (1953).

Metz, Helen Chapin, ed., *Persian Gulf States: Country Studies*, 3rd Edition, Area Handbook Series, Washington DC: U.S. Government Printing Office, 1994 Miles, Hugh, *Al-Jazeera: How Arab TV News Challenged the World*, London: Abacus, 2006.

——— 'The Al Jazeera Effect', *Foreign Policy*, 9 February 2011 http://foreignpolicy.com/2011/02/09/the-al-jazeera-effect-2/.

The Military Balance 2014, Glasgow: Routledge, 2014.

Miller, Judith, 'Stand-Off in the Gulf', *The New York Times*, 25 December 1990 'Mirages to Qatar', *Jane's Defence Weekly*, 13 October 1990.

Mistilis, Nina, and Larry Dwyer, 'Tourism Gateways and Regional Economies: The Distributional Impacts of Mice', *International Journal of Tourism Research* 1 (1999).

Moini, Joy S, Tora K Biskon, Richard C Neu, and Laura DeSisto, 'The Reform of Qatar University', Santa Monica; CA: RAND, 2009.

Monk, Ashby H B, and Adam Dixon, 'Rethinking the Sovereign in Sovereign Wealth Funds', 3 August 2010.

Moore, Jack, 'Lebanon: Nusra Front Release Army Soldier after Qatar Negotiations', *International Business Times*, 1 October 2014, http://www.ibtimes.co.uk/lebanon-nusra-front-release-army-soldier-after-qatar-negotiations-1468038.

Moran, Dominic, 'New Qatari PM, Diplomatic 'Maverick'', *International Relations and Security Network (ISN)*, 6 April 2007, http://www.isn.ethz.ch/isn/Digital-Library/Articles/Detail/?ots591=4888caa0-b3db-1461–98b9-e20e7b9c13d4&lng=en&id=53103.

Morin, Richard, 'Indentured Servitude in the Persian Gulf', *The New York Times*, 12 April 2013.

'Muslim Brotherhood Says Qatar Ousted Its Members', *The New York Times*, 13 September 2014.

'Must Do Better', *The Economist*, 12 January 2013.

Nader, Sami, 'Emir Replaces Head of Qatar Investment Authority', *Al Monitor*, 12 July 2013, http://www.al-monitor.com/pulse/originals/2013/07/qatar-emir-tamim-investment-fund-new-approach.html.

Nair, Dinesh, 'Exclusive: Qatar Bolstering Wealth Fund Team to Diversify Portfolio—Sources', Reuters, 2 September 2013, http://www.reuters.com/article/2013/09/02/us-qatar-fund-idUSBRE9810BZ20130902.

'Natural Gas Information', *IEA Statistics*, Paris: OECD, 2014 'Natural Gas Information', *IEA Statistics*, Paris: OECD, 2012 'Natural Gas Information', *IEA Statistics*, Paris: OECD, 2005 'Natural Gas Information', *IEA Statistics*, Paris: OECD, 2001 'Natural Gas Information', *IEA Statistics*, Paris: OECD, 2000.

Neate, Rupert, 'Qatar Nurtures Its City Assets: From the Shard to Glencore Shares', *The Guardian*, 27 June 2012.

Nixon, Patrick, 'Qatar: Annual Review for 1987', ed. Middle East Department, Foreign and Commonwealth Office, London: FCO, 30 December 1988.

—— 'Qatar: Annual Review for 1988', ed. Middle East Department, Foreign and Commonwealth Office, London: FCO, 31 December 1988.

—— 'Qatar: Valedictory Annual Review for 1989', ed. Middle East Department, Foreign and Commonwealth Office, London: FCO, 22 January 1990.

Nonneman, Gerd, ed., *Analyzing Middle East Foreign Policies: A Conceptual Framework*. Abingdon, UK: Routledge, 2005.

—— 'The Three Environments of Middle East Foreign Policy Making and Relations with Europe', *Analyzing Middle East Foreign Policies*, Abingdon, UK: Routledge, 2005.

Norris, Pippa, 'The Restless Searchlight: Network News Framing of the Post-Cold War World', *Political Communication* 12 (1995).

Norton-Taylor, Richard, 'Defence Chief Signals Major UK Military Presence in Gulf', *The Guardian*, 18 December 2012, http://www.guardian.co.uk/uk/defence-and-security-blog/2012/dec/18/british-army-the-gulf-defence.

Nye, Joseph S, *The Future of Power*, Philadelphia, PA: Public Affairs, 2011.

—— *Soft Power: The Means to Success in World Politics*, New York: Public Affairs, 2004.

—— 'What New World Order?', *Foreign Affairs*, 1 March 1992.

'Often the GCC Maverick, Qatar Gives 'Assured Access' to the US Military', *Gulf States Newsletter*, 28 November 2003.

Okruhlik, Gwenn, and Patrick J Conge, 'The Politics of Border Disputes on the Arabian Peninsula.' *International Journal* 54, 230 (Spring, 1999).

Olins, Wally, 'Branding the Nation—the Historical Context', *Journal of Brand Management* 9, 4–5 (2002): pp. 241–48.

Onley, James E, 'The Politics of Protection in the Gulf: The Arab Rulers and the British Resident in the Nineteenth Century', *New Arabian Studies*, eds B Pridham, J Smart and G Rex Smith, Exeter: University of Exeter Press, 2004.

Oren, Kessler, 'Qatar Punches above Its Diplomatic Weight', *The Jerusalem Post*, 3 August 2012.

Osserian, Hashem, 'Isis, Nusra Front Hand Demands to Qatari Mediators', *Daily Star*, 6 September 2014, http://www.dailystar.com.lb/News/Lebanon-News/2014/Sep-06/269762-isis-nusra-front-hand-demands-to-qatari-mediators.ashx#axzz3GV9a T9Eb.

Ottaway, David B, 'The Saudi-Qatari Clash over Syria', *The National Interest*, 2 July 2013   http://nationalinterest.org/commentary/the-saudi-qatari-clash-over-syria-8685 'Outsourcing's Third Wave', *The Economist*, 21 May 2009.

Overton, Shaun, 'Understanding the Second Houthi Rebellion in Yemen', *Terrorism Monitor*: The Jamestown Foundation, 17th June 2005.

Oweis, Khaled Yacoub, 'Saudi-Qatari Rivalry Divides Syrian Opposition', Reuters, 15 January 2014, http://www.reuters.com/article/2014/01/15/us-syria-crisis-qatar-idUSBREA0E1G720140115.

Panja, Tariq, 'Qatar Is Only "High Risk" Candidate among Nine Bidders to Host World Cup', *Bloomberg*, 18 November 2010, http://www.bloomberg.com/news/2010–11–17/qatar-is-only-high-risk-candidate-among-nine-bidders-to-host-world-cup.html.

Pantucci, Raffaello, 'The Al-Nusra Front "Merger": Underscoring the Growing Regionalisation of Al-Qa'ida', 15 April 2013, https://www.rusi.org/analysis/commentary/ref:C516C202F5D8B5/#.VJQspF4Cot.

Papachristou, Harry, and Ingrid Melander, 'Qatar Signs Deal to Invest up to $5bn in Greece', Reuters, 24 September 2010.

Papadopoulos, Nicolas, and Louise Heslop, 'Country Equity and Country Branding: Problems and Prospects', *Brand Management* 9, 4–5 (2002): pp. 294–314.

Paterson, Tony, 'German Soldiers "Stranded" in Afghanistan as More Planes Breakdown', *The Daily Telegraph*, 1 October 2014.

Pecquet, Julian, 'Congress Goes after "Frenemies" Turkey, Qatar', *Al Monitor*, 9 September 2014, http://www.al-monitor.com/pulse/originals/2014/09/turkey-qatar-congress-target-frenemies.html.

Peel, Michael, 'Al Jazeera Coverage Raises Tough Questions', *Financial Times*, 4 January 2013.

Peers, Alexandra, 'Qatar Purchases Cezannes *the Card Players* for More Than $250 Million, Highest Price Ever for a Work of Art', *Vanity Fair*, 2 February 2012 'Persian Gulf: Qatar: Use of Natural Gas', *Middle East Economic Digest*, 2 November 1960.

Personal Correspondence: Patrick Flaherty, Sovereign Wealth Fund Researcher, 15 March 2013.

Personal Interview: Doha-Based British Embassy Official, 20 February 2013 Personal

Interview: Dr Steven Wright, Qatar University, 6 February 2013 Personal Interview: Former Ambassador to Qatar, 30 November 2010 Personal Interview: Israeli Diplomat, 11 August 2010.

Personal Interview: Qatar-Based European Ambassador, 7 March 2010.

Personal Interview: Qatar-Based European Ambassador, 3 March 2010 Personal Interview: Qatar-Based European Diplomat, 6 April 2010 Personal Interview: Qatar-Based European Diplomat, 16 March 2010 Personal Interview: Qatar-Based Focus Group, 25 March 2010.

Personal Interview: Qatar-Based South American Ambassador, 21 March 2010 Personal Interview: Qatari Government Adviser, 22 October 2012.

Peterson, J E, 'The Al-Huthi Conflict in Yemen', *Arabian Peninsula Background Note* No. APBN-006 (August 2008).

———. 'Qatar and the World: Branding for a Micro-State', *The Middle East Journal* 60 (2006): pp. 732–748.

Pintak, Larry, 'The Al Jazeera Revolution', *Foreign Policy*, 2 February 2011 http://foreignpolicy.com/2011/02/02/the-al-jazeera-revolution/.

———. *The New Arab Journalist: Mission and Identity in a Time of Turmoil* [in English]. Kindle edition, London: I B Tauris, 2011.

Pipes, Daniel, 'Interview with Hamad Bin Jassim Bin Jabr Al Thani', *Middle East Quarterly*, December 1996.

Plunkett, John, and Josh Halliday, 'Al-Jazeera's Coverage of Egypt Protests May Hasten Revolution in World News', *The Guardian*, 7 February 2011.

Pons, Frédéric, 'Tripoli Sous La Loi Des "Katibas"', *Valeurs Actuelles*, 12 January 2012 http://www.valeursactuelles.com/international/tripoli-sous-loi-des-%E2%80%9C katibas%E2%80%9D20120112.html.

'Population, Total (1981–2011)', *Data*: World Bank, last accessed 26 August 2012.

Powers, Shawn, and Eytan Gilboa, 'The Public Diplomacy of Al Jazeera', *New Media and the New Middle East*, ed. Philip M Seib. Basingstoke: Palgrave Macmillan, 2007 'President Al-Assad Receives Letter from Emir of Qatar Affirming His Country's Support for Syrian Leadership's Effort to Foil Attempts at Undermining Syria's Security and Stability', *Tishreen*, 3 March 2011, http://tishreen.news.sy/tishreen/public/read/225349.

Press, The Associated, 'Qatar Doubles Aid to Egypt', *The New York Times*, 8 January 2013.

'Pro-Israel Groups to Rally against Qatar's Financing of Terror', *Haaretz*, 18 September 2014.

Prosor, Ron. 'Club Med for Terrorists', *The New York Times*, 24 August 2014 'Putting the GCC House in Order', *Inside Story: Al Jazeera*, 8 December 2014, http://www. aljazeera.com/programmes/insidestory/2014/12/putting-gcc-house-order-201412818195965828.html#.VIar6LhrAa0.facebook.

Putz, Catherine, 'Tajik Border Guards Held by Taliban to Be Released', *The Diplomat*,

16 June 2015, http://thediplomat.com/2015/06/tajik-border-guards-held-by-taliban-to-be-released/.

'Pygmy with the Punch of a Giant', *The Economist*, 5 November 2011 'Qatar's Annus Horribilis', *Al Monitor*, 26 June 2014, http://www.al-.monitor.com/pulse/originals/2014/06/qatar-saudi-muslim-brotherhood-foreign-policy.html.

'Qatar's Culture Queen', *The Economist*, 31 May 2012.

'Qatar Exports Plunge over 40 Pct in Year', *France 24*, 30 August 2015, http://www.france24.com/en/20150830-qatar-exports-plunge-over-40-pct-year 'Qatar's Foreign Policy Focuses on Promoting Communication: FM', *Gulf Times*, 17 November 2014, http://www.gulf-times.com/Mobile/Qatar/178/details/416564/Qatar%E2%80%99s-foreign-policy-focuses-on-promoting-communication%3A-FM.

'Qatar Approves Deployment of Friendly Forces', Reuters, 27 August 1990 'Qatar Boycotts Gulf Arab War Games', Reuters, 5 March 1996.

'Qatar Build-Up', *Private Eye*, 1379, 14–27 November 2014.

'Qatar Considers Ways of Keeping Iranians Off Their Rigs', *Gulf States Newsletter*, 845, 16 January 2009.

'Qatar Could Sever Ties with Israel If Part of Joint Arab Stance', *Cablegate*, Doha, Qatar: *Wikileaks*, 12 January 2009.

'Qatar Country Report', *EIU Country Report*, London: Economist Intelligence Unit, July 2013.

'Qatar Country Report', *EIU Country Report*, London: Economist Intelligence Unit, April 2013.

'Qatar Economic Outlook 2012–2013 Update', *Qatar Economic Outlook*, Doha, Qatar: General Secreteriat for Development Planning, 2012.

'Qatar Emir to Change Style but Keep Policy', *GulfNews.com*, 27 June 2013 http://gulfnews.com/news/gulf/qatar/qatar-emir-to-change-style-but-keep-policy-1.1202793.

'Qatar Gas Swap Deal with Egypt Collapses', *Gulf States Newsletter*, September 2013 'Qatar Gives $50m to Palestinians', *BBC News*, 17 April 2006 http://news.bbc.co.uk/2/hi/middle_east/4917088.stm.

'Qatar Goes on Spending Spree', *IHS Jane's 360*, 7 May 2014 http://www.janes.com/article/37584/qatar-goes-on-spending-spree.

'Qatar Investment Authority, Part One: History and Structure', *Cablegate*, 23 July 2008.

'Qatar Looks East to Singapore as a Model for Security and Economic Development', *Cablegate*, Doha, Qatar: *Wikileaks*, 17 December 2007.

'Qatar National Bank Denies Investing in Iran Oilfield', Reuters, 4 October 2009, http://www.reuters.com/article/2009/10/04/us-qnb-iran-idUSTRE59318Y20091004 'Qatar National Convention Centre Records Robust Growth', *Breaking Travel*, 21 May 2012, http://www.breakingtravelnews.com/news/article/qatar-national-convention-centre-records-robust-growth/.

'Qatar National Vision 2030', Doha, Qatar: General Secreteriat for Development Planning, July 2008.

'Qatar Opens Diplomatic Relations with China', Reuters, 9 July 1988.

'Qatar Pledges to End Naturalisation of GCC Citizens: Report', *GulfNews.com*, 16 August 2014, http://gulfnews.com/news/gulf/qatar/qatar-pledges-to-end-naturalisation-of-gcc-citizens-report-1.1372615.

'Qatar Predicts Wider Budget Deficit in 1988/89' Reuters, 17 February 1988 'Qatar Refinery Play Highlights Tunisian Agenda', *Gulf States Newsletter* 36, 924, May 2012.

'Qatar Risks Major Economic Fallout from Gulf Dispute', *Oxford Analytica Daily Brief*, 25 March 2014.

'Qatar Said to Give $50m in Aid to Hamas-Led Government', *Haaretz*, 17 April 2006, http://www.haaretz.com/news/qatar-said-to-give-50-million-in-aid-to-hamas-led-government-1.185409.

'Qatar Says It Mediated Release of Fiji Peacekeepers', *Daily Star*, 12 September 2014 http://www.dailystar.com.lb/News/Middle-East/2014/Sep-12/270456-qatar-says-it-mediated-release-of-fiji-peacekeepers.ashx#axzz3DrW0VeCz.

'Qatar Sets up Full Ties with Yugoslavia', Reuters, 24 August 1989 'Qatar to Open Office in Gaza', *The Jerusalem Post*, 31 July 1995.

'Qatar Tumps Saudi Arabia on Syrian Opposition Leader', *Al Monitor*, 21 March 2013, http://www.al-monitor.com/pulse/politics/2013/03/qatar-appoint-coalition-head-syria.html.

'Qatar Upgrades PLO Office to Embassy', Reuters, 7 January 1989.

'Qatar Varsity Students Vent Ire on Twitter', *The Peninsula*, 17 May 2012.

'Qatar, Burindi Establish Diplomatic Relations', *Cairo MENA*, 4 November 1974, C2.FBIS-MEA-74–213.

'Qatar, Israel Discuss Aviation Pact', *United Press International*, 18 November 1995 'Qatar: A Bouncy Bantam', *The Economist*, 7 September 2006.

'Qatar: In Brief', *Middle East Economic Digest*, 18 June 1976.

'Qatar: Political Modernisation', *Oxford Analytics Daily Brief Service*, 3 July 1998 'Qatari Ambassador Closes Embassy, Leaves Damascus', *France 24*, 18 July 2011, http://www.france24.com/en/20110718-qatar-ambassador-suspends-embassy-operations-leaves-damascus-khayarine-syria/.

'Qatari Crown Prince Starts Four-Day Visit to Iran', Reuters, 7 November 1991 'Qatari Interior Minister in Iran', Reuters, 10 May 1992.

'Qatari Mediation Succeeds in Releasing Maaloula Nuns', *Qatar Ministry of Foreign Affairs*, 1 September 2014 http://www.mofa.gov.qa/en/SiteServices/MediaCenter/News/Pages/News2014031008 1807.aspx.

Qatub, AbdulMajid, '*Asim Abdulmajid: 28 Nowfember Sayushaahid Tahwilaan Nuwaayan Fee Huwiya Al Thawra Al Misriyah* [Asim Abdulmajid: 28 November Will See a Qualitative Shift in the Identity of the Egyptian Revolution]', *Al Sharq*, 16 November 2014.

Quandt, William B, *Saudi Arabia in the 1980s: Foreign Policy, Security and Oil*, Washington DC: The Brookings Institution, 1981.

Rabi, Uzi, 'Qatar', *Middle East Contemporary Survey*, ed. Ami Ayalon, Boulder, Colorado: Westview Press, 1991.

———. 'Qatar's Relations with Israel: Challenging Arab and Gulf Norms', *The Middle East Journal* 63, 3 (2009).

Rabil, Robert G, 'Lebanon at the Crossroads', *Open Democracy*, 5 June 2009, http://www.opendemocracy.net/article/lebanon-at-the-crossroads.

'Rachid Ghannouchi', *The Independent*, 9 October 2012.

Rahman, Habibur, *The Emergence of Qatar*, London: Keegan Paul Ltd, 2005 '*Raiis Wuzara Qatr: Misr Akbar Min an Tishtryha...Wa Lam Naard Taajyr Al-Ahramaat Aw Al Qanaat* [Qatar's Prime Minister: Egypt Is Bigger Than We Could Afford [Sic]. We Did Not [Try to] Hire the Pyramids or the [Suez] Channel]', *Al Misry Al Youm*, 27 March 2013, http://www.almasryalyoum.com/news/details/298392

Ramadan, Bassam, 'Qatar under Pressure over Support for Brotherhood', *Al Monitor*, 23 April 2014, http://www.al-monitor.com/pulse/politics/2014/04/qatar-gcc-demand-stop-support-brotherhood.html.

Ramazani, R K, 'Iran's Foreign Policy: Both North and South', *The Middle East Journal* 46, 3 (Summer 1992).

Rathmell, Andrew, and Kirsten Schulze, 'Political Reform in the Gulf: The Case of Qatar', *Middle Eastern Studies* 36, 4 (2000): pp. 47–62.

'Rebels V Rebels', *The Economist*, 21 November 2013.

Rentz, George, *Oman and the South-Eastern Shore of Arabia*, Reading: Ithaca, 1997 'Report: UN Had Qatar Pay Off Al-Qaida Fighters for Release of Fiji Peacekeepers', *Haaretz*, 24 October 2011.

'Report on Allied Contributions to the Common Defense', US Department of Defense, March 2001.

Ricchiardi, Sherry, 'The Al Jazeera Effect', *American Journalism Review*, March–April 2011, http://www.ajr.org/article.asp?id=5077.

Richards, J B, 'British Residency Bahrain, Despatch No. 85, 17 July 1956, 17410/7/56)', in *Islamic Movements in the Arab World 1913–1966*, ed Anita L P Burdett, London: Cambridge Archive Editions, 1998.

Robert, Virginie, 'La France Pour Une Relation Plus "Normale" Avec Le Qatar', *Les Echos*, 21 June 2013, http://www.lesechos.fr/21/06/2013/LesEchos/21462–029-ECH_la-france-pour-une-relation-plus--normale—avec-le-qatar.htmRobert,%20Virginie.

Roberts, David B, 'Behind Qatar's Intervention in Libya', *Foreign Affairs*, 28 September 2011.

———. 'British National Interest in the Gulf: Rediscovering a Role?', *International Affairs* 90, 3 (2014): pp. 663–677.

———. 'Is Qatar Sponsoring Al Qa'ida in Mali', *RUSI*, 7 February 2013, http://www.rusi.org/go.php?structureID=commentary&ref=C5113B501179CB.

BIBLIOGRAPHY

————. 'Kuwait', *Power and Politics in the Persian Gulf Monarchies*, ed. Christopher Davidson, London: Hurst & Co., 2011.

————. 'News from Qatar Protest', *TheGulfBlog.com*, 16 March 2011, http://thegulf-blog.com/2011/03/16/news-from-qatar-protest/.

————. 'Punching above Its Weight', *Foreign Policy*, 12 April 2011.

———— 'Qatar's Flowering Relationship with Paris', *Financial Times*, 1 November 2012, http://www.ft.com/intl/cms/s/0/d457bbec-2342–11e2-a66b-00144feabdc0.html#axzz2MyALJUSn.

———— 'Qatar and Japan: A Marriage of Convenience?', *Kyoto-Durham Symposium*, Kyoto, Japan 2012.

———— 'Qatar and the Muslim Brotherhood: Pragmatism or Preference?', *Middle East Policy* 21, 3 (2014): pp. 84–94.

———— 'Qatari Mediation', *Gulf Research Centre Conference*, Cambridge, UK, 2010 Rolim Silva, Luis Henrique, 'The Establishment of the Qatar National Olympic Committee: Building the National Sport Identity', *The International Journal of the History of Sport* 31, 3 (2014/02/11 2014): pp. 306–319.

Rosenberg, David, 'Qatar Punches above Its Weight', *The Jerusalem Post*, 18 January 2012.

Rosenberg, Matthew, 'Taliban Opening Qatar Office, and Maybe Door to Talks', *The New York Times*, 3 January 2012.

Rother, Larry, 'Mixing Oil and Hollywood: Tribeca Festival Expands to the Persian Gulf', *The New York Times*, 23 October 2009.

Rubin, Lawrence, 'A Typology of Soft Powers in Middle East Politics', *Working Paper*, Dubai: The Dubai Initiative, December 2010.

'Ruler Replaced Seven in Major Qatar Cabinet Reshuffle', Reuters, 18 July 1989 Sahraoui, Sofiane, and Mohamed Zayani, *The Culture of Al Jazeera: Inside an Arab Media Giant*, Jefferson, NC: McFarland & Company Inc., 2007.

Salem, Mohammed, 'What Egypt Lost in the Al Jazeera Trial', *Al Monitor*, 26 August 2014 http://www.al-monitor.com/pulse/originals/2014/08/egypt-law-al-jazeera-journalists-trial.html.

Salman, Talal, 'An Old Dialogue with the Emir of Qatar in the Context Of: Israel Being a Gatekeeper of Arab Affiliation with Washington', *As Safir*, 21 October 2009.

Samuel-Azran, Tal, 'Al-Jazeera, Qatar, and New Tactics in State-Sponsored Media Diplomacy', *American Behavioral Scientist* 57, 9 (1 September 2013): pp. 1293–1311 Sands, Phil, 'GCC Rift Could Trigger New Power Struggle in Syrian Opposition', *The National*, 10 March 2014.

Sanger, Richard Harlakenden, *The Arabian Peninsula*, London: Cornell University Press; Oxford University Press, 1954.

Santiso, Javier, 'Sovereign Wealth Funds', ESADE Business School and KPMG, 2014.

'Saudi and UAE Border in Dispute over ID Cards', Reuters, 23 August 2009, http://in.reuters.com/article/2009/08/23/idINIndia-41923020090823.

'Saudi Arabia and Qatar Fight for Influence', *Huffington Post*, 22 August 2013 http:// www.huffingtonpost.com/2013/08/21/saudi-arabia-qatar-fight-influence_n_ 3792186.html.

Saudi Troops Attack Border Post; 2 Killed, Paris AFP, FBIS-NES-92–191 on 1992– 10–01, 30 September 1992.

'Saudis in Border Deal with Qatar', *BBC News*, 17 December 2008, http://news.bbc. co.uk/1/hi/world/middle_east/7788530.stm.

Sayare, Scott, 'Qatar Is Becoming a Player in French Sports', *The New York Times*, 26 October 2012.

'Scenesetter for August 26 Centcom Component Commanders Conference', *Wikileaks*, 18 August 2008, https://wikileaks.org/plusd/cables/08DOHA587_a. html Schenker, David, 'Who's Behind the Houthis?', *The Weekly Standard* vol. 15, 22, 22 February 2010.

Schmitt, Eric, 'Pentagon Construction Boom Beefs up Mideast Air Base', *The New York Times*, 18 September 2005.

Sciolino, Elaine, 'Qatar Rejects U.S. Demand for Return of Illicit Stingers', *The New York Times*, 28 June 1988, http://www.nytimes.com/1988/06/28/world/qatar-rejects-us-demand-for-return-of-illicit-stingers.html.

Scott, Victoria, 'Dfi Postpones New Film Festival after Laying Off Dozens of Employees', *Doha News*, 12 January 2014, http://dohanews.co/dfi-postpones-new-film-festival-after-laying-off-dozens-of-employees/.

'A Search for Allies in a Hostile World', *The Economist*, 4 February 2010 'Search: "Qatar"', *Google Trends*, December 2014, http://www.google.com/trends/ explore#q=qatar.

Searight, Sarah, 'Special Report on Qatar (3): This Proud Aloof Nation', *The Times*, 12 November 1985.

Seddiq, Ramin, 'Border Disputes on the Arabian Peninsula', *Policy Watch*: The Washington Institute for Near East Policy, 2001.

Shadid, Anthony, 'Qatar's Capital Glitters Like a World City, but Few Feel at Home', *The New York Times*, 29 November 2011.

——— 'Qatar Wields an Outsized Influence in Arab Politics', *The New York Times*, 14 November 2011.

Shaheen, Abdul Nabi, 'Eritrea: In Pursuit of the Truth.' *GulfNews.com*, 21 April 2012, http://gulfnews.com/news/region/eritrea/eritrea-in-pursuit-of-the-truth-1.615302.

'Shaikh Ahmed Al Thani to Visit the Soviet Union', *Middle East Economic Digest*, 16 September 1988.

Sharaf, Ayman, 'Al Jazeera Staff Resign after "Biased" Egypt Coverage', *GulfNews.com*, 8 July 2013, http://gulfnews.com/news/region/egypt/al-jazeera-staff-resign-after-biased-egypt-coverage-1.1206924.

Sharma, Kedar, 'U.S., French Advance Qatar Wargames—Diplomats', Reuters, 27 February 1996.

Sharman, Andy, 'British Land's "Super-Prime" Mayfair Penthouse Breaks Sale Record', *Financial Times*, 22 September 2014.

Sharp, Jeremy M, 'Qatar: Background and U.S. Relations', *CRS Report for Congress*, Washington DC: Congressional Research Service, 17 March 2004.

Sharp, Rob, 'Qatar Hero? The Sheikh Who Shook up the Art World', *The Independent*, 29 June 2011.

'Shaykh Receives Dprk's Chon Myong-Su', *Pyongyang KCNA*, 22 August 1975, C4. FBIS-MEA-75–164.

Sherlock, Ruth, 'Inside Jabhat Al Nusra—the Most Extreme Wing of Syria's Struggle', *The Daily Telegraph*, 2 December 2012.

Shrimp, Terence, Saeed Saimee, and Thomas Madden, 'Countries and Their Products: A Cognitive Structure Perspective', *Journal of the Academy of Marketing Science* 21, 4 (1993).

Siegel, Robert, 'How Tiny Qatar "Punches above Its Weight"', *NPR*, 23 December 2013, http://www.npr.org/blogs/parallels/2013/12/20/255748469/how-tiny-qatar-punches-above-its-weight.

Slackman, Michael, 'Privilege Pulls Qatar Towards Unhealthy Choices', *The New York Times*, 26 April 2010.

Slaughter, Anne-Marie, 'The Real New World Order', *Foreign Affairs* 76, 5 (1997) Sly, Liz, 'US-Backed Syria Rebels Routed by Fighters Linked to Al Qaeda', *Washington Post*, 2 November 2014.

Smoltczyk, Alexander, 'The Voice of Egypt's Muslim Brotherhood', *Spiegel Online International*, 15 February 2011, http://www.spiegel.de/international/world/islam-s-spiritual-dear-abby-the-voice-of-egypt-s-muslim-brotherhood-a-745526. html Smyth, Jamie, 'LNG Boom Fuels Australia Export Ambitions', *Financial Times*, 2 October 2014.

'Sotheby's Exhibition at Katara', *Gulf Times*, 22 October 2012.

Southan, Jenny, 'Doha's Ambition', *Business Traveller*, 20 August 2010 Spector, Bertram I, and Anna R Korula, 'Facilitating Mediation in International Disputes: From Research to Practical Application', Laxenburg: International Institution for Applied Systems Analysis, February 1992.

'Sports Sector Strategy (2011–2016)', Doha, Qatar: Qatar Olympic Committee, July 2011.

Spring, Jake, 'Qatar's Wealth Fund to Launch $10 Billion Investment Fund with China's Citic', Reuters, 4 November 2014, http://in.reuters.com/article/2014/11/04/qatar-china-sovereign-wealth-idINKBN0IO0QU20141104.

Sreberny-Mohammadi, Annabelle, 'The Media and Democratization in the Middle East: The Strange Case of Television', *Democratization* 5, 2 (1998).

'State of Qatar', *The Times*, 15 May 1972.

Steinberg, Guido, 'Qatar and the Arab Spring', German Institute for International and Security Affairs (SWP Berlin), February 2012.

Steinvorth, Daniel, and Alexander Szandar, 'The Victors of Beirut: Hezbollah Triumphs in Lebanon', *Spiegel Online International*, 29 May 2008, http://www.spiegel.de/international/world/the-victors-of-beirut-hezbollah-triumphs-in-lebanon-a-556353.html.

Stephens, Michael, 'Shuttle Diplomacy: Qatar Playing Politics in Palestine', *Open Democracy*, 29 October 2012, https://www.opendemocracy.net/michael-stephens/shuttle-diplomacy-qatar-playing-politics-in-palestine.

Stern, Paul C, and Daniel Druckman, *International Conflict Resolution after the Cold War*, Washington, DC; [United Kingdom]: National Academy Press, 2000.

Stoakes, Frank, 'Social and Political Change in the Third World', *The Arabian Peninsula: Society and Politics*, ed. Derek Hopwood, London: Allen and Unwin, 1972.

Stork, Joe, and Martha Wenger, 'The US in the Persian Gulf: From Rapid Deployment to Massive Deployment', *Middle East Report*, 168 (January–February 1991).

'Striving for Excellence: Shaikh Tamim Bin Hamad Al Thani, Emir of Qatar, on the Future Vision for the State', *Oxford Business Group*, November 2013, http://www.oxfordbusinessgroup.com/viewpoint/striving-excellence-sheikh-tamim-bin-hamad-al-thani-emir-qatar-future-vision-state.

'Subject: Qatar Establishing a Tourism Niche', *Cablegate*, Doha, Qatar: *Wikileaks*, 26 February 2007.

Sweetland Edwards, Haley, 'The Richest, Fattest Nation on Earth (It's Not the United States)', *The Atlantic*, 16 November 2011, http://www.theatlantic.com/health/archive/2011/11/the-richest-fattest-nation-on-earth-its-not-the-united-states/248366/.

'Swiss Ambassador's Credentials', *Doha*, 12 June 1975, C2.FBIS-MEA-75–114 'Syrian President Al-Asad in Ad-Dawhah for Talks', *Damascus Domestic Service*, 1974, page B2.FBIS-MEA-74–039, DAILY REPORT. MIDDLE EAST & AFRICA.

Taheri, Amir, 'Sudan: An Expanding Civil War with an Iran Connection', *The New York Times*, 9 April 1997, http://www.nytimes.com/1997/04/09/opinion/09ihtedamir.t.html.

Tajudin, 'After Mediation of Qatar, Eritrea Releases Djiboutian Soldier', *The Diplomat*, 19 September 2014, http://diplomat.so/2014/09/19/after-mediation-of-qatar-eritrea-releases-djiboutian-soldier-2/.

'Taliban Shuts Doha HQ over "Broken Promises"', *Al Jazeera*, 9 July 2013, http://www.aljazeera.com/news/middleeast/2013/07/201379221645539703.html Talks, TED, 'Sheikha Al Mayassa: Globalizing the Local, Localizing the Global', *TED Talks Director*, YouTube, 8 February 2012.

'Talks with Qatar Suspended', *The New York Times*, 28 July 1988.

Taremi, Kamran, 'The Role of Water Exports in Iranian Foreign Policy Towards the GCC', *Iranian Studies* 28, 2 (June 2005).

Tastekin, Fehim, 'Saudi Arabia and Qatar Vie for Influence in Syria', *Al Monitor*, 17

April 2013, http://www.al-monitor.com/pulse/ar/politics/2013/04/saudi-arabia-qatar-vie-influence-syria.html#.

Telhami, Shibley, 'Behind the Abdication of Qatar's Emir', Reuters, 26 June 2013, http://blogs.reuters.com/great-debate/2013/06/26/behind-the-abdication-of-qatars-emir/.

Teller, Matthew, 'Has Wealth Made Qatar Happy?', *BBC News Magazine*, 28 April 2014, http://www.bbc.com/news/magazine-27142647.

Tobin, Jonathan S, 'The Al Jazeera Liberal', *Commentary*, 1 April 2013, http://www.commentarymagazine.com/2013/01/04/the-al-jazeera-liberals-al-gore/

Tomlinson, Alan, and Christopher Young, *National Identity and Global Sports Events: Culture, Politics, and Spectacle*, Albany, NY: State University of New York Press, 2006.

'Too Rich for Its Own Good', *The Economist*, 7 June 2014.

Toth, Anthony, 'Qatar', *Persian Gulf States: Country Studies*, ed. Helen Chapin Metz, Washington DC: U.S. Government Printing Office, 1994.

Toumi, Habib, 'Public Sector in Qatar to Get 60 Per Cent Pay Rise', *GulfNews.com*, 7 September 2011, http://gulfnews.com/news/gulf/qatar/public-sector-in-qatar-to-get-60-per-cent-pay-rise-1.862595.

——— 'Saudi Prisoners Release from Qatar Jail Eases Relations', *Gulf News*, 27 May 2010, http://gulfnews.com/news/gulf/qatar/saudi-prisoner-release-from-qatar-jail-eases-relations-1.632852.

Trenwith, Courtney, 'Qatar to Invest $10bn in Malaysia—Report', *ArabianBusiness. com*, 30 January 2013.

'Tunisia Reportedly Recalls Its Ambassador in Qatar after TV Programme', *Zeitouna [BBC Monitoring]*, 9 March 2001.

Tuson, Penelope, *Records of Qatar: Primary Documents 1820–1960*, Slough: Archive Editions, 1991.

———, ed. *Report of Visit to Qatar: Persian Gulf Residency, Bahrain to Foreign Office, London, 18th August 1949*, Records of Qatar: Primary Documents 1820–1960: Volume 6: 1935–1949, Slough: Archive Editions, 1991.

———, ed *Report on Qatar: Political Agency, Doha to Political Resident, Bahrain—28th December 1958*, Records of Qatar: Primary Documents 1820–1960: Volume 7: 1949–1960, Slough: Archive Editions, 1991.

———, ed *Telegram: Bahrain Residency to Foreign Office, London—No.377*, Records of Qatar: Primary Documents 1820–1960: Volume 6: 1935–1949, Slough: Archive Editions, 1991.

Tyler, Patrick, 'US Drawn into Gulf Dispute', *Washington Post*, 6 October 1988 'Uganda President Amin Arrives on Visit', *Doha QNA*, 20 October 1975, C2. FBIS-MEA-75–203.

'UK to Establish £15m Permanent Mid East Military Base', *BBC News*, 6 December 2014, http://www.bbc.com/news/uk-30355953.

Ulrichsen, Kristian Coates, 'The Gulf States and South-South Cooperation, 1961–

1990: Contradictions and Commonalities', *BRISMES Annual Conference 2012*; LSE, 2012.

——— *Qatar and the Arab Spring* [in English], London: Hurst & Co. Ltd., 2014.

——— 'Qatar and the Arab Spring: Policy Drivers and Regional Implications', *Carnegie Endowment for International Peace*, September 2014, http://carnegieendowment.org/files/qatar_arab_spring.pdf.

'Umm Said Lpg Plant Disaster 03–04–77', *Scribd*, http://www.scribd.com/doc/21090127/UMM-Said-LPG-Plant-Disaster-03–04–77.

Untermeyer, Diana, 'Racing Horses Towards Modernity in Qatar', *Huffington Post*, 15 February 2012, http://www.huffingtonpost.com/diana-untermeyer/qatar-horses_b_1277243.html.

'US-Qatar Navies End Joint Military Exercises', Reuters, 17 December 1996 'US Air Force Begins Joint Exercises in Qatar', Reuters, 3 July 1996.

'US Embassy Cables: Qatari Prime Minister: "Iranians Lie to Us"', *The Guardian*, 28 November 2010, http://www.guardian.co.uk/world/us-embassy-cables-document/240782.

'US Marines Storm Qatar Beach in Military Exercises', Reuters, 18 March 1996 'US Seeks Return of Qatar's Stingers', *Janes Defence Weekly*, 6 August 1988.

Valbjorn, Morten, and Andre Bank, 'The New Arab Cold War: Rediscovering the Arab Dimension of Middle East Regional Politics', *Review of International Studies* (2011).

Van Ham, Peter, 'Place Branding: The State of the Art', *The Annals of the American Academy of Political and Social Science* 616, 1 (2008): pp. 126–149.

——— 'The Rise of the Brand State: The Postmodern Politics of Image and Reputation', *Foreign Affairs*, September–October 2001.

Vukmanovic, Oleg, 'Qatar's LNG Gift to Egypt to Find Foreign Firms', Reuters, 12 July 2013, http://www.reuters.com/article/2013/07/12/egypt-lng-idUSL6N0FE3QS20130712.

Waddington, Marc, 'Fears Liverpool Firms' Qatar World Cup Payments Funding Isis Terror', *Liverpool Echo*, 29 October 2014, http://www.liverpoolecho.co.uk/news/liverpool-news/fears-liverpool-firms-qatar-world-8016508.

Walker, Julian, 'Qatar: Annual Review for 1986', ed. Middle East Department, Foreign and Commonwealth Office, London: FCO, 4 January 1987.

Warden, Francis, 'Historical Sketch of the Uttoobee Tribe of Arabs (Bahrein) from the Year 1716 to the Year 1817', *Selections from the Records of the Bombay Government*, pp. 361–425, Bombay: London, 1856.

Weaver, Mary Anne, 'Qatar: Revolution from the Top Down', *National Geographic Magazine*, March 2003.

Whelan, John, 'Qatar Fire', *Middle East Economic Digest*, 15 April 1977.

——— 'Qatar: Cutbacks in Spending Masks Big Chances for Contractors', *Middle East Economic Digest*, 22 June 1978.

White, Jeffry, 'Rebels Worth Supporting: Syria's Harakat Hazm', 28 April 2014, http://www.washingtoninstitute.org/policy-analysis/view/rebels-worth-supporting-syrias-harakat-hazm.

Williams, Dan, 'Sudan: A Front for Israel's Proxy War on Sinai Jihadis?', Reuters, 25 October 2012, http://www.reuters.com/article/2012/10/25/us-sudan-planes-israel-idUSBRE89O1D720121025.

Williamson, Samuel H, 'Seven Ways to Compute the Relative Value of a U.S. Dollar Amount, 1774 to Present', *MeasuringWorth* (2015).

Willis, Michael, and Nizar Messari, 'Analyzing Moroccan Foreign Policy and Relations with Europe', *Analyzing Middle East Foreign Policies*, Abingdon, UK: Routledge, 2005.

Wines, Michael, and Doyle McManus, 'Gulf State of Qatar Gets Stinger Missiles', *Los Angeles Times*, 31 March 1988.

Wogan, Patrick, 'Qatar: Annual Review for 1993', ed. Middle East Department, Foreign and Commonwealth Office, London: FCO, 12 January 1994.

'World Economic Outlook Database', *World Economic and Financial Surveys*, International Monetary Fund, April 2015.

Worth, Robert F, 'Al Jazeera No Longer Nips at Saudis', *The New York Times*, 4 January 2008.

——— 'Qatar, Playing All Sides, Is a Non Stop Mediator', *The New York Times*, 9 July 2008.

Wright, David, 'Qatar: Annual Review for 1997', ed. Middle East Department, Foreign and Commonwealth Office, London: FCO.

Wu, Kang, and Jit Yang Lim, 'Supplying Asia-Pacific Oil Demand: Role of the Gulf', *Gulf Oil and Gas: Ensuring Economic Security*, Abu Dhabi: The Emirates Centre for Strategic Studies and Research, 2007.

Yaqoob, Tahira, 'Can Billion-Dollar Investment Put Qatar on the Cultural Map?', *The Independent*, 20 October 2012.

Yee, Amy, 'Qatar Sets Scene for Film Industry', *Financial Times*, 11 February 2009

'Yemen's Houthis Hold Secret Meet with Iran', *Al Arabiyya*, 13 December 2009, http://www.alarabiya.net/articles/2009/12/13/94076.html.

Yetiv, S A, 'How the Soviet Military Intervention in Afghanistan Improved the US Strategic Position in the Persian Gulf', *Asian Affairs* 17, 2 (Summer 1990).

Yilmaz, Muzaffer Ercan, '"The New World Order": An Outline of the Post-Cold War Era', *Alternatives: Turkish Journal of International Relations* 7, 4 (Winter 2008) 'You Are Either with Us or against Us', *CNN*, 6 November 2011, http://edition.cnn.com/2001/US/11/06/gen.attack.on.terror/.

Young, Michael, 'Pragmatic Diplomacy Enables Qatar to Punch above Weight', *The National*, 24 November 2011.

'Young Qataris More Proud of Their National Identity Than Ever Before: Survey', *Gulf Times*, 4 June 2013, http://www.gulf-times.com/qatar/178/details/355060/young-qataris-more-proud-of-their-national-identity-than-ever-before:-survey.

Zahlan, Rosemarie Said, *The Creation of Qatar*, London, New York: Croom Helm 1979.

Zayed, Dina, 'Feature: Al Jazeera TV Makes Waves with Tunisia Coverage', Reuters, 21 January 2011, http://www.reuters.com/article/2011/01/21/tunisia-jazeera-idAFLDE70J1YX20110121.

Zellman, Gail L, Gery W Ryan, Louay Constant, Charles A Goldman, Dominic J Brewer, Catherine H Augustine, and Cathleen Stasz, 'Education for a New Era: Design and Implementation of K-12 Education Reform in Qatar', *RAND Qatar Policy Institute*, Santa Monica; CA: RAND, 2007.

Zellman, Gail L, Gery W Ryan, Rita Karam, Louay Constant, Hanine Salem, Gabriella Gonzalez, Nate Orr et al, 'Implementation of the K-12 Education Reform in Qatar's Schools', *RAND Qatar Policy Institute*, Santa Monica; CA: RAND, 2009.

INDEX

2014 al-Jazeera Turk launched, 95; Saudi Arabia, UAE and Bahrain withdraw ambassadors, 4, 13, 25, 32, 55, 127, 151; Egypt withdraws ambassador, 130; release of Bergdahl negotiated in Afghanistan, 61, 70; *Sunday Times* World Cup bribery story, 154–5; release of Curtis negotiated in Syria, 61, 70, 135; international pressure to deport Muslim Brotherhood members, 65; German accusation of IS support, 156–7; joins airstrikes against IS, 162; release of Fijians negotiated in Syria, 61, 135; release of Turkish diplomats negotiated in Syria, 61; release of Djiboutian soldier negotiated in Eritrea, 61; al-Jazeera banned in Egypt, 155; US discussions on moving military base, 157; release of Greek Orthodox nuns negotiated in Syria, 61, 135; release of Lebanese negotiated in Syria, 135; awarded 2019 World Athletics Championship, 106; launch of *al-Arab al-Jadeed*, 128; Saudi Arabia, UAE and Bahrain return ambassadors, 152; Khalid Al Attiyah's speech at Italian Air Force Academy, 147; British accusations of terrorist support, 157; ambassador to Cairo refuses security check, 153; GCC summit, 152; Tamim bin Hamad steps down from QIA board, 83

2015 hosts first Renminbi Clearance Centre in MENA region, 85; al-Jolani appears on al-Jazeera, 135; release of Tajik border guards negotiated in Afghanistan, 61;

offer to mediate in Egypt, 153; military intervention in Yemen, 25, 67, 162–3; QTA opens conference centre, 105, 111; oil price crash, 158

2016 al-Jazeera America closed down, 95

Qatar Airways, 24, 104, 118, 151

Qatar Armed Forces, 2, 19, 20, 25, 40, 67, 84, 129, 141, 160–2
airstrikes in Iraq (2014), 162–3
and King's College London, 162
Operation Decisive Storm (2015), 25, 67, 162–3
Operation Unified Protector (2011), 129, 161–2
Stinger missiles, 27, 36, 44

Qatar Central Bank, 85

Qatar Electricity and Water Company, 22

Qatar Financial Centre (QFC), 173

Qatar Foundation (QF), 24, 41, 77, 80, 83–4, 86, 104–5, 108, 111, 122, 150, 164, 170, 173, 183

Qatar Holding, 84

Qatar Investment Authority (QIA), 23, 83–91, 97

Qatar MICE Development Institute (QMDI), 105

Qatar Museums Authority (QMA), 107, 115

Qatar National Convention Centre (QNCC), 104, 111

Qatar National Vision, 108, 110, 122, 165, 172–3, 183

Qatar Petroleum (QP), 51, 84

Qatar Petroleum International (QPI), 84, 86

Qatar Science and Technology Park (QSTP), 24, 122, 178

Qatar Sports Investment (QSI), 83, 90